OSF/Motif™
Programmer's Guide

Revision 1.2

(For OSF/Motif Release 1.2)

Open Software Foundation

P T R Prentice Hall, Englewood Cliffs, New Jersey 07632

Cover design
and cover illustration: **BETH FAGAN**

This book was formatted with troff

 Published by P T R Prentice-Hall, Inc.
A Simon & Schuster Company
Englewood Cliffs, New Jersey 07632

Printed in the United States of America
10   9   8   7   6   5   4

ISBN 0-13-643107-0

Prentice-Hall International (UK) Limited, *London*
Prentice-Hall of Australia Pty. Limited, *Sydney*
Prentice-Hall Canada Inc., *Toronto*
Prentice-Hall Hispanoamericana, S.A., *Mexico*
Prentice-Hall of India Private Limited, *New Delhi*
Prentice-Hall of Japan, Inc., *Tokyo*
Simon & Schuster Asia Pte. Ltd., *Singapore*
Editora Prentice-Hall do Brasil, Ltda., *Rio de Janeiro*

Open Software Foundation, OSF, the OSF logo, OSF/1, OSF/Motif, and Motif are trademarks of the Open Software Foundation, Inc.

DEC and DIGITAL are registered trademarks of Digital Equipment Corporation.

Hewlett-Packard and HP are trademarks of Hewlett-Packard Company.

Microsoft is a registered trademark of Microsoft Corporation.

Presentation Manager is a trademark of International Business Machines Corporation.

UNIX is a registered trademark of UNIX System Laboratories, Inc. in the U.S. and other countries.

X Window System is a trademark of the Massachusetts Institute of Technology.

Contents

List of Figures

List of Tables

Preface

The *OSF/Motif Programmer's Guide* describes how to use the OSF/Motif^{TM} application programming interface to create Motif^{TM} applications. The book gives an overview of the architecture of the Motif widget set, explains features of the Motif toolkit, and presents a model and examples for constructing Motif applications.

Audience

This document is written for designers and developers of Motif programs. It does not provide sufficient information to develop new Motif widgets, although widget developers need to be familiar with the facilities and the issues discussed in this book.

This document assumes that the reader is familiar with the American National Standards Institute (ANSI) C programming language. It also assumes that the reader has a general understanding of the X Window System, the Xlib library, and the X Toolkit Intrinsics (Xt).

Applicability

This is Revision 1.2 of this document. It applies to Release 1.2 of the OSF/Motif software system.

Purpose

The purpose of this guide is to explain how to write application programs using the Motif toolkit. After reading this book, you should have a general understanding of the Motif toolkit and the Motif widget set and should be able to write applications that use them. This guide is not intended to explain how to develop new classes of widgets.

Document Usage

This document is organized into 16 chapters and two appendixes:

- Chapter 1 introduces the book and gives an overview of the X Window System, Xlib, Xt, and Motif.

- Chapter 2 summarizes the structure of the Motif widget hierarchy and discusses general principles for writing Motif programs.

- Chapter 3 explains the structure and general elements of a Motif application.

- Chapter 4 describes the structure of a program that uses the User Interface Language (UIL) and Motif Resource Manager (MRM).

- Chapter 5 discusses most of the primitive widgets that form the building blocks of a Motif application.

- Chapter 6 describes how to use the RowColumn widget to build menus, radio boxes, and check boxes.

- Chapter 7 describes the widgets most appopriate for conducting dialogs with the user.

- Chapter 8 explains the Motif Text and TextField widgets, which provide general display and editing of text.

- Chapter 9 discusses composite widgets commonly used to contain other widgets in the application.

- Chapter 10 discusses the process of negotiating the layout of widgets and describes the layout-management policies of particular Motif widgets.

- Chapter 11 is a guide to internationalizing applications and providing text, font, and other information that is specific to particular language environments.

- Chapter 12 explains how Motif uses colors and pixmaps and how an application can provide its own.

- Chapter 13 discusses issues in handling input, including keyboard focus and traversal, translations, and actions.

- Chapter 14 describes DrawingArea, a general-purpose widget for displaying graphics and handling user input at a low level.

- Chapter 15 is an extensive discussion of the Motif drag and drop interface, with which the user transfers data by manipulating iconic representations with the pointer.

- Chapter 16 discusses communication between an application and other clients, including the Motif Window Manager (MWM), by means of resources, selections, protocols, and properties.

- Appendix A describes the Widget Meta-Language (WML) facility, which generates portions of the UIL compiler to support new widget sets.

- Appendix B is an extended example program using the drag and drop interface.

Related Documents

For additional information about OSF/Motif, refer to the following documents:

- The *OSF/Motif Programmer's Reference* provides detailed reference information for programmers writing Motif applications.

- The *Application Environment Specification — User Environment Volume* defines a stable set of routines for creating user interface applications.

- The *OSF/Motif Style Guide* explains the principles of user interface design for application developers.

- The *OSF/Motif User's Guide* explains how to interact with OSF/Motif applications.

For additional information about Xlib and Xt, refer to the following X Window System documents:

- *Xlib—C Language X Interface* is the specification for Xlib.

- *X Toolkit Intrinsics—C Language Interface* is the specification for Xt.

Typographic and Keying Conventions

This document uses the following typographic conventions:

Bold   **Bold** words or characters represent system elements that an application or user must use literally, such as functions, data types, commands, flags, and pathnames. **Bold** words also indicate the first use of a term included in the glossary.

Italic   *Italic* words or characters represent variable values and arguments that an application or user must supply.

`Constant width`
Examples and information that the system displays appear in this typeface.

< >   Angle brackets enclose the name of a key on the keyboard.

ComponentName
> Components of the user interface are represented by uppercase letters for each major word in the name of the component, such as PushButton.

Keyboard Conventions

Because not all keyboards are the same, it is difficult to specify keys that are correct for every manufacturer's keyboard. To solve this problem, this guide describes keys using a **virtual key** mechanism. The term *virtual* implies that the keys as described do not necessarily correspond to a fixed set of actual keys. Instead, virtual keys are linked to actual keys by means of **virtual bindings**. A given virtual key may be bound to different physical keys for different keyboards.

See Chapter 13 of this book for information on the mechanism for binding virtual keys to actual keys. For details see the **VirtualBindings(3X)** reference page in the *OSF/Motif Programmer's Reference*.

Mouse Conventions

Mouse buttons are described in this guide using a **virtual button** mechanism to better describe behavior independent from the number of buttons on the mouse. This guide assumes a 3-button mouse. On a 3-button mouse, the leftmost mouse button is usually defined as **BSelect**, the middle mouse button is usually defined as **BTransfer**, and the rightmost mouse button is usually defined as **BMenu**. For details about how virtual mouse buttons are usually defined, see the **VirtualBindings(3X)** reference page in the *OSF/Motif Programmer's Reference*.

Problem Reporting

If you have any problems with the software or documentation, please contact your software vendor's customer service department.

Chapter 1

Introduction

OSF/Motif is a **graphical user interface**, a means by which an application program can obtain input from and display output to a user of the application. Motif provides the intermediary mechanisms for communication between the application and the user. To both sides, these mechanisms appear as a set of objects with graphical representations on the screen. The program creates and displays objects of a variety of types provided by Motif for showing the user particular kinds of output and requesting particular kinds of input. The user supplies input by manipulating the screen representations of these objects with the pointer, the keyboard, or both.

This book explains the Motif **application programming interface**. This is the set of facilities that Motif gives an application developer to create and interact with a Motif interface for the application. This book is not a reference work; that is, it does not attempt to describe the API in exhaustive detail. Its focus is on giving an overview of the Motif architecture, explaining the concepts and conventions required to use the API, and providing examples. This book complements other volumes in the OSF/Motif documentation set:

- The *OSF/Motif Programmer's Reference* describes each element of the Motif programming interface in detail. It is organized into reference pages, one for each element of the interface.

- The *Application Environment Specification — User Environment Volume* describes which elements of the interface an application should use for maximum portability. All implementations of OSF/Motif must support the interfaces described in the AES.

- The *OSF/Motif Style Guide* describes *how* an application should use the interface for maximum consistency with other Motif applications.

- The *OSF/Motif User's Guide* describes the appearance and interaction style of Motif from the user's point of view.

The Motif API as supplied by OSF is implemented in the C programming language. Motif requires that an application written in C conform to American National Standards Institute (ANSI) C. This book assumes knowledge of ANSI C, which is explained by other published reference and tutorial books. It is also possible to write applications in other languages, including C++, but this book gives explanations and examples only for applications written in C.

1.1 The X Window System

Motif is based on the X Window System, often abbreviated as X. The X Window System is fundamentally a protocol by which an application can generate output on a computer that has a bitmapped display and can receive input from devices associated with the display.

X is based on a **client-server** computing model. The application program is the client, communicating through the X protocol with a server that handles the direct output to and input from the display. This model has several important features:

- The client and server may be running on the same machine or on different machines, communicating over a network.

- Only the server need concern itself with the display hardware. The X protocol is hardware independent, so a client can run without alteration using any kind of display that supports the protocol.

- A server may handle multiple clients on the same display at the same time. These clients may communicate with each other, using the server to transfer information.

- A client may communicate with multiple servers.

A **display** is an abstraction that represents the input and output devices controlled by a single server. Usually a display consists of a keyboard, a pointing device, and one or more **screens**. A screen is an abstraction that represents a single bitmapped output device.

Each client creates one or more **windows** on one or more screens of a given display. A window is a rectangular area of the screen on which the client displays output. Windows are arranged in hierarchies of children and parents. The server maintains a tree of windows for each screen. The top-level window is the **root window** of the screen. Each client typically creates at least one window as a child of the root window, and any other client windows are descendants of these top-level client windows. Windows may overlap, and the server maintains a stacking order for all windows on a screen. A child window may extend beyond the boundaries of its parent, but output is **clipped** or suppressed outside the parent's borders.

A client asks the server to create and destroy windows, but the windows themselves are resources controlled by the server. The server maintains other resources, including the following:

- A **pixmap** is a rectangular off-screen area into which an application can draw output. Both windows and pixmaps are **drawables** or entities on which a client can display output. The units of height and width in windows and pixmaps are **pixels**. Each pixel has a given depth, represented as a number of bits or **planes**. Thus, each pixel has an integral value whose range depends on the depth of the drawable. A one-bit-deep pixmap is called a **bitmap**. Each pixel in a bitmap has two possible values, 0 and 1.

- A **colormap** is an association between pixel values and colors. Each color is represented by a triple of red, green, and blue values that result in a particular color on a particular screen. Each window has an associated colormap that determines what color is used to display each pixel.

- A **font** is a collection of glyphs usually used to display text.

- A **cursor** is an object containing information needed for a graphical representation of the position of the pointer. It consists of a source bitmap, a shape bitmap, a **hotspot** or location representing the actual pointer position, and two colors.

- A **graphics context** or GC is a collection of attributes that determine how any given graphics operation affects a drawable. Each graphics operation on a drawable is executed using a given GC specified by the client. Some attributes of a GC are the foreground pixel, background pixel, line width, and clipping region.

- A **property** is a named data structure associated with a window. Clients often use properties to communicate with each other.

Each client opens a connection to one or more servers. Clients and servers interact by means of **requests**, **replies**, **errors**, and **events**. A client sends a request to the server asking it to take some action, such as creating a window or drawing a line into a pixmap. Some requests, such as requests for information, cause the server to generate replies to the client. A request that results in an error condition may cause the server to generate an error report to the client. The server executes requests from each client in the order in which it receives the requests from that client, although the server may execute requests from other clients at any time.

The server notifies clients of changes of state by means of **events**. An event may be a side effect of a client request, or it may have a completely asynchronous cause, such as the user's pressing a key or moving the pointer. In addition, a client may send an event, through the server, to another client.

Each client asks the server to send that client events of particular types that occur with respect to particular windows. The server generally reports an event with respect to some window. For example, the keyboard is conceptually attached to a window, known as the **focus** window. When the user presses a key, the server usually reports an event with respect to the focus window. If a client has asked the server to send it events of type **KeyPress** occurring with respect to some window, the server sends that client an event whenever the user presses a key while that window has the focus.

From the point of view of a client reading events from the server, events that result from that client's own requests arrive in the order in which it makes the requests. However, those events may be interspersed with events that result from other causes, such as user input or another client's actions. Furthermore, the client may buffer requests and the server may buffer events before actually transmitting them, so an event may arrive long after the client makes the request that generates the event.

The point is that for the most part event processing in X is inherently asynchronous. Most client applications continually loop, reading an event, processing the event (possibly making requests during the processing), and then reading another event. The client cannot assume, for example, that a given input event was generated after a given client request just because the client read the event after it made the request. Many events have **timestamps** that indicate when the server actually generated the events. A client that depends on the temporal ordering of events must often examine these timestamps.

1.2 Xlib, Xt, and Motif

Applications do not communicate with the X server directly. Instead, they use one or more libraries that provide high-level interfaces to the X protocol. The three principal libraries available to a Motif application are Xlib, the X Toolkit Intrinsics (Xt), and the Motif toolkit.

1.2.1 Xlib

X clients do not have to deal with the server at the level of the X protocol. X includes a C language client interface to the protocol, called Xlib. Among the Xlib facilities are the following:

- Routines for creating and managing the basic server resources, including windows, pixmaps, fonts, cursors, GCs, and properties

- Routines for rendering text and graphics into drawables

- Buffering of requests to the server and queuing of events from the server

- Data structures representing events of all types, and routines for selecting and reading events

- Routines for handling colormaps and for using device-independent color spaces

- Routines for generating text input and output in different locales

- The X resource manager (Xrm), a database of options specified by the user or the application

The resource manager is the keystone of a fundamental tenet of X: that the user and application should control the appearance, interaction style, and other optional characteristics of a client. For example, the background and foreground colors and the fonts used by an application might be represented as resources. Typically, an application provides default values for such resources but allows the user to override the defaults.

A resource is a triple consisting of a name, a class, and a value. A class may include a set of resources with different names. Resources may be arranged hierarchically; a name and class may consist of components, each identifying the name or class of a particular level of the hierarchy. The **fully qualified** name or class of a resource is the list of names or classes at all levels, starting with the name or class of the application and ending with the name or class of the resource itself.

The resource manager permits a user or application to specify resource values in a file, on the command line while starting the application, or by calling an Xrm routine in the program. A resource specification must include either the name or the class of the resource, but it may be either partially or fully qualified according to name, class, or a mixture of name and class components. The resulting resource database may include a variety of general and specific resource specifications. When an application queries the database for a resource value, it supplies a fully qualified name and class. The resource manager uses a search algorithm that returns the value from the most specific specification that matches the requested name and class.

1.2.2 Xt

Although Xlib provides the fundamental means of interacting with the X server, developing a complex application using only Xlib would be a formidable task. Xlib essentially supplies the primitives for an X client. A complex application needs to combine these primitives into constructs that handle aspects of interaction with the server in a more general way.

X includes a library, the X Toolkit Intrinsics (abbreviated Xt), that supplies some of these higher-level interfaces. Three of the most important Xt contributions are the following:

- Objects, known as widgets, used to hold data and present an interface to the user

- Management of widget geometry

- Dispatching and handling of events

1.2.2.1 Widgets

At the heart of Xt is a set of data abstractions built on an object metaphor. Each of these objects, called a **widget**, is a combination of state and procedure. Each instance of a widget is a member of a class. A widget **class** holds a set of procedures and data structures that are common to all widgets of that class. A widget **instance** contains the procedures and data structures that are particular to that single widget. A widget instance also has a pointer to its class.

Each widget class typically provides the general behavior associated with a particular kind of interaction with the user. For example, Motif has a widget class designed to let the user enter and edit text. This class provides the general behavior to support text input and display, including editing, selection, cutting, and pasting of text. The class has data structures related not only to the content of the text but also to the appearance of the widget's on-screen representation. To use this class, an application creates an instance of this class of widget and provides some of its own data and procedures for the widget instance.

Xt supports single inheritance of widget classes. That is, a widget class may be a subclass of another class, its superclass. A subclass is often a specialized variant of a more general superclass. The subclass may inherit, override, or supplement the procedures and data structures of its superclass. Xt generally supplies widget classes designed to be superclasses for other classes. Motif supplies the subclasses of which the the application constructs widget instances. Section 1.3 summarizes the Motif and Xt widget class hierarchy.

Widget instances form another, separate hierarchy. Every widget except the top-level widget (or widgets) in an application has a parent widget. Widgets of some classes, called **composites**, may have children. Other kinds of widgets, often called either **primitives** or **gadgets**, generally do not have children. An application constructs one or more trees of widget instances made up of composites, primitives, and gadgets. For example, a menu may consist of a composite parent representing the menu and a number of primitive children representing buttons. The menu and its children are one branch of the overall widget tree of the application.

Xt and Motif provide all the widget classes that most applications need. It is possible for an application to define new widget classes, but this requires knowledge of Xt and of Motif internals that is beyond the scope of this book. A typical application creates widget instances of the built-in classes, providing its own procedures and data for its widgets.

Xt uses an extension of the resource mechanism to represent the widget instance data that is available to an application. Each widget class defines a set of resources that apply to widgets of that class. A class may inherit or override the resources of its superclasses as well.

A widget class declares a name and a class for each of its resources. Xt and Motif give each widget class a name, and the application gives each widget instance a name. Finally, the application developer provides a name and a class for the application itself. For a given resource of a given widget, the fully qualified name is the list of names beginning with the application name, continuing with the name of the top-level widget and then with the names of descendant widgets down to the name of the given widget, and ending with the name of the resource. The fully qualified class is the list of classes beginning with the application class, continuing with the class of the top-level widget and then with the classes of descendant widgets down to the class of the given widget, and ending with the class of the resource.

The user, the application, and the widget class combine to provide values for resources and thus to control the appearance and other attributes of components of the application. Both the user and the application developer can provide either specific or general specifications for widget resources in several resource files and on the command line. They can also supply different resource specifications depending on the locale, the characteristics of the screen, or arbitrary customization criteria.

When the application starts up, Xt combines these specifications into an initial resource database. When the application creates a widget, Xt assigns initial values to the widget's resources using a specification from the database, from values supplied by the application at creation time, or from defaults supplied by the widget class. After creating a widget, the application can use the **XtGetValues** routine to retrieve the value of a widget resource and the **XtSetValues** routine to supply a new value for a resource.

1.2.2.2 Widget Geometry

Most widgets either have an associated window or occupy a defined rectangular area of their parent's window. Each widget has a height, width, and a position with respect to its parent, expressed as the x and y coordinates of the upper left corner of the widget. Specification of the dimensions of widgets and their positions with respect to each other constitutes the layout or **geometry** of the application.

Application geometry results from the interaction of several factors:

- The user or application may supply values for resources that influence geometry, such as the height and width of a widget.

- A **window manager**, a special client that controls the positions and sizes of top-level windows, runs on most displays. Motif provides a window manager called the Motif Window Manager (MWM). The user can change the size of most top-level windows by means of window manager facilities.

- A child widget may have preferences about its size. For example, a widget that displays a label may wish to be wide enough to display all the text of the label.

- A parent widget may have preferences about the sizes and locations of its children. For example, a menu widget may wish to lay out its button children aligned in a given number of rows or columns.

The process of accounting for all these factors and determining widget layout is known as **geometry management**. Xt provides the essential means of handling geometry management:

- All widgets have resources that specify, either directly or indirectly, the geometry intended by the user or the application.

- Xt has special widgets known as **shells** whose function is largely to handle interaction between the application and outside agents such as window managers.

- Widget class procedures may ask the widget's parent to change the widget's geometry, may calculate a preferred size, and may recalculate the widget's layout when the widget is given a new size.

- Parent widgets have ultimate control over the geometry of their children. A widget class procedure of a parent may accept or reject a child's/p request to change its geometry. In general a parent may change a child's geometry at any time.

A child is **managed** when it and its parent are prepared to negotiate geometry. In general, widgets are eligible to appear on the screen only after they are managed.

See Chapter 10 for more information on geometry management and the specific management policies of Motif widgets.

1.2.2.3 Event Handling

Xt has an event-handling procedure that reads events from the server and dispatches them to appropriate widgets. Each widget that has an associated window may also have a **translation table**. This table maps descriptions of events to names of procedures, known as **actions**. When Xt reads an event associated with a widget, it looks up the event description in the translation table and dispatches the event to the associated action routine.

An application can provide its own action routine, but most such routines are supplied by the widget class. An action routine often takes some action on its own and then notifies the application by invoking an application procedure known as a **callback**. Many widgets have resources whose value is a list of callback procedures. The widget invokes the procedures on these lists at specified times, often when the widget receives certain kinds of events. Xt supplies other means for an application to receive and respond to events, but many applications need only add appropriate callback procedures. These callbacks do most of the "work" of the application in the course of interacting with the user.

The Xt event-handling mechanism leads naturally to an event-driven structure for an application program. Most applications have the same general form:

- Initialize the application

- Create and manage the application widgets

- Provide callback procedures to be invoked by widgets

- Enter the Xt event-dispatching loop, which usually does not return

See Chapter 3 for more information about the structure of a Motif application.

1.2.3 Motif

Xt provides the substrate for creating a set of widgets responsible for specific aspects of a user interface. Motif uses the Xt substrate to build both base classes and specialized subclasses of widgets for a variety of purposes. Section 1.3 outlines the Motif widget set.

In addition to supplying widgets, Motif adds a number of features that are of general use to applications and users. The following sections summarize some of these features.

1.2.3.1 Visual Style

Motif widgets have a distinctive visual style. Many widgets have **shadows** with a three-dimensional look that makes the widget appear to be raised above or depressed below the background. A widget that has keyboard focus may have a rectangular **highlight** border. When the user presses the **BSelect** mouse button and focus is in a button, the color of the button face changes to indicate that the user has selected or "pressed" the button.

Motif automatically generates default colors for widget foregrounds, shadows, highlights, and selections states. The user or application can supply its own colors or pixmaps as values for widget resources.

See Chapter 12 for more information on colors and pixmaps in Motif.

1.2.3.2 Selections and Drag and Drop

The X Window System establishes conventions for clients to follow in allowing the user to transfer data from one application to another. These transfers operate through **selections** of several kinds, including primary, secondary, and clipboard selections. A selection is a shared resource that can be owned by only one client at a time for a given display. When the user wants to transfer data from one application to another, the receiving client asks the selection owner to convert the data into a form the receiving client understands, and then the receiver inserts the data. This mechanism can also transfer data between one widget and another in the same application.

The Motif Text and TextField widgets support primary, secondary, and clipboard selections. Motif also has routines that handle the clipboard selection, allowing an application to copy data easily to and from the clipboard. Xt provides more general routines for transferring data by means of selections.

Motif has an extensive **drag and drop** mechanism for transferring data. The user begins a transfer by pressing the **BTransfer** mouse button with the pointer over a data source. The user then drags an iconic representation of the data to a spot that can receive the data, called a drop site. When the user releases **BTransfer** the data is moved, copied, or linked to the drop site.

The Motif Text, TextField, List, and Label subclasses automatically support drag and drop transfer of textual and some pixmap data. Motif includes an extensive programming interface of objects and routines that allow an application to establish its own drag sources and drop sites, control negotiation between sender and receiver, customize the visual elements, and convert arbitrary kinds of data.

See Chapter 16 for information on selections and the Motif clipboard interface. See Chapter 15 for an extensive discussion of drag and drop.

1.2.3.3 Keyboard Traversal

Motif provides two styles of transferring keyboard focus from widget to widget. In one style, the widget that contains the pointer has focus. In the other style, the user presses a key or the **BSelect** button to move focus to another widget, and the pointer location does not otherwise affect the focus.

In the second style, Motif distinguishes between traversal to a composite or a widget with internal navigation, called a **tab group**, and navigation to a widget or element within a tab group. Motif has a number of resources and routines to control traversal using this style.

See Chapter 13 for more information on keyboard traversal and other input issues.

1.2.3.4 Compound Strings and Font Lists

Motif represents much textual data using a data type called a **compound string**. This is a byte stream consisting of components representing text, a display direction, and a **font list element tag**. A compound string can have multiple text segments, possibly with different directions and font list element tags. Motif uses compound strings to represent all text except that in the Text and TextField widgets.

For each widget that can contain text, Motif maintains font information using a data type called a **font list**. This is a list of entries, each consisting of a font list element tag and either a font or a font set. A font set is a construct representing a group of fonts needed to display text in the locale of the application.

When Motif displays the text of a compound string segment, it matches the segment's font list element tag with a font list element tag from the widget's font list. It then uses the associated font or font set to display the text of the segment. A special font list element tag indicates text to be parsed in the encoding of the locale and displayed using the fonts needed in that locale.

See Chapter 11 for more information on compound strings and font lists, particularly for information on preparing an application for different language environments.

1.2.3.5 Motif Window Manager

The Motif Window Manager (MWM) is a Motif client that is capable of managing windows of either Motif or non-Motif applications. MWM provides window decorations and functions for moving, resizing, raising, lowering, maximizing, and minimizing windows. The user can display icons either on the root window or in an icon box. MWM has many resources that permit the user to customize its appearance and behavior.

See Chapter 16 for more information on the application interfaces to MWM. See the **mwm(1X)** reference page in the *OSF/Motif Programmer's Reference* for information on MWM resources and functions.

1.2.3.6 UIL and MRM

Motif has a specification language called the User Interface Language (UIL). The developer uses UIL to define widgets and data in a text file. The developer then compiles this file into a binary format. At run time the application, using Motif Resource Manager (MRM) routines, retrieves the widget descriptions and data definitions from the binary file, and MRM creates the widgets and data structures from these descriptions.

UIL and MRM work in conjunction with the Motif toolkit. The application defines callback procedures and interacts with the widgets as if it were using the Motif toolkit alone. By using UIL to define the program's widget hierarchies, the developer can separate the user interface specification from the application code. A developer can change the interface by editing and recompiling a text file without recompiling and relinking the application program. As with resource files, a developer can use separate UIL files to contain text, font lists, and other data specific to particular locales.

See Chapter 4 for information on using UIL and MRM in an application. See the **UIL(5X)** reference page in the *OSF/Motif Programmer's Reference* for information on UIL syntax.

1.2.4 Using Xlib, Xt, and Motif

Xt is built atop Xlib, and Motif is built atop Xt. One goal of Xt is to give applications a set of high-level interfaces and objects that relieve the program of the need to deal with many primitive Xlib routines. A goal of Motif is to give applications still higher-level interfaces and, particularly, a versatile set of widgets to relieve the program of the need to define its own widgets for most tasks.

However, Xt does not strive to replace all Xlib interfaces, and Motif does not strive to replace all Xt interfaces. Even a simple Motif application must use basic Xt routines to initialize the toolkit, manage widgets, create windows for widgets, get and set resources, add callback routines, and enter the event-dispatching loop.

Many Motif applications do not need to call Xlib routines. However, Motif does not have its own graphics routines, color-space facilities, or support for application management of input methods. Programs that need these features must either use vendor-supplied tools or call Xlib routines directly.

As a general rule, an application should use the highest-level interfaces sufficient for the tasks at hand. Not only does this usually result in a concise program, but it also ensures that the program functions as intended when a higher-level procedure supersedes a lower-level procedure.

For example, Xlib, Xt, and Motif all have routines to set keyboard focus to a window or widget. Xt and Motif both maintain internal state that keeps track of focus changes. If a Motif application uses the Xt or Xlib routine, it may cause Motif or Xt to become internally inconsistent.

By convention, the names of Xlib routines and data structures begin with "X"; the names of Xt routines and data structures begin with "Xt"; and the names of Motif routines and data structures begin with "Xm".

This book does not document Xlib or Xt interfaces. A Motif application developer must have a working knowledge of basic Xt application interfaces and should have at least general familiarity with Xlib. For more information on Xlib, see the X Consortium Standard *Xlib—C Language X Interface*. For more information on Xt, see the X Window System document *X Toolkit Intrinsics—C Language Interface*.

1.3 Widget Classes and Hierarchy

This section gives a brief overview of the hierarchy of widget classes in Xt and Motif. Chapter 2 discusses this hierarchy in more detail.

1.3.1 Xt Classes

Xt defines the base classes for all widgets. **Core** is the fundamental class for all widgets that can have windows. **Core** has basic resources for a widget's geometry, background color, translations, and sensitivity to input. Widgetlike objects—called **gadgets** in Motif—that do not have windows are subclasses of **RectObj**. This class has geometry resources but no colors or translations.

Composite is the base class for all widgets that can have children. This class maintains a list of its children and is responsible for managing their geometry. **Constraint** is a subclass of **Composite** that maintains additional data for each child, represented by **constraint resources** for the child.

Shell is the base class for shell widgets. Shells envelop other widgets whose windows are children of the root window. Shells are responsible for interaction with the window manager. **Shell** is a subclass of **Composite**. Xt has the following subclasses of **Shell**:

OverrideShell
> Envelops widgets that the window manager should ignore, such as menus

WMShell   Superclass for shells that need to interact specifically with the window manager

VendorShell Subclass of **WMShell** that implements toolkit-specific behavior

TransientShell
> Subclass of **VendorShell** for widgets such as dialogs that appear briefly on behalf of other widgets

TopLevelShell
> Subclass of **VendorShell** for top-level widgets for components of the application

ApplicationShell
> Subclass of **TopLevelShell** for the top-level widget that represents the application as a whole

1.3.2 Motif Classes

Motif has three broad groups of widgets: primitives and gadgets, managers, and shells.

1.3.2.1 Primitives and Gadgets

Primitives are widgets that have no children. They are commonly the fundamental units of input and output, and they are usually building blocks for composite widgets. **XmPrimitive**, a subclass of **Core**, is the base class for all primitives. **XmPrimitive** has basic color resources and provides keyboard traversal behavior.

XmPrimitive is used only as a superclass for classes with more specific behavior. Following are the subclasses of Motif primitives:

XmSeparator
> Used to separate other widgets; usually appears as a line.

XmLabel
> Displays text or a pixmap. As a superclass for buttons, provides specialized behavior, such as keyboard traversal, inside menus.
>
> **XmLabel** subclasses **XmCascadeButton**, **XmDrawnButton**, **XmPushButton**, and **XmToggleButton** perform some action when activated or "pressed" by the user. Subclasses have roles as menu activators, toggles, pushbuttons, and small graphics areas.

XmScrollBar
> Control that moves a scroll widget horizontally or vertically with respect to a fixed viewport on the scroll.

XmList
> Array of textual items from which the user can select one or more entries.

XmText
> Widget for display and possible editing of text. **XmText** may be multiline or constrained to a single line. **XmTextField** is a variant optimized for single-line text.

Gadgets are variants of primitives that have no windows. Gadgets have geometry, but they inherit colors from their parents and depend on their parents to dispatch input events to them. **XmGadget**, a subclass of **RectObj**, is the base class for gadgets. Gadget variants exist for separators, labels, and most button classes.

See Chapter 8 for more information on the Text and TextField widgets. See Chapter 5 for more information on other primitives.

1.3.2.2 Managers

A manager is a widget that generally has children and manages their geometry. **XmManager**, a subclass of **Constraint**, is the base class for managers. This class has special responsibilities when it has gadget children. It provides color resources that its gadget children inherit, and it dispatches input events to appropriate gadgets. Following are the subclasses of Motif managers:

XmFrame   Surrounds a child with a shadow and a margin.

XmScale   Displays a value within a range and optionally allows the user to supply a new value.

XmPanedWindow

    Arranges children, called panes, vertically from top to bottom. May insert a control called a sash that lets the user adjust the size of a pane.

XmScrolledWindow

    Provides a viewport onto a child widget that behaves as a virtual scroll. Manages ScrollBars to move the scroll with respect to the viewport.

XmMainWindow

    Subclass of ScrolledWindow that provides support for a MenuBar and other specialized areas.

XmRowColumn

    Implements menus, RadioBoxes, and CheckBoxes, usually consisting of button children. Can be used to lay out arbitrary widgets in rows, columns, or two-dimensional formations.

XmBulletinBoard

    Superclass for dialogs, widgets that present information to the user or seek information from the user. The dialog widget may be a BulletinBoard, which provides general behavior, or a specialized subclass. Common subclasses present a list from which the user makes a selection, display filenames and allow the user to choose one, ask the user to enter a command, and display a message. One subclass, **XmForm**, performs general constraint-based geometry management for its children.

XmDrawingArea
> General-purpose manager suitable for use as a canvas for graphics operations.

See the following chapters for more information on Motif manager widgets:

RowColumn
> Chapter 6 for menus; Chapter 10 for geometry management

BulletinBoard subclasses
> Chapter 7 for dialogs; Chapter 10 for geometry management

ScrolledWindow, MainWindow, PanedWindow, Frame
> Chapter 9

DrawingArea
> Chapter 14

1.3.2.3 Shells

Motif has three shell classes:

VendorShell
> Motif-specific implementation of the Xt class. Among other responsibilities, manages communication with MWM.

XmDialogShell
> Subclass of **TransientShell** that envelops dialogs. Cooperates with BulletinBoard in popping up and positioning transient dialogs.

XmMenuShell
> Subclass of **OverrideShell** that envelops menus.

1.3.2.4 Other Motif Classes

Motif uses a number of specialized objects that are not intended to be used in creating widgets. These objects exist primarily to hold resources and other information that would be difficult to make available in another way. **XmDisplay** holds resources specific to a given display, and **XmScreen** holds resources specific to each screen on which the application has created a widget. The drag and drop interface includes objects representing several aspects of a drag and drop transaction, including the general context, drop sites, drag icons, and data transfers.

1.4 Header Files and Libraries

Xlib, Xt, and Motif all have header files that an application must include. However, the Motif header files themselves include the required Xt files, which in turn include the required Xlib files. An application usually needs to include only the proper Motif files.

All Motif applications must include the file **<Xm/Xm.h>**. This file contains definitions that all applications need. Each Motif widget also has an include file. An application must include the header files for all widgets it creates. In addition, some groups of Motif routines have their own header files. Required include files for each Motif widget and routine are documented in the *OSF/Motif Programmer's Reference*.

Instead of using a large number of include files for particular widgets and routines, an application can include **<Xm/XmAll.h>**. This file incorporates all documented Motif header files.

When building a Motif application, a developer must link the program with the appropriate libraries. Xlib, Xt, the Motif toolkit, and MRM have separate libraries. An application that does not use MRM must be linked with the Motif toolkit, Xt, and Xlib libraries. An application that uses MRM must be linked with these libraries and also with the MRM library. A developer might also need to link the application with additional libraries, depending on the platform and operating system. Consult your system administrator and vendor documentation for more information on the libraries required for Motif applications.

Chapter 2

The Motif Programming Model

OSF/Motif accommodates a variety of application programming styles. An application can accomplish most tasks, such as handling a particular kind of user input or displaying a particular kind of output, in more than one way. While this flexibility is one of the strengths of OSF/Motif, the toolkit has been designed with a set of programming principles in mind. This chapter explains at a general level the intended uses of Motif widgets and other features of the toolkit. The next chapter outlines the structure of common Motif programs, and succeeding chapters explain toolkit features in more detail.

The following general principles make sense in writing any Motif program:

- Adopt a user-centered perspective. In most Motif programs, the application does its work in response to commands or other input from the user. An important part of interface design is deciding precisely which commands, options, and other information the user can give the application. The interface then consists largely of procedures that execute the user's commands or otherwise respond to the user's input.

- Separate the design of the core application and the user interface. The core application should not depend on a particular user interface. Often it's a good idea to specify a set of generic routines and data structures for obtaining input and displaying output. The developer can then implement these routines in different ways to provide different user interfaces for the application.

- Follow the *OSF/Motif Style Guide* in designing the user interface. Although an application can use Motif widgets in many configurations, users find some more common, intuitive, and comfortable than others. The *OSF/Motif Style Guide* contains requirements and recommendations for compliant applications, and it offers more advice on application design.

- Outline the widget hierarchy. Once you have settled on one or more combinations of widgets, you may find the implementation more tractable if you sketch a genealogy of all the widgets the program uses. Constructing a widget tree can reveal gaps and awkwardness in the design. Attaching dialogs and menus to the hierarchy may help ensure consistency and completeness in the presentation and solicitation of information.

- Use high-level interfaces when possible. A Motif application must use some X Toolkit Intrinsics (Xt) interfaces, and it may call other public Xt and Xlib routines. For some tasks, such as drawing graphics, an application must call lower-level routines. However, Motif provides interfaces such as resources, callback lists, and convenience routines to handle many common tasks. Motif also includes both simple and composite widgets that do most of the work related to their specific functions, such as text editing or constraint-based geometry management. Using a high-level Motif interface instead of a comparable series of lower-level calls can make code simpler and more maintainable.

- Use resource files and the User Interface Language (UIL) to specify characteristics of the interface. Avoid locking the user-interface specification and data into the application code. Using resources gives the user the power to override application-supplied default behavior. UIL provides the opportunity to separate the widget hierarchy from the application. With both resources and UIL, the developer can change the interface without recompiling the application code. These mechanisms also provide the means to tailor the interface and data for particular language environments.

2.1 A User-Centered Model

A basic principle of Motif and Xt programming is that the user is in charge of the application. Except in unusual circumstances, the program takes action in response to commands or other input from the user. In fact, a typical Motif program spends most of its real time waiting for the user to provide input.

The fundamental object type in a Motif interface is the **widget**. Some widgets can display output or process input or both; some widgets serve to contain other widgets. A widget is usually associated with a **window** or a rectangular area of the screen. A widget also has attributes, called **resources**, which can often be set by the user or the application. An application organizes widgets into one or more hierarchies or trees of parent widgets and their children.

Motif and Xt define a set of widget types or **classes**. A widget class may be a subclass of another class; in that case it inherits some of the attributes and behavior of the superclass. Motif has three basic classes of widgets:

- **Primitives** are the basic units of input and output. Primitives usually do not have children. Specialized Motif primitives include labels, separators, buttons, scroll bars, lists, and text widgets. Some primitive classes have equivalent objects called **gadgets**. These are just like primitives except that, to enhance performance, they have no associated windows.

- **Managers** are composite widgets that contain primitives, gadgets, or other managers. Managers are responsible for the geometrical arrangement of their children. They also process and dispatch input to their gadget children. Specialized Motif managers include frames, scrolled and paned windows, menus, constraint-based geometry managers, and several kinds of dialogs.

- **Shells** are widgets whose main purpose is to communicate with the window manager. Most shells have only one child, and they maintain the same size and position as the child. Specialized Motif shells exist to envelop applications, dialogs, and menus.

Defining a widget hierarchy is one of the two main tasks of a Motif application. The other is to define a set of **callback procedures**. Callbacks are the primary means by which the application responds to user input. When the user takes an action like pressing a key or a mouse button, the X server sends the application an **event**. Xt dispatches these events to the appropriate widget, usually the one to which the user directed the input. Xt maps the event to one or more widget **action routines**. The action may change the state of the widget and, if the application has asked to be notified of that action, may "call back" to the program by invoking an application callback procedure.

Many Motif widgets have resources that are lists of callback procedures. Motif invokes a list of callbacks when the user takes an action that has a particular meaning. For example, most buttons have callbacks that Motif invokes when the user **activates** the button. The user may activate the button in a number of ways, such as by pressing the **KSelect** key or the **BSelect** mouse button. The events that constitute activation and other meaningful user actions are defined in a general way in the *OSF/Motif Style Guide* and are documented for specific widgets in the *OSF/Motif Programmer's Reference*.

The user action may cause Motif to change to the state and appearance of a widget. For example, when the user presses **KSelect** in a PushButton, Motif may make the button appear to be depressed and then released, like a mechanical push button. The action may have other effects depending on the context. For example, Motif has a dialog widget called a FileSelectionBox, used for finding and selecting files. When the user activates the "filter" PushButton in a FileSelectionBox, Motif searches for and displays the names of files that match a pattern displayed elsewhere in the FileSelectionBox.

In general Motif takes care of changing the state and appearance of a widget to correspond to the user's action. By default, though, this action has no effect on the application. The application programmer must interpret the meaning of the action for the application by providing a callback routine, which Motif invokes when the user takes that action. The callback routine may change the state of the application, for example, by changing the value of a variable when the user selects a new value from a Scale widget. The callback may cause the application to take an action. It may also change the state of one or more widgets itself, or it may create an entirely new widget hierarchy.

When both Motif and the application have finished responding to a user action, the application waits for the user to provide more input. Xt provides a routine in which applications spend most of their time. This routine waits for an event, dispatches it to the appropriate widget, and then waits for another event. After initializing the toolkit and creating the initial widget hierarchy, most applications enter this loop and remain there until the user terminates the program.

Motif and Xt provide other ways for applications to direct and respond to events, but for simple programs, virtually the entire interface between the user and the application consists of callback routines.

2.2 Separating Interface from Application

A widely accepted principle of application design is that a core application should not rely on a specific user interface. Separating the application from the interface allows developers to work on the two components independently. It also allows the program to run with different interfaces without changes in the core application. This makes it easier to port the application to more than one interface and to experiment with different configurations of a single interface.

Many applications need to collect input from the user and to display output in some form. It may be easier to separate the core application from the user interface if the developer specifies a set of generic input and output routines along with any necessary data structures. If these generic interfaces have no dependence on specific user interfaces, they can be implemented in different ways for different interfaces without changing the core application. They form a module for communication between the core application and the interface.

The Motif implementation of the interface module consists of code to perform the following tasks:

- Initialize the Intrinsics
- Create the widget hierarchy
- Define callback procedures
- Make widgets visible
- Enter a loop that waits for and responds to user input

These steps are explained in detail in Chapter 3.

The User Interface Language (UIL) helps enforce the separation of the interface from the core application. With UIL, the developer defines widgets and their characteristics in a text file and then compiles the text file into a binary format. At run time, the application uses Motif Resource Manager (MRM) routines to retrieve the widget descriptions from the binary file, and MRM creates the widgets from these descriptions. The UIL file can also define data such as text strings and colors, and MRM can retrieve the data at run time.

In this way, an application can remove the description of the widget hierarchy from the program code. In its source code, the application defines callback procedures and interacts with the widgets as if it were using the Motif toolkit alone. If the application has defined all the callback procedures it needs, a developer can change the widget hierarchy by editing and recompling the UIL file without recompiling and relinking the source program.

2.3 Building Blocks: Primitive Widgets and Gadgets

Primitive widgets are the fundamental units of input and output in Motif. Primitives are commonly the widgets at the leaves of an application's widget hierarchy. These widgets do not have children of their own. The name *primitive* does not imply simplicity; some primitives, such as the Text widget, have quite complicated behavior. *Primitive* is meant to contrast with *manager*, a widget that usually has children. It also suggests a basic component from which composite widgets are built. Primitives are often referred to as **controls**.

The **XmPrimitive** Motif widget class is the superclass for all primitives. **XmPrimitive** is itself a subclass of the fundamental Xt widget class, **Core**. **Core** has resources that describe the widget's width, height, and x and y coordinates with respect to its parent. Other **Core** resources control characteristics of the window, such as its background color; whether or not the widget can receive input events; and the mapping that Xt uses to translate events into calls to the widget's action routines.

XmPrimitive adds two groups of features to the **Core** class. One group consists of resources to control additional visual characteristics, including the characteristic three-dimensional shadow and a highlighting rectangle that can appear when the widget is the focus for keyboard input. The second group controls **keyboard traversal**, the use of the keyboard to move focus from one widget to another. This group includes several resources and a set of translations and actions that allow the user to move the keyboard focus to another widget by pressing an arrow key. **XmPrimitive** also provides callbacks to let the application provide help information when the user presses **KHelp**.

The **XmGadget** widget class is the superclass for all gadgets. **XmGadget** is a subclass of the Xt widget class **RectObj**. This class provides resources to determine the dimensions and position of the gadget's rectangular area inside its parent. **XmGadget** is equivalent to **XmPrimitive**, with two exceptions:

- Gadgets have no color or pixmap resources; they inherit these from their parents.

- Gadgets do not have translations or actions. A gadget's parent controls keyboard traversal from the gadget to another widget, and it dispatches events to the gadget when appropriate.

XmPrimitive and **XmGadget** are used only as superclasses for other classes of widgets. **XmPrimitive** and **XmGadget** are not **instantiable**; that is, an application cannot create an actual widget that is an instance of either of these classes. Motif has several specialized subclasses of primitives and gadgets, summarized in the following sections.

2.3.1 Label and Separator

Labels provide the ability to display static (uneditable) text or a pixmap. A Label or LabelGadget itself is useful for displaying a message, title, or description. Label and LabelGadgets are also superclasses for buttons used as menu items, toggles, or controls.

A Label can display either text or a pixmap. When a Label displays text, it uses a construct called a **compound string**. This is a stream of bytes that represents zero or more pieces of text, each with an associated tag and display direction. When Motif displays the compound string, it matches each tag with a tag in the widget's **font list** and uses the corresponding font or fonts from the font list to display the text.

A Separator or SeparatorGadget separates controls or groups of controls. It usually appears as a horizontal or vertical line and supports several styles of line drawing.

Labels and Separators are described in more detail in Chapter 5.

2.3.2 Buttons

A button is a basic control that performs some action when the user activates it. Buttons commonly appear in menus, RadioBoxes and CheckBoxes, SelectionBoxes and MessageBoxes. Motif has the following classes of buttons:

- A CascadeButton or CascadeButtonGadget is used inside a menu and, when activated, usually causes a PulldownMenu to appear.

- A PushButton or PushButtonGadget can appear either inside or outside a menu. It performs some action determined by the application. When a PushButton is armed, or ready to be activated, it changes its appearance so that it looks as if the user has pressed it in. When it is disarmed, it reverts to the appearance of extending out.

- ToggleButtons and ToggleButtonGadgets have one of two states: like toggle switches, they are either on or off. They can appear in menus or in nonmenu RowColumn WorkAreas, including RadioBoxes and CheckBoxes.

- A DrawnButton is an empty button surrounded by a shadow border. It is intended to be used as a PushButton but with graphics drawn by the application.

Buttons are described in more detail in Chapter 5.

2.3.3 ScrollBar

A widget can act as a viewport onto a virtual scroll. The scroll is a plane with text, graphics, a list of items, or other contents. The viewport is a fixed-size window onto a portion of the scroll.

A ScrollBar is the control that moves the viewport horizontally or vertically relative to the underlying scroll. A ScrollBar consists of a rectangle, called the scroll region, representing the full size of the scroll. It has a smaller rectangle, called the slider, within the scroll region, representing the position and size of the viewport relative to the full scroll. The ScrollBar usually has arrow graphics at both ends of the larger rectangle.

ScrollBars are described in more detail in Chapter 5.

2.3.4 List

A List is an array of textual items from which the user selects one or more entries. Each item is a compound string. A List has four modes for selecting items: two that allow the user to select one item at a time, and two that allow the user to select more than one item in either contiguous or discontiguous ranges.

Lists are described in more detail in Chapter 5.

2.3.5 Text

Text is a widget for displaying and possibly editing text. When the Text is editable and the user presses a key that represents a text character, that character is inserted into the text. Other translations and actions allow the user to navigate or to select, cut, copy, paste, or scroll the text.

The text in a Text widget can be multiline or constrained to be a single line. In a single-line widget, actions that move up and down one line in a multiline widget instead traverse to another widget, and pressing **KTab** moves the keyboard focus to another group of widgets instead of inserting a **Tab** character. A TextField is essentially the same as a Text widget in single-line mode, except that its performance is optimized for single-line text operations.

Text is described in more detail in Chapters 5 and 8.

2.4 Managers

A manager is a widget that usually contains children, either primitives or other managers. One responsibility of a manager is to position and shape its children so that the configuration of the children is appropriate for the manager's specialized purpose. Another responsibility is to determine whether a gadget child should process an input event and, if so, to dispatch the event to that child.

The **XmManager** Motif widget class is the superclass for all managers. **XmManager** is a subclass of **Core**. Like **XmPrimitive**, **XmManager** has resources to control colors or pixmaps used for the foreground, shadows, and highlighting rectangle. Most managers do not have shadows or highlighting rectangles, but gadget children inherit the related resources. Managers also have resources that control keyboard traversal, and they provide callbacks for processing user requests for help. In addition, they have translations and actions for dispatching input events to gadget children, usually to the child that is the current focus of keyboard events.

XmManager is not an instantiable widget class; it is used only as a subclass for other widgets. Motif has several specialized subclasses of managers, summarized in the following sections.

2.4.1 Frame

A Frame is a simple manager that surrounds a single child with a shadow and a margin. A Frame can also have another child that appears as a title for the Frame.

Frames are discussed in more detail in Chapter 9.

2.4.2 Scale

A Scale is a manager that functions as a control. It displays a value within a range and optionally allows the user to supply a new value. Its appearance and behavior are much like those of a ScrollBar without arrows. It also has a title and can display the current value next to the slider. If the application adds other children to a Scale, the Scale positions them evenly along the rectangular area that represents the range of values, and these children then act as tic marks or value labels.

Scales are discussed in more detail in Chapter 5.

2.4.3 PanedWindow

A PanedWindow arranges its children vertically from top to bottom and forces them all to have the same width. Each child is a **pane** of the window. Between each pair of panes, PanedWindow inserts an optional Separator and a control called a **sash**. By manipulating a sash with the mouse or keyboard, the user can increase or decrease the height of the pane above. PanedWindow has resources to control the margins, the spacing between panes, and the appearance of the sashes. Each pane of a PanedWindow has resources specifying a maximum and minimum height and whether or not either the pane itself or the PanedWindow should be allowed to resize the pane without user intervention.

PanedWindow is discussed in more detail in Chapter 9.

2.4.4 ScrolledWindow and MainWindow

A ScrolledWindow manages a viewport and ScrollBars to implement a window onto a virtual scroll. The user can move the viewport to display different portions of the underlying scroll using the ScrollBars or keyboard scrolling commands.

ScrolledWindow is capable of performing scrolling operations automatically. In this mode, the application creates the widget that represents the scroll as a child of the ScrolledWindow. The ScrolledWindow then creates a clipping window to act as the viewport, creates and manages the ScrollBars, and moves the viewport with respect to the scroll when the user issues a scrolling command.

ScrolledWindow can also allow the application to perform scrolling operations. In this mode, the application must create and manage the ScrollBars and must change the contents of the viewport in response to the user's scrolling commands.

List and Text widgets are often used as virtual scrolls. Motif has convenience routines to create List and Text widgets inside ScrolledWindows, and the resulting ScrolledList and ScrolledText widgets perform scrolling operations without intervention by the application.

MainWindow is a subclass of ScrolledWindow that is intended as the primary window in an application. In addition to a viewport and ScrollBars, MainWindow includes an optional MenuBar and an optional command window and message window.

The ScrolledWindow and MainWindow widgets are described in more detail in Chapter 9.

2.4.5 RowColumn

RowColumn implements both menus and nonmenu WorkAreas. Menus are widgets that allow the user to make choices among actions or states. Motif offers four basic kinds of menu:

- A MenuBar usually appears in the application's MainWindow and sometimes in other components. It most often consists of a row of CascadeButtons that, when activated, cause PulldownMenus to appear.

- A PopupMenu contains a set of choices that apply to a component of the application. The menu is not visible until the user takes an action that posts it, It can contain buttons that take action directly or CascadeButtons that cause PulldownMenus to appear.

- A PulldownMenu is associated with a CascadeButton in a MenuBar, a PopupMenu, or another PulldownMenu. The menu is not visible until the user posts it by activating the associated CascadeButton. Like a PopupMenu, a PulldownMenu can contain buttons that take action directly or CascadeButtons that cause other PulldownMenus to appear.

- An OptionMenu allows the user to choose among one set of choices, usually mutually exclusive attributes or states. It consists of a label, a CascadeButtonGadget whose label shows the currently selected option, and a PulldownMenu containing buttons that represent the set of options.

One use for a nonmenu RowColumn WorkArea is to contain a set of ToggleButtons constituting a RadioBox or a CheckBox. When the user selects a ToggleButton, its state changes from on to off or from off to on. Another use is to lay out an arbitrary set of widgets in a row, column, or two-dimensional formation.

RowColumn is discussed in more detail in Chapter 6.

2.4.6 BulletinBoard, Form, MessageBox, SelectionBox

Dialogs are container widgets that provide a means of communicating between the user and the application. A dialog widget usually asks a question or presents some information to the user. In some cases, the application is suspended until the user provides a response.

The usual superclass for a dialog widget is **XmBulletinBoard**. The dialog widget can be either a BulletinBoard itself or one of its more specialized subclasses. BulletinBoard is a container with no automatically created children; it supplies general behavior needed by most dialogs. Its subclasses provide child widgets and specific behavior tailored to particular types of dialogs:

- A SelectionBox is a BulletinBoard subclass that allows the user to select a choice from a list. It usually contains a List, an editable text field displaying the choice, and three or four buttons for accepting or canceling the choice and seeking help.

- A FileSelectionBox is a specialized SelectionBox for choosing a file from a directory. It contains two text fields, one containing a file search pattern and the other containing the selected filename; two lists, one displaying filenames and the other displaying subdirectories; and a set of buttons.

- A Command is a specialized SelectionBox for entering a command. Its main components are a text field for editing the command and a list representing the command history.

- A MessageBox is a BulletinBoard subclass for displaying messages to the user. It usually contains a message symbol, a message label, and up to three buttons. Motif provides distinct symbols for several kinds of messages: errors, warnings, information, questions, and notifications that the application is busy.

- A TemplateDialog is a specialized MessageBox that allows the application to build a custom dialog with additional children, such as a MenuBar and added buttons.

- A Form is a BulletinBoard subclass that performs constraint-based geometry management. The children of a Form have resources that represent attachments to other children or to the Form, offsets from the attachments, and relative positions within the Form. The Form calculates the positions and sizes of its children based partly on these constraints. This layout function makes Form useful outside dialogs as well.

Dialogs are discussed in more detail in Chapter 7.

2.4.7 DrawingArea

A DrawingArea is a manager suited for use as a canvas containing graphical objects. An application must interact with a DrawingArea at a somewhat lower level than with other Motif widgets, but a DrawingArea provides the application with more fine-grained information about events. DrawingArea has callbacks to notify the application when the widget is exposed or resized and when it receives keyboard or mouse input. An application generally must use Xlib routines to draw into the DrawingArea, and the application is responsible for updating the contents when necessary. The flexibility of a DrawingArea makes it a useful widget for implementing both graphical and text features not provided by other Motif widgets.

DrawingArea is discussed in more detail in Chapter 15.

2.5 Shells

Users of X Window System applications normally employ a window manager, a special application that may control the positions, sizes, and border decorations of top-level windows on the display. Motif supplies its own window manager, the Motif Window Manager (MWM), but Motif applications can cooperate with other window managers as well.

A window manager communicates with other applications through a protocol defined in an X Window System document, the *Inter-Client Communication Conventions Manual* (ICCCM). Xt and Motif define a group of widgets whose main responsibility is to envelop other widgets and communicate with the window manager. These widgets are called shells.

A shell is nearly invisible to the application. Each shell has a single managed child, and the shell's window usually remains coincident with the child's window. The application must create shells when needed, but many Motif convenience routines that create widgets also create shells automatically. Once it has created a shell, the application may not need to handle the shell again. For example, an application can position or resize a Motif shell by positioning or resizing the child widget.

Each widget with a top-level window—that is, a window whose parent is the root window of the screen—needs to be enclosed in a shell. This is true of the main application widget, but it is also true of dialogs, menus, and any top-level widgets other than the main application widget. Motif provides three classes of shell: VendorShell, DialogShell, and MenuShell.

2.5.1 VendorShell

VendorShell is the shell class that provides Motif-specific behavior for shells other than those surrounding menus. It is responsible for communication between the application and MWM. VendorShell is a superclass for other classes. TopLevelShell is an Xt subclass of VendorShell that surrounds a top-level widget in an application. ApplicationShell is another Xt subclass of VendorShell that surrounds the main widget in the application.

Many applications create only one ApplicationShell. A program can create this shell explicitly, or it can use the Xt convenience routine

XtAppInitialize to initialize the application and automatically create the ApplicationShell.

2.5.2 DialogShell

XmDialogShell is a VendorShell subclass that envelops dialogs. Although the window manager takes account of dialogs, they are usually transient; they appear to provide information to or solicit information from the user, and then they disappear. DialogShell is a subclass of the Xt TransientShell class, which keeps track of the application to which the dialog belongs. Users cannot iconify a dialog separately from the main application window.

DialogShell is designed to have a child that is a subclass of BulletinBoard. Most Motif convenience routines that create dialogs create DialogShell parents automatically.

2.5.3 MenuShell

XmMenuShell is the class of shell that surrounds PopupMenus and PulldownMenus. MenuShell is a subclass of the Xt OverrideShell class. This class enables the shell to bypass the window manager. Most Motif convenience routines that create PopupMenus and PulldownMenus create MenuShell parents automatically.

2.6 Applications, Top-Level Widgets, and Dialogs

Primitives, managers, and shells are the components Motif provides for building an interface. A developer assembles these components into the broadest units of the program: dialogs, top-level widgets, and the application itself.

One approach to this construction is to specify the connection between the core application and the user interface. The developer determines what information the application needs to obtain from and present to the user. From this assessment, the developer specifies a generic interface to the application and then implements a Motif version using particular combinations of widgets.

Another approach is to design the user interface from the application level down to specific widgets. The developer decides what the top-level components of the application should be and how they relate to each other. From this assessment, the developer designs a combination of widgets that presents the application clearly to the user and permits a graceful transition from one task to another. The developer can then finely adjust the visual appearance of the interface.

In practice, a developer is likely to use both the bottom-up and top-down approaches at different stages of the program design. The approaches converge at the level of the application.

2.6.1 Applications

The application is the highest level of abstraction of a Motif program. In one sense the application embodies the entire program. In another sense, the application is the primary widget in the program. The user may cause other widgets to appear, but the application is the focus of activity and is usually the first widget to appear when the user starts the program.

The widget that represents the application is commonly a MainWindow. For many applications, the essential operations should be available from the MenuBar at the top of the MainWindow. By browsing through the MenuBar, the user can quickly determine what general functions the application provides. The activation callbacks for the buttons in menus that are pulled down from the MenuBar initiate the general operations of the application. The *OSF/Motif Style Guide* contains requirements and recommendations for the contents of the application MenuBar and its PulldownMenus.

The MainWindow usually contains a large scrollable work area. Single-component applications usually perform most of their work using this region. Other applications may require more than one work area.

An ApplicationShell encloses the main widget of an application. The developer can use the Xt function **XtAppCreateShell** to create an ApplicationShell directly or can let Xt create the shell during a call to **XtAppInitialize**.

Usually a program has only one application, but sometimes a program is made up of multiple logical applications. In this case, the program may have more than one main window, each enveloped in a separate ApplicationShell.

2.6.2 Top-Level Widgets

Although it is unusual for a program to have more than one logical application, it is more common for an application to require multiple top-level widgets. For example, a mail-processing program may consist of a component for reading mail and another for composing and sending it.

Each major component of an application may reside in a top-level widget. Each top-level widget must be enclosed in a TopLevelShell or an ApplicationShell. One approach is to have a single ApplicationShell for the application, with each TopLevelShell a **popup** child of the ApplicationShell. The program does not create a window for the ApplicationShell. Another approach is to designate one top-level widget the application, enclosed in an ApplicationShell, and make the other TopLevelShells popup children of the ApplicationShell. A popup child is one whose window is a child of the root window and whose geometry is not managed by its parent widget.

Multiple top-level widgets are discussed in more detail in Chapter 3.

2.6.3 Dialogs

Dialogs are transient components used to display information about the current state of the application or to obtain specific information from the user. A dialog widget is usually a BulletinBoard or one of its subclasses, enclosed in a DialogShell. The DialogShell is a popup child of another widget in the hierarchy. Its window is a child of the root window, but the user cannot iconify a dialog separately from the main application.

A dialog can be **modal**—that is, it can prevent other parts of the application from processing input while the dialog is active. It can also be **modeless**, so that the user can interact with the rest of the application while the dialog is visible. Motif has convenience routines that create both the dialog widget and the DialogShell for several kinds of information.

Dialogs are discussed in more detail in Chapter 7.

2.7 Resources: User and Program Customization

A widget, a class of widgets, and an application as a whole have a set of attributes that the program can examine and that the user and program may be able to specify. These attributes are implemented as X **resources**. Xlib has a facility called the X resource manager (Xrm) whose purpose is to establish and query databases of resources. Xt and Motif build on Xrm to make resources the repository of publicly available attributes of widgets as well as applications.

Xt maintains databases of resources that apply to several levels:

- To the application as a whole
- To the display on which an application is running
- To the screen on which a widget hierarchy is created
- To a class of widgets
- To an individual widget

The user can specify resources at any of these levels through resource files or the command line used to start the program. The application can also specify resources through resource files.

Each application has a name and a class; each widget within an application has a name and a class; and each resource has a name and a class. When supplying resource values in a file or on the command line, the user or the application specifies the scope of the resource value by qualifying the resource according to its name or class. For example, a user might specify that all resources of the class Background should have a particular value for all widgets; or the user might specify that only the resource named background within a particular hierarchy of named widgets should have a particular value. The qualification mechanism allows resource values to be specified at any level.

Most widget classes define a set of resources, by name and class, that apply to those classes. Subclasses inherit superclass resources, unless a subclass overrides the superclass resource specification. A widget class also defines a default value for each of its resources, used in case the user and the application do not provide another value.

When an application starts up, Xt constructs an initial database of resource values. This database is derived from a combination of user and application resource files and the command line. Some resources in the database may have different values depending on the display or the screen on which the application is running. When an application creates a widget, Xt uses this initial database in combination with the widget class resource defaults to supply values for the widget's resources. The application can override these values by supplying arguments to the routine that creates the widget. It can set a resource value after creating the widget by using the Xt function **XtSetValues**.

Setting resources is the primary means by which an application changes the attributes of a widget. However, an application should be careful not to override the user's specification of many resources governing characteristics such as visual appearance and the policy for determining which widget has keyboard focus. In general, the application should set only those resources necessary for the proper functioning of the program. An application can specify preferences for other resource values in an application defaults file. Xt reads this file when an application starts up, but a user can override the values supplied there.

The process by which Xt creates the initial resource database is discussed in more detail in Chapter 3.

2.8 Handling Input and Output

The X server communicates input to a client through input **events** associated with a window. In the simplest case, when a keyboard or pointer event occurs, the X server sends the event to the client that has expressed interest in events of that type on the window that contains the pointer. However, processing can be more complex. A client can **grab** a pointer button or key, the pointer or keyboard, or the entire server; the client then receives the relevant events. A client can set the **input focus** to some window, and the X server then reports events with respect to this window even if the pointer is outside this window.

To insulate applications from such complexities, Xt and Motif supply facilities for low-level processing of user input to an application:

- A VendorShell resource, **XmNkeyboardFocusPolicy**, allows the user or application to determine whether keyboard events go to the widget that contains the pointer or the widget in which the user presses **BSelect** (a "click-to-type" policy).

- In the click-to-type model, the user can also use keys to navigate from widget to widget or from one group of widgets to another.

- Xt provides the basic event-dispatching loop used by most applications. Xt takes events out of the application's queue and dispatches them to the appropriate widget, usually the widget that has input focus. Xt usually invokes an **action** associated with the particular event through a table of **translations** from event specifications to action routines. The action, in turn, often invokes a callback list.

- Motif and Xt provide **mnemonics** and **accelerators**, which are shortcuts for taking actions associated with a widget when the widget does not have input focus. A **mnemonic** is a keysym for a key that activates a visible button in a menu. An **accelerator** is a description for an event that invokes an action routine through a translation.

Most applications can use these high-level interfaces, allowing Xt and Motif to process user input at lower levels. If an application needs more control, it can also provide its own **event handler**, a routine invoked by the Xt dispatching loop when the widget receives events of the specified type. An application can also provide its own event-dispatching loop.

Issues of input, focus, and keyboard navigation are discussed in more detail in Chapter 13.

For most widgets, Xt and Motif handle low-level output processing as well. For example, in a Label or Text widget, when an application changes the text to be displayed, Motif automatically redisplays the contents of the widget. Most widgets have resources that control the appearance of the output, such as the fonts used to display text.

Motif provides the DrawingArea widget for applications that need to produce graphic output or that need more control or flexibility in displaying text. DrawingArea is discussed in more detail in Chapter 15.

Chapter 3

Structure of a Motif Program

OSF/Motif uses the same event-driven programming model as the X Toolkit Intrinsics. At its core, a Motif application waits for the user to provide input, usually by pressing a key, moving the mouse, or clicking a mouse button. Such an action by the user causes the X server to generate one or more X Window System events. Xt listens for these events and dispatches them to the appropriate Motif widget, usually the widget to which the user directed the input. The widget may take some action as a result of the user input. If the application has asked to be notified of that action, the widget "calls back" to the application—that is, it invokes an application callback procedure. When both Motif and the application have finished responding to the user input, the application waits for the user to provide more input. This cycle of user-initiated events and application response, called the **event loop,** continues until the user terminates the application.

For simple applications, the Intrinsics and Motif toolkits do everything necessary for dispatching user input to widgets. The application must take the following actions:

- Include the required header files
- Initialize the Intrinsics
- Create one or more widgets

- Define callback procedures and attach them to widgets

- Make the widgets visible

- Enter the event loop

This chapter discusses each of these actions. The following table summarizes these steps and some of the procedures the application needs to call. Note that some of these steps are different when the application uses UIL and MRM. See Chapter 4 for more information.

Table 3-1. Steps in Writing Widget Programs

Step	Description	Related Functions
1	Include required header files.	**#include <Xm/Xm.h>** **#include <Xm/***widget***.h>**
2	Initialize Xt Intrinsics	**XtAppInitialize()**
	Do steps 3 and 4 for each widget.	
3	Create widget	**XtSetArg()** **XtCreateManagedWidget()** *or* **XmCreate***<WidgetName>***()** followed by **XtManageChild(***widget***)**
4	Add callback routines	**XtAddCallback()**
5	Realize widgets	**XtRealizeWidget(***parent***)**
6	Enter event loop	**XtAppMainLoop()**

3.1 Including Header Files

All Motif applications must include the file **<Xm/Xm.h>**. This file contains definitions that all applications need. It also includes the Xt header files **<X11/Intrinsic.h>** and **<X11/StringDefs.h>**.

Each Motif widget also has an include file. An application must include the header files for all widgets it creates. In addition, some groups of Motif routines have their own header files. For example, an application that uses any of the Motif clipboard routines must include the file **<Xm/CutPaste.h>**. Required include files for each Motif widget and routine are documented in the *OSF/Motif Programmer's Reference*.

Following is an example of including header files for an application that uses only a Text widget:

```
#include <Xm/Xm.h>
#include <Xm/Text.h>
```

3.2 Initializing the Intrinsics

The first task of a Motif application is to initialize the Intrinsics. Most applications can perform the initialization by calling the routine **XtAppInitialize**. This is a convenience routine that combines several initialization steps, each of which the application can take separately by calling a specialized Xt routine:

1. Initialize the state of the Intrinsics. An application can also do this by calling **XtToolkitInitialize**.

2. Create an application context. Xt uses this construct to contain the information it associates with each instance of an application. Its purpose is to allow multiple instances of an application to run in a single address space. Most applications need only create an application context and pass it to Intrinsics routines that take an application context as an argument. The data type is **XtAppContext**. An application can create an application context explicitly by calling **XtCreateApplicationContext**.

3. Open a connection to a display and attach it to an application context. When an application uses **XtAppInitialize**, the display specification comes from the command line invoking the application or from the user's environment. After opening the display, Xt builds a resource database by processing resource defaults and command-line options. The construction of this database is described in the next section. An application can perform these steps explicitly by calling **XtOpenDisplay**. If an application already has an open display as a result of calling **XOpenDisplay**, it can attach the display to an application context and build the initial resource database by calling **XtDisplayInitialize**.

4. Create a top-level shell widget for the application. **XtAppInitialize** creates an ApplicationShell and returns it as the function's return value. An application can create a top-level shell by calling **XtAppCreateShell**.

Following is an example of a simple call to **XtAppInitialize**:

```
int main(int argc, char **argv)
{
    Widget          app_shell;
    XtAppContext    app;
    app_shell = XtAppInitialize(&app, "Example",
        (XrmOptionDescList) NULL, 0, &argc, argv,
        (String *) NULL, (ArgList) NULL, 0);
}
```

3.2.1 The Initial Resource Database

The **XtDisplayInitialize** routine builds the initial resource database for the application. An application rarely needs to call this routine directly; it is called by **XtOpenDisplay**, which in turn is called by **XtAppInitialize**.

XtDisplayInitialize builds a separate resource database for each display connection. The initial database combines resource settings from the command line, the display, an application class defaults file, and user defaults files that may be specialized according to the application or the host on which the application is running. The application class defaults and the user's per-application defaults may be further specialized according to the language environment and possibly according to a general-purpose

customization resource. The resources in the initial database may pertain to particular widgets or widget classes or to the application as a whole. When the application creates widgets, the resource settings from the database are often the source for the initial values of widget resources.

The remainder of this section describes the order in which **XtDisplayInitialize** loads each component of the database and how it derives the location of that component.

3.2.1.1 File Search Paths

In loading the application class defaults and the user's per-application defaults, **XtDisplayInitialize** calls **XtResolvePathname** to determine which files to read. **XtResolvePathname** uses file search paths. Each path is a set of patterns that may contain special character sequences for which **XtResolvePathname** substitutes runtime values when it searches for a file. It uses the following substitutions in building the path:

- **%N** is replaced by class name of the application, as specified by the *application_class* argument to **XtAppInitialize**, **XtOpenDisplay**, or **XtDisplayInitialize**.

- **%C** is replaced by the value of the **customization** resource.

- **%L** is replaced by the display's language specification. This may come from the **xnlLanguage** resource, the locale of the application, or an application callback procedure. See Chapter 11 for more information. The format of the language specification is implementation dependent; it may have language, territory, and codeset components.

- **%l** is replaced by the language part of the language specification.

- **%t** is replaced by the territory part of the language specification.

- **%c** is replaced by the codeset part of the language specification.

- **%%** is replaced by %.

If the language specification is not defined, or if one of its parts is missing, a % element that references it is replaced by NULL.

The paths contain a series of elements separated by colons. Each element denotes a filename, and the filenames are looked up left-to-right until one of them succeeds. Before doing the lookup, substitutions are performed.

Note: The Intrinsics use the X/Open convention of collapsing multiple adjoining slashes in a filename into one slash.

3.2.1.2 Initial Database Components

The **XtDisplayInitialize** function loads the resource database by merging in resources from these sources, in order of precedence (that is, each component takes precedence over the following components):

- The application command line
- Per-host user environment resource file on the local host
- Screen-specific resources for the default screen of the display
- Resource property on the server or user preference resource file on the local host
- Application-specific user resource file on the local host
- Application-specific class resource file on the local host

3.2.1.3 Command-Line Specifications

XtDisplayInitialize calls the X Resource Manager function **XrmParseCommand** to extract resource settings from the command line by which the user invoked the application. The arguments and number of arguments on the command line come from the *argv* and *argc* arguments to **XtAppInitialize**, **XtOpenDisplay**, or **XtDisplayInitialize**. Xt maintains a standard set of command-line options, such as **-background** and **-geometry**, for specifying resource settings. An application can specify additional options in arguments to **XtAppInitialize**, **XtOpenDisplay**, or **XtDisplayInitialize**. The user can supply the **-xrm** option to set any resource in the database.

3.2.1.4 Per-Host User Resources

To load the per-host user environment resources, **XtDisplayInitialize** uses the filename specified by the **XENVIRONMENT** environment variable. If **XENVIRONMENT** is not defined, **XtDisplayInitialize** looks for the file **$HOME/.Xdefaults-***host*, where *host* is the name of the host on which the application is running (that is, the name of the client host, not the server host).

3.2.1.5 Screen-Specific Resources

To load screen-specific resources, **XtDisplayInitialize** looks for a SCREEN_RESOURCES property on the root window of the default screen of the display. The SCREEN_RESOURCES property typically results from invoking the **xrdb** command when some resources are not defined for all screens.

Note: When Xt needs to fetch resources for a screen other than the default screen of the display—for example, when the application creates a widget on another screen—it uses the SCREEN_RESOURCES property of that screen instead of the SCREEN_RESOURCES property of the default screen.

3.2.1.6 Server or User-Preference Resources

To load the server resource property or user preference file, **XtDisplayInitialize** first looks for a RESOURCE_MANAGER property on the root window of the display's screen 0. The RESOURCE_MANAGER property typically results from invoking the **xrdb** command when some resources are defined for all screens. If that property does not exist, **XtDisplayInitialize** looks for the file **$HOME/.Xdefaults**.

3.2.1.7 User Application File

To load the user's application resource file, **XtDisplayInitialize** performs the following steps:

1. Use **XUSERFILESEARCHPATH** to look up the file, performing appropriate substitutions.

2. If that fails, or if **XUSERFILESEARCHPATH** is not defined, and if **XAPPLRESDIR** is defined, use an implementation-dependent search path containing at least seven entries, in the following order and with the following directory prefixes and substitutions:

   $XAPPLRESDIR with **%C, %N, %L** or with **%C, %N, %l, %t, %c**
   $XAPPLRESDIR with **%C, %N, %l**
   $XAPPLRESDIR with **%C, %N**
   $XAPPLRESDIR with **%N, %L** or with **%N, %l, %t, %c**
   $XAPPLRESDIR with **%N, %l**
   $XAPPLRESDIR with **%N**
   $HOME with **%N**

   where **$XAPPLRESDIR** is the value of the **XAPPLRESDIR** environment variable and **$HOME** is the user's home directory.

3. If **XAPPLRESDIR** is not defined, use an implementation-dependent search path containing at least six entries, in the following order and with the following directory prefixes and substitutions:

   $HOME with **%C, %N, %L** or with **%C, %N, %l, %t, %c**
   $HOME with **%C, %N, %l**
   $HOME with **%C, %N**
   $HOME with **%N, %L** or with **%N, %l, %t, %c**
   $HOME with **%N, %l**
   $HOME with **%N**

3.2.1.8 Application Class Resource File

To load the application-specific class resource file, **XtDisplayInitialize** performs the appropriate substitutions on the path specified by the **XFILESEARCHPATH** environment variable. If that fails, or if **XFILESEARCHPATH** is not defined, **XtDisplayInitialize** uses an implementation-dependent search path containing at least six entries, in the following order and with the following substitutions:

%C, %N, %S, %T, %L or %C, %N, %S, %T, %l, %t, %c
%C, %N, %S, %T, %l
%C, %N, %S, %T
%N, %S, %T, %L or %N, %S, %T, %l, %t, %c
%N, %S, %T, %l
%N, %S, %T

where the substitution for **%S** is usually NULL and the substitution for **%T** is usually **app-defaults**.

If no application-specific class resource file is found, **XtDisplayInitialize** looks for any fallback resources that may have been defined by a call to **XtAppInitialize** or **XtAppSetFallbackResources**.

3.3 Creating Widgets

The top-level widget returned by **XtAppInitialize** or **XtAppCreateShell** is the root of a program's widget hierarchy for a given display or logical application. After initializing the Intrinsics, the application can proceed to create the remainder of the widget hierarchy it needs to start the program.

Widget creation is a two-stage process. In the first stage, the application creates the widget hierarchy but does not assign windows to the widgets. In the second stage, the application assigns windows and makes them visible. These stages are separate because, otherwise, window geometry might have to be recomputed each time a child is added. This computation can require a great deal of communication with the X server and take a long time. Instead, initial window geometry is computed only once. For more information, see Section 3.5.

The general routine for creating a widget is **XtCreateWidget**. The required arguments to this routine are the widget's name, class, and parent widget. You can also provide initial resource values for the widget, as discussed in the next section. **XtVaCreateWidget** is a version of **XtCreateWidget** that uses a variable-length argument list.

Motif has a convenience routine for creating a widget of each Motif class. The name of such a routine is usually **XmCreate**<*widget*>, where *widget* represents the widget class. For example, the convenience routine for creating a Text widget is **XmCreateText**. These routines do not require the widget-class argument.

Some convenience routines, such as **XmCreateMenuBar**, create specialized widgets. These routines usually set some initial resource values to configure the widget for a particular use—for example, to configure a RowColumn widget for use as a MenuBar. In some cases, such as **XmCreatePulldownMenu** and **XmCreateScrolledList**, these routines create a widget hierarchy rather than a single widget. The documentation for each convenience routine in the *OSF/Motif Programmer's Reference* explains what the routine does.

Using a Motif creation routine is generally preferable to calling **XtCreateWidget**. In addition to creating multiple widgets and setting appropriate resources, these routines sometimes perform optimizations. For example, some convenience routines add **XmNdestroyCallback** procedures to free memory when the widget is destroyed.

Note: Every widget except a top-level widget must have a parent at the time the widget is created.

An application can use **XtDestroyWidget** to destroy a widget.

3.3.1 Specifying Resource Values

An application can specify values for resources when it creates a widget and anytime thereafter. It can retrieve resource values after creating a widget.

3.3.1.1 Widget Initialization

When an application creates a widget, the creation routine sets the widget's initial resource values from the following sources, in order (that is, each succeeding component takes precedence over preceding components):

- Default values for resources specified by the widget class and its superclasses
- Resource values from the initial resource database

- Resource values specified by the application in its call to the widget creation routine

Each widget class can have its own **initialize** procedure. After setting the initial resource values, the widget creation routine calls the **initialize** procedure for each class in the widget's class hierarchy, in superclass-to-subclass order. The **initialize** procedure can set new values for resources, possibly based on other resource values in the widget or its ancestors. In some cases, an **initialize** procedure forces a resource to have a particular value, regardless of whether the user or application has specified another value. In other cases, the **initialize** procedure might set a resource value only if the user or application has not specified another value.

The documentation for each widget class in the *OSF/Motif Programmer's Reference* lists the data type and default value for each resource. For resources whose default values are computed dynamically, the documentation describes how the default values are determined.

3.3.1.2 Arguments that Specify Resource Values

To specify initial resource values in a call to a widget creation routine, an application supplies two arguments: a list of elements representing resource settings and an integer specifying the number of elements in the list. Each element in the list is a structure of type **Arg**. This structure has two members: a string representing the name of the resource, and a value specifier representing the resource value. The value specifier is of type **XtArgVal**. This is a data type large enough to hold a **long** or one of several types of pointers to other data. If the resource value is of a type small enough to fit into an **XtArgVal**, the value specifier contains the resource value itself; otherwise, it contains a pointer to the actual value. For most resources, an application supplies integer values (including such types as **Position** and **Dimension**) directly in the value specifier; otherwise, the application supplies a pointer to the value.

The most common way to set up a list of resource specifications is to declare a list of **Arg** elements large enough to hold all the specifications and then to use **XtSetArg** to insert each specification into the list.

An application should always use a sequence of calls to **XtSetArg** in the following way to avoid mistakes in building the list:

```
...
Widget      text;
Arg         args[10];
Cardinal    n;

n = 0;
XtSetArg(args[n], XmNrows, 10);          n++;
XtSetArg(args[n], XmNcolumns, 80);       n++;
text = XmCreateText("text", parent, args, n);
```

Instead of using lists of **Arg** structures, the variable-argument routines that specify resource values take a variable number of pairs of resource names and values as arguments. The resource value in each pair is of type **XtArgVal**, with the same meaning as the value in an **Arg** structure. The application can provide two special strings in place of a resource name. If the name is **XtVaNestedList**, the next argument is interpreted as a nested list of name-value pairs. If the name is **XtVaTypedArg**, the next four arguments supply the resource value and cause it to be converted from one data type to another, as described in the following sections.

3.3.1.3 Setting Resource Values

To specify resource values after a widget has been created, an application uses **XtSetValues** or **XtVaSetValues**. **XtSetValues** takes a list of resource specifications in the same format as that used when creating a widget:

```
...
Arg         args[10];
Cardinal    n;

n = 0;
XtSetArg(args[n], XmNrows, 10);          n++;
XtSetArg(args[n], XmNcolumns, 80);       n++;
XtSetValues(text, args, n);
```

Each widget class can have its own **set_values** procedure. After setting the values specified in the argument list, **XtSetValues** calls the **set_values** procedure for each class in the widget's class hierarchy, in superclass-to-subclass order. The **set_values** procedure can set new values for resources other than those specified in the arguments to **XtSetValues**. This usually happens when the value of one resource depends on the value of another. Setting a new value for a resource that affects the widget's geometry can also cause Motif to recompute the widget's layout. In some cases a **set_values** procedure forces a resource to have a particular value, regardless of whether the application has specified another value.

3.3.1.4 Retrieving Resource Values

To retrieve resource values, an application uses **XtGetValues** or **XtVaGetValues**. The arguments are the same as those for **XtSetValues**, except that in place of a value for each resource is an address in which Motif stores the requested value:

```
...
Arg          args[10];
Cardinal     n;
short        nrows, ncolumns;

n = 0;
XtSetArg(args[n], XmNrows, &nrows);            n++;
XtSetArg(args[n], XmNcolumns, &ncolumns);      n++;
XtGetValues(text, args, n);
```

3.3.1.5 Resource Value Data Types

The documentation for each widget class in the *OSF/Motif Programmer's Reference* lists the data types to use when setting and retrieving values for resources. The user and application do not always have to supply data of the type documented. Motif has routines, called converters, that convert resource values from one data type to another. For example, when a value for the resource database comes from a file or the command line, Motif processes the value as a string. Motif and Xt have routines to convert strings to most common resource types, including **Boolean**, **Dimension**, **Position**, **Pixel**, and **XmFontList**.

When using the standard widget creation routines, **XtSetValues**, and **XtGetValues**, an application must supply resource values or addresses of the types the widget expects. But when using the variable-argument versions of these routines, the application can supply values of any types for which routines exist to convert data of those types into values of the expected types. To provide for a resource conversion, the application supplies **XtVaTypedArg** in place of a resource name in the argument list. In place of the resource value, the application supplies four arguments:

- The resource name

- A string representing the type of the value supplied

- The value itself (of type **XtArgVal**)

- An integer representing the number of bytes in the value

For example, the following call converts the string supplied into the compound string that Motif expects for a PushButton label:

```
...
char *label = "Button";

XtVaSetValues(button, XtVaTypedArg, XmNlabelString,
    XmRString, label, strlen(label) + 1, NULL);
```

3.3.1.6 Resource Values and Memory Management

The application is responsible for allocating and freeing memory needed for resource values it supplies when initializing a widget or setting new values. For most resources whose values are not immediate data, including strings, compound strings, and font lists, Motif makes copies of values the application supplies when it creates a widget or calls **XtSetValues**. The application can free the allocated memory anytime after the widget creation routine executes or **XtSetValues** returns:

```
...
char    *label = "Button";
XmString  label_cs;
```

```
label_cs = XmStringCreateSimple(label);
XtVaSetValues(button, XmNlabelString, label_cs, NULL);
XmStringFree(label_cs);
```

For resources whose values are not immediate data, **XtGetValues** sometimes makes a copy of values and sometimes does not. For example, Motif always makes copies of compound strings retrieved by **XtGetValues**, but it does not make copies of lists of compound strings (data of type **XmStringTable**). Motif usually copies simple strings retrieved by **XtGetValues**. An application should free compound strings retrieved by **XtGetValues**, but in general it should not free values of other types unless the documentation for the particular resource in the *OSF/Motif Programmer's Reference* says the application must free that value.

The standard routines an application should use to allocate memory are **XtMalloc** and **XtNew**. The standard routine to free memory is **XtFree**. Some Motif data types have memory-management routines that an application should use instead of the more general Xt routines. For example, use **XmStringFree** to free memory for a compound string, and use **XmFontListFree** to free memory for a font list.

3.4 Adding Callback Procedures

Callback routines are the heart of a Motif application. Many widget classes have resources whose values are lists of callback procedures. When the user acts on a widget—for example, pressing a PushButton—Motif invokes the callback routines in the corresponding callback list. If an application needs to take some action when the user presses a PushButton, it supplies a callback routine and adds that routine to the appropriate callback list.

Callbacks are not the only means Motif uses to notify an application of a user action. An application can also supply its own action routines and event handlers. The main difference between these kinds of procedures is the level of abstraction at which Motif or Xt invokes the procedures:

- The Xt event dispatcher calls an event handler whenever an event of a particular type occurs in a specified widget.

- The Xt translation manager calls an action routine when an event sequence matches an event specification in a widget translation table.

In a translation table, actions are associated with event specifications. More than one event sequence can invoke the same action routine.

- A Motif widget invokes callback procedures when user input signifies an action that is meaningful to the widget, such as activating a PushButton. Widgets often invoke callbacks from action routines. More than one action can invoke the same callback list.

Most applications use only callback procedures. Action routines and event handlers are discussed in Chapter 13.

Each callback procedure is a function of type **XtCallbackProc**. The procedure takes three arguments: a widget and two pointers to data. The first pointer is to data that the application has told the widget to pass back to the application when the callback procedure is invoked. The second pointer is to data that the widget passes to all callbacks on the callback list. A callback procedure returns no value.

The application data argument is primarily for passing data that the application maintains separately from the widget itself. The widget data argument for most Motif widgets is a pointer to a structure containing information that varies by widget class. For example, when the user changes the value of a ToggleButton, Motif invokes callback procedures with a pointer to an **XmToggleButtonCallbackStruct** structure as the third argument. This structure has three members:

- An integer indicating the reason for invoking the callback. When the user changes the value, the reason is **XmCR_VALUE_CHANGED**. Usually the reason is identified by a symbol beginning with the characters **XmCR**.

- A pointer to the **XEvent** that triggered the callback.

- An integer that indicates the new state of the ToggleButton, either selected or unselected.

Documentation for each widget class in the *OSF/Motif Programmer's Reference* describes any callback structures that the widget passes to callback procedures as widget data. A callback procedure can change the values of some members of these structures. Because the order of procedures in a callback list is unspecified, an application using multiple callback procedures in the same list must use caution in changing these values.

Following is a simple callback procedure that an application might use to set the state of a valve when the user changes the value of a ToggleButton.

The application data passed in the callback in this example might be a pointer to a valve object associated with the ToggleButton:

```
void ToggleValueChangedCB(Widget toggle, XtPointer app_data,
    XtPointer widget_data)
{
    Valve *valve_p = (Valve *) app_data;
    XmToggleButtonCallbackStruct *toggle_info =
        (XmToggleButtonCallbackStruct *) widget_data;
    ChangeValveState(*valve_p,
        ((Boolean) toggle_info->set == TRUE) ?
                            VALVE_ON : VALVE_OFF);
}
```

To register a callback procedure with a widget, an application uses **XtAddCallback** or **XtAddCallbacks** after declaring the callback procedure and creating the widget. The following code fragment creates a ToggleButton for each valve in a global list of valves:

```
...
    char      name[20];
    Widget    toggles[N_VALVES];
    int       i;
    Valve     *valve_p;

    for(i = 0, valve_p = valves; i < N_VALVES;
                                    i++, valve_p++) {
        sprintf(name, "valve_state_%d", i);
        toggles[i] = XmCreateToggleButton(parent, name,
            (ArgList) NULL, 0);
        XtAddCallback(toggles[i], XmNvalueChangedCallback,
            (XtCallbackProc) ToggleValueChangedCB,
            (XtPointer) valve_p);
    }
```

To remove a callback procedure from a callback list, use **XtRemoveCallback** or **XtRemoveCallbacks**. Because Motif sometimes adds its own callbacks to callback lists, do not use **XtRemoveAllCallbacks** to remove all callbacks from a list.

3.5 Making Widgets Visible

Creating a widget does not by itself make the widget visible. Widgets become visible when the following conditions exist:

- The widget and its ancestors are **managed**. A widget is managed when the Xt and Motif geometry managers take account of the widget when computing the positions and sizes of widgets they display.

- The widget and its ancestors are **realized**. A widget is realized when it has an associated window.

- The widget and its ancestors are **mapped**. A widget is mapped when its window is displayed.

An application can manage, realize, and map widgets in separate steps, but each of these actions affects the others.

3.5.1 Managing Widgets

Parent widgets are responsible for managing the geometry of their children. A child can ask the parent to be given some size or position, but the parent decides whether or not to grant the request. A parent can move or resize a child without the child's permission. The process by which parent and child widgets interact to determine widget geometry is described in Chapter 10.

An application tells a widget to manage a child widget's geometry by calling **XtManageChild** or **XtManageChildren**. If the parent is realized, **XtManageChild** calls the parent class's **change_managed** procedure. This procedure can change the size or position of any of the parent's children. After calling the parent's **change_managed** procedure, **XtManageChild** realizes the child and, if the child's **XmNmappedWhenManaged** resource is True, maps it.

If the parent is not realized, **XtManageChild** marks the child as managed. Xt defers calling the parent's **change_managed** procedure until the parent is realized.

When managing more than one child of a realized parent, it is more efficient for an application to call **XtManageChildren** than to call **XtManageChild** separately for each child being managed. Widget layout can be computationally expensive, and **XtManageChild** invokes the parent's **change_managed** procedure each time it is called. **XtManageChildren** calls the parent's **change_managed** procedure only once for all children being managed.

An application tells a widget not to manage a child widget's geometry by calling **XtUnmanageChild** or **XtUnmanageChildren**. By managing and unmanaging widgets, an application can alternately display more than one set of children without having to create and destroy widgets each time the configuration of the application changes. In addition, managing a Motif dialog or PopupMenu causes the widget to pop up, and unmanaging it causes the widget to pop down.

To create a widget and then manage it in the same call, an application can use **XtCreateManagedWidget** or **XtVaCreateManagedWidget**. The Motif routines that create widgets of particular classes return unmanaged widgets. When using these routines, the application must manage the widgets using **XtUnmanageChild** or **XtUnmanageChildren**.

3.5.2 Realizing Widgets

An application uses **XtRealizeWidget** to realize a widget. This routine does the following:

- In post-order, traverses the tree whose root is the widget and calls the class **change_managed** procedure for any widget in the tree that has managed children.

- Recursively traverses the tree whose root is the widget and calls the class **realize** procedure for any widget in the tree that is managed. The **realize** procedure creates the widget's window.

- Maps the widget's managed children whose **XmNmappedWhenManaged** resource is True. If the widget is a top-level widget whose **XmNmappedWhenManaged** resource is True, **XtRealizeWidget** maps the widget.

Note these implications:

- Geometry negotiation proceeds from the bottom up; then window creation proceeds from the top down.

- After a widget is realized, all its managed descendants are realized and, by default, mapped.

- If no widget in the tree is realized, all geometry negotiation between parents and their managed children takes place before any widget is realized.

When making a widget tree visible for the first time, an application should usually manage all children before realizing any widgets, then realize only the top-level widget. This causes all initial sizing and positioning of children to take place and the overall size of the top-level window to be determined before any windows exist, minimizing interaction with the X server. It also allows the application to realize all widgets with a single call to **XtRealizeWidget**.

3.5.3 Mapping Widgets

Most applications do not explicitly map or unmap widgets' windows. Mapping usually takes place as part of the process of managing or realizing widgets. But it is possible to keep Xt from mapping windows at these times by setting a widget's **XmNmappedWhenManaged** to False. In this case, the application must explicitly use **XtMapWidget** to map the widget. An application can use **XtUnmapWidget** to unmap a widget.

The effect of making a widget managed but unmapped is different from the effect of making a widget unmanaged. When a widget is unmanaged, its parent takes no account of it in laying out its children. When a widget is managed, its parent is likely to leave room for it in the widget layout. When the parent is mapped, the space allocated for a managed but unmapped child is filled with the parent's background rather than the child's window.

3.5.4 Multiple Screens, Displays, and Applications

An application can run on more than one display. In this case, it must use **XOpenDisplay** to open a connection to each display and must then call **XtDisplayInitialize** separately for each display connection. It need not create a separate application context for each display.

Note: **XtDisplayInitialize** modifies its *argv* and *argc* arguments. If an application needs to call **XtDisplayInitialize** more than once, it must save these arguments before the first call and use a copy of the saved arguments on each call.

The application should use **XtAppCreateShell** to create at least one top-level widget for each display on which it runs. Because Xt maintains a separate resource database for each display, a child widget running on a different display from that of its parent would use incorrect initial resource settings.

An application can also run on more than one screen within a display. Such an application opens and initializes the display only once, no matter how many screens it uses within the display. However, the application also needs a widget on each screen, whose window is a child of the root window for that screen, to serve as the root of the widget hierarchy for the screen.

One approach to using multiple screens is to create a single, unrealized ApplicationShell for the display. The application then creates one TopLevelShell for each screen as a **popup** child of the ApplicationShell. Although a shell normally has only one managed child, it can have more than one popup child. The application uses **XtAppCreateShell** to create the ApplicationShell and **XtCreatePopupShell** to create each TopLevelShell. If no screen is specified for the ApplicationShell, **XtAppCreateShell** sets the **XmNscreen** resource for this widget to the default screen of the display. In the argument list passed to **XtCreatePopupShell**, the application must specify the proper value for **XmNscreen** for each TopLevelShell so that the shell is created on the intended screen.

The application does not manage the TopLevelShells. To realize and map the TopLevelShells, the program uses **XtPopup** with a *grab_kind* argument of **XtGrabNone**.

```
int main(int argc, char **argv)
{
    Widget          app_shell, top_shell;
    XtAppContext    app;
    Display         *display;
    char            name[20];
    Arg             args[5];
    Cardinal        n;
    int             i;
```

```
app_shell = XtAppInitialize(&app, "Example",
    (XrmOptionDescList) NULL, 0, &argc, argv,
    (String *) NULL, (ArgList) NULL, 0);
display = XtDisplay(app_shell);
for (i = 0; i < ScreenCount(display); i++) {
    sprintf(name, "top_shell_%d", i);
    n = 0;
    XtSetArg(args[n], XmNscreen,
        ScreenOfDisplay(display, i));     n++;
    top_shell = XtCreatePopupShell(name,
                    topLevelShellWidgetClass, app_shell,
                    args, n);
    /* Create and manage descendants of top shell */
    ...
    /* Realize and map the top shell */
    XtPopup(top_shell, XtGrabNone);
}
...
}
```

It is possible for a program to have multiple logical applications on the same display. In this case, it can use **XtAppCreateShell** to create a separate top-level widget for each logical application.

3.6 Entering the Event Loop

The last step in a Motif application is to enter the event loop. Most applications simply call **XtAppMainLoop**. This routine waits for user input and dispatches the resulting events to the appropriate event-handling procedures, usually in the widget in which the input occurs. **XtAppMainLoop** is an infinite loop; it never returns. An application should provide for a user action to terminate the program and should exit as a result of that action, usually in a callback routine.

Chapter 4
Structure of a Program Using UIL and MRM

The User Interface Language (UIL) allows an application developer to separate the specification of particular widget hierarchies from the application source code. The application defines widgets and their characteristics in a text file, which the developer compiles into a User Interface Definition (UID) file in binary format. At run time the application, using Motif Resource Manager (MRM) routines, retrieves the widget descriptions from the binary file, and MRM creates the widgets from these descriptions. The application defines callback procedures and interacts with the widgets as if it were using the Motif toolkit alone.

UIL offers several advantages over toolkit-only applications:

- UIL enforces the separation of the user interface specification from the application.

- A developer can change the interface by editing and recompiling a text file without recompiling and relinking the application program.

- The UIL compiler generates warnings for errors that the developer otherwise would not discover until running the program, if then. For example, the UIL compiler checks the spelling of resource names.

- The toolkit may handle large databases more efficiently when they are represented as UID files rather than resource files.

An application that uses UIL has two separate components: the UIL file and the application program.

The UIL file consists mainly of definitions of the application's widget hierarchy. The declaration for each widget typically includes the following components:

- Widget type

- Widget children

- Initial resource values

- Declarations for callback procedures

The UIL file can also define values for data such as compound strings, colors, and icons.

The structure of the application program is similar to that of a toolkit-only program. The chief difference is that instead of explicitly creating each widget, the program uses MRM routines to retrieve widget definitions from the UID file and to create the widgets themselves. The program might also use MRM routines to retrieve data values defined in the UIL file. An application program using UIL must take the following actions:

- Include the required header files

- Initialize the Intrinsics

- Initialize MRM

- Open the UID file

- Register the names of callback procedures and values of identifiers specified in the UID file

- Retrieve and create widgets and data defined in the UID file

- Close the UID file

- Define callback procedures

- Make the widgets visible

- Enter the event loop

4.1 Structure of a UIL Module

A UIL module is a block of declarations and definitions for the values, procedures, literals, and objects that make up a user interface specification. Each UIL file contains either one complete module or, if the file is to be included in another UIL file, at least one complete top-level construct within a module.

Each module has the following structure:

- **module** clause
- Zero or more declarations for the module as a whole
- Zero or more **include** directives
- Zero or more **value** declarations
- Zero or more **identifier** declarations
- Zero or more **procedure** declarations
- Zero or more **object** declarations
- Zero or more **list** declarations
- **end module** clause

This section discusses the components of a UIL module, but it does not describe the UIL syntax in detail. For more information, see the **UIL(5X)** reference page in the *OSF/Motif Programmer's Reference*.

4.1.1 module Clause

Each module begins with the declaration **module** *name*. The keyword **module** must be in lowercase.

4.1.2 Module-Level Declarations

Several optional declarations at the beginning of the module modify characteristics of the module as a whole:

names   The **names** declaration specifieso whether names in the UIL file are stored in a case-sensitive or case-insensitive way. The following declaration, the default, means that names are stored as they appear in the UIL file, and all UIL keywords must be in lowercase:

```
names = case_sensitive
```

The following declaration means that all names are stored in uppercase, and UIL keywords can be in uppercase, lowercase, or mixed case:

```
names = case_insensitive
```

The entire **names** declaration itself must be in lowercase, and it affects only the part of the module that follows it.

character_set

The **character_set** clause declares the default character set for strings and compound strings specified in the module by double quotes ("*string*"). If this clause is not present, UIL derives the default character set from the language environment in which the UIL file is compiled. This does not affect the character set of strings specified in the module by single quotes ('*string*'). UIL derives the character set of these strings from the language environment in which the UIL file is compiled. The character set in this clause must be either a keyword representing one of the character sets UIL knows about or a character set returned by the **character_set** function.

objects   The **objects** clause specifies whether UIL should define objects of the specified types as widgets or gadgets. For example, this declaration specifies that UIL should define objects of type **XmPushButton** to be gadgets:

```
objects = { XmPushButton = gadget; }
```

A declaration for an individual object can override this specification.

4.1.3 include Directive

The **include** directive includes the contents of a file in the current module. The directive consists of the keywords **include file** followed by a string representing the filename. If the filename has a full directory specification, UIL searches that directory for the file. Otherwise, UIL searches the directory of the main UIL source file and then the directory of the current UIL source file. The **-I** option to the **uil** command adds a directory to the search list.

Included files are useful for definitions common to more than one UIL module. In conjunction with the **-I** option to **uil**, they are also useful in internationalizing applications. Localized definitions for strings, font lists, and the like can reside in files included from different directories depending on language environment. In this case, the **include** directives should not specify the directories; instead, you can use the **-I** option to **uil** to compile files for different language environments without editing or duplicating UIL files.

4.1.4 value Declaration

The **value** clause defines one or more names and associates them with values. The names can stand for values elsewhere in the module.

The specification for each value is either a literal expression or a call to a UIL function that generates a value. Each value has a UIL type that depends on the representation of the literal or the type of value returned by the UIL function. For more information on UIL types, literals, and functions, see the **UIL(5X)** reference page in the *OSF/Motif Programmer's Reference*.

By default, the names and their associated values are private to the module. The **value** declaration can also export a value to other modules or import a value from another module. For each name declared to be imported, MRM assigns the value from the corresponding exported declaration at run time.

In this example, the value **id_1** is exported:

```
value
    id_1            : exported 1;
    label_1         : compound_string('Off');
```

Another module can use the value **id_1** as follows:

```
value
    id_1            : imported integer;
```

4.1.5 identifier Declaration

An **identifier** clause declares one or more names that can appear elsewhere in the module. At run time, MRM assigns values to these names from data defined in the application program. The application uses the **MrmRegisterNames** or **MrmRegisterNamesInHierarchy** routine to establish the correspondence between UIL identifier names and application-defined data. The UIL compiler performs no type checking on identifiers.

The following example identifies names for x and y values that the application defines at run time:

```
identifier
    app_x_value;
    app_y_value;
```

4.1.6 procedure Declaration

A **procedure** clause declares names of callback procedures or of creation routines for user-defined widgets. The application program itself defines the actual procedures. As with identifiers, the application must use **MrmRegisterNames** or **MrmRegisterNamesInHierarchy** to associate the procedure names with the actual procedures at run time.

For a callback procedure, the **procedure** declaration can also specify the type of data represented by the second argument (the application data pointer) to the callback routine:

```
procedure
    toggle_cb (integer);
    push_button_cb (integer);
```

4.1.7 object Declaration

An **object** clause defines a widget or gadget and assigns a name that can stand for the object elsewhere in the UIL module. As with values, an object definition by default is private to the UIL module, but the **object** clause can declare it to be exported or imported. In addition to the UIL name, the **object** clause specifies the object's type and a list (enclosed in braces) that can define children, initial resource values, and callback procedures.

4.1.7.1 Object Type

The object type specification is a keyword that is usually the same as the name of the corresponding toolkit widget class. For example, the type keyword for a MainWindow is **XmMainWindow** and for a PushButton is **XmPushButton**. UIL also allows type specifications that correspond to toolkit convenience routines for creating some kinds of specialized widgets, including menus, dialogs, ScrolledList, and ScrolledText. For example, the keyword **XmPulldownMenu** specifies a PulldownMenu, and the keyword **XmPromptDialog** specifies a PromptDialog.

The **object** clause can also specify that the object is to be either a widget or a gadget, overriding the default specified by the **objects** clause. For example, the following defines a PushButtonGadget:

```
object
    pb : XmPushButton gadget {};
```

Alternately, an **object** clause can specify a gadget by using the gadget class name (for example, **XmPushButtonGadget**) as the type specification.

4.1.7.2 Children

An **object** clause can specify the children of a composite widget. This specification appears inside the object list section and consists of the keyword **controls** followed by a list of child declarations. The declaration for each child consists of an object type and, usually, a name that refers to the definition for the child widget in its own **object** clause. Instead of a name for the child, the declaration can contain an entire local definition for the child widget in the form of an object list section. The child declaration can optionally begin with the keyword **managed** or **unmanaged**, which specifies whether or not MRM should manage the child after creating it. The default is to manage the child.

Some manager widgets automatically create children. For example, MainWindow creates three separators to separate its main components. The **controls** list can contain declarations for these children so that the UIL file can specify resource values for them. The declaration for an automatically created child begins with a specification of the name of the child, formed by prepending **Xm_** to the actual name of the child widget. The names of automatically created children are documented in the reference pages for the manager widgets in the *OSF/Motif Programmer's Reference*.

Following is an example of specifications for child widgets:

```
object
    main_win : XmMainWindow {
        controls {
            XmMenuBar main_menu;
            Xm_Separator1 sep_1;
            XmScrolledText text_win;
        };
    };
```

In general, a child widget can be of any type the Motif toolkit allows for a child of the parent widget. In some cases, the type of the child differs from the Motif toolkit class. For example, dialogs and menus require shells as their parents, but in UIL a dialog or menu is declared to be a direct child of its parent, with no intervening shell. MRM creates the shell at run time. In this way, UIL and MRM act like the Motif convenience routines for creating dialogs and menus.

Some widget hierarchies in UIL are slightly different from the corresponding hierarchies in the toolkit. For example, in UIL a PulldownMenu in an OptionMenu is described as a child of the OptionMenu, not of the OptionMenu's parent as it is in the toolkit. In a PulldownMenu system from a MenuBar or a PopupMenu, each PulldownMenu is a child of the associated CascadeButton, not of the CascadeButton's parent as it is in the toolkit. For more information, see Chapter 6.

4.1.7.3 Resource Values

An **object** clause can specify resource values for MRM to pass to the widget's creation function. This specification appears inside the object list section and consists of the keyword **arguments** followed by a list of resource declarations. The declaration for each resource consists of the name of the resource as in the toolkit (for example, **XmNheight**) followed by = (equals sign) and a value for the resource. The type of the value must be of the proper UIL type for that resource. For information on the required UIL type for each resource, see Appendix C of the *OSF/Motif Programmer's Reference*.

Following is an example of specifications for initial resource values:

```
object
    main_win : XmScrolledText {
        arguments {
            XmNrows = 10;
            XmNwordWrap = true;
            XmNbackground = color('red');
        };
    };
```

In some cases, UIL provides a value for a resource related to a resource that appears in a specification. For example, if a specification contains a value for **XmNitems** in a List, UIL provides the appropriate value for **XmNitemCount**.

4.1.7.4 Callback Procedures

An **object** clause can specify procedures to appear in callback lists for the object. This specification appears inside the object list section and consists of the keyword **callbacks** followed by a list of callback list declarations. The declaration for each callback list consists of the name of the callback resource as in the toolkit (for example, **XmNactivateCallback**) followed by = (equals sign) and a value specification for the resource.

In addition to appropriate toolkit resources, the specification can include the special callback list name **MrmNcreateCallback**. MRM invokes callback procedures on this list when it creates the widget. These procedures provide a means for the application to identify the widget ID of a widget created by MRM.

The value specification can be one of two forms:

- If the callback list contains only one procedure, the specification consists of the keyword **procedure** followed by the procedure name and, optionally, a value in parentheses for the application data argument to the procedure.

- If the callback list contains more than one procedure, the specification consists of the keyword **procedures** followed by a list of procedure specifications. Each specification consists of the procedure name and, optionally, a value in parentheses for the application data argument to the procedure.

The UIL compiler issues a warning if a procedure specification contains an application data argument whose type does not match the argument type in the corresponding **procedure** declaration.

The application uses the **MrmRegisterNames** routine or the **MrmRegisterNamesInHierarchy** routine to establish the correspondence between UIL procedure names and the application-defined procedures.

Following is an example of specifications for a callback list:

```
object
    pb : XmPushButton {
        callbacks {
            XmNactivateCallback =
                procedure pb_activate_cb (pb_ident);
        };
    };
```

4.1.8 list Declaration

A **list** clause defines one or more lists of specifications for resources, callbacks, procedures, or widget children. Each list has a symbolic name that the application can use to refer to the list elsewhere in the UIL file, usually in an **object** declaration. The main use for this clause is to define lists of specifications that are common to more than one object definition.

A **list** clause consists of the keyword **list** followed by one or more list specifications. Each list specification contains the name, type, and contents of the list. Following are the four kinds of lists:

- A list of resources consists of the keyword **arguments** followed by a list of resource specifications.

- A list of callbacks consists of the keyword **callbacks** followed by a list of callback specifications.

- A list of procedures consists of the keyword **procedures** followed by a list of procedure specifications.

- A list of widget children consists of the keyword **controls** followed by a list of specifications for the children.

In each case, the form of the list is the same as that of the corresponding clause of an **object** declaration.

Following is an example of a **list** declaration:

```
list
    pb_activate_procs : procedures {
        pb_ac_proc_1 ();
        pb_ac_proc_2 ();
    };

list
    pb_callbacks : callbacks {
        XmNactivateCallback = pb_activate_procs;
        XmNarmCallback = procedure pb_arm_proc ();
    };
list
    pb_args : arguments {
        XmNheight = 10;
```

```
                XmNbackground = color('red');
            };

    object
        pb_1 : XmPushButton {
            arguments {
                arguments pb_args;
                XmNlabelString = pb_label_1;
            };
            callbacks pb_callbacks;
          };

    object
        pb_2 : XmPushButton {
            arguments {
                arguments pb_args;
                XmNlabelString = pb_label_2;
            };
            callbacks pb_callbacks;
          };

    list
        menu_items : controls {
            XmPushButton pb_1;
            XmPushButton pb_2;
        };

    object
        menu_1 : XmPulldownMenu {
            controls menu_items;
        };
```

4.1.9 end module Clause

Each UIL module must end with an **end module** clause.

4.2 Structure of a Program Using MRM

4.2.1 Including Header Files

An application that uses MRM must include all the header files it would need if it did not use MRM. These include **<Xm/Xm.h>**, header files specific to each widget the program uses, and any header files needed by Motif routines. In addition, the application must include the file **<Mrm/MrmPublic.h>**. This file contains definitions that the MRM routines need.

Following is an example of including header files for an application that uses only a Text widget and MRM:

```
#include <Mrm/MrmPublic.h>
#include <Xm/Xm.h>
#include <Xm/Text.h>
```

4.2.2 Initializing the Intrinsics

An application initializes the Intrinsics as in any other program, usually by calling **XtAppInitialize**. The application must call **XtDisplayInitialize** either directly or indirectly before opening any UID files.

4.2.3 Initializing MRM

An application that uses MRM must initialize MRM by calling **MrmInitialize** before fetching any widgets from UID files. It is a good idea to call **MrmInitialize** before using any other MRM routines.

4.2.4 Opening UID Files

After initializing MRM and the Intrinsics, an application uses **MrmOpenHierarchyPerDisplay** to find and open one or more UID files that contain the widget definitions and other information to be loaded. **MrmOpenHierarchyPerDisplay** uses search paths in much the same way **XtDisplayInitialize** uses them to build the initial resource database. One argument to **MrmOpenHierarchyPerDisplay** is a list of UID filenames, each of which represents either a full pathname or a name to be substituted in a file search path. The search path comes from the **UIDPATH** environment variable or, if **UIDPATH** is not set, from a series of default paths. **MrmOpenHierarchyPerDisplay** calls **XtResolvePathname** to search these paths. When it uses a search path, **MrmOpenHierarchyPerDisplay** looks for files first using a suffix of **.uid** and then using a NULL suffix.

As with the initial resource database, UID files can reside in different directories depending on the language environment. The search paths can include these substitutions, as well as others recognized by **XtResolvePathname**:

- **%N** is replaced by the class name of the application.

- **%L** is replaced by the display's language specification.

- **%l** is replaced by the language part of the language specification.

- **%U** is replaced by the current filename from the list of filenames passed as an argument to **MrmOpenHierarchyPerDisplay**.

MrmOpenHierarchyPerDisplay returns an ID that identifies the list of open UID files for subsequent calls to routines that load data from the files. On each request to load data, MRM searches the list of files in order. This ordered list of open files is the UID hierarchy. The program can retrieve data from the hierarchy until it calls **MrmCloseHierarchy**.

Following is an example of a call to **MrmOpenHierarchyPerDisplay**. The
example initializes MRM and the Intrinsics, opens a UID hierarchy, and
closes the hierarchy.

```
int main(int argc, char **argv)
{
    Widget        app_shell;
    XtAppContext  app;
    static String file_names[] = { "app_1", "app_2" };
    MrmHierarchy  hierarchy_id;

    app_shell = XtAppInitialize(&app, "Example",
        (XrmOptionDescList) NULL, 0, (Cardinal *) &argc, argv,
        (String *) NULL, (ArgList) NULL, 0);
    MrmInitialize();
    switch (MrmOpenHierarchyPerDisplay(XtDisplay(app_shell),
            (MrmCount) XtNumber(file_names), file_names,
            (MrmOsOpenParamPtr *) NULL, &hierarchy_id)) {
    case MrmSUCCESS:
        if (MrmCloseHierarchy(hierarchy_id) == MrmSUCCESS) {
            exit 0;
        } else {
            fprintf(stderr,
                    "Unable to close UID hierarchy.\n");
            exit 1;
        }
    case MrmNOT_FOUND:
        fprintf(stderr, "Unable to open UID files.\n");
        exit 1;
    default:
        fprintf(stderr, "Unable to open UID hierarchy.\n");
        exit 1;
    }
}
```

4.2.5 Registering Callbacks and Identifiers

The application must register the names of all callback procedures and identifiers defined in the UIL files. Registering the names associates the symbolic names in the UIL files with procedures and data defined in the program. **MrmRegisterNames** and **MrmRegisterNamesInHierarchy** accomplish this task. Names registered by **MrmRegisterNames** are global to all UID hierarchies, whereas names registered by **MrmRegisterNamesInHierarchy** are local to a particular hierarchy. When MRM looks up the program-defined value associated with a name in a given hierarchy, it searches first for an association local to the hierarchy and then for a global association.

Following is an example using **MrmRegisterNames**:

```
void PBActivateCB_1(Widget pb, XtPointer app_data,
    XtPointer widget_data);
void PBActivateCB_2(Widget pb, XtPointer app_data,
    XtPointer widget_data);
void PBArmCB(Widget pb, XtPointer app_data,
    XtPointer widget_data);

static MrmRegisterArg cb_list[] = {
    { "pb_ac_proc_1",    (XtPointer) PBActivateCB_1 },
    { "pb_ac_proc_2",    (XtPointer) PBActivateCB_2 },
    { "pb_arm_proc",     (XtPointer) PBArmCB }
};


...

    if (MrmRegisterNames(cb_list,
                    (MrmCount) XtNumber(cb_list))
        == MrmSUCCESS) {
        ...
    } else {
        ...
    }
```

4.2.6 Fetching Information from UID Files

MRM can fetch the following information from UID files:

- Named widgets, defined by **object** clauses, and their descendants. Use **MrmFetchWidget** or **MrmFetchWidgetOverride**.

- Named color literals, defined by **color** or **rbg** functions and appearing in **value** clauses. Use **MrmFetchColorLiteral**.

- Named icon literals, defined by **icon** functions and appearing in **value** clauses. Use **MrmFetchIconLiteral**.

- Other named literals appearing in **value** clauses. Use **MrmFetchLiteral** or **MrmFetchSetValues**.

MRM can fetch literals appearing in **value** clauses only if they are defined as **exported**.

After creating a top-level shell, using **XtAppInitialize** or **XtAppCreateShell**, the application can use **MrmFetchWidget** to fetch the child of the top-level shell and its descendants. For each widget in the tree, **MrmFetchWidget** does the following:

- Calls the appropriate widget creation routine, passing it the initial resource values defined in the **arguments** specification in the **object** clause

- Adds the callback routines defined in the **callbacks** specification of the **object** clause

- Calls any **MrmNcreateCallback** callbacks

- Manages all child widgets unless they are defined to be **unmanaged**

The application does not have to fetch all widgets at the beginning of the program. To create widgets such as menus and dialogs as needed, the application can call **MrmFetchWidget** at any time.

The application can fetch the same widget definition more than once. MRM creates a new widget each time, essentially using the UIL definition as a template. **MrmFetchWidgetOverride** is useful here, as it allows the application to override the initial resource values specified in the UIL file.

Following is a simple example using **MrmFetchWidget** to create the main widget hierarchy for an application:

```
int main(int argc, char **argv)
{
    Widget          app_shell, top_level;
    XtAppContext    app;
    static String   file_names[] = { "app_1", "app_2" };
    MrmHierarchy    hierarchy_id;
    MrmType         top_level_class;

    MrmInitialize();
    app_shell = XtAppInitialize(&app, "Example",
        (XrmOptionDescList) NULL, 0, (Cardinal *) &argc, argv,
        (String *) NULL, (ArgList) NULL, 0);
    switch (MrmOpenHierarchyPerDisplay(XtDisplay(app_shell),
            (MrmCount) XtNumber(file_names), file_names,
            (MrmOsOpenParamPtr *) NULL, &hierarchy_id)) {
    case MrmSUCCESS:
        if (MrmFetchWidget(hierarchy_id, "top_level",
            app_shell, &top_level, &top_level_class)
                                          != MrmSUCCESS) {
            fprintf(stderr,
                    "Unable to fetch top-level widget.\n");
        }
        if (MrmCloseHierarchy(hierarchy_id) == MrmSUCCESS) {
            exit 0;
        } else {
            fprintf(stderr,
                    "Unable to close UID hierarchy.\n");
            exit 1;
        }
    case MrmNOT_FOUND:
        fprintf(stderr, "Unable to open UID files.\n");
        exit 1;
    default:
        fprintf(stderr, "Unable to open UID hierarchy.\n");
        exit 1;
    }
}
```

4.2.7 Closing the UID File

MrmCloseHierarchy closes all files in the specified UID hierarchy. The application can close and reopen a hierarchy, but usually it does not close a hierarchy until it is finished reading data from the UID files. When the application uses multiple hierarchies, operating system limits on the number of open files may make it necessary to close one hierarchy before opening another.

4.2.8 Defining Callback Procedures

An application that uses MRM defines callback procedures in the same way as an application that uses only the toolkit. For callbacks delared in UIL files, the application must use **MrmRegisterNames** or **MrmRegisterNamesInHierarchy** to associate the UIL callback procedure names with the actual procedures defined in the program.

An application can create widgets, such as dialogs and PopupMenus, as the program needs them. If these widgets are defined in UIL files, a callback procedure can call **MrmFetchWidget** to fetch them from UID files.

4.2.9 Making Widgets Visible

MrmFetchWidget never manages the widget the application is fetching. It does manage all other widgets in the tree whose root is the widget being fetched, except for widgets declared **unmanaged** in the UIL file. **MrmFetchWidget** does not realize any widgets in the tree.

The application must manage any unmanaged widgets created by **MrmFetchWidget**, and it must realize all widgets it wants to make visible. In the simple case where the application fetches the entire widget hierarchy at the beginning of the program, it typically manages the widget it fetches and then realizes the top-level shell:

```
int main(int argc, char **argv)
{
    Widget          app_shell, top_level;
    XtAppContext    app;
    static String   file_names[] = { "app_1", "app_2" };
```

```
MrmHierarchy    hierarchy_id;
MrmType         top_level_class;

MrmInitialize();
app_shell = XtAppInitialize(&app, "Example",
    (XrmOptionDescList) NULL, 0, (Cardinal *) &argc, argv,
    (String *) NULL, (ArgList) NULL, 0);
switch (MrmOpenHierarchyPerDisplay(XtDisplay(app_shell),
        (MrmCount) XtNumber(file_names), file_names,
        (MrmOsOpenParamPtr *) NULL, &hierarchy_id)) {
case MrmSUCCESS:
    if (MrmFetchWidget(hierarchy_id, "top_level", app_shell,
            &top_level, &top_level_class) == MrmSUCCESS) {
        XtManageChild(top_level);
        XtRealizeWidget(app_shell);
    } else {
        fprintf(stderr,
                "Unable to fetch top-level widget.\n");
    }
    if (MrmCloseHierarchy(hierarchy_id) == MrmSUCCESS) {
        exit 0;
    } else {
        fprintf(stderr,
                "Unable to close UID hierarchy.\n");
        exit 1;
    }
case MrmNOT_FOUND:
    fprintf(stderr, "Unable to open UID files.\n");
    exit 1;
default:
    fprintf(stderr, "Unable to open UID hierarchy.\n");
    exit 1;
}
}
```

4.2.10 Entering the Event Loop

As with toolkit applications that do not use MRM, a program using MRM typically calls **XtAppMainLoop** to enter the event loop after realizing the top-level shell.

Chapter 5

Basic Controls

Controls are widgets and gadgets with which the user interacts directly. They form the leaves of the widget tree whose root is the application's top-level shell. In most cases, controls are subclasses of **XmPrimitive** or **XmGadget**, and their parents are subclasses of **XmManager**. (**XmScale** is a manager, but in many ways the application treats it as a primitive.) Motif provides the following basic controls:

- Labels, buttons, and separators
- ScrollBar
- Scale
- List
- Text and TextField

5.1 Core, RectObj, XmPrimitive, and XmGadget Classes

Nearly all the basic controls are subclasses of **XmPrimitive** or **XmGadget**. **XmPrimitive**, in turn, is a subclass of the Intrinsics **Core** class, and **XmGadget** is a subclass of the Intrinsics **RectObj** class.

5.1.1 Core

The **Core** class provides basic attributes of all widgets that have associated windows. It has the following groups of resources:

- Specifications of the widget's x and y coordinates, width and height, and border width

- A resource specifying whether or not the widget is sensitive or able to receive input events from the Intrinsics event manager

- Characteristics of the window, including background and border color or pixmap, colormap, depth, and screen

- A resource controlling whether or not the Intrinsics map the window when the widget is managed

- A table associating translations with actions

- A set of accelerators, which is a translation table bound in the context of a particular widget

5.1.2 RectObj

RectObj is the foundation for gadget classes; it is essentially **Core** without the attributes related to having a window. **RectObj** resources control the position and dimensions of the gadget's rectangular area within its parent widget. A **RectObj** resource also determines whether or not the gadget is sensitive.

5.1.3 XmPrimitive

XmPrimitive is the fundamental Motif class for all basic control widgets—widgets that do not have children. It includes the following resources and behavior:

- Foreground color, top and bottom shadow colors or pixmaps, and shadow thickness

- Thickness and color or pixmap for the highlighting rectangle, which is displayed when the widget has keyboard focus

- Resources to determine whether the user can traverse to the widget and whether or not it is a tab group

- A resource to determine what unit of measurement the widget uses for size and position resources

- Callbacks for the widget to invoke when the user presses **KHelp**

- A resource for the application to use in associating arbitrary data with the widget

- Translations and actions for keyboard traversal to another widget

5.1.4 XmGadget

XmGadget is the fundamental Motif class for all basic control gadgets. It is equivalent to **XmPrimitive**, with two major exceptions:

- It has no resources for colors or pixmaps. A gadget inherits these from its parent; therefore, all gadgets within a Manager have the same colors or pixmaps.

- It has no translations or actions. The Manager parent controls traversal between its gadget children, keeps track of gadgets that have input focus, and dispatches events to them.

5.2 Labels, Buttons, and Separators

Labels, buttons, and separators are simple widgets built on **XmPrimitive**.

5.2.1 Labels

Labels provide the ability to display static (uneditable) text or a pixmap. A Label or LabelGadget itself is useful for displaying a message, title, or description. Label and LabelGadget are also superclasses for buttons used as menu items, toggles, or controls.

The application can specify the following characteristics of Labels, LabelGadgets, and their subclasses:

- A compound string or pixmap to be displayed. When using a pixmap, the application can supply a separate pixmap to be displayed when the widget is insensitive.

- A font list for displaying the compound string.

- Resources to determine the positioning of the text or pixmap within the widget. One sets of resources determines the space allocated for the margins; another determines the distance between the margins and the text or pixmap inside. The **XmNalignment** and **XmNstringDirection** resources together determine whether the text or pixmap is centered or is left or right justified within the widget.

- A resource, **XmNrecomputeSize**, that determines whether the widget attempts to remain large enough to contain the text or pixmap. When this resource is True and a resource that affects the size of the text or pixmap, the margins, or the widget itself is changed, the widget tries to resize itself to be just large enough to contain the text or pixmap.

In addition, Label and LabelGadget provide the following facilities for button subclasses in menus:

- A keysym used as a mnemonic to select the button. The user can activate the button by pressing the mnemonic key when the button is visible.

- An accelerator, a **KeyPress** event by which the user can activate the button whether or not it is visible. Accelerators are supported only for PushButtons and ToggleButtons in PulldownMenus and PopupMenus.

- Translations and actions for keyboard traversal within the menu or menu system.

5.2.2 Buttons

A button is a basic control that performs some action when the user activates it. Buttons commonly appear in menus, RadioBoxes, CheckBoxes, SelectionBoxes, and MessageBoxes. This section describes some of the functions of each subclass.

5.2.2.1 CascadeButtons

A CascadeButton or CascadeButtonGadget is used inside a menu and, when activated, usually causes a PulldownMenu to appear. CascadeButtons have the following resources and behavior:

- A pixmap displayed at one end of the widget in a PopupMenu or PulldownMenu to indicate that activating the CascadeButton posts another menu.

- A resource, **XmNsubMenuId**, that holds the widget ID of the PulldownMenu posted when the user activates the button.

- **XmNactivateCallback** callbacks, which the widget invokes when the user activates it, and **XmNcascadingCallback** callbacks, which the widget invokes just before posting a PulldownMenu.

- A resource to provide a delay between the time the mouse enters the widget and the time it posts a menu.

- Translations and actions to activate the widget and to post and unpost PulldownMenus. In general, pressing **BSelect** or dragging **BSelect** into the widget posts the PulldownMenu. Releasing **BSelect** in the widget causes the PulldownMenu to remain posted and enables keyboard traversal. When keyboard traversal is enabled, pressing **KActivate** or **KSelect** in the widget posts the PulldownMenu and enables keyboard traversal in that menu.

5.2.2.2 PushButtons

A PushButton or PushButtonGadget can appear either inside or outside a menu. It performs some action determined by the application. When a PushButton is armed, or ready to be activated, it changes its appearance so that it looks as if the user has pressed it in. When it is disarmed it reverts to the appearance of extending out. PushButtons provide the following behavior:

- Callbacks that the widget invokes when it is armed, disarmed, and activated. The application usually provides only an **XmNactivateCallback** procedure to perform the action associated with the button.

- Resources to provide a color or pixmap to be displayed when the button is armed and not inside a menu. When a button in a menu is armed, the top and bottom shadows switch colors.

- A resource to determine whether or not the widget considers multiple mouse clicks distinct from single mouse clicks.

- A resource to determine whether or not the button is marked as the default button when outside a menu. In a BulletinBoard, the default button is the one activated when the user presses **KActivate** and no other button has keyboard focus. The default button has a distinctive shadow whose thickness is controlled by the **XmNdefaultButtonShadowThickness** resource.

- Translations to arm, disarm, and activate the button. In general, pressing **BSelect** on a button or, in a menu, dragging **BSelect** or traversing to a button arms it. Releasing **BSelect** or pressing **KActivate** (in a menu) or **KSelect** in the widget activates and disarms it.

5.2.2.3 ToggleButtons

ToggleButtons and ToggleButtonGadgets have one of two states: like toggle switches, they are either "on" or "off". They can appear in menus or in nonmenu RowColumn WorkAreas, including RadioBoxes and CheckBoxes. In a RadioBox only one ToggleButton at a time can be on; in a CheckBox more than one ToggleButton can be on. ToggleButtons can have indicators with distinctive shapes to distinguish whether or not more than one button at a time can be set. However, it is the RowColumn parent, not the

ToggleButton, that controls this behavior.

ToggleButtons have the following characteristics:

- Callbacks that the widget invokes when it is armed or disarmed and when it changes state. The widget invokes the **XmNvalueChangedCallback** callbacks when the button's state changes from on to off or from off to on.

- Resources to control the appearance of the indicator. If **XmNindicatorOn** is False or if **XmNvisibleWhenOff** is False and the button is in the off state, no indicator is displayed. Otherwise, **XmNindicatorType** determines whether the indicator shows that only one or more than one button at a time can be on.

- A color or pixmap to be displayed when the button is armed and **XmNfillOnSelect** is True.

- Pixmaps to be displayed when the button is selected and the Label or LabelGadget superclass's **XmNlabelType** is **XmPIXMAP**.

- Translations to arm and disarm the button and to change its state. In general, pressing **BSelect** on a button or, in a menu, dragging **BSelect** or traversing to a button arms it. Releasing **BSelect** or pressing **KActivate** (in a menu) or **KSelect** in the widget changes its state and disarms it.

5.2.2.4 DrawnButtons

A DrawnButton is an empty button surrounded by a shadow border. It is intended to be used as a PushButton but with graphics drawn by the application. Like a PushButton, it has translations and actions to arm, disarm, and activate the button and invoke the corresponding callbacks. If **XmNpushButtonEnabled** is True, it draws the shadow so that the button appears pressed in when armed and popped out when disarmed.

Other than this, the application must manage the button's visual appearance. It has **XmNexposeCallback** and **XmNresizeCallback** callbacks to notify the application that the button has been exposed or resized and therefore needs to be redrawn. The application must be careful not to draw within the button's shadows or highlight areas. The application can use a clipping rectangle in the widget's graphics context that takes account of the button's **XmNhighlightThickness** and **XmNshadowThickness**.

5.2.2.5 ArrowButtons

An ArrowButton or ArrowButtonGadget is a button with an arrow graphic and a shadow. A resource controls the direction of the arrow. Unlike other buttons, it is not a subclass of **XmLabel** or **XmLabelGadget**, but is has some of the same behavior as other buttons. It has callbacks that the widget invokes when armed, disarmed, or activated. It has translations and actions similar to those of other buttons to arm, disarm, or activate the button.

5.2.3 Separators

A Separator or SeparatorGadget separates controls or groups of controls. It usually appears as a horizontal or vertical line and supports several styles of line drawing. Resources control its orientation and the type of line it draws. One line style consists of no line at all. This allows the application to control the appearance of the separator by setting its **XmNbackgroundColor** or **XmNbackgroundPixmap**.

5.3 ScrollBar

A widget can act as a viewport onto a virtual scroll. The ScrollBar is the control that moves the viewport horizontally or vertically relative to the underlying scroll. A ScrollBar consists of a rectangle, called the scroll region, representing the full size of the scroll. It has a smaller rectangle, called the slider, within the scroll region, representing the position and size of the viewport relative to the full scroll. The ScrollBar usually has arrow graphics at both ends of the larger rectangle.

A ScrollBar has translations and actions that allow the user to move the slider. By clicking on an arrow, the user moves the slider one small increment in the direction of the arrow. By clicking in the scroll region between an arrow and the slider, the user moves the slider a larger increment (the page increment) in the direction of the arrow. When the ScrollBar has keyboard focus the user can use the keyboard to move the slider in this way. The user can also drag the slider using the mouse.

By itself, the ScrollBar does not have an association with a widget acting as a viewport onto a scroll. Most applications use a ScrolledWindow, a

Manager widget with a child to be scrolled and possibly with one or two ScrollBars to control the scrolling. ScrolledWindow can automatically control the interaction between the scrolled child and the ScrollBars, or it can allow the application to control the interaction. For more information see Chapter 9.

ScrollBar has a number of resources that allow the application to use it to control scrolling:

- A minimum value (**XmNminimum**), representing the position of the slider at one end of the scroll region, and a maximum value (**XmNmaximum**), representing the position of the slider at the other end of the scroll region. These values can be in any integral units the application chooses so long as the maximum is greater than the minimum.

- The length of the slider (**XmNsliderSize**) between 1 and (**XmNmaximum** - **XmNminimum**).

- A value (**XmNvalue**), ranging between **XmNminimum** and (**XmNmaximum** - **XmNsliderSize**), representing the current position of the slider between the maximum and minimum values.

- Values for the increment (**XmNincrement**) and page increment (**XmNpageIncrement**) by which the user can move the slider.

- A resource (**XmNprocessingDirection**) that determines whether the minimum value is on the left or right for horizontal ScrollBars or is on the bottom or top for vertical ScrollBars.

- Distinct callbacks that the widget invokes when the user moves the slider by one increment in either direction, by one page increment in either direction, or all the way to either end of the scroll region. The widget invokes other callbacks as the user drags the slider and when the user stops dragging the slider. The application does not have to provide routines for all these callback lists; if it provides only an **XmNvalueChangedCallback** procedure, the widget invokes that procedure whenever the ScrollBar value changes (except during interactive dragging of the slider).

- Resources to control the color of the scroll region, whether the ScrollBar is horizontal or vertical, and whether or not the ScrollBar has arrows.

- Resources to control the delays before the widget moves the slider continuously as the user presses and holds **BSelect** on an arrow or the scroll region.

Two convenience routines, **XmScrollBarGetValues** and **XmScrollBarSetValues**, allow the application to get and set the value, slider size, increment, and page increment in one call.

5.4 Scale

A Scale displays a value within a range and optionally allows the user to supply a new value. Its appearance and behavior are much like those of a ScrollBar without arrows. It also has a title and can display the current value next to the slider.

Like a ScrollBar, a Scale has minimum, maximum, and current integral values. The application has no access to the slider size, and the current value ranges between the minimum and maximum. The increment by which the arrow keys move the slider is always 1, but the application can supply a multiple increment (**XmNscaleMultiple**) analogous to ScrollBar's **XmNpageIncrement**. Scale has two callback lists: **XmNvalueChangedCallback** is invoked when the user changes the value but is not in the process of dragging the slider, and **XmNdragCallback** is invoked when the user changes the value while dragging the slider.

Scale also has resources controlling whether the orientation is vertical or horizontal and which end of the Scale represents the minimum value. Other resources control aspects of the Scale's appearance, including the width and height, the title string, whether or not the Scale displays the current value next to the slider, the number of decimal places in the displayed value, and a font list for the title and value.

Two convenience routines, **XmScaleGetValue** and **XmScaleSetValue**, allow the application to get and set the value.

By default, a Scale has no labels or tic marks along the rectangle in which the slider moves. The application can add these by creating a series of widgets—such as LabelGadgets or SeparatorGadgets—as children of the Scale. For example, LabelGadgets could display values at intervals between the minimum and maximum, or SeparatorGadgets could display short lines as tic marks. The Scale positions any children, in order of creation, along the rectangle containing the slider, as follows:

- A single child appears in the middle of the rectangle

- If there are two children, the first appears at the top (for a vertical Scale) or left (for a horizontal scale) of the rectangle, and the other child appears at the bottom or right of the rectangle

- If there are more than three children, they appear at equal intervals along the rectangle ranging from top to bottom or from left to right

The following example creates a Scale with five tic marks:

```
#define NUM_TICS 5
Widget          parent, scale, tics[NUM_TICS];
Arg             args[10];
Cardinal        i, n;
unsigned char   scale_orientation, tic_orientation;
Dimension       tic_long_dim = 10, tic_short_dim = 5;
Dimension       tic_width, tic_height;
char            tic_name[10];
...
scale = XmCreateScale(parent, "scale", args, n);
XtManageChild(scale);
...
n = 0;
XtSetArg(args[n], XmNorientation, &scale_orientation);   n++;
XtGetValues(scale, args, n);
if (scale_orientation == XmHORIZONTAL) {
    tic_orientation = XmVERTICAL;
    tic_width = tic_short_dim;
    tic_height = tic_long_dim;
} else {
    tic_orientation = XmHORIZONTAL;
    tic_width = tic_long_dim;
    tic_height = tic_short_dim;
}

for (i = 0; i < NUM_TICS; i++) {
    sprintf(tic_name, "tic_%d", i);
    n = 0;
```

```
        XtSetArg(args[n], XmNseparatorType, XmSINGLE_LINE);   n++;
        XtSetArg(args[n], XmNorientation, tic_orientation);   n++;
        XtSetArg(args[n], XmNwidth, tic_width);               n++;
        XtSetArg(args[n], XmNheight, tic_height);             n++;
        tics[i] = XmCreateSeparatorGadget(scale, tic_name,
                                          args, n);
    }
    XtManageChildren(tics, NUM_TICS);
    ...
```

5.5 List

A List is an array of textual items from which the user selects one or more entries. Each item is a compound string. List has four modes, controlled by the **XmNselectionPolicy** resource, for selecting items:

Single Select

> At most one item is selected. Performing the selection action on an item toggles the selection state of the item and deselects any other selected item.

Browse Select

> At most one item is selected. Performing the selection action on an item selects the item and deselects any other selected item. Dragging **BSelect** through the list moves the selection along with the cursor.

Multiple Select

> Any number of items can be selected. Performing the selection action on an item toggles the selection state of the item but does not deselect any other selected item.

Extended Select

> Any number of items can be selected. The user can select either continuous or discontinuous ranges of items, depending on the mouse buttons used or, when using the keyboard, on whether the List is in Normal Mode or Add Mode:
>
> - Pressing **BSelect** or, in Normal Mode, **KSelect** on an item selects the item and deselects any other selected item. Dragging **BSelect** or pressing or dragging **BExtend**

following a **BSelect** action selects all items between the item under the pointer and the item on which **BSelect** was pressed. In Normal Mode, **KExtend** and shifted navigation have the same effect as pressing **BExtend** following a **BSelect** action.

- Pressing **BToggle** or, in Add Mode, **KSelect** on an item toggles the selection state of the item but does not deselect any selected item. Dragging **BToggle** or pressing or dragging **BExtend** following a **BToggle** action sets the selection state of all items between the item under the pointer and the item on which **BToggle** was pressed to the state of the item on which **BToggle** was pressed. In Add Mode, **KExtend** and shifted navigation have the same effect as pressing **BExtend** following a **BToggle** action.

When the user makes a selection, the List invokes one of four callback lists, depending on the selection policy:

Selection Policy	Callback List
Single Select	**XmNsingleSelectionCallback**
Browse Select	**XmNbrowseSelectionCallback**
Multiple Select	**XmNmultipleSelectionCallback**
Extended Select	**XmNextendedSelectionCallback**

By default, the List does not invoke a callback list when the List is in Single Select or Extended Select mode and the user drags the mouse cursor over a new item. It does invoke the callbacks when the user releases the mouse button. If **XmNautomaticSelection** is True, the List invokes the callbacks while the user is dragging the mouse.

The widget data passed to selection callback routines contains both the selected items—the compound strings—and integers representing the positions within the list of the selected items. The first item in the list is at position 1, the second item at position 2, and so on.

List has another callback list, **XmNdefaultActionCallback**, which it invokes when the user double clicks or presses **KActivate** on an item. The widget data passed to these callback routines contains only the item at the location cursor and its position, not the selected items. When the user performs the default action via a double click, the List calls the appropriate selection callbacks on the first click and the **XmNdefaultActionCallback** callbacks on the second click.

List includes several other sets of resources:

- Arrays and counts of the List items and selected items

- The number of items, **XmNvisibleItemCount**, that the list can display at one time, and the position in the List of the first visible item

- Several resources that affect the appearance of the list items: font list, justification (**XmNstringDirection**), spacing between items, and margins between the items and the List border

- The maximum time interval between clicks for a double click

- A resource (**XmNlistSizePolicy**) that determines what the List does when an item is too wide to fit into the List: it can keep its size and, if it is a ScrolledList, add a horizontal ScrollBar; grow to accommodate the item; or try to grow and, if it fails to accommodate the item but is a ScrolledList, add a ScrollBar

- A resource that determines whether the ScrollBars in a ScrolledList are displayed at all times or only when needed

A ScrolledList is a List inside a ScrolledWindow. The application can use **XmCreateScrolledList** to create one.

In addition to its resources, List has a variety of convenience routines that allow the application to add, remove, select, and deselect items; specify the first or last visible item; find the position of an item or the positions of the selected items; set Add Mode; and scroll the List horizontally.

5.6 Text and TextField

Text is a widget for displaying and, optionally, editing text. When the Text is editable and the user presses a key that represents a text character, that character is inserted into the text. Other translations and actions allow the user to navigate or to select, cut, copy, paste, or scroll the text.

For more information on Text and TextField, see Chapter 8.

Chapter 6

Menus and Options

A menu is a widget that allows the user to make a choice among actions or states. When the menu is visible, the user makes a choice by activating a button in the menu, usually by pressing **BSelect**, **KSelect**, or **KActivate** on the button. Some buttons also have mnemonics that allow the user to activate them by pressing the mnemonic keys when the menu is visible. Buttons can also have accelerators, which activate the buttons whether or not the menu is visible.

Motif has four basic kinds of menu:

- MenuBar. This menu is normally always managed within some component of an application, often the MainWindow. It usually consists of a row of CascadeButtons. When the user activates a button in the menu, a PulldownMenu menu appears with one set of top-level choices that apply to the application component.

- PopupMenu. This menu contains a set of choices that apply to a component of the application. The menu is not visible until the user takes an action that posts it, usually pressing **BMenu** in the associated component or pressing **KMenu** when the component has keyboard focus. A PopupMenu can contain buttons that take action or change state directly. It can also contain CascadeButtons that cause PulldownMenus to appear.

- PulldownMenu. This menu is associated with a CascadeButton in a MenuBar, a PopupMenu, or another PulldownMenu. The menu is not visible until the user posts it by activating the associated CascadeButton. Like a PopupMenu, a PulldownMenu can contain buttons that take action or change state directly. It can also contain CascadeButtons that cause other PulldownMenus to appear.

- OptionMenu. This menu allows the user to choose among one set of choices, usually mutually exclusive attributes or states. It consists of a label, a selection area, and a PulldownMenu. The selection area is a CascadeButtonGadget whose label shows the currently selected option. The PulldownMenu contains the set of options. The user posts the PulldownMenu by activating the CascadeButtonGadget or by pressing **MAlt** along with a mnemonic. When the user activates a button in the PulldownMenu, that button becomes the newly selected option.

RowColumn is the widget that Motif uses as a menu. A RowColumn can also be a nonmenu WorkArea. One use for a WorkArea is to contain a set of ToggleButtons constituting a RadioBox or a CheckBox. When the user selects a ToggleButton, its state changes from on to off or from off to on. In a RadioBox, only one ToggleButton at a time can be on; in a CheckBox, more than one ToggleButton can be on.

RowColumn performs special geometry management to align and lay out its children in a variety of ways. An application can use a RowColumn WorkArea to take advantage of the RowColumn geometry management for a set of widgets. For details see Chapter 10.

6.1 Menu Components: Buttons, RowColumn, MenuShell

A menu is a three-level hierarchy:

- Buttons represent the menu selections.

- A RowColumn widget is the manager that contains the buttons.

- A MenuShell envelops each PulldownMenu and PopupMenu.

6.1.1 Buttons

The user makes a choice in a menu by activating one of the buttons in the menu. CascadeButtons, PushButtons, and ToggleButtons and their gadget variants are most commonly used in menus.

Note: Motif does not support DrawnButtons or ArrowButtons in menus, though they can appear in a RowColumn WorkArea. To give a menu button a distinctive appearance, use a PushButton with a label type of **XmPIXMAP** and supply **XmNlabelPixmap** and **XmNlabelInsensitivePixmap** resources.

The application learns of the user's choice through the appropriate button callback lists:

- When the user activates a CascadeButton, the button calls the **XmNcascadingCallback** callbacks. If the button has an attached PulldownMenu after these callbacks return, the button posts the menu. Otherwise, the button calls the **XmNactivateCallback** callbacks.

- When the user activates a PushButton, the button calls the **XmNactivateCallback** callbacks.

- When the user activates a ToggleButton, the button calls the **XmNvalueChangedCallback** callbacks.

Buttons in a menu have translations and actions that arm, disarm, and activate the buttons. These actions also post and unpost menus in the hierarchy at appropriate times. The buttons inherit menu traversal translations and actions from **XmLabel**. These actions allow the user to move from button to button within a menu and from menu to menu within the menu hierarchy.

6.1.2 RowColumn

The parent of the buttons in a menu is a RowColumn widget. RowColumn interacts with its button children in these ways:

- In a menu (but not a WorkArea), it ensures that all children are CascadeButtons, PushButtons, ToggleButtons, Labels, or Separators (or their gadget variants). If the **XmNisHomogeneous** resource is True, it ensures that all children are of the class specified by **XmNentryClass**.

6–3

- It lays out its children and, if **XmNisAligned** is True, aligns the labels of children that are **XmLabel** or **XmLabelGadget** subclasses.

- It stores the widget ID of the last menu item selected in the **XmNmenuHistory** resource.

- It allows the application to supply a single callback list for all button children. If **XmNentryCallback** is not NULL, it disables the **XmNactivateCallback** and **XmNvalueChangedCallback** callbacks for its button children and arranges for the buttons to call the **XmNentryCallback** callbacks instead.

- If **XmNradioBehavior** is True, it ensures that only one ToggleButton at a time is normally selected. It also changes the default values for **XmNindicatorType** and **XmNvisibleWhenOff** for its ToggleButton children to the one-of-many, always-displayed style.

- It has additional resources for MenuBars and OptionMenus, described in the following sections.

In addition to **XmNentryCallback**, RowColumn also has **XmNmapCallback** and **XmNunmapCallback** callbacks. These callbacks apply only to PopupMenus and PulldownMenus. The **XmNmapCallback** callbacks are called just before the menu is posted, and the **XmNunmapCallback** callbacks are called just after the menu is unposted. They are useful for changing the menu to reflect the current state of the application. For example, an **XmNmapCallback** callback can use **XtSetSensitive** to make some menu items insensitive if they are not applicable in the current state of the program.

6.1.3 MenuShell

The window's associated with PopupMenus and PulldownMenus are top-level windows. That is, the parent window of such a menu is the root window of the screen, not the window associated with the parent widget. This allows the menu to appear anywhere on the screen without being clipped by the parent widget's window.

The parent widget of each PopupMenu and PulldownMenu RowColumn must be a MenuShell. It is actually the MenuShell's window that is the top-level window. **XmMenuShell** is a subclass of OverrideShell, so the window manager ignores MenuShell's windows.

A MenuShell is often invisible to the application. The Motif convenience routines for creating PopupMenus and PulldownMenus automatically create MenuShell parents for these menus. When a PulldownMenu is the child of a PopupMenu or another PulldownMenu, the child's MenuShell is actually the child of the parent's MenuShell. The convenience routines for creating PulldownMenus manage these relations automatically.

Motif arranges for the RowColumn's window to coincide with the MenuShell's window. Setting **XmNheight**, **XmNwidth**, or **XmNborderWidth** for either a MenuShell or its child sets that resource to the same value in both the parent and the child. For a child of a MenuShell, setting **XmNx** or **XmNy** sets the corresponding resource of the parent but does not change the child's position relative to the parent. **XtGetValues** for the child's **XmNx** or **XmNy** yields the value of the corresponding resource in the parent. The x and y coordinates of the child's upper left outside corner relative to the parent's upper left inside corner are both zero minus the value of **XmNborderWidth**.

To change any geometry-related resources of a PopupMenu or PulldownMenu, an application should always specify these resources for the RowColumn child, not the MenuShell parent.

If an application needs to create a MenuShell explicitly, it should create the MenuShell as a popup child of its parent (using **XtCreatePopupShell** or **XtVaCreatePopupShell**). All Motif convenience routines that create MenuShells do this automatically, and an application rarely needs to create a MenuShell directly.

6.2 MenuBar

All children of a MenuBar must be CascadeButtons or CascadeButtonGadgets. The MenuBar attempts to place its button children in a single row. If it does not have enough room, it tries to wrap the remaining children into additional rows.

An application should treat specially the button, if any, that pulls down a help menu. The application should set the MenuBar RowColumn's **XmNmenuHelpWidget** to the widget ID of this button. The MenuBar attempts to place this button at one of the lower corners of the MenuBar, as specified by the *OSF/Motif Style Guide*.

In a MenuBar, all buttons typically have associated PulldownMenus. Each PulldownMenu associated with a button in a MenuBar must be a child of the MenuBar. (More precisely, each PulldownMenu's MenuShell must be a child of the MenuBar.) Each button's **XmNsubMenuId** resource must be set to the widget ID of the associated PulldownMenu. Set **XmNsubMenuId** to the widget ID of the PulldownMenu RowColumn, not of the PulldownMenu's MenuShell.

The routines **XmCreateMenuBar**, **XmCreateSimpleMenuBar**, and **XmVaCreateSimpleMenuBar** all create MenuBars.

6.3 PopupMenu

A PopupMenu is normally invisible. When the user takes some action—usually pressing **BMenu** or **KMenu**—in a widget that has a PopupMenu, the menu is posted. The user moves from item to item in the menu by dragging **BMenu** or, when keyboard traversal is enabled, by keyboard traversal actions. Motif unposts the menu when the user activates an item in the menu system (other than a CascadeButton), presses **KCancel**, or releases or clicks **BMenu** outside a menu item.

A PopupMenu RowColumn must have a MenuShell parent. The parent of the MenuShell is the widget with which the PopupMenu is associated. Because the MenuShell is a popup child of its parent, the parent can be any widget (but not a gadget); it does not have to be a subclass of **Composite**. The Motif convenience routines that create PopupMenus automatically create a MenuShell as the parent of the PopupMenu RowColumn.

The PopupMenu's **XmNmenuPost** resource specifies the button event that posts the menu. The event can be any button press, possibly with modifiers. To allow the user to post a PopupMenu using the mouse, the application has to take these actions:

- Provide an event handler (using **XtAddEventHandler**) for button press events for the widget with which the PopupMenu is associated. The second argument (the *client_data* argument) to the event handler should be the PopupMenu RowColumn.

- In the event handler, call **XmMenuPosition** to locate the PopupMenu at the point where the user pressed the mouse button, or position the menu itself.

- In the event handler, manage the PopupMenu RowColumn. If the button event matches the event description in the RowColumn's **XmNmenuPost** resource, Motif makes the PopupMenu visible when the application manages it. Otherwise, Motif unmanages the PopupMenu and does not post it.

The PopupMenu is realized, if necessary, the first time it is posted.

Following is an example:

```
void ButtonEventHandler(Widget widget, XtPointer popup,
                        XEvent *event, Boolean *continue)
{
    XmMenuPosition((Widget) popup, (XButtonPressedEvent *)
                event);
    XtManageChild((Widget) popup);
}


    Widget        parent, popup;
    popup = XmCreatePopupMenu(parent, "popup", args, n);
    XtAddEventHandler(parent, ButtonPressMask, False,
                (XtEventHandler) ButtonEventHandler,
                (XtPointer) popup);
...
```

Posting a PopupMenu through the keyboard is controlled by the PopupMenu's **XmNmenuAccelerator** and **XmNpopupEnabled** resources. **XmNmenuAccelerator** specifies a key event that may post the menu. **XmNpopupEnabled** specifies whether or not this event actually posts the menu. It also determines whether or not accelerators and mnemonics in the PopupMenu and its submenus are enabled.

An application can have only one active PopupMenu at a time for a particular widget. If the widget has more than one PopupMenu, the application should set **XmNpopupEnabled** to True for the active menu and set **XmNpopupEnabled** to False for all inactive menus. The application must also arrange for its button event handler to manage the proper PopupMenu on a popup button event. One possible implementation is for the event handler to call a function that returns the appropriate PopupMenu, depending on the state of the application.

6.4 PulldownMenu

A PulldownMenu is always associated with another RowColumn. It becomes visible when the user activates a CascadeButton in the associated RowColumn. It becomes invisible when the user traverses upward or laterally in the menu hierarchy, activates a button in the hierarchy (other than a CascadeButton in the menu or a descendant), presses **KCancel**, or clicks or releases a mouse button outside a menu item.

A PulldownMenu must have the following relations with other widgets:

- It must be the value of the **XmNsubMenuId** resource of the CascadeButton that is to post the menu.

- It must have a MenuShell as its parent. The Motif convenience routines that create PulldownMenus create MenuShell parents automatically.

- The MenuShell must have the proper parent, depending on the kind of RowColumn with which the PulldownMenu is associated. The MenuShell is a popup child of its own parent. Following are the required parents of the MenuShell:

  — If the PulldownMenu is to be pulled down from a MenuBar, the parent must be the MenuBar.

  — If the PulldownMenu is to be pulled down from a PopupMenu or another PulldownMenu, the parent must be that PopupMenu or PulldownMenu. Actually, the parent is the other menu's MenuShell; but the *parent* parameter to the Motif convenience routines that create PopupMenus must be the other menu itself (the RowColumn), not its MenuShell parent.

  — If the PulldownMenu is to be pulled down from an OptionMenu, the parent must be the parent of the OptionMenu.

6.5 OptionMenu

An OptionMenu lets the user choose among a set of usually mutually exclusive options. The OptionMenu is always visible. It consists of a label (a LabelGadget), a selection area (a CascadeButtonGadget), and an associated PulldownMenu. The label of the CascadeButtonGadget displays the currently selected option, one of the items in the PulldownMenu. When the user activates the CascadeButtonGadget, the PulldownMenu becomes visible with the currently selected item directly above the selection area. When the user activates an item in the PulldownMenu, the PulldownMenu is unposted and the item the user chose becomes the currently selected option.

The PulldownMenu normally contains only PushButtons. It must not contain any ToggleButtons, and Motif does not support CascadeButtons.

RowColumn has a number of resources for use specifically with an OptionMenu:

XmNlabelString

> The text of the label. Setting this resource also sets the **XmNlabelString** of the LabelGadget.

XmNmnemonic

> A keysym that, when pressed along with the **MAlt** modifier, posts the PulldownMenu. Motif underlines the first character in the label string that matches the mnemonic and that is in a segment whose font list element tag matches **XmNmnemonicCharSet**. Setting this resource also sets the **XmNmnemonic** of the LabelGadget.

XmNmnemonicCharSet

> The font list element tag used for underlining the mnemonic. Setting this resource also sets the **XmNmnemonicCharSet** of the LabelGadget.

XmNsubMenuId

> The widget ID of the PulldownMenu. Setting this resource also sets the **XmNsubMenuId** of the CascadeButtonGadget.

If the application needs to get or set any of these four resources for the LabelGadget or CascadeButtonGadget, it should always get or set it in the OptionMenu RowColumn, not the gadget itself. To get or set other resources for the gadgets, the application should use

XmOptionLabelGadget or XmOptionButtonGadget and then call XtGetValues or XtSetValues on the returned widget ID. A user or application can also specify resource values in resource files by using the names of the gadgets, "OptionLabel" and "OptionButton".

Setting the XmNmenuHistory resource also has a special effect in OptionMenus. Setting XmNmenuHistory to an item in the PulldownMenu makes that item the currently selected option. It updates the label of the CascadeButtonGadget and causes the PulldownMenu to appear, when posted, with the selected item over the CascadeButtonGadget.

XmCreateOptionMenu creates an OptionMenu RowColumn and its LabelGadget and CascadeButtonGadget children. It does not create the associated PulldownMenu.

The following example creates a simple OptionMenu with three options:

```
Widget          parent, pulldown, option, pb1, pb2, pb3;
Arg             args[10];
Cardinal        n;
...
  n = 0;
  pulldown = XmCreatePulldownMenu(parent, "option_pd",
                                  args, n);
  pb1 = XmCreatePushButtonGadget(pulldown, "option_pb1",
                                  args, n);
  pb2 = XmCreatePushButtonGadget(pulldown, "option_pb2",
                                  args, n);
  pb3 = XmCreatePushButtonGadget(pulldown, "option_pb3",
                                  args  n);
  XtSetArg(args[n], XmNsubMenuId, pulldown);      n++;
  XtSetArg(args[n], XmNmenuHistory, pb2);         n++;
  option = XmCreateOptionMenu(parent, "option_rc", args, n);
...
```

The following application-class defaults file provides labels and mnemonics for an English-language locale:

```
*option_pb1.labelString    :    Option 1
*option_pb2.labelString    :    Option 2
*option_pb3.labelString    :    Option 3
*option_rc.labelString     :    Options
*option_rc.mnemonic        :    O
```

6.6 RadioBox and CheckBox

RadioBoxes and CheckBoxes are collections of ToggleButtons. The difference is that in a RadioBox only one ToggleButton at a time can be set; in a CheckBox more than one ToggleButton can be set.

RadioBoxes and CheckBoxes are usually implemented as WorkAreas, though it is possible to implement them as menus. Usually the application intends for the box to remain visible after the user sets a ToggleButton, particularly in a CheckBox. The application can implement a transient RadioBox or CheckBox by placing a WorkArea inside a dialog.

The following RowColumn resources specifically control the behavior of a RadioBox or CheckBox:

XmNradioBehavior

> When True, the RowColumn ensures that at most one ToggleButton is set at a time. Setting this resource to True also causes the ToggleButton resource **XmNindicatorType** to default to **XmONE_OF_MANY** and **XmNvisibleWhenOff** to default to True.

XmNradioAlwaysOne

> When both this resource and **XmNradioBehavior** are True, RowColumn ensures that one ToggleButton is always set. The user is not allowed to unset a ToggleButton when no other ToggleButton is set.

For a RadioBox implemented as a WorkArea, the default value for **XmNisHomogeneous** is True, and by default RowColumn allows only ToggleButton and ToggleButtonGadget children.

Note that the application can foil the RowColumn's enforcement of **XmNradioBehavior** and **XmNradioAlwaysOne**, even when these resources are True. The application can use **XtSetValues** to set the state of the ToggleButtons, and it can manage and unmanage ToggleButtons regardless of their state. The behavior of a RadioBox is undefined if the application takes actions that contradict **XmNradioBehavior** or **XmNradioAlwaysOne**.

XmCreateRadioBox creates a WorkArea RadioBox and initializes **XmNradioBehavior** to True.

A CheckBox is most often a collection of ToggleButtons in a WorkArea with **XmNradioBehavior** set to False. By default, the ToggleButton **XmNindicatorType** is **XmN_OF_MANY** and **XmNvisibleWhenOff** is True.

6.7 TearOffMenus

An application can allow the user to "tear off" a PulldownMenu or PopupMenu. When the user tears off a menu, Motif unposts that menu and any posted menu descendants. It gives the menu a TransientShell parent and then maps the parent as a top-level window. The torn-off menu has window-manager decorations, and its title is the label of the CascadeButton that posts the menu in the original menu system.

The user can interact with the torn-off menu just as in the menu hierarchy. When the user activates buttons in a torn-off menu, the actions take effect but the torn-off menu remains posted. When the user takes an action that unposts the torn-off menu, such as pressing **KCancel**, the menu returns to its original position in the menu hierarchy. If the user reposts the original menu from the menu hierarchy while the torn-off menu is posted, an inactive representation of the torn-off menu remains visible, but the menu itself is unposted and then reposted within the menu hierarchy.

When a menu in a menu system can be torn off, a distinctive tear-off button appears at the beginning of the menu. The user can tear off the menu by activating the tear-off button as with any other button in the menu. The user can also tear off the menu by pressing **BTransfer** in the tear-off button. The user can then drag the torn-off menu to another position on the screen and fix its position by releasing **BTransfer**.

Menus cannot be torn off by default. The application must allow the user to tear off a menu by setting the RowColumn resource **XmNtearOffModel** to **XmTEAR_OFF_ENABLED**. When the user tears off a menu, the **XmNtearOffMenuActivateCallback** callbacks are invoked just before the **XmNmapCallback** callbacks. When the user unposts a torn-off menu, the **XmNtearOffMenuDeactivateCallback** callbacks are invoked just after the **XmNunmapCallback** callbacks.

Chapter 7

Dialogs

Dialogs are container widgets that provide a means of communicating between the user and the application. A dialog widget usually asks a question or presents some information to the user. In some cases, the application is suspended until the user provides a response.

Dialogs are similar to menus. Both seek input from the user. Like PopupMenus and PulldownMenus, dialogs appear in top-level windows and are more or less transient. Making a selection typically unposts a PopupMenu or PulldownMenu and often pops down a dialog. There are two chief differences:

- Unless torn off, menus are usually **modal**: the user must make a selection from the menu or unpost it before interacting with other parts of the application. Dialogs can be either modal or **modeless**. In a modeless dialog, the user can interact with other parts of the application before returning to the dialog.

- Menu components are limited to buttons, labels, and separators. Dialogs can contain other, sometimes arbitrary, kinds of widgets, such as List and Text. Dialogs permit more complex interaction with the user and allow the application to solicit a broader range of information.

Menus are well suited to allowing the user to make a single choice from a constrained set. Dialogs are appropriate for displaying information about a transient or unusual state of the program and for obtaining complex input from the user. Whether to use a dialog or a menu is not always clear. In fact, a TearOffMenu combines aspects of both. For more information on using menus and dialogs, see the *OSF/Motif Style Guide*.

7.1 BulletinBoard and DialogShell

From the application's point of view, a dialog is a widget that is a subclass of **XmBulletinBoard** inside a DialogShell. BulletinBoard is intended to be the usual superclass for a dialog widget. The dialog widget can be either a BulletinBoard itself or one of its more specialized subclasses. BulletinBoard is a container with no automatically created children; it supplies general behavior needed by most dialogs. Its subclasses provide child widgets and specific behavior tailored to particular types of dialogs.

BulletinBoard and its subclasses can also function outside a DialogShell, as part of the application's main window. One subclass, Form, is particularly useful in providing constraint-based geometry management for a collection of child widgets.

7.1.1 BulletinBoard

BulletinBoard provides the following resources and behavior:

- Activation and cancellation of the dialog. BulletinBoard installs accelerators for **KActivate** and **KCancel**. Unless focus is in another button, **KActivate** activates the **XmNdefaultButton** if it is sensitive. **KCancel** activates the **XmNcancelButton** if it is sensitive. Subclasses set the **XmNdefaultButton** and **XmNcancelButton**.

- A resource, **XmNdialogStyle**, that determines whether the dialog is modal or modeless. Three modal styles exist:

Primary application modal
> Among the dialog and its ancestors, input goes only to the dialog, but the user can iteract with other parts of the application or with other applications.

Full application modal

> Within the application, input goes only to the dialog, but the user can interact with other applications.

System modal

> Input goes only to the dialog; the user cannot interact with other applications.

- Callbacks invoked when the BulletinBoard is mapped and unmapped and when it gains input focus.

- Geometry-management resources and class methods that implement several resizing policies and that allow the BulletinBoard to interact with its subclasses in managing complex collections of descendant widgets. The geometry-related resources are **XmNmarginHeight**, **XmNmarginWidth** and **XmNresizePolicy**. For more information on BulletinBoard's geometry management, see Chapter 10.

7.1.2 Activation, Cancellation, and Help

Often a dialog has one or more actions, associated with buttons, that apply to the dialog as a whole. Some common actions are "activate," "cancel," and "help." BulletinBoard deals specially with activation and cancellation. BulletinBoard allows the user to "activate" or "cancel" the dialog from anywhere within the BulletinBoard (except, in the case of activation, when a button has the focus).

BulletinBoard has a resource, **XmNdefaultButton**, whose value is a button descendant that represents the default activation action. When the user presses **KActivate** in a button that has keyboard focus, that button's **KActivate** actions are called. If the user presses **KActivate** and no button has focus, BulletinBoard calls the **KActivate** actions for the **XmNdefaultButton** if it is sensitive. If the user presses **KActivate** in a List, Text, or TextField descendant, the **KActivate** actions for that widget are invoked first, and then BulletinBoard calls the **KActivate** actions for the **XmNdefaultButton**.

BulletinBoard has another resource, **XmNcancelButton**, whose value is a button descendant that represents the default cancellation action. When the user presses **KCancel** anywhere within the BulletinBoard, BulletinBoard calls the **KActivate** actions for the **XmNcancelButton** if it is sensitive.

The help action works differently. Often the application represents help for the dialog as a whole by providing a Help button. When the user activates this button, the application provides help for the dialog. In general the application can provide help through an **XmNactivateCallback** procedure for the Help button. Some BulletinBoard subclasses create Help buttons automatically. These widgets add a procedure to the Help button's **XmNactivateCallback** list that invokes the dialog's **XmNhelpCallback** procedures when the Help button is activated. In these cases, the application can provide help through the dialog's **XmNhelpCallback** procedures.

If the user presses **KHelp** elsewhere in the BulletinBoard, this action usually invokes the **XmNhelpCallback** callbacks for the widget with the focus. If this widget has no **XmNhelpCallback** procedures, Motif looks up the widget hierarchy for the first ancestor with a non-NULL **XmNhelpCallback** list and invokes those procedures. By providing an **XmNhelpCallback** procedure for the dialog itself, the application can ensure that the user sees help for the dialog as a whole when the descendant widget with focus has no help information of its own.

7.1.3 DialogShell

DialogShell is the Motif shell widget that contains dialogs. It is a subclass of TransientShell, which is a subclass of VendorShell. DialogShell inherits much of VendorShell's behavior in interacting with the window manager and in providing geometry management for off-the-spot input methods.

DialogShell cooperates extensively with BulletinBoard, and some of DialogShell's features for containing dialogs assume that its child is a BulletinBoard or BulletinBoard subclass. Often the application does not need to deal directly with the DialogShell at all. The Motif convenience routines that create dialogs automatically create a DialogShell as the popup child of the parent shell.

To pop up the dialog, the application does not call **XtPopup** on the DialogShell, but instead manages the child of the DialogShell. DialogShell's **change_managed** procedure pops up the dialog when the child is managed and pops it down when the child is unmanaged, providing that the child's **XmNmappedWhenManaged** resource is True. If a BulletinBoard child's **XmNautoUnmanage** resource is initialized to True, the BulletinBoard is automatically unmanaged when its OK and cancel buttons are activated.

DialogShell notifies its BulletinBoard child using the **XmNmapCallback** and **XmNunmapCallback** procedures when the child is about to be mapped and unmapped.

Like VendorShell, DialogShell ensures that when no off-the-spot input method exists the DialogShell window remains coincident with the child window. Setting **XmNx** and **XmNy** for the child sets these resources for the shell, without changing the child's position relative to the child. Setting **XmNheight**, **XmNwidth** and **XmNborderWidth** for the child usually sets these resources to the same value in the DialogShell. When a BulletinBoard child is managed with its **XmNdefaultPosition** resource set to True, DialogShell centers the dialog with respect to the parent.

BulletinBoard has two resources that allow the user or application to customize a parent DialogShell's interaction with the window manager. **XmNdialogTitle** provides a title for the window manager, and **XmNnoResize** determines whether or not the dialog MWM frame includes resize controls. To affect other aspects of interaction with the window manager, the user or application must set the appropriate DialogShell resources.

XmCreateBulletinBoardDialog creates a BulletinBoard and a parent DialogShell.

7.1.4 Initial Focus

When the **XmNkeyboardFocusPolicy** of a shell is **XmEXPLICIT**, Motif uses the Manager resource **XmNinitialFocus** in determining which component of a manager receives initial focus in these circumstances:

- When the manager is the child of a shell and the shell hierarchy receives focus for the first time

- When focus is inside the shell hierarchy, the manager is a composite tab group, and the user traverses to the manager using the keyboard

Following are the default values of **XmNinitialFocus** for BulletinBoard and its subclasses:

- For BulletinBoard, Form, and MessageBox, the default is the value of **XmNdefaultButton**

• For SelectionBox and its subclasses, the default is the text edit area

7.2 Making a Selection: SelectionBox

SelectionBox is a BulletinBoard subclass that generally allows the user to select an item from a list. By default, a SelectionBox includes the following children:

• A scrolling list of alternatives

• An editable text field for the selected alternative

• Labels for the list and text field

• Three or four buttons

The default buttons are OK, Cancel, and Help. By default, an Apply button is also created. If the parent of the SelectionBox is a DialogShell, it is managed; otherwise, it is unmanaged.

An application can add additional children to the SelectionBox. The first child is used as a work area. The value of **XmNchildPlacement** determines whether the work area is placed above or below the Text area, or above or below the List area. Additional children are laid out in the following manner:

MenuBar   The first MenuBar child is placed at the top of the window

Buttons   All **XmPushButton** widgets or gadgets and their subclasses are placed after the OK button in the order of their creation

Others   The layout of additional children that are not in these categories is undefined

The user can select an item in two ways: by scrolling through the list and selecting the desired item or by entering the item name directly into the text edit area. Selecting an item from the list causes that item name to appear in the selection text edit area. SelectionBox installs accelerators, the value of **XmNtextAccelerators**, on the text edit widget. The default accelerators bind **KUp**, **KDown**, **KBeginLine**, **KEndLine**, and **KRestore** events in the text edit widget to SelectionBox actions that select an item in the List and replace the text edit widget value with that List item.

SelectionBox provides **XmNokCallback**, **XmNcancelCallback**, **XmNhelpCallback**, and **XmNapplyCallback** lists, which the SelectionBox invokes when the corresponding button is activated. Activation of the OK button may invoke either the **XmNokCallback** list or the **XmNnoMatchCallback** list. When the user activates the OK button and either the **XmNmustMatch** resource is False or the text in the text edit area matches a List item, SelectionBox invokes the **XmNokCallback** procedures. When the user activates the OK button, **XmNmustMatch** is True, and the text in the text edit area does not match a List item, SelectionBox invokes the **XmNnoMatchCallback** procedures.

SelectionBox has two subclasses, FileSelectionBox and Command, which are described in later sections. **XmCreateSelectionDialog** creates a standard SelectionBox and a DialogShell parent. **XmCreatePromptDialog** creates a variant SelectionBox dialog containing a text edit area and label and OK, Cancel, and Help buttons. A PromptDialog has an unmanaged Apply button, and it has no List or List label. It is intended for the application to prompt the user for brief text input.

The **XmNdialogType** resource determines which of the standard SelectionBox children are created and managed. The value usually depends on the application's use of the SelectionBox:

- **XmDIALOG_SELECTION** usually indicates a standard SelectionBox dialog.

- **XmDIALOG_WORK_AREA** indicates a SelectionBox outside a DialogShell. The Apply button is unmanaged.

- **XmDIALOG_PROMPT** indicates a PromptDialog.

- **XmDIALOG_COMMAND** indicates a Command subclass.

- **XmDIALOG_FILE_SELECTION** indicates a FileSelectionBox subclass.

SelectionBox has resources for supplying text, label strings, and list items for its children. The widget IDs of the children of a SelectionBox and its subclasses are not available as resources. The application can retrieve the widget IDs of the automatically created children by using **XtNameToWidget** or by calling one of the convenience routines Motif provides for this purpose: **XmSelectionBoxGetChild**, **XmFileSelectionBoxGetChild**, and **XmCommandGetChild**.

7.3 Choosing a Pathname: FileSelectionBox

FileSelectionBox is a subclass of SelectionBox designed for finding and selecting files. By default, a FileSelectionBox contains the same children as a standard SelectionBox, with the addition of a second ScrolledList, a second text edit area, and the corresponding labels. By default, the Apply button is labeled "Filter".

One of the text areas, the directory mask area, holds a directory mask specifying a base directory to be searched and a search pattern. The other text area, the selection area, holds the name of the selected file. One of the Lists, the directory list, displays the subdirectories of the current base directory. The other List, the file list, displays all the files, subdirectories, or both in the base directory that match the search pattern.

The user can select a new base directory to examine by scrolling through the list of directories and selecting the desired directory or by editing the directory mask. Selecting a new directory from the directory list does not change the search pattern. A user can select a new search pattern by editing the directory mask. Double clicking or pressing **KActivate** on a directory in the directory list initiates a search for files and subdirectories in the new directory, using the current search pattern.

Activating the Filter button, the directory list, or the directory mask text area causes the FileSelectionBox to initiate a file search. The FileSelectionBox uses three procedures, each the value of a resource, in conducting the search: the **XmNqualifySearchDataProc**, the **XmNdirSearchProc** and the **XmNfileSearchProc**. The **XmNqualifySearchDataProc** extracts the base directory and the search pattern from the directory mask. The **XmNdirSearchProc** uses the data returned by the **XmNqualifySearchDataProc** to update the directory list. The **XmNfileSearchProc** uses the data returned by the **XmNqualifySearchDataProc** to update the file list.

The user can select a file by scrolling through the list of filenames and selecting the desired file or by entering the filename directly into the text edit area. Selecting a file from the list causes that filename to appear in the file selection text edit area. The user confirms the selection by activating the OK button, the file list, or the selection text area.

FileSelectionBox uses the SelectionBox callback lists to notify the application when the user activates one of the buttons. The application can also provide one or more of the three procedures that FileSelectionBox uses to conduct a search. For a specification of the input to and output from these routines, see the **XmFileSelectionBox(3X)** reference page in the *OSF/Motif Programmer's Reference*.

The application can remove the directory list, the file list, or both. The application must unmanage the ScrolledWindow parent of the List and the corresponding label. An application can also add additional children to a FileSelectionBox, which manages any additional children in the same way as SelectionBox.

XmCreateFileSelectionDialog creates a FileSelectionBox and a parent DialogShell.

7.4 Command

Command is a SelectionBox subclass intended for entering a command. It contains the SelectionBox text edit area, List, and List label, but no buttons. The application can add only one additional work area child to the Command. A Command usually appears as part of the application's main window rather than as a dialog.

The user specifies a command by adding text to the text area or by selecting an item from the List, which represents the command history. Whenever the text edit area changes, Command invokes the **XmNcommandChangedCallback** procedures. The user enters a command by activating the List or the text edit area. When the user enters a command, Command appends the command to the history list and invokes the **XmNcommandEnteredCallback** procedures.

Command has a number of resources that are aliases for SelectionBox resources dealing with the List and text edit area. Command also has an **XmNhistoryMaxItems** resource, which specifies the maximum length of the history list. After the list reaches this length, Command deletes the first item in the list before appending a newly entered command.

7.5 MessageBox

MessageBox is a BulletinBoard subclass intended for a dialog consisting of a single user interaction. By default, a MessageBox has the following components:

- A LabelGadget with a pixmap label symbolizing the type of interaction the MessageBox represents

- A LabelGadget with a compound string label representing the text of the message

- A SeparatorGadget separating the message symbol and text from the other children

- Three buttons: OK, Cancel, and Help

Typically the message symbol and text are on top and the buttons on the bottom, with the separator between. The application can add additional children to a MessageBox. Additional children are laid out in the following manner:

- The first MenuBar child is placed at the top of the window.

- All **XmPushButton** widgets or gadgets, and their subclasses are placed after the OK button in the order of their creation.

- A child that is not in these categories is treated as a work area and is placed above the row of buttons. If a message label exists, the child is placed below the label. If a message pixmap exists, but a message label is absent, the child is placed on the same row as the pixmap. The child behaves as a work area and grows or shrinks to fill the space above the row of buttons. The layout of multiple work area children is undefined.

Several convenience routines create MessageBox widgets with DialogShell parents for particular kinds of interactions. For most of these routines, the principal difference in the type of MessageBox they create is that each uses a distinct default symbol pixmap. When it creates the symbol pixmap, MessageBox uses **XmGetPixmapByDepth** to find a pixmap with a name that corresponds to the type of interaction. Each dialog type is also associated with a value of the **XmNdialogType** resource. The following table shows the correspondence between creation routine, **XmNdialogType**, and symbol pixmap name:

Table 7–1. MessageBox Routines, Dialog Types, and Pixmaps

Convenience Routine	XmNdialogType	Pixmap Name
XmCreateErrorDialog	XmDIALOG_ERROR	xm_error
XmCreateInformationDialog	XmDIALOG_INFORMATION	xm_information
XmCreateMessageDialog	XmDIALOG_MESSAGE	
XmCreateQuestionDialog	XmDIALOG_QUESTION	xm_question
XmCreateTemplateDialog	XmDIALOG_TEMPLATE	
XmCreateWarningDialog	XmDIALOG_WARNING	xm_warning
XmCreateWorkingDialog	XmDIALOG_WORKING	xm_working

A MesssageDialog and a TemplateDialog have no default symbol pixmap. A TemplateDialog is a special MessageBox variant that is intended for application customization and that, by default, has no children except the separator.

Like SelectionBox, MessageBox has **XmNokCallback**, **XmNcancelCallback**, and **XmNhelpCallback** lists to inform the application when the user activates a button. MessageBox has resources for supplying label strings and the symbol pixmap for its children. The widget IDs of the children of a MessageBox are not available as resources. The application can retrieve the widget IDs of the automatically created children by using **XtNameToWidget** or by calling **XmMessageBoxGetChild**.

7.6 Form

Form is a BulletinBoard subclass whose main purpose is to provide constraint-based geometry management for arbitrary children. Form has a number of constraint resources that it uses to place children with respect to the Form, positions within the form, and other children. Most Form-specific behavior is related to this geometry management. Form has no default children of its own. But as a BulletinBoard subclass, Form is an appropriate container for use in dialogs. **XmCreateFormDialog** creates a Form and a DialogShell parent.

For information on Form's geometry management, see Chapter 10.

Chapter 8

Text

OSF/Motif has widgets for displaying two kinds of text: static text, as in labels and messages, and editable text. Static text usually appears in Label widgets or Label subclasses, including buttons, and in Lists. The application or user can specify initial text for Labels or Lists using resource or UIL files, but the user cannot edit the text. The application can replace the text during the program by setting the appropriate resources. In Labels and Label subclasses and in Lists, Motif represents text as compound strings. These are byte streams that contain the text itself and tags that the toolkit matches with tags in font lists in order to select the appropriate fonts or font sets to display the text.

For editing text, Motif provides Text and TextField widgets. The displayed text in these widgets may or may not be editable, depending on the value of the **XmNeditable** resource. When the Text is editable and the user enters a text character, that character is inserted into the text. Other translations and actions allow the user to navigate or to select, cut, copy, paste, or scroll the text. In Text and TextField widgets, Motif represents text as strings of either multibyte (**char**) or wide (**wchar_t**) characters. The Text widget uses a single font or font set from a font list to display the text.

This chapter discusses the Text and TextField widgets. Labels and their subclasses are discussed in Chapter 5, and compound strings, font lists, and localization of text are discussed in Chapter 11. It is possible for an application to construct its own text-editing widget using a DrawingArea. This is discussed in Chapter 14.

8.1 Text and TextField

The text in a Text widget can be multiline or constrained to be a single line, depending on the value of the **XmNeditMode** resource. In multiline Text, pressing **KUp** moves the insertion cursor, the point at which new text is inserted, to the previous line, and pressing **KDown** moves the insertion cursor to the next line. Other actions move the insertion cursor forward and backward by paragraphs. Pressing **KSpace**, **KTab**, or **KEnter** causes the corresponding character to be inserted into the text. For this reason, some virtual key bindings are different in Text from those in other widgets, as shown in the following table:

Table 8–1. Text Virtual Key Bindings

Virtual Key	Actual Key Events
KActivate	Ctrl<Key>Return <Key>osfActivate
KExtend	Ctrl Shift<Key>space Shift<Key>osfSelect
KNextField	Ctrl<Key>Tab
KSelect	Ctrl<Key>space <Key>osfSelect

In a single-line widget, pressing **KSpace** still inserts a space into the text. However, **KUp** and **KDown** now move keyboard focus to the previous or next traversable widget, and **KTab** traverses to the next tab group. **KEnter** invokes the **XmNactivateCallback** callbacks. The actions for moving by paragraphs have no effect. In other words, a single-line Text widget acts more as a simple control than a field control.

A TextField is essentially the same as a Text widget in single-line mode, except that its performance is optimized for single-line text operations. Although TextField has a complete set of convenience routines of its own, the widget argument to the Text convenience routines can be either a Text or a TextField widget.

8.2 Selection

Both Text and TextField allow the user to cut, copy, and paste text using the clipboard, primary transfer, or secondary transfer. The user can also drag and drop text within a widget, between widgets, or from a Label or List widget to a Text or TextField widget. In all cases, the user first selects text in some widget and then inserts the selected text into a Text or TextField widget.

This section explains how selection works in Text and TextField. Understanding selection requires understanding of several concepts: **primary selection**, **secondary selection**, **clipboard selection**, the **destination** widget, the **insertion cursor**, the selection **anchor**, and **pending delete**.

Selections are the primary means of exchanging data between X clients. A selection is a piece of data. Each display may have several kinds of selections, but only one selection of each kind can exist at any time on the display. A client owns each selection, and the selection is attached to a window. Clients can acquire or give up ownership of a selection and can request that the owner convert the selection into some data type and place the results on a property of a particular window. This mechanism makes it possible to select and then cut, copy, or paste data from one client to another. Selections are discussed in detail in the X Window System *Inter-Client Communication Conventions Manual* (ICCCM).

Text and TextField support transfers using the three kinds of selection common to all X clients:

Primary   The primary selection is the principal selection on the display. Unless they are qualified, the terms *selecting text* and *the selection* refer to the primary selection.

Secondary   The secondary selection is used to transfer data without disturbing the primary selection. Text and TextField use the secondary selection for *quick* transfer, in which the user selects and then moves or copies text using a single series of mouse gestures.

Clipboard   The clipboard selection usually holds data cut or copied from one client and available to be pasted into another. Text and TextField provide actions for cutting and copying text to the clipboard and for pasting text from the clipboard.

The **destination** is the widget that, at any particular time, would receive the selection if the user were to invoke a move, copy, or paste operation. A Text or TextField widget must be both sensitive and editable to become the destination. When the **XmNkeyboardFocusPolicy** of the shell is **XmEXPLICIT**, an editable widget becomes the destination when it receives keyboard focus. When the **XmNkeyboardFocusPolicy** is **XmPOINTER**, an editable widget becomes the destination when it receives any mouse button or keyboard input. If the destination widget becomes insensitive or uneditable, there is no destination widget.

The **insertion cursor** is an I-beam cursor that shows where text, including a selection, would be inserted in a Text or TextField widget. The insertion cursor appears as a solid I-beam when the widget is in **normal mode** (explained below) and when it is either the widget with keyboard focus or the destination widget. Otherwise, the insertion cursor appears as a stippled I-beam.

The **anchor** is a position in the text of a widget that marks one boundary of a selection or a potential selection. For example, the user can select a range of text by pressing, dragging, and releasing **BSelect**. The anchor is set at the point of the button press, and the selection extends to the point of the button release. When the user takes an action to extend an existing selection, Motif first adjusts the anchor using a balance-beam method: it moves the anchor to the end of the existing selection that is farthest from the point of the button or key press that initiates the extend action.

Text and TextField have an **XmNpendingDelete** resource. When the value of this resource is True, as it is by default, some user actions cause a selection to be deleted. When a selection exists and the insertion cursor is not disjoint from it, an operation that inserts text, including a transfer of the secondary or clipboard selection, deletes the primary selection before inserting the text. Also, when a selection exists and the insertion cursor is not disjoint from it, an operation that deletes text deletes the primary selection instead of the text that would otherwise be removed. When **XmNpendingDelete** is False, these operations do not delete the selection.

8.2.1 Mouse Selection

The user makes a primary selection with **BSelect**. Pressing **BSelect** deselects any existing selection and moves the insertion cursor and the anchor to the position in the text where the button is pressed. Dragging **BSelect** selects all text between the anchor and the pointer position, deselecting any text outside that range. Releasing **BSelect** moves the insertion cursor to the position where the button is released. Clicking **BSelect** deselects any existing selection and moves the insertion cursor and the anchor to the position where **BSelect** is released.

BExtend extends a selection using the balance-beam method. When the user presses **BExtend**, the selection becomes anchored at the edge of the selection farthest from the pointer position. When the user releases **BExtend**, the selection extends from the anchor to the position where **BExtend** is released, and any text outside that range is deselected. The insertion cursor moves to the position where **BExtend** is released.

Clicking **BToggle** moves the insertion cursor to the position where **BToggle** is released without affecting the selection.

Clicking **BTransfer** moves the insertion cursor to the position where **BTransfer** is released. Then, unless the insertion cursor is in the midst of the selection, it copies the primary selection to the insertion cursor and moves the insertion cursor to the end of the copied text. The original selection remains selected. Clicking **MShift BTransfer** has the same effect except that it moves the primary selection to the insertion cursor, deleting the original selection if possible.

Dragging **MAlt BTransfer** outside of the primary selection starts a secondary selection consisting of all text between the position of the pointer and the position where **MAlt BTransfer** was pressed. Releasing **MAlt BTransfer** copies the secondary selection to the insertion cursor in the destination widget. Before copying the secondary selection, if the destination contains the primary selection and the insertion cursor is not disjoint from it, releasing **MAlt BTransfer** deletes the primary selection. Dragging **MAlt MShift BTransfer** also makes a secondary selection, and releasing **MAlt MShift BTransfer** moves the secondary selection to the destination widget.

Dragging **BTransfer** with the insertion cursor positioned within a primary selection initiates a drag operation. The user may press a modifier key to indicate whether the drag is a copy, move, or link operation. Releasing

BTransfer either in the same Text widget or a different widget moves the insertion cursor to the position where **BTransfer** is released, drops the selected text at that point, and moves the insertion cursor to the end of the dropped text.

Pressing **KCancel** during the operation aborts the operation and no data exchange occurs. If the user presses **KHelp** over a drop site, the user has the option to continue or to cancel the drop operation in response to the help information that the application provides.

8.2.2 Keyboard Selection

Selection operations available with the mouse, except secondary selection, are also available from the keyboard. Text has two keyboard selection modes, Normal Mode and Add Mode. In Normal Mode, if text is selected, a navigation operation deselects the selected text and moves the anchor to the current position of the insertion cursor before navigating. In Add Mode, navigation operations have no effect other than navigation. In both modes, pressing **KSelect** has the same effect as pressing **BSelect** at that position.

In Normal mode, when the widget contains the primary selection and the insertion cursor is disjoint from it, any operation that inserts or pastes text into the widget (except a transfer of the primary selection from the same widget) first deselects the primary selection. In Add Mode, such an operation does not deselect the primary selection.

Pressing **KExtend** extends the current selection to the insertion cursor using the balance-beam method. The current selection becomes anchored at the edge of the selection farthest from the insertion cursor. The selection then extends from the anchor to the insertion cursor, and any text outside that range is deselected.

Shifted navigation operations also extend a selection. In Normal Mode, if no text is selected, a shifted navigation operation moves the anchor to the insertion cursor, navigates, selects the navigated text, and deselects any text outside that range. In the remaining cases—Normal Mode and Add Mode with any selection—a shifted navigation operation extends the selection using the balance-beam method. Before navigation, the current selection becomes anchored at the edge of the selection farthest from the insertion cursor. After navigation, the selection extends from the anchor to the insertion cursor, and any text outside that range is deselected.

KPrimaryCopy copies the primary selection to the insertion cursor. **KPrimaryCut** cuts the primary selection to the insertion cursor.

KCopy copies the current selection in the Text widget to the clipboard; **KCut** cuts the selection; and **KPaste** inserts the contents of the clipboard at the insertion cursor.

8.3 Text Editing and Callbacks

Text has a number of callback lists for communication with the application. Text invokes callbacks whenever the widget gains or loses focus, when it gains or loses the primary selection, before the insertion cursor is moved or text is modified, and when the text string changes or the **activate()** action is invoked.

Text passes these callbacks a pointer to either an **XmAnyCallbackStruct** or an **XmTextVerifyCallbackStruct** (or **XmTextVerifyCallbackStructWcs**) structure. The two verification structures contain the current and new positions of the insertion cursor, the starting and ending positions of the text to be modified, a pointer to an **XmTextBlockRec** (or **XmTextBlockRecWcs**) structure with information about the text to be modified, and a Boolean in/out **doit** member that the callback procedure can set to tell the widget whether or not to go ahead with the modification.

Following is a summary of the callbacks:

XmNmotionVerifyCallback

> Text invokes this list, passing a pointer to an **XmTextVerifyCallbackStruct** as the widget data, before moving the insertion cursor. The application can prevent the action by setting the **doit** member of the callback struct to False.

XmNmodifyVerifyCallback or **XmNmodifyVerifyCallbackWcs**

> Text invokes this list, passing a pointer to an **XmTextVerifyCallbackStruct** structure (or an **XmTextVerifyCallbackStructWcs** structure) as the widget data, before deleting or inserting any text. The application can prevent the action by setting the **doit** member of the callback struct to False.

XmNvalueChangedCallback

> Text invokes this list, passing a pointer to an **XmAnyCallbackStruct** as the widget data, after text is inserted or deleted.

XmNfocusCallback

> Text invokes this list, passing a pointer to an **XmAnyCallbackStruct** as the widget data, when the widget gains input focus.

XmNlosingFocusCallback

> Text invokes this list, passing a pointer to an **XmTextVerifyCallbackStruct** as the widget data, before the widget loses input focus. The application can prevent the action by setting the **doit** member of the callback struct to False.

XmNgainPrimaryCallback

> Text invokes this list, passing a pointer to an **XmAnyCallbackStruct** as the widget data, when the widget gains ownership of the primary selection.

XmNlosePrimaryCallback

> Text invokes this list, passing a pointer to an **XmAnyCallbackStruct** as the widget data, when the widget loses ownership of the primary selection.

XmNactivateCallback

> Text invokes this list, passing a pointer to an **XmAnyCallbackStruct** as the widget data, when the **activate()** action is invoked. By default no translations are bound to this action, but in a single-line Text widget or a TextField widget, pressing **KEnter** invokes the **XmNactivateCallback** callbacks.

These callbacks provide a great deal of flexibility for an application to alter the behavior of the Text widget. For example, an application can prevent text from being inserted, as when the user types a password, using the **XmNmodifyVerifyCallback** or **XmNmodifyVerifyCallbackWcs** callbacks. The application can prevent any text from appearing by setting the **doit** member of the **XmTextVerifyCallbackStruct** (or **XmTextVerifyCallbackStructWcs**) to False. The application can also alter the text that will appear by creating a new text string and setting the **ptr** member of the **XmTextBlockRec** structure (or the **wcsptr** member of the

XmTextBlockRecWcs structure) to the new string.

Following is an example of an **XmNmodifyVerifyCallback** that substitutes a string of characters for any text a user enters. Because the **XmNmodifyVerifyCallback** procedures are most commonly invoked after the user enters a character, this routine usually substitutes the replacement string for each character the user types. This example could be used with a single-line Text widget as part of a simple password-entry program. In this case, the **XmNmodifyVerifyCallback** procedure would need additional code to save the characters the user types, and the program would need an **XmNactivateCallback** procedure to check whether the saved characters match the password.

```
/* XmNmodifyVerifyCallback procedure that
 * replaces text the user enters
 * with a replacement string passed in as
 * application data. */
void ModifyVerifyCB(Widget w, XtPointer app_data,
                    XtPointer widget_data)
{
  char *replace_string = (char *) app_data;
  XmTextVerifyCallbackStruct *widget_info =
    (XmTextVerifyCallbackStruct *) widget_data;
  if (widget_info->text->length > 0) {
    widget_info->text->length = strlen(replace_string);
    widget_info->text->ptr = replace_string;
  }
}
```

Text and TextField differ from most other Motif widgets in that calling some convenience routines and setting some resources causes the widget to invoke callback procedures. In general

- Setting resources or calling convenience routines that change the contents of the text invokes the **XmNmodifyVerifyCallback** and **XmNmodifyVerifyCallbackWcs** callbacks. If these procedures allow the text to be modified, the **XmNvalueChangedCallback** callbacks are invoked.

- Setting resources or calling convenience routines that change the position of the insertion cursor invokes the **XmNmotionVerifyCallback** callbacks.

- Setting resources or calling convenience routines that cause the widget to gain the primary selection invokes the **XmNgainPrimaryCallback** callbacks.

- Setting resources or calling convenience routines that cause the widget to lose the primary selection invokes the **XmNlosePrimaryCallback** callbacks.

If the application needs to distinguish between callbacks invoked as a result of user action and callbacks invoked as a result of application action (such as setting a resource or calling a convenience routine), it needs to set a flag before taking the application action and clear the flag afterward.

8.4 Text Resources and Geometry

In addition to the resources discussed in the previous section, Text has many others, including the following:

- The text itself, **XmNvalue** or **XmNvalueWcs**. The text is represented to the application as an array of either **char** elements (for **XmNvalue**) or **wchar_t** elements (for **XmNvalueWcs**). The application can set or get either resource.

- Resources representing the insertion cursor position and blink rate, the position of text at the top of the window, and whether the insertion cursor is always visible. A text position (of type **XmTextPosition**) is an integer representing the number of characters from the beginning of the buffer.

- A resource (**XmNmaxLength**) representing the maximum length of the text string that the user can enter.

- A resource (**XmNwordWrap**) that specifies whether lines are broken at word boundaries. Breaking a line at a word boundary does not insert a newline into the text.

In addition, Text and TextField have several resources that determine the geometry of the widget:

- Two resources, **XmNmarginHeight** and **XmNmarginWidth**, that determine the margins between the text and the shadow, if present. Text and TextField also use the Primitive resources that determine shadow and highlight appearance.

- The font list (**XmNfontList**) that the widget uses to select a font or font set to display the text.

- Resources that specify the number of rows of text (**XmNrows**) and the number of horizontal character positions (**XmNcolumns**). Single-line Text and TextField always have one row.

- Resources that determine whether or not the widget grows vertically (**XmNresizeHeight**) or horizontally (**XmNresizeWidth**) to accommodate all its text. **XmNresizeHeight** does not apply to single-line Text or TextField.

- Resources that apply only when the widget is inside a ScrolledWindow whose XmNvisualPolicy is **XmVARIABLE**. **XmNscrollHorizontal** determines whether or not the widget should have a horizontal ScrollBar and should scroll horizontally instead of growing when the text expands beyond the width allocated for it. **XmNscrollVertical** determines whether or not the widget should have a vertical ScrollBar and should scroll vertically instead of growing when the text expands beyond the height allocated for it. **XmNscrollLeftSide** and **XmNscrollTopSide** determine which side of the widget receives the corresponding ScrollBar. These resources do not apply to TextField, and **XmNscrollVertical** and **XmNscrollLeftSide** do not apply to single-line Text.

XmNresizeWidth is initialized to False when **XmNscrollHorizontal** is True or **XmNwordWrap** is True. **XmNresizeHeight** is initialized to False when **XmNscrollVertical** is True.

If the user or application initializes or sets a specific height (**XmNheight**) or width (**XmNwidth**), that value is used as the corresponding dimension of the widget. In addition, if a height is specified, **XmNrows** is recalculated based on that height, and if a width is specified, **XmNcolumns** is recalculated based on that width.

If the user or application initializes or sets **XmNrows** but not **XmNheight**, the geometry calculation depends on the value of **XmNresizeHeight**. If **XmNresizeHeight** is True, the height of the widget is the greater of the height needed to display **XmNrows** of text and the height needed to display all the text. If **XmNresizeHeight** is False, as it is by default, the height of the widget is the height needed to display all the text. The same relations hold for **XmNcolumns**, **XmNwidth**, and **XmNresizeWidth**.

If the user or application does not initialize either **XmNrows** or **XmNheight**, the geometry calculation depends on the value of **XmNresizeHeight**. If **XmNresizeHeight** is True, the height of the widget is the height needed to display all the text. If **XmNresizeHeight** is False, the height of the widget is the height needed to display the default for **XmNrows**, which is one row of text. The same relations hold for **XmNcolumns**, **XmNwidth**, and **XmNresizeWidth**, except that the default number of columns is 20.

If the contents of the text (**XmNvalue** or **XmNvalueWcs**) change, as a result of user editing or an action by the application, the geometry calculation depends on the value of **XmNresizeHeight**. If **XmNresizeHeight** is True, the height of the widget is the height needed to display all the text. If **XmNresizeHeight** is False, the height of the widget does not change. The same relations hold for **XmNvalue**, **XmNvalueWcs**, **XmNresizeWidth**, and the width of the widget.

If the application sets another resource that affects the height needed by the widget, such as **XmNmarginHeight** or **XmNfontList**, the geometry calculation depends on the value of **XmNresizeHeight**. If **XmNresizeHeight** is True, the height of the widget is the height needed to display all the text with the new resource values. If **XmNresizeHeight** is False, the height of the widget is the height needed to display **XmNrows** of text using the new resources. The same relations hold for these resources, **XmNresizeWidth**, **XmNcolumns**, and the width of the widget.

8.5 Convenience Routines

Text has convenience routines to permit the application to perform many functions, including these:

- Insert and replace text.

- Cut, copy, and paste using the clipboard.

- Get and set the editable state, the insertion cursor position, the maximum length of text, the primary selection and its position, the source, the text string, and the position of the first character displayed. All routines that have parameters or return values that are strings have both **char** * and **wchar_t** * versions.

- Convert between a text position and x and y coordinates.
- Display text at a given position and scroll the text.

8.6 ScrolledText

ScrolledText is a Text widget inside a ScrolledWindow. The application can use **XmCreateScrolledText** to create one. This routine creates both Text and ScrolledWindow widgets and forces the following initial values for ScrolledWindow resources:

- **XmNscrollingPolicy** is set to **XmAPPLICATION_DEFINED**.
- **XmNvisualPolicy** is set to **XmVARIABLE**.
- **XmNscrollBarDisplayPolicy** is set to **XmSTATIC**.
- **XmNshadowThickness** is set to 0.

8.7 Storing Text in a File

A common requirement of many text editors is the ability to read text from a file, allow the user to edit the text, and then store the text in a file. An application usually obtains pathnames from the user by means of a FileSelectionBox, often invoked as a dialog from a MenuBar File Menu. Following are very simple routines that use ANSI C input/output facilities to read text from a file into a Text widget and save text from a Text widget into a file:

```
void ReadTextFromFile(Widget w, char *filename)
{
  FILE           *file;
  char            buffer[MAXSIZE];
  char           *ptr, *end;
  XmTextPosition  last_pos;
  if (file = fopen(filename, "r")) {
    XmTextSetString(w, "");
    ptr = buffer;
```

```
        end = buffer + MAXSIZE - 1;
        while((val = getc(file)) != EOF) {
          if (ptr < end) {
            *ptr++ = (char) val;
          } else {
            *ptr = '\0';
            last_pos = XmTextGetLastPosition(w);
            XmTextReplace(w, last_pos, last_pos, buffer);
            ptr = buffer;
          }
        }
        if (ptr > buffer) {
          *ptr = '\0';
          last_pos = XmTextGetLastPosition(w);
          XmTextReplace(w, last_pos, last_pos, buffer);
        }
        (void) fclose(file);
    }
}


void SaveTextToFile(Widget w, char *filename)
{
    FILE    *file;
    char    *text;
    if (file = fopen(filename, "w")) {
      text = XmTextGetString(w);
      (void) fputs(text, file);
      (void) fclose(file);
      XtFree(text);
    }
}
```

8.8 Sharing Text Sources

Each Text widget has a data structure of type **XmTextSource** that functions as the source and sink of text for the widget. The source is the value of the **XmNsource** resource.

Two or more Text widgets can share the same source. In this case, editing of Text in one widget changes the text of the source and therefore the text of all widgets that share that source. For example, an application might use a PanedWindow with multiple text widgets, each functioning as a "window" onto a single text source. Editing changes in one pane are reflected in all Text panes that share the same source.

An application creates a Text source by creating a Text widget. The program uses **XmTextGetSource** or **XtGetValues** for the **XmNsource** resource to obtain that widget's source. The application then creates another Text widget, supplying the source obtained from the first widget using **XmTextSetSource**, the initialization argument list, or **XtSetValues** of the **XmNsource** resource.

Setting a Text source destroys the existing source of the widget if no other widgets are sharing that source. To replace a Text source but keep it for later use, the application can create an unmanaged Text widget and set its source to the Text source the program wants to keep.

If the application does not supply a source, Text creates a default string source.

Chapter 9

Scrolling, Panes, and Frames

Chapters 6 and 7 discuss the OSF/Motif Manager widgets used to construct menus and dialogs. Motif also provides more general-purpose managers intended for use in main application windows and some dialogs. This chapter discusses widgets that perform the following functions:

- Establishing a viewport for a larger underlying scroll

- Providing a main application window with a combination of standard and custom components

- Placing a shadowed frame around a widget and an optional title at the top

- Creating multiple subwindows for a composite with adjustable boundaries between the subwindows

9.1 ScrolledWindow

Frequently a collection occupies an area that is too large to display within an application or that may grow or shrink as the user adds or deletes data. Examples include text in a Text widget, items in a List, and graphical objects in a DrawingArea or other canvas. Three approaches exist for handling this problem:

- Set a fixed size for the widget. The disadvantage of this approach is that when the collection grows beyond the bounds of the widget, part of the collection is not visible.

- Allow the widget to make geometry requests to expand or contract, perhaps up to some maximum or down to some minimum size. The disadvantages of this approach are that it may disrupt the application's visual layout and that the widget is able to grow only within limits, perhaps not at all.

- Treat the collection as a virtual scroll, with the widget acting as a (more or less) fixed-size viewport onto the scroll. The user can move the viewport to expose obscured portions of the scroll.

The ScrolledWindow widget implements the last approach. It is a Manager with one or two ScrollBar children, a child widget that acts as the virtual scroll, and in some cases another child that acts as a viewport onto the scroll. By using the ScrollBars or keyboard scrolling commands, the user moves the viewport to expose part of the scroll.

9.1.1 Automatic and Application-Defined Scrolling

ScrolledWindow implements two scrolling models: automatic and application defined.

In automatic scrolling, the application creates a widget to serve as the virtual scroll, and the ScrolledWindow creates the ScrollBars and a widget to serve as a fixed-size viewport onto the scroll. The application adjusts the size of the scroll widget as necessary to contain the entire collection. The ScrolledWindow adjusts the appropriate ScrollBar resources so that the size and position of the slider reflect the position of the viewport in relation to the scroll and the proportion of the scroll's entire size that the viewport represents. The ScrolledWindow also handles the user's interaction with the ScrollBars, moving the viewport in relation to the scroll as the user manipulates the ScrollBars. Usually the application need have no interaction with the ScrollBars or the widget that serves as the viewport.

In application-defined scrolling, the application must create the ScrollBars as well as the widget that acts as the virtual scroll and, if necessary, a separate viewport widget. The application must determine how large to make the viewport widget and what portion of the data to display in the viewport. The application handles all interaction with the ScrollBars. It must adjust the appropriate ScrollBar resources if it wants the size and position of the slider to reflect the relation of the viewport to the underlying scroll. It must also move the viewport in relation to the scroll as the user interacts with the ScrollBars.

The ScrolledWindow resource **XmNscrollingPolicy** determines the scrolling model. Possible values for this resource are **XmAUTOMATIC** and **XmAPPLICATION_DEFINED**. The default value is **XmAPPLICATION_DEFINED**.

9.1.2 Other Resources

In addition to **XmNscrollingPolicy**, ScrolledWindow has two sets of resources.

One set of resources holds the components of the ScrolledWindow. An application usually does not have to set any of these resources; the ScrolledWindow examines the class and other characteristics of each child as it is created and sets the appropriate resource. If the application needs to supply a new ScrollBar or scroll widget after creating the initial component, it can use either **XtSetValues** or **XmScrolledWindowSetAreas**.

Following are the resources that hold components of the ScrolledWindow:

XmNclipWindow
> The value is the ID of the viewport widget created by the ScrolledWindow in automatic scrolling. This resource applies only when the **XmNscrollingPolicy** is **XmAUTOMATIC**. It is a read-only resource; the application cannot set a new value.

XmNhorizontalScrollBar
> The value is the ID of the horizontal ScrollBar. The

ScrolledWindow creates this ScrollBar and sets the value of this resource when the **XmNscrollingPolicy** is **XmAUTOMATIC**. In application-defined scrolling, the application must create and manage the ScrollBar, but the ScrolledWindow automatically sets the value of this resource to its widget ID.

XmNverticalScrollBar

The value is the ID of the vertical ScrollBar. The ScrolledWindow creates this ScrollBar and sets the value of this resource when the **XmNscrollingPolicy** is **XmAUTOMATIC**. In application-defined scrolling, the application must create and manage the ScrollBar, but the ScrolledWindow automatically sets the value of this resource to its widget ID.

XmNworkWindow

The value is the ID of the widget that serves as the scroll. The application has to create and manage this widget, but it usually does not have to set this resource. When the application creates a child of the ScrolledWindow that is not a ScrollBar, the ScrolledWindow automatically sets the value of this resource to its widget ID.

The second set of resources specifies the layout of the ScrolledWindow:

XmNscrollBarDisplayPolicy

This resource determines whether the ScrolledWindow always displays managed ScrollBars or displays them only when the corresponding dimensions of the scroll exceed those of the viewport. Possible values are **XmAS_NEEDED** and **XmSTATIC**. The value is forced to **XmSTATIC** when the scrolling policy is **XmAPPLICATION_DEFINED** and defaults to **XmAS_NEEDED** when the scrolling policy is **XmAUTOMATIC**.

XmNscrollBarPlacement

This resource determines where the ScrolledWindow places the horizontal and vertical ScrollBars. The possible values are constants that specify on which sides of the viewport the ScrolledWindow places the two ScrollBars: **XmTOP_LEFT**, **XmTOP_RIGHT**, **XmBOTTOM_LEFT**, and **XmBOTTOM_RIGHT**.

XmNscrolledWindowMarginHeight

> This resource specifies the margins between the top and bottom sides of the ScrolledWindow and the first child on each side.

XmNscrolledWindowMarginWidth

> This resource specifies the margins between the left and right sides of the ScrolledWindow and the first child on each side.

XmNspacing

> This resource specifies the distance between each ScrollBar and the viewport.

9.2 Automatic Scrolling

In the automatic scrolling model, the ScrolledWindow creates a fixed-size viewport and handles all interaction with the ScrollBars. The application usually needs to take only the following steps:

- Create and manage a ScrolledWindow, supplying a value of **XmAUTOMATIC** for **XmNscrollingPolicy** in the argument list passed to the creation function

- Create and manage a widget child of the ScrolledWindow to serve as the scroll

- Adjust the size of the scroll widget, typically using **XtSetValues** of **XmNheight** and **XmNwidth**, as necessary to contain all the data in the scroll

The ScrolledWindow automatically creates a widget to serve as the viewport and sets **XmNclipWindow** to the ID of this widget. It also creates horizontal and vertical ScrollBars and sets **XmNhorizontalScrollBar** and **XmNverticalScrollBar** to the appropriate IDs of the ScrollBars. The ScrolledWindow attaches callback procedures to the ScrollBars to handle user interaction with the ScrollBars.

The ScrolledWindow sets the ScrollBar resource **XmNincrement** to a small fraction of the height or width of the viewport. It sets the ScrollBar resource **XmNpageIncrement** to a large fraction of the height or width of the viewport. If the ScrolledWindow resizes the viewport, it recomputes the values of these resources.

The ScrolledWindow sets the ScrollBar resources **XmNmaximum**, **XmNminimum**, and **XmNsliderSize** so that the size of the slider reflects the proportion of the entire scroll that the viewport represents. If the application resizes the scroll or if the ScrolledWindow resizes the viewport, the ScrolledWindow recomputes the values of some or all of these resources.

If the value of **XmNscrollBarDisplayPolicy** is **XmAS_NEEDED**, as it is by default in automatic scrolling, the ScrolledWindow displays a ScrollBar only if the size of the scroll exceeds the size of the viewport in the relevant dimension. If the value of **XmNscrollBarDisplayPolicy** is **XmSTATIC**, the ScrolledWindow always displays both ScrollBars.

As the user manipulates a ScrollBar and changes its **XmNvalue**, the ScrolledWindow moves the scroll with respect to the viewport. For example, if the user moves the slider down in a vertical ScrollBar, the ScrolledWindow moves the scroll up with respect to the viewport.

The ScrolledWindow may need to move the scroll (and set a ScrollBar's **XmNvalue**) in circumstances other than the user's interaction with the ScrollBar. For example, if the viewport is at the bottom of the scroll and the application reduces the height of the scroll, the ScrolledWindow must move the scroll down with respect to the viewport. In this case, it reduces the ScrollBar's **XmNmaximum** and **XmNvalue**.

In automatic scrolling, the application should not try to set any of the following resources:

- The **XmNx** or **XmNy** of any child of the ScrolledWindow

- Any geometry resources of the viewport (the **XmNclipWindow**)

- The **XmNmaximum**, **XmNminimum**, **XmNvalue**, **XmNincrement**, or **XmNpageIncrement** of a ScrollBar

The application can add callbacks of its own to a ScrollBar, but because the ScrolledWindow adds its own callbacks, the application must not call **XtRemoveAllCallbacks** for a ScrollBar.

The application or user can specify other resources, such as those that determine appearance, for the ScrolledWindow or its children. The names of the automatically created ScrollBars are "HorScrollBar" and "VertScrollBar".

9.2.1 Traversing to Obscured Widgets

By default, it is not possible to use keyboard traversal to move to a widget that is inside the scroll but outside the viewport. For example, if the user presses **KNextField** and the next field is not within the viewport, focus does not move to that field. The user must first use the ScrollBars or a scrolling command to position the viewport so the target widget is not obscured.

ScrolledWindow has a callback list, **XmNtraverseObscuredCallback**, that allows an application to make it possible to traverse to widgets that are in the scroll but not in the viewport. The callback list is invoked when the user tries to traverse to such a widget in a ScrolledWindow with automatic scrolling. The callback procedure is passed a pointer to an **XmTraverseObscuredCallbackStruct** structure, which contains the reason (**XmCR_OBSCURED_TRAVERSAL**), the event, the widget that is the target of the traversal, and the traversal direction passed to **XmProcessTraversal**.

Usually the callback procedure can allow traversal to the target widget simply by calling **XmScrollVisible**. This function takes as arguments the ScrolledWindow, the target widget, and requested margins between the target widget and the edges of the viewport. The function moves the work area with respect to the viewport to make the obscured widget visible. This function applies only to ScrolledWidgets with automatic scrolling.

When ScrolledWindows are nested and focus is in an inner ScrolledWindow, the **XmNtraverseObscuredCallback** callbacks of the inner ScrolledWindow are invoked first if necessary. If the destination widget remains outside the viewport of the first ancestor ScrolledWindow, that ScrolledWindow's **XmNtraverseObscuredCallback** callbacks are invoked, and so on up the widget hierarchy.

9.2.2 Example of Automatic Scrolling

This section contains the scrolling-related portions of an example program that uses a ScrolledWindow with an automatic scrolling policy. The ScrolledWindow is actually a MainWindow, a subclass of ScrolledWindow that is often the containing manager for the primary window of an application. (MainWindow is discussed in Section 9.4.) The scroll widget is a DrawingArea.

The application allows the user to create a simple map in the DrawingArea. The user can use the mouse to establish points representing cities and to draw lines between the cities. The application contains a TextField that allows the user to enter the name of a city and then to create a button child of the DrawingArea located at the city and containing the city's name as its label. The user can adjust the size of the DrawingArea by manipulating two Scales, one for the height of the DrawingArea and the other for the width. Other parts of the application save and retrieve the map data.

This section contains only the portions of the application that relate directly to creating and maintaining the ScrolledWindow. These include:

- Creating the MainWindow with an automatic scrolling policy

- Creating the DrawingArea child of the ScrolledWindow

- Resizing the DrawingArea in response to the user's interaction with the Scales

- Establishing an **XmNtraverseObscuredCallback** procedure

```
/*--------------------------------------------------------------
**  Create a Main Window with a menubar, a command panel
**  containing 2 scales and a textfied, and a workarea.
**  Also put in the graphic structure the workarea info and the
**  textfield ids.
*/
void CreateApplication (
Widget          parent,
Graphic *       graph )
{
    Widget main_window, menu_bar, menu_pane, cascade,
            button, comw, scale ;
    Arg args[5];
    int n ;

    /*  Create automatic MainWindow.
     */
    n = 0;
    XtSetArg (args[n], XmNscrollingPolicy, XmAUTOMATIC); n++;
    main_window = XmCreateMainWindow (parent, "main_window",
                    args, n);

    XtAddCallback (main_window, XmNtraverseObscuredCallback,
```

```
                        TravCB, NULL);

        XtManageChild (main_window);

...

        /*  Create work_area in MainWindow
         */
        n = 0;
        XtSetArg (args[n], XmNresizePolicy, XmRESIZE_NONE); n++ ;
        XtSetArg (args[n], XmNmarginWidth, 0); n++ ;
        XtSetArg (args[n], XmNmarginHeight, 0); n++ ;
        graph->work_area = XmCreateDrawingArea(main_window,
                                        "work_area", args, n);
        XtAddCallback (graph->work_area, XmNexposeCallback, DrawCB,
                    (XtPointer)graph);
        XtAddCallback (graph->work_area, XmNresizeCallback, DrawCB,
                    (XtPointer)graph);
        XtAddCallback (graph->work_area, XmNinputCallback, DrawCB,
                    (XtPointer)graph);
        XtManageChild (graph->work_area);

        /*  Create a commandWindow in MainWindow with text and
            scales */
        n = 0;
        comw = XmCreateRowColumn(main_window, "comw", args, n);
        XtManageChild (comw);
        n = 0;
        XtSetArg (args[n], XmNcommandWindow, comw);  n++;
        XtSetValues (main_window, args, n);

        /* find initial size of the work_area and report to the
            scales */
        n = 0;
        XtSetArg (args[n], XmNwidth, &graph->old_width);  n++;
        XtSetArg (args[n], XmNheight, &graph->old_height);  n++;
        XtGetValues (graph->work_area, args, n);

        n = 0;
        XtSetArg (args[n], XmNorientation, XmHORIZONTAL);  n++;
        XtSetArg (args[n], XmNvalue, graph->old_width);  n++;
```

```
                 /* scale_w is the name */
                 scale = XmCreateScale(comw, "scale_w", args, n);
                 XtAddCallback (scale, XmNvalueChangedCallback, ValueCB,
                            (XtPointer)graph->work_area);
                 XtManageChild (scale);

                 n = 0;
                 XtSetArg (args[n], XmNorientation, XmHORIZONTAL);  n++;
                 XtSetArg (args[n], XmNvalue, graph->old_height);  n++;
                 scale = XmCreateScale(comw, "scale_h", args, n);
                 XtAddCallback (scale, XmNvalueChangedCallback, ValueCB,
                            (XtPointer)graph->work_area);
                 XtManageChild (scale);

                 n = 0;
                 graph->textf = XmCreateTextField(comw, "textf", args, n);
                 XtManageChild (graph->textf);

                 /*  Set MainWindow areas
                  */
                 XmMainWindowSetAreas (main_window, menu_bar, comw, NULL,
                                  NULL, graph->work_area);
             }


    /*-------------------------------------------------------------
    **      TravCB            - callback for traverseObscure
    */
    void TravCB (
    Widget          w,              /*  widget id             */
    XtPointer       client_data,    /*  data from application  */
    XtPointer       call_data )     /*  data from widget class */
    {
        XmTraverseObscuredCallbackStruct * tocs =
            (XmTraverseObscuredCallbackStruct *) call_data ;

        XmScrollVisible(w, tocs->traversal_destination, 20, 20) ;
    }


    /*-------------------------------------------------------------
    **      ValueCB           - callback for scales
    */
```

```
void ValueCB (
Widget          w,              /*  widget id              */
XtPointer       client_data,    /*  data from application  */
XtPointer       call_data )     /*  data from widget class */
{

    Arg args[5];
    int n ;
    int value ;
    Widget workarea = (Widget) client_data ;

    /* get the value outof the Scale */
    n = 0;
    XtSetArg (args[n], XmNvalue, &value);  n++;
    XtGetValues (w, args, n);

    n = 0;
    if (strcmp(XtName(w), "scale_w") == 0 ) { /* width scale */
        XtSetArg (args[n], XmNwidth, value);  n++;
    } else {
        XtSetArg (args[n], XmNheight, value);  n++;
    }
    XtSetValues (workarea, args, n);
}
```

9.3 Application-Defined Scrolling

In application-defined scrolling, the application is responsible for all aspects of the interactions among the scroll, the viewport, and the ScrollBars. The ScrolledWindow remains responsible for geometry and layout, but the application must adjust both the ScrollBars and the scroll position in response to the user's scrolling actions.

Because this model requires more work on the part of the application, it is most suitable for programs in which automatic scrolling is not adequate.

For example, an application may contain a text editor or browser that reads only enough of a file to fill the viewport. This application must be informed of the user's scrolling actions so that it can read more of the file when necessary.

The application implements a scheme of its choosing for the relationship between the scroll and the viewport. Following are two common models:

- A fixed-size viewport widget as the parent of a variable-sized scroll widget that contains the data. The application resizes the scroll widget as necessary to contain all the data. As the user interacts with the ScrollBar, the application moves the scroll widget with respect to the viewport, which clips the scroll. This is the model that ScrolledWindow uses for automatic scrolling.

- A single widget that serves as the viewport, with the scroll contained in internal data structures or a combination of data structures and files. The application expands the internal structures as necessary to contain all the data. As the user interacts with the ScrollBar, the application retrieves the appropriate portion of the data from the internal structures or files and displays that portion of the data in the viewport. This is the model that the Motif ScrolledList and ScrolledText widgets use.

In both models, the application must be notified when the viewport is resized. It may need to adjust the scroll with respect to the viewport, and it must recompute ScrollBar resources to reflect the new relation between the viewport and the scroll. If the viewport is a DrawingArea the application can use the **XmNresizeCallback** callbacks for this purpose. Otherwise, the application can establish an event handler for **ConfigureNotify** events.

The application needs to take the following steps to use application-defined scrolling:

- Create and manage a ScrolledWindow, horizontal and vertical ScrollBar children, and a child to serve as the viewport.

- If the application is using a separate widget as the scroll, create and manage that widget as a child of the viewport widget.

- Add callbacks to the ScrollBars to notify the application when the user interacts with the ScrollBars. The application should at least provide a procedure for the **XmNvalueChangedCallback** list.

- Add a callback (such as the DrawingArea **XmNresizeCallback**) or an event handler to the viewport widget to notify the application when the widget is resized.

- Based on the initial relationship between the viewport and the scroll, supply initial values for the ScrollBars' **XmNincrement**, **XmNpageIncrement**, **XmNmaximum**, **XmNminimum**, **XmNvalue**, and **XmNsliderSize** resources.

- Adjust the size of the scroll widget or internal data structures as necessary to contain the data in the scroll.

- As the data in the scroll changes, recompute the ScrollBars' **XmNmaximum** and **XmNsliderSize** and perhaps **XmNminimum** and **XmNvalue** to reflect the new relation between the viewport and the scroll.

- When the viewport is resized, reposition and resize the scroll with respect to the viewport if necessary. Recompute the ScrollBars' **XmNsliderSize** and **XmNpageIncrement** and possibly other resources to reflect the new relationship between the viewport and the scroll.

- As the user interacts with the ScrollBars, if a separate scroll widget exists, reposition the scroll with respect to the viewport. If no separate scroll widget exists, bring in additional data from files if necessary, recompute which portion of the data to make visible, and redisplay the viewport. If the size of the scroll has changed, recompute the ScrollBar resources to reflect the new relationship between the viewport and the scroll.

9.3.1 Example of Application-Defined Scrolling

This section contains the scrolling-related portions of an example program that uses a ScrolledWindow with an application-defined scrolling policy. As in the example of automatic scrolling, the ScrolledWindow is a MainWindow, and the scroll widget is a DrawingArea. In this example, the scroll widget also serves as the viewport widget, and the scroll data is maintained in internal data structures.

The application is a simple file browser for C source code. The user selects a filename. The program reads the file and parses it (in the C locale) into an internal table of lines. The application displays in the DrawingArea as many lines as will fit into the current dimensions of the DrawingArea.

The application uses only a vertical ScrollBar, which allows the user to browse through the file. After reading the file, the program sets the ScrollBar's **XmNminimum** and **XmNvalue** to 0, its **XmNmaximum** to the number of lines in the file, and its **XmNsliderSize** to the lesser of the number of lines in the file and the number of lines that can be displayed in the viewport.

The program establishes a ScrollBar **XmNvalueChangedCallback** and a DrawingArea **XmNexposeCallback** that redisplay the lines in the viewport. The redisplay procedure fetches and displays lines from the internal data structure, starting with the line indicated by the ScrollBar's **XmNvalue** and proceeding to the last line that fits in the viewport. The program also establishes a DrawingArea **XmNresizeCallback** that recomputes the ScrollBar's **XmNsliderSize** and **XmNvalue** based on the number of lines that can be displayed in the viewport. The application does not resize the DrawingArea itself.

This section contains only the portions of the application that relate directly to creating and maintaining the ScrolledWindow. These include:

- Creating the MainWindow with an application-defined scrolling policy

- Creating the DrawingArea and vertical ScrollBar children of the ScrolledWindow

- Establishing an **XmNactivateCallback** callback for the OK button of the FileSelectionBox invoked from the file menu Open button

- Establishing a ScrollBar **XmNvalueChangedCallback** callback

- Establishing a DrawingArea **XmNexposeCallback** callback and an **XmNresizeCallback** callback

```
/*------------------------------------------------------------
**        Internal data structure to hold file info.
*/
typedef struct {
    Widget work_area  ;
    Widget v_scrb ;
    String file_name ;
    XFontStruct * font_struct ;
    GC draw_gc ;
```

```
    char ** lines ;
    int num_lines ;
} FileData ;

/*-------------------------------------------------------------
** Create a MainWindow with a MenuBar to load a file.
** Add the vertical scrollbar and the workarea to filedata.
*/
void CreateApplication (
Widget          parent,
FileData *      filedata )
{
    Widget main_window, menu_bar, menu_pane, cascade,
           button ;
    Arg args[5];
    int n ;

    /*  Create app_defined MainWindow.
     *  XmAPPLICATION_DEFINED is the default; not necessary
     *  to specify it here.
     */
    n = 0;
    XtSetArg (args[n], XmNscrollingPolicy,
              XmAPPLICATION_DEFINED);  n++;
    main_window = XmCreateMainWindow (parent,
                               "main_window", args, n);
    XtManageChild (main_window);

    /*  Create MenuBar in MainWindow.
     */

...

    /* Create "File" PulldownMenu with Open and Quit buttons
     */

    n = 0;
    menu_pane = XmCreatePulldownMenu (menu_bar,
                               "menu_pane", args, n);

    n = 0;
```

```
button = XmCreatePushButton (menu_pane, "Open...",
                                args, n);
XtManageChild (button);


/* pass the file data to the Open callback */
XtAddCallback (button, XmNactivateCallback,
            OpenCB, (XtPointer)filedata);
n = 0;
button = XmCreatePushButton (menu_pane, "Quit", args, n);
XtManageChild (button);
XtAddCallback (button, XmNactivateCallback, QuitCB, NULL);


n = 0;
XtSetArg (args[n], XmNsubMenuId, menu_pane);  n++;
cascade = XmCreateCascadeButton (menu_bar, "File",
                                args, n);
XtManageChild (cascade);


/*  Create "Help" PulldownMenu with Help button.
 */


...


/*  Create vertical scrollbar only
 */
 n = 0;
XtSetArg (args[n], XmNorientation, XmVERTICAL);  n++;
filedata->v_scrb = XmCreateScrollBar (main_window,
                                "v_scrb", args, n);
XtAddCallback (filedata->v_scrb, XmNvalueChangedCallback,
            ValueCB, (XtPointer)filedata);
XtManageChild (filedata->v_scrb);


/*  Create work_area in MainWindow
 */
n = 0;
filedata->work_area = XmCreateDrawingArea(main_window,
                                "work_area", args, n);
XtAddCallback (filedata->work_area, XmNexposeCallback,
            DrawCB, (XtPointer)filedata);
XtAddCallback (filedata->work_area, XmNresizeCallback,
```

```
                    DrawCB, (XtPointer)filedata);
        XtManageChild (filedata->work_area);

        /*  Set MainWindow areas
         */
        XmMainWindowSetAreas (main_window, menu_bar, NULL, NULL,
                         filedata->v_scrb,
                         filedata->work_area);

}

/*-----------------------------------------------------------
**      OpenCB                     - callback for Open button
*/
void OpenCB (
Widget          w,                 /*  widget id            */
XtPointer       client_data,       /*  data from application   */
XtPointer       call_data )        /*  data from widget class  */
{
        static Widget fsb_box = NULL ;

        if (!fsb_box) {
            fsb_box = XmCreateFileSelectionDialog (w,
                                 "Load file", NULL, 0);
            /* just propagate the file information */
            XtAddCallback (fsb_box, XmNokCallback, ReadCB,
                                        client_data);
        }

        XtManageChild (fsb_box);
}

/*-----------------------------------------------------------
**      ReadCB  - callback for fsb activate
*/
void ReadCB (
Widget          w,                 /*  widget id            */
XtPointer       client_data,       /*  data from application   */
XtPointer       call_data )        /*  data from widget class  */
{
    FileData * filedata = (FileData *) client_data ;
```

```
        String file_name ;
        Arg args[5];
        int n, slider_size ;
        Dimension height ;

        file_name = XmTextGetString(
                XmFileSelectionBoxGetChild(w, XmDIALOG_TEXT));

        if (!BuildLineTable(filedata, file_name)) {
            WarnUser (w, "Cannot open %s0, file_name);
        } else {
            filedata->file_name = file_name ;

            /* ok, we have a new file, so reset some values */
            n = 0;
            XtSetArg (args[n], XmNheight, &height);  n++;
            XtGetValues (filedata->work_area, args, n);

            slider_size = (height - 4) /
                            (filedata->font_struct->ascent
                            + filedata->font_struct->descent);
            if (slider_size <= 0) slider_size = 1 ;
            if (slider_size > filedata->num_lines)
                slider_size = filedata->num_lines ;

            n = 0 ;
            XtSetArg (args[n], XmNsliderSize, slider_size);  n++;
            XtSetArg (args[n], XmNmaximum, filedata->num_lines);
                        n++;
            XtSetArg (args[n], XmNvalue, 0);  n++;
            XtSetValues (filedata->v_scrb, args, n);

            /* clear and redraw */
            XClearWindow(XtDisplay(filedata->work_area),
                        XtWindow(filedata->work_area));
            ReDraw (filedata);
        }
    }


/*------------------------------------------------------------
**      ValueCB              - callback for scrollbar
```

```
*/
void ValueCB (
Widget          w,              /*  widget id             */
XtPointer       client_data,    /*  data from application   */
XtPointer       call_data )     /*  data from widget class  */
{
    FileData * filedata = (FileData *) client_data ;

    /* clear and redraw, dumb dumb.. */
    XClearWindow(XtDisplay(filedata->work_area),
                XtWindow(filedata->work_area));
    ReDraw(filedata);
}

/*-------------------------------------------------------------
**      DrawCB                      - callback for drawing area
*/
void DrawCB (
Widget          w,              /*  widget id             */
XtPointer       client_data,    /*  data from application   */
XtPointer       call_data )     /*  data from widget class  */
{

    XmDrawingAreaCallbackStruct * dacs =
        (XmDrawingAreaCallbackStruct *) call_data ;
    FileData * filedata = (FileData *) client_data ;
    XSetWindowAttributes xswa;

    static Boolean first_time = True ;

    switch (dacs->reason) {
    case XmCR_EXPOSE:
        if (first_time) {
            /* Change once the bit gravity of the
                Drawing Area; default is north west and we
                want forget, so that resize always
                generates exposure events */
            first_time = False ;
            xswa.bit_gravity = ForgetGravity ;
            XChangeWindowAttributes(XtDisplay(w), XtWindow(w),
                                CWBitGravity, &xswa);
```

```
            }

        ReDraw(filedata) ;

        break ;
    case XmCR_RESIZE:
        ReSize(filedata) ;

        break ;
    }
}

void ReDraw(
FileData * filedata )
{
    /* Display as many line as slider_size actually shows,
        since slider_size is computed relative to the
        work_area height */

    Cardinal i ;
    int value, slider_size ;
    Arg args[5];
    int n ;
    Position y ;

    if (filedata->num_lines == 0) return ;

    n = 0;
    XtSetArg (args[n], XmNvalue, &value);  n++;
    XtSetArg (args[n], XmNsliderSize, &slider_size);  n++;
    XtGetValues (filedata->v_scrb, args, n);

    for (i = value, y = 2 + filedata->font_struct->ascent;
            i < value + slider_size ;
            i++, y += (filedata->font_struct->ascent
                    + filedata->font_struct->descent)) {
        XDrawString(XtDisplay(filedata->work_area),
                XtWindow(filedata->work_area),
                filedata->draw_gc,
                4, y,
                filedata->lines[i],
```

```
                        strlen(filedata->lines[i]));
    }
}

void ReSize(
FileData * filedata )
{
    /* Just update the scrollbar internals here, don't
       bother to redisplay since the gravity is none */

    Arg args[5];
    int n ;
    int value, slider_size ;
    Dimension height ;

    if (filedata->num_lines == 0) return ;

    n = 0;
    XtSetArg (args[n], XmNheight, &height);  n++;
    XtGetValues (filedata->work_area, args, n);

    /* sliderSize is the number of visible lines */
    slider_size = (height - 4) /
                        (filedata->font_struct->ascent
                         + filedata->font_struct->descent);
    if (slider_size <= 0) slider_size = 1 ;
    if (slider_size > filedata->num_lines)
        slider_size = filedata->num_lines ;

    n = 0;
    XtSetArg (args[n], XmNvalue, &value);  n++;
    XtGetValues (filedata->v_scrb, args, n);

    /* value shouldn't change that often but there are cases
       where it matters */
    if (value > filedata->num_lines - slider_size)
        value = filedata->num_lines - slider_size;

    n = 0;
    XtSetArg (args[n], XmNsliderSize, slider_size);  n++;
    XtSetArg (args[n], XmNvalue, value);  n++;
```

```
XtSetArg (args[n], XmNmaximum, filedata->num_lines); n++;
XtSetValues (filedata->v_scrb, args, n);
}
```

9.4 MainWindow

Motif provides a widget, MainWindow, that serves as a template for the
primary window of most applications. MainWindow is a subclass of
ScrolledWindow. In addition to the viewport and ScrollBar components of
the ScrolledWindow, MainWindow has an optional MenuBar, Command
window, and Message window.

MainWindow lays out these components in a manner compliant with the
OSF/Motif Style Guide specifications for the primary window of an
application. The MenuBar, if present, spans the top of the MainWindow
horizontally. By default, the Command window, if present, spans the
MainWindow horizontally just below the MenuBar. The ScrolledWindow
viewport and ScrollBars are below the Command window, and the Message
window is below the ScrolledWindow viewport or horizontal ScrollBar. If
the MainWindow resource **XmNcommandWindowLocation** is set to
XmCOMMAND_BELOW_WORKSPACE at the time the MainWindow
is created, the Command window is located below the ScrolledWindow
viewport or horizontal ScrollBar.

If the MainWindow resource **XmNshowSeparator** is True, the
MainWindow automatically creates up to three SeparatorGadgets to
separate the components. The names of these automatically created
SeparatorGadgets are "Separator1", "Separator2", and "Separator3". The
application can retrieve the widget IDs of the SeparatorGadgets by using the
functions **XmMainWindowSep1**, **XmMainWindowSep2**, and
XmMainWindowSep3.

In addition to the ScrolledWindow resources that hold the widget IDs of the
ScrollBars, scroll widget, and viewport widget, MainWindow has resources
that hold the widget IDs of the other MainWindow components:

XmNcommandWindow

> The value is the widget ID of the Command window. If a
> child is a Command widget and no Command window exists,

MainWindow automatically sets the value of this resource to the child's widget ID.

XmNmenuBar

The value is the widget ID of the MenuBar. If a child is a MenuBar and no MainWindow MenuBar exists, MainWindow automatically sets the value of this resource to the child's widget ID.

XmNmessageWindow

The value is the widget ID of the Message window. After creating the Message window, the application must use **XtSetValues** to set the value of this resource to the child's widget ID.

MainWindow has a convenience routine, **XmMainWindowSetAreas**, to establish both the MainWindow and the ScrolledWindow components. **XmMainWindowSetAreas** does not set the Message window; an application must use **XtSetValues** of **XmNmessageWindow** to set the Message window. An application that has no Message window and uses only standard components for the other MainWindow children may not need to call **XmMainWindowSetAreas** or **XtSetValues** for the component resources, but it is good practice to make these calls. If an application uses a Message window or has additional MainWindow children beyond the standard components, it must call **XmMainWindowSetAreas** and **XtSetValues** for **XmNmessageWindow**.

An application takes the following steps to use MainWindow:

- Create and manage the MainWindow, usually as a child of the ApplicationShell. If the scrolling mode is to be automatic, supply an initial value of **XmAUTOMATIC** for **XmNscrollingPolicy**.

- Create and manage the components of the MainWindow.

- If necessary, call **XmMainWindowSetAreas** or **XtSetValues** for the MainWindow components.

- Take any other actions needed to regulate the ScrolledWindow components. These actions are discussed in the previous descriptions of automatic and application-defined scrolling.

For examples of using MainWindow with both automatic and application-defined scrolling policies, see the ScrolledWindow examples in the previous sections.

9.5 Frame

Frame is a simple manager that encloses a child and displays a shadow around it. An application usually uses a Frame to provide a shadow for a widget, such as a RowColumn WorkArea, that does not display a shadow itself. The Frame resource **XmNshadowType** determines the type of shadow to draw. The resources **XmNmarginHeight** and **XmNmarginWidth** specify the margin between the shadow and the border of the child.

Frame can also have one other child that serves as a title. Frame places the title above the principal child of the Frame. The following constraint resources determine the Frame's treatment of the child:

XmNchildType

The value is a constant that tells the Frame whether the child is the work area child, the title, or another kind of child. Following are the possible values:

XmFRAME_WORKAREA_CHILD

This value specifies that the child is the principal (work area) component. This is the default.

XmFRAME_TITLE_CHILD

This value specifies that the child is the Frame title.

XmFRAME_GENERIC_CHILD

This value specifies that the child is a component other than the work area and the title. When the value is **XmFRAME_GENERIC_CHILD**, Frame does not include the child in its layout.

XmNchildHorizontalAlignment

The value specifies the alignment of the title with respect to the left and right inner edges of the Frame (determined by the child's **XmNchildHorizontalSpacing**). Following are the possible values:

XmALIGNMENT_BEGINNING

This value specifies that the title is placed at the left inner edge when the Frame's **XmNstringDirection** has the value

XmSTRING_DIRECTION_L_TO_R;
otherwise, the title is placed at the right inner edge. This is the default.

XmALIGNMENT_END

This value specifies that the title is placed at the right inner edge when the Frame's **XmNstringDirection** has the value **XmSTRING_DIRECTION_L_TO_R**; otherwise, the title is placed at the left inner edge.

XmALIGNMENT_CENTER

This value specifies that the title is centered between the edges.

XmNchildHorizontalSpacing

The value is the minimum distance between the title and the shadow along the left and right edges of the Frame. The default is the Frame's **XmNmarginWidth**.

XmNchildVerticalAlignment The value specifies the alignment of the title with respect to the shadow along the top edge of the Frame. Following are the possible values:

XmALIGNMENT_BASELINE_BOTTOM

The baseline of the last line of text in the title is even with the shadow along the top edge of the Frame.

XmALIGNMENT_BASELINE_TOP

The baseline of the first line of text in the title is even with the shadow along the top edge of the Frame.

XmALIGNMENT_CENTER

The center of the title is even with the shadow along the top edge of the Frame. This is the default.

XmALIGNMENT_WIDGET_BOTTOM

The bottom edge of the title is even with the shadow along the top edge of the Frame.

XmALIGNMENT_WIDGET_TOP

> The top edge of the title is even with the shadow along the top edge of the Frame.

Following is a UIL specification for an example Frame with a Label title and a Form child (not defined here):

```
object exampleFrame : XmFrame {
  controls {
      XmLabel  { arguments {
          XmNchildType = XmFRAME_TITLE_CHILD;
          XmNchildHorizontalSpacing = 4;
          XmNchildVerticalAlignment = XmALIGNMENT_WIDGET_BOTTOM;
      }; };
      XmForm exampleForm;
    };
};
```

9.6 PanedWindow

PanedWindow is a manager that lays out its children vertically from top to bottom and, by default, places a separator between each pair of children. Each child spans the width of the PanedWindow, which resizes children to be as wide as the widest child. When possible, the PanedWindow grows to accommodate the width of the widest child and the heights of all the children.

Usually PanedWindow allows the user to adjust the height of each pane. When a pane is adjustable, PanedWindow creates a control called a sash and places it below the pane that it controls. By manipulating the sash with the mouse or keyboard commands, the user changes the height of the pane above. This may also change the height of a pane below the sash.

PanedWindow has the following resources to control general appearance:

XmNmarginHeight

> The value specifies the margin between the PanedWindow's top and bottom shadows and the children nearest those shadows.

XmNmarginWidth

> The value specifies the margin between the PanedWindow's left and right shadows and the children nearest those shadows.

XmNseparatorOn

> The value determines whether or not PanedWindow displays a separator between each pair of panes.

XmNspacing

> The value is the distance between each pane.

The following PanedWindow resources control the appearance of the sashes:

XmNsashHeight

> The value specifies the height of each sash.

XmNsashIndent

> The value specifies the distance between each sash and the inner margin of the left or right side of the PanedWindow. If the value is positive, the sash is offset from the near (left) side of the PanedWindow. If the value is negative, the sash is offset from the far (right) side of the PanedWindow. If the value is greater than the width of the PanedWindow minus the width of the sash, the sash is placed flush against the near side of the PanedWindow.

XmNsashShadowThickness

> The value specifies the shadow thickness for each sash.

XmNsashWidth

> The value specifies the width of each sash.

PanedWindow has one other resource, **XmNrefigureMode**. When this resource is set to False, the PanedWindow does not recompute its layout when either the user or the application resizes a pane or when the PanedWindow is resized.

PanedWindow children have a number of constraint resources that PanedWindow uses to determine the positions and size limitations of the panes:

XmNallowResize

> The value specifies whether the PanedWindow grants resize requests from the pane. When the value is False (the default) and the pane is realized, PanedWindow refuses such requests,

but it allows the user to resize the pane if it is adjustable. For example, if the application attempts to change the height or width of the pane using **XtSetValues**, PanedWindow does not allow the change. If the value is True or if the pane is not realized, PanedWindow grants requests by the pane to change its size if possible.

XmNpaneMaximum

The value is the maximum height to which the user or application can resize the pane. If this value is the same as the value of **XmNpaneMinimum**, the pane cannot be resized at all, and PanedWindow does not display a sash at the bottom of the pane.

XmNpaneMinimum

The value is the minimum height to which the user or application can resize the pane. If this value is the same as the value of **XmNpaneMaximum**, the pane cannot be resized at all, and PanedWindow does not display a sash at the bottom of the pane.

XmNpositionIndex

The value is the ordinal position of the pane in the PanedWindow's list of pane children. The application or user can specify the value as an integer between 0 and the number of children already in the list, or as the value **XmLAST_POSITION** (the default), which means the child is inserted at the end of the list. If specifying a new value causes the order of children in the list to change, PanedWindow recomputes its layout according to the new order of children: the first pane is displayed at the top of the PanedWindow, the second child below the first, and so on.

XmNskipAdjust

The value specifies whether or not the PanedWindow resizes the pane when the PanedWindow itself is resized or when the user resizes another pane. When the value is True, PanedWindow does not resize this pane under these circumstances, but the user can still resize the pane if **XmNpaneMaximum** is greater than **XmNpaneMinimum**. The default is False.

Chapter 10

Managing Geometry

The geometry of a widget consists of its size, location, and stacking order. Widgets often have preferred sizes and perhaps locations. For example, a Label widget may prefer to be just large enough to display the text of the label. But composite widgets usually have preferences or constraints in laying out their children, and these may conflict with the preferences of the child widgets. Furthermore, the user or the application can change a widget's geometry at any time, for example, by resizing the top-level window. Geometry management is the process by which the user, parent widgets, and child widgets negotiate the actual sizes and locations of the widgets in the application.

Following are some common occasions for geometry changes:

- The application manages or unmanages a child widget.

- The application sets a geometry resource.

- The application sets a resource that causes one of the geometry resources to change. For example, setting a new label for a Label widget may cause a geometry change.

- The user resizes a top-level window using the window manager.

- The user resizes a pane of a PanedWindow.

Following are the basic Core and RectObj resources that determine widget geometry:

XmNx   Specifies the x coordinate of the upper left outside corner (outside the border) of the widget's window. The value is relative to the upper left inside corner (inside the border) of the parent window.

XmNy   Specifies the y coordinate of the upper left outside corner (outside the border) of the widget's window. The value is relative to the upper left inside corner (inside the border) of the parent window.

XmNwidth   Specifies the inside width (excluding the border) of the widget's window.

XmNheight   Specifies the inside height (excluding the border) of the widget's window.

XmNborderWidth
     Specifies the width of the border that surrounds the widget's window on all four sides.

10.1 Xt and Geometry Management

The Intrinsics provide the basic mechanisms and policies that underlie geometry management in Motif. The fundamental principle of geometry management is that parent widgets control the geometry of their children. Child widgets *request* changes to their geometry; parent widgets *respond* to requests from their children and *change* the geometry of their children directly.

10.1.1 Widget Class Procedures

Six widget class procedures, two in the parent and four in the child, handle most of the work of geometry management:

- The parent's **change_managed** procedure. When a child is managed or unmanaged, the parent often must move or resize some of its children. In the **change_managed** procedure, the parent can move a child by calling **XtMoveWidget**, resize a child by calling **XtResizeWidget**, or both move and resize a child by calling **XtConfigureWidget**. These functions update the appropriate geometry resources of the child and, if the child is realized, reconfigure the child's window.

- The parent's **geometry_manager** procedure. This function receives and acts on requests from child widgets to change their geometry. The **geometry_manager** procedure can grant a request, deny a request, or suggest a compromise to the child. If the procedure grants the request, it updates the appropriate geometry resources of the child. If the child is realized, the parent can either reconfigure the child's window itself or let the Intrinsics reconfigure the window. To make all geometry changes itself, the procedure can call **XtMoveWidget**, **XtResizeWidget**, or **XtConfigureWidget**.

- The child's **set_values** procedure. Whenever the application or user sets one of the basic geometry resources—**XmNx**, **XmNy**, **XmNwidth**, **XmNheight**, or **XmNborderWidth**—Xt automatically makes a request to the widget's parent for the geometry change. In the **set_values** procedure the widget can determine whether a change to another resource requires a geometry change. If so, it can simply change one or more of the geometry resources, and Xt makes the appropriate geometry request of the parent. If the parent denies the request, Xt restores the geometry resources to the values they had before the call to **XtSetValues**.

- The child's **set_values_almost** procedure. When the user or the application sets one of the widget's geometry resources, the parent may suggest a compromise geometry change. The child's **set_values_almost** procedure determines whether to accept the compromise, reject the compromise, or request an alternate geometry change.

- The child's **resize** procedure. When a parent calls **XtResizeWidget** or **XtConfigureWidget** with a size change, Xt makes the changes to the child's geometry resources and window and then invokes the child's **resize** procedure to inform the child of the size change. This procedure makes any internal changes necessary to conform to the new dimensions. If the child is itself a composite widget, its **resize** procedure may move or resize its own children.

- The child's **query_geometry** procedure. A parent widget may take account of a child's preferred geometry in determining its layout. The parent calls **XtQueryGeometry**, which invokes the child's **query_geometry** procedure. The child can accept the parent's intended geometry change, inform the parent of the child's preferred geometry, or indicate that the child's current geometry is its preferred geometry. The parent can use the results however it wants.

10.1.2 Geometry Change Requests

A widget uses **XtMakeGeometryRequest** to make a request to its parent for a change in its geometry. The widget can also use **XtMakeResizeRequest**, a simple interface to **XtMakeGeometryRequest** for requests to change width or height. Primitive widgets seldom invoke **XtMakeGeometryRequest** directly. They usually generate geometry requests indirectly when the application sets a resource that requires a geometry change. Composite widgets often make geometry requests when they try to accommodate requests from their children. For example, when a child asks to grow, the parent may ask its own parent to grow as well. In such cases the parent's **geometry_manager** procedure invokes **XtMakeGeometryRequest** directly.

If the requesting widget is unmanaged, its parent is not realized, or the requested geometry resource values are the same as the current values, **XtMakeGeometryRequest** makes the requested changes and returns **XtGeometryYes**. If the widget is being destroyed, it returns **XtGeometryNo**. Otherwise, it invokes the parent's **geometry_manager** procedure. If the **geometry_manager** procedure approves the request, **XtMakeGeometryRequest** returns **XtGeometryYes**. If the **geometry_manager** procedure denies the request, **XtMakeGeometryRequest** returns **XtGeometryNo**. If the **geometry_manager** procedure suggests a compromise geometry, **XtMakeGeometryRequest** returns **XtGeometryAlmost**. In this case the widget can accept the compromise by immediately making another geometry request with the compromise parameters.

The second argument to **XtMakeGeometryRequest** is a pointer to an **XtWidgetGeometry** structure. This structure contains the parameters of the widget's geometry request: the intended x, y, width, height, border width, and stacking mode. The structure also contains a bitmask with a bit for each parameter. If a bit is set, the widget intends to set the corresponding parameter to the intended value. If a bit is not set, the widget does not care about the corresponding parameter, and the parent is free to change it.

The third argument to **XtMakeGeometryRequest** is a pointer to another **XtWidgetGeometry** structure. This argument is valid only when the return value is **XtGeometryAlmost**. In that case the argument, if not NULL, returns the parameters of the parent's compromise geometry.

10.1.3 The geometry_manager Procedure

When a managed child widget makes a geometry request of a realized parent, **XtMakeGeometryRequest** invokes the parent's **geometry_manager** procedure. The arguments are the same as those to **XtMakeGeometryRequest**. This routine examines the bitmask (the **request_mode** member) and the requested geometry parameters in the **XtWidgetGeometry** structure provided by the child. If the **geometry_manager** routine can satisfy the request, it has two choices:

- Change the appropriate geometry resources of the child and return **XtGeometryYes** to **XtMakeGeometryRequest**. If the child is a widget, **XtMakeGeometryRequest** then calls **XConfigureWindow** to change the geometry of the child's window. If the child is not a widget, **XtMakeGeometryRequest** clears both the old and the new areas occupied by the child. **XtMakeGeometryRequest** does not call the child's **resize** procedure. It returns **XtGeometryYes** to the child.

- Call **XtConfigureWidget**, **XtMoveWidget**, or **XtResizeWidget** on the child, and return **XtGeometryDone** to **XtMakeGeometryRequest**. **XtConfigureWidget**, **XtMoveWidget**, and **XtResizeWidget** configure the child's window or clear the old and new areas occupied by the child, and when the child's size changes, they call its **resize** procedure. **XtMakeGeometryRequest** returns **XtGeometryYes** to the child.

To satisfy a child's geometry request, the **geometry_manager** routine may need to move or resize other children. It uses **XtConfigureWidget**, **XtMoveWidget**, or **XtResizeWidget** to do this. A **geometry_manager** procedure that returns **XtGeometryDone** calls these routines on the child making the request as well. The difference between answers of **XtGeometryDone** and **XtGeometryYes** is as follows:

- **XtGeometryDone** means that the **geometry_manager** routine has called the child's **resize** procedure if the child's size changes. **XtGeometryYes** means that neither the **geometry_manager** routine nor

XtMakeGeometryRequest calls the child's **resize** procedure. The caller of **XtMakeGeometryRequest** must call the child's **resize** procedure if necessary.

- **XtGeometryDone** means that the **geometry_manager** routine has configured the child's window or cleared the old and new areas occupied by the child. **XtGeometryYes** means that **XtMakeGeometryRequest** should do this.

Note: The **geometry_manager** procedures for Motif widgets return **XtGeometryYes**, not **XtGeometryDone**, and they do not call the **resize** procedure of the child making the geometry request.

The **geometry_manager** procedure may be able to satisfy some but not all of a child's request. For example, it may be able to grant the requested width, but not the requested height. In this case the **geometry_manager** procedure may offer the child a compromise geometry. It fills in the reply **XtWidgetGeometry** structure with the parameters it intends to allow, and it sets the corresponding bit in the reply bitmask for any parameter it intends to change from the value requested. It then caches these parameters and returns **XtGeometryAlmost** to the child. If the child immediately makes another geometry request using the compromise parameters, the **geometry_manager** procedure must grant the request if it can.

10.1.4 Intermediate Geometry Requests

Often a parent widget must change its own geometry in order to satisfy a child's request. The parent's **geometry_manager** procedure uses **XtMakeGeometryRequest** to ask its own parent for a geometry change. If **XtMakeGeometryRequest** to the grandparent returns **XtGeometryYes**, the parent's actions depend on whether the widget set's policy is for a **geometry_manager** procedure to return **XtGeometryDone** or **XtGeometryYes** when it grants a request:

- With an **XtGeometryDone** policy, the **geometry_manager** procedure calls the requesting widget's **resize** procedure. During a successful intermediate request, the grandparent's **geometry_manager** procedure calls the parent's **resize** procedure. The parent widget's **geometry_manager** and **resize** procedures must cooperate to ensure that, before the child's request is granted, the child is given the geometry it requested and the child's **resize** procedure is called. The parent's **geometry_manager** procedure then returns **XtGeometryDone**.

- With an **XtGeometryYes** policy, the **geometry_manager** procedure does not call the requesting widget's **resize** procedure. During a successful intermediate request, the grandparent's **geometry_manager** procedure does not call the parent's **resize** procedure. The parent widget's **geometry_manager** procedure updates the requesting child's geometry fields and may resize other children, but it should not call the requesting child's **resize** procedure. The parent may call its own **resize** procedure so long as that routine does not call the requesting child's **resize** procedure. The parent's **geometry_manager** procedure then returns **XtGeometryYes**.

Sometimes the parent needs to make a geometry request to its own parent just to find out whether the grandparent will accept a proposed change. For example, the parent may intend to offer a compromise geometry to the child but must first determine whether the grandparent will allow the parent to change its own geometry in order to offer the compromise. In this case the parent does not want the grandparent actually to make the proposed change; it just wants the grandparent to tell the parent whether the change is acceptable.

In making its own geometry request to the grandparent, the parent sets the **XtCWQueryOnly** bit in the request bitmask. The grandparent can return **XtGeometryYes**, but it must not actually change any of its children. The parent then returns **XtGeometryAlmost** to the child, along with its compromise parameters. If the child accepts the compromise, the parent repeats its request to the grandparent without setting **XtCWQueryOnly**. The grandparent should grant the parent's request, and the parent can then grant the child's request.

If the grandparent's response is **XtGeometryAlmost** and the parent still wishes to offer a compromise to the child, it caches the grandparent's reply and returns **XtGeometryAlmost** to the child. If the child accepts this compromise, the parent then makes another request of the grandparent, using the cached compromise parameters from the grandparent and without setting **XtCWQueryOnly**. The grandparent should grant the parent's request, and the parent can then grant the child's request.

10.1.5 XtSetValues

When a user or application invokes **XtSetValues** on a geometry resource, **XtSetValues** makes a geometry request. After invoking all the widget's **set_values** procedures, **XtSetValues** checks for changes to any geometry resources. If any of those resources have changed, it sets their values to those in effect before **XtSetValues** was called and then makes a geometry request with the new values as the requested geometry parameters. If the geometry request returns **XtGeometryYes**, **XtSetValues** calls the widget's **resize** procedure. If the parent's **geometry_manager** procedure returns **XtGeometryDone**, **XtSetValues** does not call the widget's **resize** procedure.

If the geometry request returns **XtGeometryNo** or **XtGeometryAlmost**, **XtSetValues** calls the widget's **set_values_almost** procedure, passing it the request and reply **XtWidgetGeometry** structures. If the request returns **XtGeometryNo**, the bitmask in the reply structure is 0. The **set_values_almost** procedure can accept a compromise geometry by copying the reply parameters into the request structure. It can also construct another request by altering the request structure, or it can end the negotiation by setting the request bitmask to 0. If the request bitmask is nonzero when the **set_values_almost** procedure returns, **XtSetValues** makes another geometry request and treats the result in the same way as for the original request.

A widget's **set_values** procedure can initiate a geometry request by changing any of the geometry resources. For example, if **XtSetValues** is invoked on a Label's text, the **set_values** procedure can calculate how large the widget should be to contain the new text and then set the relevant geometry fields accordingly. The **set_values** procedure should not do any resizing itself; in particular, it should not resize any child widgets, because the geometry request might be denied. Resizing is usually done in the widget's **resize** procedure. The widget's **set_values_almost** procedure may need to restore some widget state in the event the geometry request is denied.

10.1.6 The resize Procedure

A widget's **resize** procedure is invoked in the following circumstances:

- By **XtConfigureWidget** or **XtResizeWidget** when the parent resizes the widget

- By **XtSetValues** when the widget's geometry resources are changed and the resulting geometry request returns **XtGeometryYes**

- By the parent's **geometry_manager** procedure when it grants the widget's geometry request and is about to return **XtGeometryDone**

In addition, a shell's **resize** procedure is invoked when the size of the shell is changed, often by a user through the window manager.

When the **resize** procedure is called, the widget's geometry resources contain the new values. The **resize** procedure uses these values to recalculate the widget's layout. In the process, it may move or resize child widgets. The **resize** procedure must take its geometry resource values as given; it may not issue a geometry request.

A composite widget's **resize** procedure may need coordination with its **geometry_manager** procedure in handling a geometry request from a child when the parent must make its own geometry request to accommodate the child. If the widget set's **geometry_manager** procedures return **XtGeometryYes**, a parent's **geometry_manager** procedure may call the parent's **resize** procedure after a successful request to the grandparent. In this case, the **resize** procedure should not resize the child widget making the original geometry request. This problem can be avoided if the **geometry_manager** and **resize** procedures call a common subroutine that performs layout, taking as an argument the child that is making the request (if any) so that the layout routine can avoid resizing that child.

If the widget set's **geometry_manager** procedures return **XtGeometryDone**, the grandparent's **geometry_manager** procedure calls the parent's **resize** procedure during a successful request to the grandparent. In this case, the child's geometry resources may be different from the geometry parameters it is requesting at the time the parent's **resize** procedure is called. This problem can be avoided if the parent's **geometry_manager** procedure sets the child's geometry resources to the requested values before making its own geometry request, setting them back to the original values if the parent's request is refused.

10.1.7 Preferred Size and Location

When calculating its layout, a parent widget may take account of a child's preferred size and location. The parent uses **XtQueryGeometry** to inquire about a child's preferred geometry. The parent passes to **XtQueryGeometry** pointers to two **XtWidgetGeometry** structures, one containing the parameters that the parent intends to impose and the other containing the preferred parameters returned by the child. **XtQueryGeometry** then calls the child's **query_geometry** procedure with pointers to these two **XtWidgetGeometry** structures.

The child's **query_geometry** procedure determines the widget's preferred geometry and stores the parameters into the return **XtWidgetGeometry** structure, setting corresponding bits in the bitmask for fields that it cares about. It then returns one of these values:

- If the parent's intended geometry is acceptable, it returns **XtGeometryYes**.

- If the parent's and child's parameters differ for some field that both widget care about, or if the child has expressed interest in a field that the parent does not care about, it returns **XtGeometryAlmost**.

- If the child's preferred geometry is the same as its current geometry, it returns **XtGeometryNo**.

After the **query_geometry** procedure returns, **XtQueryGeometry** fills in any fields in the return **XtWidgetGeometry** structure that the child does not care about with the current values of the resources in the child widget. **XtQueryGeometry** returns the value returned by the **query_geometry** procedure.

Most composite widgets should call **XtQueryGeometry** whenever they intend to change the geometry of a child that is not in the process of making a geometry request. A **geometry_manager** procedure should not call **XtQueryGeometry** for the child making the request. For a widget making a geometry request, the requested geometry is the preferred geometry.

This can be problem for widget sets whose **geometry_manager** procedures call the **resize** procedure for the child making the request and then return **XtGeometryDone**. During a successful intermediate geometry request, the grandparent calls the parent's **resize** procedure. This procedure in turn may resize the child making the original request, but it cannot reliably use **XtQueryGeometry** to determine the child's preferred geometry. Indeed, the parent's **resize** procedure may not know which child is making the request or even that it is being invoked as a result of a child's geometry request. The parent widget's **geometry_manager** procedure may need to arrange to communicate this information to the parent's **resize** procedure.

10.1.8 Exposure and Redisplay

A widget may recompute its layout in its **resize**, **set_values**, or **geometry_manager** procedure, but usually it does not actually generate the window contents in those procedures. A widget usually regenerates its window contents in response to an **Expose** event, which causes the widget's **expose** procedure to be invoked. This procedure takes as arguments the widget, the event, and the set of rectangles to be redisplayed. Using the current state of the widget (including its geometry resources), the **expose** procedure generates the contents of either the affected rectangles or the window as a whole.

XtConfigureWidget, **XtResizeWidget**, and **XtMoveWidget** call **XConfigureWindow**, **XMoveWindow**, or **XClearArea** as appropriate. These functions cause the server to generate **Expose** events when necessary. **XtMakeGeometryRequest** also calls **XConfigureWindow** or **XClearArea** when the parent's **geometry_manager** procedure returns **XtGeometryYes**. When the **geometry_manager** procedure returns **XtGeometryDone** it must call **XConfigureWindow** or **XClearArea** itself (perhaps indirectly).

10.2 Shells and Their Children

Shell widgets encapsulate application widgets, principally to communicate with the window manager. Motif has three shell classes based on Intrinsics shell classes:

VendorShell

> Subclass of **WMShell** and superclass for other shell classes that contain both persistent top-level widgets and dialogs

XmDialogShell

> Subclass of **TransientShell** (which is a subclass of **VendorShell**) used to contain dialog widgets, commonly subclasses of **XmBulletinBoard**

XmMenuShell

> Subclass of **OverrideShell** used to contain RowColumn PulldownMenu and PopupMenu widgets

A shell has only one managed child. Except when a shell contains an off-the-spot input method, the shell's window is coincident with the child's window. The **geometry_manager** procedures of the shell classes treat geometry requests from the child as geometry requests for the shell, and the **resize** procedures of the shell classes make the child the same size as the shell. Applications should usually change the geometry of the child, not of the shell.

In particular, setting **XmNheight**, **XmNwidth**, or **XmNborderWidth** for either a shell or its child sets that resource to the same value in both the parent and the child. For a child of a shell, setting **XmNx** or **XmNy** sets the corresponding resource of the parent but does not change the child's position relative to the parent. **XtGetValues** for the child's **XmNx** or **XmNy** yields the value of the corresponding resource in the parent. The x and y coordinates of the child's upper left outside corner relative to the parent's upper left inside corner are both zero minus the value of **XmNborderWidth**.

The exception is a VendorShell or DialogShell that contains an off-the-spot input method. In this case, the input method appears inside the shell and below the application widget. The conventions for geometry parameters are the same as for other shells, except that the values of **XmNheight** for the child and the shell are not identical. The height of the shell is the sum of the height and border width of the application window and the height of the area occupied by the input method.

When the Shell resource **XmNallowShellResize** is False, a shell's **geometry_manager** procedure returns **XtGeometryNo** for all geometry requests from a realized child.

10.3 Manager Widgets and Their Children

Each Primitive widget has resources that determine its layout or contents. For example, the size of a Text widget depends on the values of the **XmNrows**, **XmNcolumns**, **XmNmarginHeight**, and **XmNmarginWidth** Text resources; the **XmNhighlightThickness** and **XmNshadowThickness** Primitive resources; and the basic Core geometry resources. In addition, when the Text **XmNresizeHeight** or **XmNresizeWidth** resource is True, the size of the widget can depend on the size of the text (the **XmNvalue** resource). Setting any of these resources can cause Text to generate a geometry request.

Manager widgets have their own layout policies, which they use in responding to geometry requests from their children or to resizing by their parents. These policies are determined by the Manager's own resources and, for some Managers, by its constraint resources.

Constraints are resources defined by the Manager but associated with each child. An application or user initializes, sets, or gets constraint resources for the child as if they were resources defined by the child's class. Initialization, **XtSetValues**, and **XtGetValues** for the child operate on the parent's constraint resources associated with that child. The Manager has constraint **initialize** and **set_values** procedures that allow it to set other constraints and recompute its layout.

Motif uses constraints in determining the layout of Form, PanedWindow, and Frame widgets. Motif also uses constraints to adjust the positions of child widgets in PanedWindow and RowColumn. The Form widget is discussed in Section 10.6. PanedWindow and Frame are discussed in Chapter 9.

10.4 Managing Geometry Using RowColumn

In addition to its role as the menu widget, RowColumn provides general-purpose layout and geometry management for child widgets arranged in rows, columns, or grids. The default RowColumn type, **XmWORK_AREA**, provides the layout features but not the menu semantics.

RowColumn's layout is controlled by two sets of resources. One set determines the position of children within the parent. The other set specifies whether RowColumn adjusts the internal layout characteristics of the children, such as margins and text alignment.

The two primary resources that control child positioning are **XmNorientation** and **XmNpacking**. **XmNorientation** determines whether RowColumn lays out its children in rows or columns. When **XmNorientation** is **XmVERTICAL**—the default for a WorkArea—the layout is column-major. When **XmNorientation** is **XmHORIZONTAL** the layout is row-major.

XmNpacking controls the general style of the layout. The resource has three possible values:

XmPACK_TIGHT

> RowColumn places children one after the other along the major dimension (for example, in a column when **XmNorientation** is **XmVERTICAL**). It proceeds until no more children fit along that dimension and then begins a new row or column. When **XmNorientation** is **XmVERTICAL** and the vertical distance remaining in the current column is too small to accommodate the child being placed, RowColumn begins a new column if **XmNresizeHeight** is False or the RowColumn cannot become larger. When placing children in a column, RowColumn does not alter their heights, but it makes the width of each child in the column equal to the width of the widest child in that column. Analogous rules apply to row-major layouts. **XmPACK_TIGHT** is the default value for **XmNpacking** in a WorkArea.

XmPACK_COLUMN

> RowColumn makes the width and height of each child identical. The width is the maximum width of all children, and the height is the maximum height. RowColumn uses the value of **XmNnumColumns** to determine the maximum number of columns (in **XmVERTICAL** orientation) or rows (in **XmHORIZONTAL** orientation) to produce. RowColumn tries to create **XmNnumColumns** columns (or rows) with an equal number of children in each column (or row).

XmPACK_NONE

> RowColumn does not change the position of any child. Unless **XmNresizeWidth** is False, it tries to grow large enough to

enclose the greatest x extent of any child. Unless **XmNresizeHeight** is False, it tries to grow large enough to enclose the greatest y extent of any child.

Several other resources influence the position and size of children:

XmNadjustLast
> This resource applies only when **XmNpacking** is **XmPACK_TIGHT** or **XmPACK_COLUMN**. When this resource is True and the orientation is vertical, RowColumn increases the widths of children in the last column when necessary so that all children extend to the right edge of the RowColumn. When this resource is True and the orientation is horizontal, RowColumn increases the heights of children in the last row when necessary so that all children extend to the bottom edge of the RowColumn.

XmNentryBorder
> When this resource is nonzero, it specifies the border width for all children of the RowColumn. When this resource is zero, RowColumn does not alter the border width of its children.

XmNmarginHeight
> This resource specifies the amount of space between the top edge of the RowColumn and the first item in each column, and between the bottom edge of the RowColumn and the last item in each column.

XmNmarginWidth
> This resource specifies the amount of space between the left edge of the RowColumn and the first item in each row, and between the right edge of the RowColumn and the last item in each row.

XmNresizeHeight
> When this resource is True, RowColumn adjusts its own height when possible to accommodate its children. When this resource is False, RowColumn does not request a new height during layout.

XmNresizeWidth
> When this resource is True, RowColumn adjusts its own width when possible to accommodate its children. When this resource is False, RowColumn does not request a new width during layout.

XmNspacing

> This resource applies only when **XmNpacking** is **XmPACK_TIGHT** or **XmPACK_COLUMN**. It specifies the amount of vertical space between each child in a vertical orientation and the amount of horizontal space between each child in a horizontal orientation.

RowColumn also has several resources that can cause the RowColumn to change the internal layout of some classes of children:

XmNadjustMargin

> This resource applies only to children that are subclasses of **XmLabel** and **XmLabelGadget**. When this resource is True and the orientation is vertical, RowColumn sets the **XmNmarginLeft** and **XmNmarginRight** for all children to the maximum values for those resources among all children. When this resource is True and the orientation is horizontal, RowColumn sets the **XmNmarginTop** and **XmNmarginBottom** for all children to the maximum values for those resources among all children. In PopupMenus and PulldownMenus RowColumn this resource is adjusts the margins only for button children, not for labels.

XmNentryAlignment

> This resource applies only to children that are subclasses of **XmLabel** and **XmLabelGadget**. When **XmNisAligned** is True, RowColumn sets the **XmNalignment** of all children to the value specified by **XmNentryAlignment**. Following are the possible values:

> **XmALIGNMENT_BEGINNING**
>> The child's text or pixmap is aligned with the left edge of the child's window.

> **XmALIGNMENT_CENTER**
>> The child's text or pixmap is aligned with the center of the child's window.

> **XmALIGNMENT_END**
>> The child's text or pixmap is aligned with the right edge of the child's window.

> In menus RowColumn sets the alignment only for button children, not for labels.

XmNentryVerticalAlignment

This resource applies only to children that are subclasses of **XmLabel**, **XmLabelGadget**, **XmText**, and **XmTextField**. It also applies only when **XmNpacking** is **XmPACK_COLUMN** (in either orientation) or when **XmNpacking** is **XmPACK_TIGHT** and the orientation is horizontal. The value specifies a reference point for aligning the children in any row:

XmALIGNMENT_BASELINE_BOTTOM

Causes the last baseline of each child in a row to align with the last baseline of the tallest child in the row. This value is applicable only when all children in a row contain textual data.

XmALIGNMENT_BASELINE_TOP

Causes the first baseline of each child in a row to align with the first baseline of the tallest child in the row. This value is applicable only when all children in a row contain textual data.

XmALIGNMENT_BOTTOM

Causes the bottom edge of the last line of text contained in each child to align with the bottom edge of the last line of text of the tallest child in the row.

XmALIGNMENT_CENTER

Causes the center of each child to align vertically with the center point established by the tallest child in the row.

XmALIGNMENT_TOP

Causes the top edge of the first line of text contained in each child to align with the top edge of the first line of text of the tallest child in the row.

XmNisAligned

When True, RowColumn sets the **XmNalignment** resources of children that are subclasses of **XmLabel** or **XmLabelGadget** to the value specified by **XmNentryAlignment**.

10.5 Managing Geometry Using BulletinBoard and DrawingArea

BulletinBoard and DrawingArea are two container widgets with similar geometry policies. These widgets have three geometry-related resources in common:

XmNmarginHeight

Specifies the amount of space between the top shadow of the widget and the top edge of any child, and between the bottom shadow of the widget and the bottom edge of any child. When the value of this resource is greater than 0, the widget ensures that the top edges of all children are below the widget's top margin.

XmNmarginWidth

Specifies the amount of space between the left shadow of the widget and the left edge of any child, and between the right shadow of the widget and the right edge of any child. When the value of this resource is greater than 0, the widget ensures that the left edges of all children are to the right of the widget's left margin.

XmNresizePolicy

Determines the widget's policy with regard to resize requests from its children. Following are the possible values:

XmRESIZE_NONE

The widget has a fixed size determined by its **XmNwidth** and **XmNheight**. The widget does not accept any geometry requests that would cause it to grow, but it may accept requests (without changing its own size) that would not cause it to grow. The widget also reports its current size as its own preferred size.

XmRESIZE_GROW

The widget can grow but not shrink. If its own parent approves, the widget accepts geometry requests that cause it to grow in order to enclose its children. It may accept requests (without changing its own size) that would not cause it to grow. When queried about its own preferred size, the widget calculates its layout and reports as its preference the greater of the calculated width and height and the current width and height.

XmRESIZE_ANY

The widget tries to accommodate geometry requests that would cause it to grow or shrink in order to enclose its children, requesting changes to its own size when necessary. When queried about its own preferred size, the widget calculates its layout and reports the calculated width and height as its preference.

In addition to these policies, BulletinBoard has geometry facilities that allow it to interact with subclasses in laying out complex collections of children. For example, SelectionBox has a List containing choices, a Text selection area, labels for the list and selection area, and three or four buttons. Usually the list appears above the selection area. The buttons appear equally spaced in a row below the selection area.

Additional children may be added to the SelectionBox after creation. The first child is used as a work area. The value of **XmNchildPlacement** determines if the work area is placed above or below the Text area, or above or below the List area. Additional children are laid out in the following manner:

MenuBar   The first MenuBar child is placed at the top of the window.

Buttons   All **XmArrowButton**, **XmDrawnButton**, **XmPushButton**, and **XmToggleButton** widgets or gadgets, and their subclasses are placed after the OK button in the order of their creation.

Others   The layout of additional children that are not in the above categories is undefined.

10.6 Managing Geometry Using Form

Form is a container widget that provides the most comprehensive facilities for controlling the layout of children. Constraints are placed on children of the Form to define attachments for each of the child's four sides. These attachments can be to the Form, to another child widget or gadget, to a relative position within the Form, or to the initial position of the child. The attachments determine the layout behavior of the Form when resizing occurs. Form is a subclass of BulletinBoard, so the resources and general geometry policies of BulletinBoard apply to Form as well.

Each child has 17 Form constraint resources, four for each side of the child and one, **XmNresizable**, that applies to the child as a whole. Following is a description of **XmNresizable** and the constraint resources that apply to the top side of a child:

XmNresizable

> This Boolean resource specifies whether or not a child's request for a new size is (conditionally) granted by the Form. If this resource is set to True, the request is granted if possible. If this resource is set to False, the request is always refused.

> If a child has both left and right attachments, its width is completely controlled by the Form, regardless of the value of the child's **XmNresizable** resource. If a child has a left or right attachment but not both, the child's **XmNwidth** is used in setting its width if the value of the child's **XmNresizable** resource is True. These conditions are also true for top and bottom attachments, with height acting like width.

XmNtopAttachment

> Specifies attachment of the top side of the child. It can have the following values:

> **XmATTACH_NONE**

>> Do not attach the top side of the child. If **XmNbottomAttachment** is also **XmATTACH_NONE**, this value is ignored and the child is given a default top attachment.

> **XmATTACH_FORM**

>> Attach the top side of the child to the top side of the Form.

XmATTACH_OPPOSITE_FORM

Attach the top side of the child to the bottom side of the Form. **XmNtopOffset** can be used to determine the visibility of the child.

XmATTACH_WIDGET

Attach the top side of the child to the bottom side of the widget or gadget specified in the **XmNtopWidget** resource. If **XmNtopWidget** is NULL, **XmATTACH_WIDGET** is replaced by **XmATTACH_FORM**, and the child is attached to the top side of the Form.

XmATTACH_OPPOSITE_WIDGET

Attach the top side of the child to the top side of the widget or gadget specified in the **XmNtopWidget** resource.

XmATTACH_POSITION

Attach the top side of the child to a position that is relative to the top side of the Form and in proportion to the height of the Form. This position is determined by the **XmNtopPosition** and **XmNfractionBase** resources.

XmATTACH_SELF

Attach the top side of the child to a position that is proportional to the current y value of the child divided by the height of the Form. This position is determined by the **XmNtopPosition** and **XmNfractionBase** resources. **XmNtopPosition** is set to a value proportional to the current y value of the child divided by the height of the Form.

XmNtopOffset

Specifies the constant offset between the top side of the child and the object to which it is attached. The relationship established remains, regardless of any resizing operations that occur.

XmNtopPosition

This resource is used to determine the position of the top side of the child when the child's **XmNtopAttachment** is set to

XmATTACH_POSITION. In this case, the position of the top side of the child is relative to the top side of the Form and is a fraction of the height of the Form. This fraction is the value of the child's **XmNtopPosition** resource divided by the value of the Form's **XmNfractionBase**. For example, if the child's **XmNtopPosition** is 50, the Form's **XmNfractionBase** is 100, and the Form's height is 200, the position of the top side of the child is 100.

XmNtopWidget

Specifies the widget or gadget to which the top side of the child is attached. This resource is used if **XmNtopAttachment** is set to either **XmATTACH_WIDGET** or **XmATTACH_OPPOSITE_WIDGET**.

These constraint resources interact with the following resources of the Form itself:

XmNfractionBase

Specifies the denominator used in calculating the relative position of a child widget using **XmATTACH_POSITION** constraints. The value must not be 0.

If the value of a child's **XmNleftAttachment** (or **XmNrightAttachment**) is **XmATTACH_POSITION**, the position of the left (or right) side of the child is relative to the left side of the Form and is a fraction of the width of the Form. This fraction is the value of the child's **XmNleftPosition** (or **XmNrightPosition**) resource divided by the value of the Form's **XmNfractionBase**.

If the value of a child's **XmNtopAttachment** (or **XmNbottomAttachment**) is **XmATTACH_POSITION**, the position of the top (or bottom) side of the child is relative to the top side of the Form and is a fraction of the height of the Form. This fraction is the value of the child's **XmNtopPosition** (or **XmNbottomPosition**) resource divided by the value of the Form's **XmNfractionBase**.

XmNhorizontalSpacing

Specifies the offset for right and left attachments.

XmNrubberPositioning

Indicates the default near (left) and top attachments for a child of the Form.

Note: Whether this resource actually applies to the left or right side of the child and its attachment may depend on the value of the **XmNstringDirection** resource.)

The default left attachment is applied whenever initialization or **XtSetValues** leaves the child without either a left or right attachment. The default top attachment is applied whenever initialization or **XtSetValues** leaves the child without either a top or bottom attachment.

If this Boolean resource is set to False, **XmNleftAttachment** and **XmNtopAttachment** default to **XmATTACH_FORM**, **XmNleftOffset** defaults to the current x value of the left side of the child, and **XmNtopOffset** defaults to the current y value of the child. The effect is to position the child according to its absolute distance from the left or top side of the Form.

If this resource is set to True, **XmNleftAttachment** and **XmNtopAttachment** default to **XmATTACH_POSITION**, **XmNleftPosition** defaults to a value proportional to the current x value of the left side of the child divided by the width of the Form, and **XmNtopPosition** defaults to a value proportional to the current y value of the child divided by the height of the Form. The effect is to position the child relative to the left or top side of the Form and in proportion to the width or height of the Form.

XmNverticalSpacing
Specifies the offset for top and bottom attachments.

Following are some important considerations in using a Form:

- Every child must have an attachment on either the left or the right. If initialization or **XtSetValues** leaves a widget without such an attachment, the result depends upon the value of **XmNrubberPositioning**.

  If **XmNrubberPositioning** is False, the child is given an **XmNleftAttachment** of **XmATTACH_FORM** and an **XmNleftOffset** equal to its current x value.

  If **XmNrubberPositioning** is True, the child is given an **XmNleftAttachment** of **XmATTACH_POSITION** and an

XmNleftPosition proportional to the current x value divided by the width of the Form.

In either case, if the child has not been previously given an x value, its x value is taken to be 0, which places the child at the left side of the Form.

- If you want to create a child without any attachments, and then later (for example, after creating and managing it, but before realizing it) give it a right attachment using **XtSetValues**, you must set its **XmNleftAttachment** to **XmATTACH_NONE** at the same time.

- The **XmNresizable** resource controls only whether a geometry request by the child will be granted. It has no effect on whether the child's size can be changed because of changes in geometry of the Form or of other children.

- Every child has a preferred width, based on geometry requests it makes (whether they are granted or not).

- If a child has attachments on both the left and the right sides, its size is completely controlled by the Form. It can be shrunk below its preferred width or enlarged above it, if necessary, due to other constraints. In addition, the child's geometry requests to change its own width may be refused.

- If a child has attachments on only its left or right side, it will always be at its preferred width (if resizable, otherwise at is current width). This may cause it to be clipped by the Form or by other children.

- If a child's left (or right) attachment is set to **XmATTACH_SELF**, its corresponding left (or right) offset is forced to 0. The attachment is then changed to **XmATTACH_POSITION**, with a position that corresponds to the x value of the child's left (or right) edge. To fix the position of a side at a specific x value, use **XmATTACH_FORM** or **XmATTACH_OPPOSITE_FORM** with the x value as the left (or right) offset.

- Unmapping a child has no effect on the Form except that the child is not mapped.

- Unmanaging a child unmaps it. If no other child is attached to it, or if all children attached to it and all children recursively attached to them are also all unmanaged, all of those children are treated as if they did not exist in determining the size of the Form.

- When using **XtSetValues** to change the **XmNx** resource of a child, you must simultaneously set its left attachment to either **XmATTACH_SELF** or **XmATTACH_NONE**. Otherwise, the request is not granted. If **XmNresizable** is False, the request is granted only if the child's size can remain the same.

- A left (or right) attachment of **XmATTACH_WIDGET**, where **XmNleftWidget** (or **XmNrightWidget**) is NULL, acts like an attachment of **XmATTACH_FORM**.

- If an attachment is made to a widget that is not a child of the Form, but an ancestor of the widget is a child of the Form, the attachment is made to the ancestor.

All these considerations are true of top and bottom attachments as well, with top acting like left, bottom acting like right, y acting like x, and height acting like width.

Chapter 11

Internationalization

Internationalization is a method of application development that allows the application to be run in many different languages without having to be rewritten or recompiled. This chapter describes how to design applications to use Motif's internationalization capability. It is not a general discussion of internationalization.

11.1 Issues in Internationalized Applications

There are several important issues to keep in mind when designing an application so that it takes advantage of Motif's internationalization capabilities.

11.1.1 Internationalization and Localization

An internationalized application contains no code that is dependent on the user's language, the characters needed to represent that language, or any formats (such as date and currency) that the user expects to see and interact with. Motif accomplishes this by storing language and custom dependent information outside the application.

The following figure shows the kinds of information that should be external to an application to simplify internationalization.

Figure 11-1. Information External to the Application

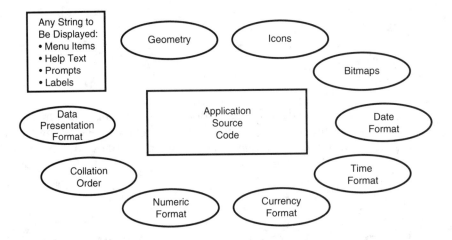

Because the language and culture dependent information is separate from the application source code, the application does not need to be rewritten or recompiled to be marketed in a different countries. Instead, the only requirement is for the external information to be **localized** to accommodate local language and custom.

Localizing the application includes the process of translating certain parts of the external information into the appropriate language and storing the translated information in files that are then accessed by the application. In addition, the application may be told the format to use to display time, date, and the other language or culture dependent formats shown in the previous figure.

Every language consists of a set of characters that, either individually or in combination, represents meaningful words or concepts in the language. The set of characters is called a **character set**. The set of binary values needed to represent all the characters in a language is called a coded character set or, more simply, a **code set**.

Several attempts were started long ago to standardize character sets and continue to this day. The most commonly used code set for English is the American National Standard Code for Information Interchange (ASCII). It originally used a 7-bit encoding scheme plus an eighth bit for error control. Using 7 bits for character representation allows 128 unique binary values. Later versions use the eighth bit as a code bit allowing 255 characters. Both are fine for English and some other alphabetic languages, but neither is suitable for ideographic languages such as Chinese, Japanese, and Korean. Ideographic languages represent a concept or an idea as a single character; consequently, there are thousands of characters in these languages, and two or more bytes are needed to represent the characters.

Other standard code sets have been developed to accommodate other languages. The ISO8859 standard is perhaps the most commonly used of these. Different versions of the ISO8859 standard exist for various areas of the world. The following table shows a typical language and character set relationship for various areas.

Table 11-1. Areas and Typical Character Sets

Area or Language	Character Set
English	ASCII, ISO8859-1
Western Europe	ISO8859-1
Eastern Europe	ISO8859-2
Northern Europe	ISO8859-3
Russia (Cyrillic)	ISO8859-5
Hebrew	ISO8859-6
Greek	ISO8859-7, 8, 9
Japan	Shift JIS
Japan	UJIS

See the specifications for the American National Standards Institute (ANSI) C programming language and the *X/Open Portability Guide, Issue 3* (XPG3) for more information on standards involved in internationalization.

11.1.2 Obtaining Input

Special considerations must be made for the user of an application to input characters in the local written language. Virtually all applications require some action on the part of the user, often asking for input in one form or another. For example, an application can ask the user to input information in text form, such as name, home address, and so on. The user must then enter this information by typing it on the keyboard in the normal manner. This is done with relative ease in an English-based application but can become more complex when other language text is desired.

Motif uses Xlib functions to provide the basic support for obtaining input in a Text widget.

11.1.2.1 The Problems

Many languages are expressed by means of an alphabet made up of characters or letters. The letters are arranged in groups to form meaningful words. A keyboard suitable for the language normally contains all the letters of the alphabet, plus the standard numerals and punctuation marks. The problem arises when the keyboard does *not* have all the alphabet characters. This can happen when a German user is using an English-based keyboard and needs a German character such as "β."

A far more involved example is the case of defining a keyboard to use for the ideographic languages. Because thousands of characters are needed to represent an ideographic language, no reasonable keyboard can be constructed with a single key for each character.

11.1.2.2 The Solution

Motif solves these input problems by using an **input method**, which is a layer of mapping between the keyboard keys (or combinations of keys) that the user types and the text data that is passed to the application. For example, the Swedish user with an English keyboard who needs the letter "∅" must enter a *combination* of keystrokes (this varies among vendors but could be **<Extend char> <O> </>** as an example) rather than just one keystroke. This is very similar to the act of using the **<Shift>** key to access uppercase letters.

An ideographic language's input method is often based on the language's phonetics, but there are also input methods based on a common graphics property of certain characters. The graphics method involves defining a key to map to a common graphic symbol that is the basis for multiple characters. The phonetic method is more commonly used. It requires a phonetic (alphabet-based) writing system. The number of phonetic signs or characters is few enough that a unique key is assigned to each phoneme. Characters are entered by pressing the appropriate phonetic keys. In several popular input methods, the user types a phonetic representation of a spoken word and the input method determines which characters are pronounced that way. If only one character meets this criterion, it is displayed. If more than one character meets the criterion, a list of all characters found is displayed and the user chooses the desired one. It is then passed to the application. See Section 11.4.1 for more information on input methods.

11.1.3 Displaying Output

Displaying the output produced by an application intended for international use also requires some consideration. To display text, it must have the appropriate content, encoding and fonts. For example, many languages, especially ideographic ones, require more than one font. Bitmaps and pixmaps must be localized as well. An icon that is an appropriate or meaningful symbol in one country may be totally inappropriate or meaningless in another.

11.1.4 Locales and Localization

A locale is the language environment determined by the application at run time. XPG3 defines locale as a means of specifying three characteristics of a language environment that may be needed for localization: language, territory, and code set. Motif supports only one locale per application; that is, an application can set the locale only once, at start-up time.

Motif uses the locale to help find:

- Resource files
- UID files

- Bitmap files

- Fonts used to display text and labels

- Text input method

The ANSI C method of setting the locale in an application is to use the function **setlocale**. How **setlocale** obtains a language when the language is not explicitly referenced in the call to **setlocale** is system dependent. For example, on POSIX systems, the environment variable **LANG** is used. The locale name is also used to establish a path to the localized files of information. How this is actually accomplished is explained in Section 11.3.

11.2 Compound Strings, Fonts, and Text Display

A **compound string** is a means of encoding text so that it can be displayed in many different languages or fonts without changing anything in the program. Motif uses compound strings to display all text except that in the Text and TextField widgets. This section describes the structure of a compound string and the interaction between a compound string and a font list that determines how the compound string is displayed.

11.2.1 Compound String Components

A compound string is a byte stream in ASN.1 encoding, consisting of tag-length-value segments. Semantically, a compound string has components that contain the text to be displayed, a tag (called a font list element tag) that will be matched with an element of a font list, and an indicator denoting the direction in which it is to be displayed.

A compound string component can be one of four types:

- A font list element tag.

  — The font list element tag **XmFONTLIST_DEFAULT_TAG** indicates that the text is encoded in the codeset of the current locale.

  — Other font list element tags are used later to match text with particular entries in a font list.

- A direction identifier.

- The text of the string. For internationalized applications, the text falls into two broad categories: either the text requires localized treatment or it does not.

- A separator.

The following section describes each of the compound string components:

Font list element tag
> The font list element tag is a string value that correlates the text component of a compound string to a font or a font set in a font list.

Direction
> The relationship between the order in which characters are entered on the keyboard and the order in which the characters are displayed on the screen. For example, the display order is left to right in English, French, German, and Italian and right to left in Hebrew and Arabic.

Text
> The text to be displayed.

Separator
> A separator is a special form of a compound string component that has no value. It is used to separate other segments.

Motif uses the specified font list element tag identified in the text component to display the compound string. A specified font list element tag is used until a new font list element tag is encountered. Motif provides a special font list element tag, **XmFONTLIST_DEFAULT_TAG**, that matches a font that is correct for the current codeset. It identifies the default entry in a font list. See Section 11.2.3 for more information.

The direction segment of a compound string specifies the direction in which the text is displayed. Direction can be left-to-right or right-to-left.

11.2.1.1 Compound Strings and Resources

Compound strings are used to display all text except that in the Text and TextField widgets. The compound string is set into the appropriate widget resource so that it can be displayed. For example, the label for the PushButton widget is inherited from the Label widget, and the resource is

XmNlabelString, which is type **XmString**. This means that the resource expects a value that is a compound string. A compound string can be created programmatically or defined in a resource file.

11.2.1.1.1 Setting a Compound String Programmatically

An application can set this resource programmatically by creating the compound string using one of the compound string convenience functions. There are several such functions:

XmStringCreate

        This function creates a compound string with text and a font list element tag, both of which are arguments in the function call.

XmStringCreateLocalized

        This function creates a compound string in the encoding of the current locale and automatically sets the font list entry tag to **XmFONTLIST_DEFAULT_TAG**.

The following code segment shows one way to set **XmNlabelString** for a PushButton programmatically:

```
Widget    button;
Args      args[10];
int       n;
XmString  button_label;
        .
        .
button_label = XmStringCreateLocalized (locvar,
            XmFONTLIST_DEFAULT_TAG);
/* locvar is a variable assumed to contain
 * locale-encoded text.
 * Create an argument list for the button */
n = 0;
XtSetArg (args[n], XmNlabelString, button_label); n++;

/* Create and manage the button */
button = XmCreatePushButton (toplevel, "button", args, n);
XtManageChild (button);
XmStringFree (button_label);
```

11.2.1.1.2 Setting a Compound String in a Defaults File

In an internationalized program, the label string for the button label should be obtained from an external source. For example, the button label can come from a resource file instead of the program. For this example, assume that the PushButton is a child of a Form widget called "form1".

```
*form1.button.labelString:   Push Here
```

Here, Motif's string-to-compound-string converter produces a compound string from the resource file text. This converter always uses **XmFONTLIST_DEFAULT_TAG**.

11.2.1.2 Compound Strings in UIL

Three basic mechanisms exist for specifying strings in UIL files:

- String literals, which may be stored in UID files as either NULL-terminated strings or compound strings

- Compound strings

- Wide-character strings

Both string literals and compound strings consist of text, a character set, and a writing direction. For string literals and for compound strings with no explicit direction, UIL infers the writing direction from the character set. The UIL concatenation operator (&) concatenates both string literals and compound strings.

Whether UIL stores string literals in UID files as NULL-terminated strings or as compound strings, it stores information about each string's character set and writing direction along with the text. In general, UIL stores string literals or string expressions as compound strings in UID files under the following conditions:

- When a string expression consists of two or more literals with different character sets or writing directions

- When the literal or expression is used as a value that has a compound string data type (such as the value of a resource whose data type is compound string)

UIL recognizes a number of keywords specifying character sets. UIL associates parsing rules, including parsing direction and whether characters have 8 or 16 bits, for each character set it recognizes. It is also possible to define a character set using the UIL **character_set** function.

The syntax of a string literal is one of the following:

'[*character_string*]'
[#*char_set*]"[*character_string*]"

For each syntax, the character set of the string is determined as follows:

- For a string declared as '*string*', the character set is the codeset component of the **LANG** environment variable if it is set in the UIL compilation environment, or the value of **XmFALLBACK_CHARSET** if **LANG** is not set or has no codeset. By default, the value of **XmFALLBACK_CHARSET** is ISO8859-1, but vendors may supply different values.

- For a string declared as #*char_set*"*string*", the character set is *char_set*.

- For a string declared as "*string*", the character set depends on whether or not the module has a **character_set** clause and on whether or not the UIL compiler's **use_setlocale_flag** is set:

  — If the module has a **character_set** clause, the character set is the one specified in that clause.

  — If the module has no **character_set** clause but the **uil** command was invoked with the **-s** option or the **Uil** function was invoked with the **use_setlocale_flag** set, UIL calls **setlocale** and parses the string in the current locale. The character set of the resulting string is **XmFONTLIST_DEFAULT_TAG**.

  — If the module has no **character_set** clause and the **uil** command was invoked without the **-s** option or the **Uil** function was invoked without the **use_setlocale_flag**, the character set is the codeset component of the **LANG** environment variable if it is set in the UIL compilation environment; if **LANG** is not set or has no codeset, the character set is the value of **XmFALLBACK_CHARSET**.

UIL always stores a string specified using the **compound_string** function as a compound string. This function takes as arguments a string expression and optional specifications of a character set, direction, and whether or not to append a separator to the string. If no character set or direction is specified, UIL derives it from the string expression, as described above.

Note that certain predefined escape sequences, beginning with a backslash, may appear in string literals, with these exceptions:

- A string in single quotes can span multiple lines, with each newline escaped by a backslash. A string in double quotes cannot span multiple lines.

- Escape sequences are processed literally inside a string that is parsed in the current locale (a localized string).

For more information on UIL string and compound string syntax, see the **UIL(5X)** reference page in the *OSF/Motif Programmer's Reference*.

11.2.2 Fonts, Font Lists, and Font Sets

Motif uses font sets and font lists to display text. A font defines set of glyphs that represent the characters in a given language. A font set is a group of fonts that are needed to display text for a given locale. A font list is a list of fonts, font sets, or a combination of the two, that may be used. Motif has convenience functions to create a font list.

11.2.2.1 Font List Structure

Motif requires a font list for text display. A font list is a list of font structures, font sets, or both, each of which has a tag to identify it. A font set ensures that all characters in the current language can be displayed. With font structures, the responsibility for ensuring that all characters can be displayed rests with the programmer.

Each entry in a font list is in the form of a {tag, element} pair, where *element* can be either a single font or a font set. The application can create a font list entry from either a single font or a font set. For example, the following code segment creates a font list entry for a font set:

```
char font1[] =
    "-adobe-courier-medium-r-normal--10-100-75-75-M-60";
XmFontListEntry font_list_entry;
font_list_entry = XmFontListEntryLoad (display,
                   font1, XmFONT_IS_FONT, "font_tag");
```

XmFontListEntryLoad loads a font or creates and loads a font set. There are four arguments to the function:

display The display on which the font list is to be used

font_name A string that represents either a font name or a base font name list, depending on the *type* argument

type   A value that specifies whether *font_name* refers to a font name or a base font name list

tag   A string that represents the tag for this font list entry

If *type* is **XmFONT_IS_FONTSET**, **XmFontListEntryLoad** creates a font set in the current locale from the value in *font_name*. The character set(s) of the fonts specified in the font set are dependent on the locale. If *type* is **XmFONT_IS_FONT**, **XmFontListEntryLoad** opens the font found in *font_name*. In either case, the font or font set is placed into a font list entry.

Now, the following code creates a font list, using the font list entry just created:

```
XmFontList font_list;
XmFontListEntry font_list_entry;
    .

    .
font_list = XmFontListAppendEntry (NULL, font_list_entry);
XmFontListEntryFree (font_list_entry);
```

The code example above creates a new font list and appends the entry *font_list_entry* to it.

Once a font list has been created, **XmFontListEntryAppend** adds a new entry to it. The following example uses **XmFontListEntryCreate** to create a new font list entry for an existing font list:

```
XFontSet font2;
char *font_tag;
XmFontListEntry font_list_entry2;
    .

    .
font_list_entry2 = XmFontListEntryCreate (font_tag,
                XmFONT_IS_FONT_SET,
                (XtPointer) font2);
```

font2 specifies an **XFontSet** returned by **XCreateFontSet**. The arguments to **XmFontListEntryCreate** are *font_tag*, **XmFONT_IS_FONTSET**, and *font2*, which are the tag, type, and font, respectively. The tag and the font set are the {tag, element} pair of the font list entry.

Now, to add this entry to the font list, use **XmFontListAppendEntry** again, only this time its first parameter specifies the existing font list:

```
font_list = XmFontListAppendEntry(font_list, font_list_entry2);
XmFontListEntryFree(font_list_entry2);
```

11.2.2.2 Font Lists and Resources

The syntax for specifying a font list in a resource file depends on whether the list contains fonts, font sets, or both.

- To obtain a font, specify a font and an optional font list element tag. If the tag is present, it should be preceded by an equal sign (=). If the tag is not present, do not use the equal sign. Entries specifying more than one font are separated by commas.

- To obtain a font set, specify a base font list and an optional font list element tag. The tag should be preceded by a colon (:) instead of an equal sign. If the tag is not present, the colon *must* still be present, because this is what distinguishes a font from a font set in the resource declaration. Fonts specified in the base font list are separated by semicolons (;). Entries specifying more than one font set are separated by commas.

If the font list element tag is not present in either case, Motif uses the default **XmFONTLIST_DEFAULT_TAG**. Here are some examples:

- Specifying a font:

  — Using the default font list element tag:

```
*fontList:  fixed
*fontList:\
  -adobe-courier-medium-r-normal--10-100-75-75-M-60-iso8859-1
```

  — Specifying a font list element tag:

```
    *fontList:  fixed=ROMAN, 8x13bold=BOLD
```

  — Specifying two fonts, one with the default font list element tag and one with an explicit tag:

```
    *fontList:  fixed, 8x13bold=BOLD
```

- Specifying a font set:

  — List the fonts explicitly without specifying a font list element tag:

```
    *fontList:\
      -JIS-Fixed-Medium-R-Normal--26-180-100-100-C-240;\
      -JIS-Fixed-Medium-R-Normal--26-180-100-100-C-120;\
      -GB-Fixed-Medium-R-Normal--26-180-100-100-C-240;\
      -Adobe-Courier-Bold-R-Normal--25-180-100-100-M-150:
```

  — Let Xlib select the fonts without specifying a font list element tag:

```
    *fontList:  -*-*-*-R-Normal--*-180-100-100-*-*:
```

  — List the fonts explicitly and specify a font list element tag as MY_TAG:

```
*fontList:\
  -JIS-Fixed-Medium-R-Normal--26-180-100-100-C-240;\
  -JIS-Fixed-Medium-R-Normal--26-180-100-100-C-120;\
  -GB-Fixed-Medium-R-Normal--26-180-100-100-C-240;\
  -Adobe-Courier-Bold-R-Normal--25-180-100-100-M-150:MY_TAG
```

— Let Xlib select the fonts and specify a font list element tag as
MY_TAG:

```
*fontList:  -*-*-*-R-Normal--*-180-100-100-*-*:MY_TAG
```

— List the fonts explicitly and specify a font list element tag for bold
fonts, but use the default font list element tag for medium fonts:

```
*fontList:\
  -JIS-Fixed-Medium-R-Normal--26-180-100-100-C-240;\
  -JIS-Fixed-Medium-R-Normal--26-180-100-100-C-120;\
  -GB-Fixed-Medium-R-Normal--26-180-100-100-C-240;\
  -Adobe-Courier-Bold-R-Normal--25-180-100-100-M-150:,\
  -JIS-Fixed-Medium-R-Normal--26-180-100-100-C-240;\
  -JIS-Fixed-Medium-R-Normal--26-180-100-100-C-120;\
  -GB-Fixed-Medium-R-Normal--26-180-100-100-C-240;\
  -Adobe-Courier-Bold-R-Normal--25-180-100-100-M-150:BOLD
```

— Let Xlib select the fonts and specify a font list element tag for bold
fonts and use the default font list element tag for the others:

```
*fontList:  -*-*-*-R-Normal--*-180-100-100-*-*:,\
            -*-*-Bold-R-Normal--*-180-100-100-*-*:BOLD
```

11.2.2.3 Font List Resource Defaults

A font list resource exists for a number of different widgets. Motif uses a
hierarchy system to determine the font list it should use. There are several
font list resources for **VendorShell**, **XmBulletinBoard**, and **XmMenuShell**.
These resources can be set, either programmatically or in resource files.
VendorShell and **XmMenuShell** have some common font list resources but
one of them, **XmNdefaultFontList**, exists only for compatibility with
earlier Motif releases. The widgets that have a font list resource (or
resources) are listed in the following table. Note that in some cases the
resource is *not* named **XmNfontList**.

Table 11–2. Widgets With Font List Resources

Widget	Resource Name
VendorShell	XmNbuttonFontList
VendorShell	XmNdefaultFontList
VendorShell	XmNlabelFontList
VendorShell	XmNtextFontList
XmBulletinBoard	XmNbuttonFontList
XmBulletinBoard	XmNlabelFontList
XmBulletinBoard	XmNtextFontList
XmLabel	XmNfontList
XmLabelGadget	XmNfontList
XmList	XmNfontList
XmMenuShell	XmNbuttonFontList
XmMenuShell	XmNdefaultFontList
XmMenuShell	XmNlabelFontList
XmScale	XmNfontList
XmText	XmNfontList
XmTextField	XmNfontList

The three resources **XmNbuttonFontList**, **XmNlabelFontList**, and **XmNtextFontList** are used to specify a font list for descendants of a type associated with the resource. For example, **XmNbuttonFontList** specifies the font list used for button descendants of **VendorShell**, **XmBulletinBoard**, and **XmMenuShell**. If a button's **XmNfontList** is NULL at initialization, the font list for the button is set by searching the parent hierarchy of the button widget or gadget for an ancestor that is a subclass of **VendorShell**, **XmBulletinBoard**, or **XmMenuShell**. If such an ancestor is found, the button's font list is set to the value of **XmNbuttonFontList** in the ancestor widget. If no such ancestor is found, the result is implementation dependent.

11.2.2.4 Font Lists in UIL

UIL has three functions for use in creating font lists: **font**, **fontset**, and **font_table**. The **font** and **fontset** functions create font list entries. The **font_table** function creates a font list from these font list entries.

The **font** function creates a font list entry containing a font specification. The argument is a string representing an XLFD font name. The **fontset** function creates a font list entry containing a font set specification. The argument is a comma-separated list of XLFD font names representing a base name font list.

Both **font** and **fontset** have optional **character_set** parameters that specify the font list element tag for the font list entry. In both cases, if no **character_set** parameter is specified, UIL determines the font list element tag as follows:

- If the module contains no **character_set** declaration and if the **uil** command was invoked with the **-s** option or the **Uil** function was invoked with the **use_setlocale_flag** set, the font list element tag is **XmFONTLIST_DEFAULT_TAG**.

- Otherwise, the font list element tag is the codeset component of the **LANG** environment variable if it is set in the UIL compilation environment, or the value of **XmFALLBACK_CHARSET** if **LANG** is not set or has no codeset.

The **font_table** function creates a font list from a comma-separated list of font list entries, created by **FONT** or **FONTSET**. The resulting font list can be used as the value of a font list resource. If a single font list entry is supplied as the value for such a resource, UIL converts the entry to a font list.

11.2.3 Compound Strings and Font Lists

When Motif displays a compound string, it associates each segment with a font or font set by means of the font list element tag for that segment. The application must have loaded the desired font or font set, created a font list that contains that font or font set and its associated font list element tag, and created the compound string segment with the same tag.

Motif follows a set search procedure when when it binds a compound string to a font list entry:

1. Motif searches the font list for an exact match with the font list element tag specified in the compound string. If it finds a match, the compound string is bound to that font list entry.

2. If the above does not provide a binding between the compound string and the font list, Motif binds the compound string to the first element in the font list, regardless of its font list element tag.

For backward compatibility, if an exact match is not found, **XmFONTLIST_DEFAULT_TAG** in either a compound string or a font list matches the tag that would result from creating a compound string or font list entry with a tag of **XmSTRING_DEFAULT_CHARSET**.

The following figure shows the relationships between a compound string, a font set, and a font list when the font list element tag is set to something other than **XmFONTLIST_DEFAULT_TAG**.

Figure 11–2. Compound String and Explicit Tag

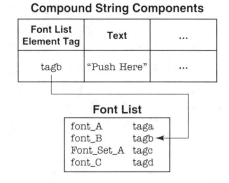

The following example shows how to use a tag called *tagb*.

```
XFontStruct      *font1;
XmFontListEntry font_list_entry;
XmFontList font_list;
XmString  label_text;
char *tagb;  /* Font list element tag */
char *fontx; /* Initialize to XLFD or font alias */
char *button_label;   /* Contains button label text */
          .
          .
font1 = XLoadQueryFont (XtDisplay(toplevel), fontx);
font_list_entry = XmFontListEntryCreate (tagb, XmFONT_IS_FONT,
       (XtPointer)font1);
```

```
font_list = XmFontListAppendEntry (NULL, font_list_entry);
XmFontListEntryFree (font_list_entry);

label_text = XmStringCreate (button_label, tagb);
```

XLoadQueryFont loads the font and then **XmFontListEntryCreate** creates a font list entry. The application must create an entry and then append it to an existing font list or create a new font list, in either case using **XmFontListAppendEntry**. Because there is no font list in place, the previous code example has NULL for the font list argument. **XmFontListAppendEntry** creates a new font list called *font_list* with a single entry, *font_list_entry*. To add another entry to *font_list*, the application can follow the same procedure but supply a non-NULL font list argument.

The following figure shows the relationships between a compound string, a font set, and a font list when the font list element tag is set to **XmFONTLIST_DEFAULT_TAG**. In this case, the value field is locale text.

Figure 11–3. Compound String and XmFONTLIST_DEFAULT_TAG

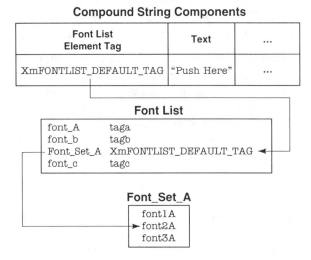

11.2.4 Text and TextField Widgets and Font Lists

The Text and TextField widgets display text information. To do so, they must be able to select the correct font in which to display the information. The Text and TextField widgets follow a set search pattern to find the correct font:

1. Search the font list for an entry that is a font set and has a font list element tag of **XmFONTLIST_DEFAULT_TAG**. If a match is found, use that font list entry. No further searching occurs.

2. Search the font list for an entry that specifies a font set. Use the first one found.

3. If no font set is found, use the first font in the font list.

A font set is desired because that insures that there are glyphs for every character in the locale.

11.3 Localizing Applications

An internationalized application can be tailored to operate in many areas of the world, each with its own requirements for the language and customs to be used. This section explains some methods for localizing an application.

The following section describes how the user, the application developer, and the implementation combine to establish the language environment of the application. It then discusses two general approaches to localizing applications. Succeeding sections focus on four aspects of localizing information in Motif programs:

- Resource files

- UID files

- Message catalogs

- X bitmap files

Many aspects of localization depend on the particular operating system, Motif implementation, and user environment in which the application runs.

The following must all cooperate for correct localization to occur:

- The operating system's locale mechanism, if any
- The Motif implementation
- The application itself
- The user's system administrator
- The user's language environment

11.3.1 Techniques for Localization

Although there are different methods for localizing an application, there are some common considerations:

- The application should not explicitly code any language-dependent information in the application. This includes strings, fonts, and language-dependent pixmaps.
- The application should isolate text, fonts, and pixmaps, and translate them into the languages needed. Usually this information is stored in separate directories by language.

11.3.1.1 Establishing the Language Environment

The term *language environment* refers to the set of localized data that the application needs in order to run correctly in the user specified locale. A language environment supplies the rules associated with a specific language. In addition, the language environment consists of any externally stored data, such as localized strings or text used by the application. For example, the menu items displayed by an application might be stored in separate files for each language supported by the application. This type of data can be stored in resource files, UID files, or, on XPG3-compliant systems, message catalogs.

A single language environment is established when an application executes. The actual language environment in which an application operates is specified by the application user, often either by setting an environment variable (**LANG** on POSIX-based systems) or by setting the **xnlLanguage** resource. The application then sets the language environment based on the user's specification. The application can do this either by using **setlocale** in a language procedure established by **XtSetLanguageProc**, or by using a method that does not call **setlocale**. In either case, Xt caches a per-display language string that is used by **XtResolvePathname** to find resource, bitmap, and UIL files.

An application that supplies a language procedure may either provide its own or use an Xt default procedure. In either case, the application establishes the language procedure by calling **XtSetLanguageProc** before calling **XtAppInitialize**. When a language procedure is installed, Xt calls it in the process of constructing the initial resource database. Xt uses the value returned by the language procedure as its per-display language string.

The default language procedure performs the following tasks:

- Sets the locale. On ANSI C-based systems, this is done by using the following code:

  ```
  setlocale(LC_ALL, language);
  ```

  where *language* is the value of **xnlLanguage** or the empty string ("") if **xnlLanguage** is not set. When **xnlLanguage** is not set, the locale is generally derived from an environment variable (**LANG** on POSIX-based systems).

- Calls **XSupportsLocale** to verify that the locale just set is supported. If not, a warning message is issued and the locale is set to "C."

- Calls **XSetLocaleModifiers** specifying the empty string.

- Returns the value of the current locale. On ANSI C-based systems, this is the result of calling:

  ```
  setlocale(LC_ALL, NULL);
  ```

The application can use the default language procedure by making the call to **XtSetLanguageProc** in this manner:

```
XtSetLanguageProc(NULL, NULL, NULL);
      .
      .
      .
toplevel = XtAppinitialize(...);
```

By default, Xt does not install any language procedure. If the application does not call **XtSetLanguageProc**, Xt uses as its per-display language string the value of the **xnlLanguage** resource if it is set. If **xnlLanguage** is not set, Xt derives the language string from the environment. On POSIX-based systems, this is the value of the **LANG** environment variable.

It is important to note that the per-display language string that results from this process is implementation dependent and that Xt provides no public means of examining the language string once it is established. The following vary by operating system and by Motif implementation:

- The mechanism, if any, used to set the locale

- On ANSI C-based systems, the value returned by **setlocale**

- The possible values of any environment variables used to establish the language environment

- Whether or not **xnlLanguage** is used and, if so, its possible values

Furthermore, by supplying its own language procedure, an application may use any procedure it wants for setting the language string.

11.3.1.2 Using Locales

The locale provides local information to an application based on the user's language, territory, and codeset. Both language and territory are needed because some languages are spoken in more than one country and more than one language may be spoken in some countries (Belgium, Canada, and Switzerland are examples).

Information in resource, UID, and image files can be localized and stored in separate directories by language. The Xt function **XtResolvePathname** uses the run-time locale to determine the proper directory to use.

On XPG3-compliant systems, an application can use message catalogs to localize text and messages. A message catalog file exists for each language, and each is usually stored in a separate directory by language.

The locale method of localizing compound strings and font lists consists of the following steps:

1. Establish a language procedure before calling **XtAppInitialize**. The language procedure calls **setlocale**.

2. Localize the compound strings and font lists using resource files, message catalogs, or UID files. Normally, do not specify any font list element tags other than **XmFONTLIST_DEFAULT_TAG**.

3. Use font sets in resource or UID file font lists.

4. Use **XmStringCreateLocalized** to create compound strings in the program. This function only has one argument, a text string, and automatically sets the font list element tag to **XmFONTLIST_DEFAULT_TAG**.

The run-time locale determines which fonts are used to display text. This is accomplished in the following manner:

*   Motif calls **XtResolvePathname** to load resource or UID files that specify the names of fonts for font sets. **XtResolvePathname** uses a file search path that may vary depending on the display's language string.

*   **XCreateFontSet** uses the locale to determine the fonts to be used from the base font name and the locale charset.

In this method, the application usually does not specify font list element tags other than **XmFONTLIST_DEFAULT_TAG**. It is possible to supply explicit font list element tags with locale-dependent text. For example, text might be displayed using large and small fonts or bold and italic fonts. The application can do this with special tags in both the compound string and the font list associated with it. In the font list, match the tag with a font set specification that supplies the desired attribute (point size, for example). When the application creates the font set, the charset comes from the locale. For example, a resource file might specify a font list in the following manner to obtain fonts with a different point size:

```
*fontList:   -*-*-*-R-Normal--*-120-100-100-*-*:,\
             -*-*-*-R-Normal--*-180-100-100-*-*:BIG,\
             -*-*-*-R-Normal--*-80-100-100-*-*:SMALL
```

In this case, the application should also map the tags to **XmFONTLIST_DEFAULT_TAG** in the Motif registry of font list element tags. See Section 11.4.2 for more information.

11.3.1.3 Localization Without Locales

In this method, the locale is not set in the program, and a language procedure is not needed. Instead, the user specifies the language environment using either **xnlLanguage** or an environment variable such as **LANG**. Resource, UID, and image files are localized and stored in separate directories by language, as they are when the application uses locales. **XtResolvePathname** uses the display's language string in the same way to determine the proper locations of these files. Message catalogs are not used in this method. Also, in this case Text and TextField cannot accommodate 16-bit data. The nonlocale method of localizing compound strings and font lists consists of these steps:

1. Localize compound strings using UIL files. Note that resource files cannot be used for compound strings because the string-to-compound-string converter always uses the font list element tag **XmFONTLIST_DEFAULT_TAG**. Localized font lists can appear in resource files.

2. Specify explicit font list element tags *other* than **XmFONTLIST_DEFAULT_TAG** in both compound strings and font lists.

3. Use font names with explicit charset components in resource or UIL files. Do not use font sets.

4. To create compound strings in the program, use **XmStringCreate** with the font list element tag set to something other than **XmFONTLIST_DEFAULT_TAG**.

11.3.2 Resources and Localization

The resources used in an application that are subject to internationalization are stored in files external to the application. These resources include

- All labels, particularly those that identify controls. Such labels are defined as type **XmString**, meaning they are compound strings.

- Text strings; that is, strings of text that are not compound strings.

- Font lists.

11.3.2.1 Initial Resource Database

The information in the external resource files is used when Xt builds the initial resource database. The **XtDisplayInitalize** function loads the resource database by merging in resources from the following sources, in order of precedence (that is, each component takes precedence over the following components):

- The application command line
- A per-host user environment resource file on the local host
- Screen-specific resources for the default screen of the display
- A resource property on the server or user preference resource file on the local host
- An application-specific user resource file on the local host
- An application-specific class resource file on the local host

Localization applies to two components of the initial resource database— the application-specific user and class resources. Localized resources that are controlled by the programmer are in the application class resource file, and localized resources that are controlled by the user are in the user resource file. Note that the user resources take precedence over the application class resources.

11.3.2.2 Resource File Locations

XtDisplayInitialize calls **XtResolvePathname** to load both the user and the class resources.

To load the user's application resource file, **XtDisplayInitialize** uses the value of the **XUSERFILESEARCHPATH** environment variable as the search path. If that variable is not set or if the search path fails to find the file, and if the environment variable **XAPPLRESDIR** is defined, **XtDisplayInitialize** next tries an implementation-dependent search path with a number of entries that include **XAPPLRESDIR** and the user's home directory. If **XAPPLRESDIR** is not set or if that search path fails, **XtDisplayInitialize** tries another implementation-dependent search path with a number of entries that include the user's home directory.

To load the application-specific class resource file, **XtDisplayInitialize** uses the value of the **XFILESEARCHPATH** environment variable as the search path. If that variable is not set or if the search path fails to find the file, **XtDisplayInitialize** tries an implementation-dependent search path.

The search paths for both resource files may contain any substitutions recognized by **XtResolvePathname**. That routine substitutes the display's language string for **%L**. In an implementation-dependent manner, it substitutes the language, territory, and codeset components of the language string for **%l**, **%t**, and **%c**, respectively. This mechanism allows Xt to load different resource files for different languages, as specified by the display's language string.

The display's language string is determined by the application's language procedure, if present, or else by the value of the **xnlLanguage** resource or by the environment. The language string associated with any particular language and the search paths used to find the resource files depend on the system vendor, the Motif vendor, the application, and the user's system administrator. Determining the actual directories in which localized resource files reside requires coordination among all these sources.

In general, an application developer prepares a set of localized application class resource files, one for each language the application supports. The developer may also need to supply a language procedure appropriate for one or more of the systems on which the application will run. The application vendor must arrange for the resource files to be installed in the correct directories, depending on the operating system and the Motif implementation on which the application will run.

11.3.2.3 An Example

Following is an example of an application class defaults file for a simple program that creates a MainWindow with a Text widget. The font list specification includes a single font set with a default tag. This resource file would be appropriate for an application that uses locales.

```
*fontList:                    -*-*-*-R-Normal--*-180-100-100-*-*:
*Text1.value:\
Hier ist etwas Text fur das Text Widget.\n\
Gemischter 8-und 16-bit Text.
*version_box.messageString:    Dies ist i18n Demo Version
*version_box.okLabelString:    Schliessen
*version_box.dialogTitle:      I18n Demo Version
*pgm_ver_btn.labelString:      I18n Demo Version
*events_btn.labelString:       Aktionen
*help_btn_menu.labelString:    Hilfe
*help_btn_cascade.labelString: Hilfe
*help_box.messageString:       Leider ist keine Hilfe hier.
*help_box.okLabelString:       Schliessen
*help_box.dialogTitle:         i18n Demo Hilfe
*stop_btn.labelString:         Enden
```

11.3.3 UIL and Localization

The general models for localizing applications using UIL are the same as those for applications that do not use UIL. An application developer creates separate UIL files, each containing string and resource values for a particular language. UIL files can also be used in conjuction with localized resource and pixmap files. As with localization of resource files, there are two basic approaches to localizing UIL files: one that uses locales and one that does not.

11.3.3.1 Preparing Localized UID Files

When using locales with UIL, an application developer should take the following steps:

- Do not use a **character_set** declaration for the module.

- When creating compound strings in a UIL file, use double quotes and no character set specification for the text.

- When creating font lists in a UIL file, use font sets, not fonts. Do not specify character sets for the font sets.

- Before compiling a UIL file using the **uil** command, set up any environment variables (such as **LANG**) or other mechanisms the system vendor recommends to establish the locale that is appropriate for the UIL file to be compiled. Invoke the **uil** command with the **-s** option. This enables the UIL compiler to set the locale and parse double quoted strings without explicit character sets in the locale's encoding. It also ensures that localized compound strings and font list entries are created with font list element tags of **XmFONTLIST_DEFAULT_TAG**.

- Before using the **Uil** function to compile a UIL file, set the locale that is appropriate for the UIL file to be compiled. In the **Uil_command_type** structure that is the first argument to the **Uil** function, set the **use_setlocale_flag** member to 1. This has the same effect as invoking the **uil** command with the **-s** option.

When localizing UIL files without using locales, an application developer should take the following steps:

- When using single quotes for the text of compound strings, supply a **character_set** declaration for the module.

- When using double quotes for the text of compound strings, supply an explicit character set for each segment.

- When creating font lists in a UIL file, use fonts, not font sets. Specify an explicit character set for each font.

- When compiling a UIL file using the **uil** command, do not invoke the command with the **-s** option. The UIL compiler does not set the locale, and it parses each string using rules derived from the explicitly specified character set for that string.

- When compiling a UIL file using the **Uil** function, set the **use_setlocale_flag** member of the **Uil_command_type** structure to 0. This has the same effect as invoking the **uil** command without the **-s** option.

The UIL compiler processes a single source file for each invocation of the **uil** command or the **Uil** function. However, UIL has an **include file** directive that is similar to the C preprocessor's **#include** directive. If the file argument for this directive is not an absolute pathname, the compiler searches for the file in a series of directories. These include the directory of the main UIL source file and any directories specified via the **-I** option to the **uil** command or the **include_dir** member of the **Uil_command_type** structure for the **Uil** function.

One strategy for maintaining localized UIL source files is to place only language-independent information in the main UIL source file and to put all language-dependent information in included files that are in separate directories for each language. Then a developer can compile the UIL files for different languages without editing any UIL files. When using locales, a developer first sets up the environment for the intended locale. Whether using locales or not, the developer then invokes the UIL compiler with the proper include directory for the intended language.

In general, a developer can mix localized UIL files with localized resource files. For example, the developer might specify compound strings in UIL files and font lists in resource files. Note one exception: it is not practical to use resource files to localize compound strings without using locales. This is because no resource file syntax exists for supplying an explicit font list element tag for a compound string.

For resource values that the user may override, the developer must use resource files or fallback resources, or must in some way ensure that the user's resource settings can override the developer's settings from the UIL file.

11.3.3.2 MRM and Localized UID Files

Once the developer has generated localized UID files, the vendor and the user's system administrator must arrange for these files to be installed in the appropriate directories for the system where the program is to run. As with resource files, these directories depend on configurations established by the operating system vendor, the Motif vendor, and the system administrator.

MrmOpenHierarchyPerDisplay takes as an argument a list of names of UID files. It calls **XtResolvePathname** to find each file the list. If a filename is an absolute pathname, that pathname is the search path for **XtResolvePathname**. Otherwise, **MrmOpenHierarchyPerDisplay** constructs a search path in the following way:

- If the environment variable **UIDPATH** is set, the value of that variable is the search path.

- If **UIDPATH** is not set, but **XAPPLRESDIR** is set, **MrmOpenHierarchyPerDisplay** uses a default search path with entries that include **$XAPPLRESDIR**, the user's home directory, and vendor-dependent system directories.

- If neither **UIDPATH** nor **XAPPLRESDIR** is set, **MrmOpenHierarchyPerDisplay** uses a default search path with entries that include the user's home directory and vendor-dependent system directories.

These paths may include the substitution field **%U**. In each call to **XtResolvePathname**, **MrmOpenHierarchyPerDisplay** substitutes the current filename from the list of UID files for **%U**. The paths may also include other substitution fields accepted by **XtResolvePathname**. In particular, **XtResolvePathname** substitutes the display's language string for **%L**, and it substitutes the components of the display's language string (in a vendor-dependent way) for **%l**, **%t**, and **%c**. If necessary **MrmOpenHierarchyPerDisplay** searches the path twice, first with **%S** mapped to **.uid** and then with **%S** mapped to NULL. The substitution field **%T** is always mapped to **uid**.

The usual mechanism for employing localized UID files is to use a search path that contains one of the substitutions derived from the display's language string. As with resource files, the vendor and system administrator must ensure that the directories where the localized UID files reside match the display's language string (or the appropriate component of the language string).

11.3.4 Message Catalogs and Localization

On an XPG3-compliant system, an application can use message catalogs to localize text. The format of message catalogs is implementation dependent, and the application must take steps to coordinate the locations of the message catalogs with the locations of resource, UID, and image files. Use of message catalogs requires the following steps:

- Using an implementation-dependent method, prepare a separate message catalog containing text to be localized for each language.

- Arrange to have the message catalogs installed in the appropriate directories on the systems on which the application will run.

- Arrange for the user's environment to be set up correctly so that the application can read the message catalog appropriate to the language.

- In the program, use the **catopen** function to open a message catalog and the **catclose** function to close it.

- Use the **catgets** function to read text from an open message catalog.

- If necessary, convert the text to the target format (such as a compound string) and, for resources, supply the text in the appropriate widget creation argument list or call to **XtSetValues**.

The **catopen** function takes as an argument the name of the message catalog file. If this is an absolute pathname, **catopen** opens that file. Otherwise, **catopen** uses the value of the **NLSPATH** environment variable as a search path. This path can contain a number of substitution fields. The filename passed to **catopen** is substituted for **%N**. The value of the **LANG** environment variable is substituted for **%L**, and its language, territory, and codeset components are substituted for **%l**, **%t**, and **%c**, respectively.

Note that these values may not be the same as the display's language string or its components. An application and software vendor that use message catalogs must coordinate the locations of message catalogs with those of localized resource, UID, and image files, which usually depend on the display's language string. One possible strategy is to call **catopen** with an absolute pathname constructed by calling **XtResolvePathname** with the value of **NLSPATH** as the search path argument. **XtResolvePathname** substitutes the display's language string and its components for **%L**, **%l**, **%t**, and **%c** in **$NLSPATH**. In this way, the application can use a single mechanism, the display's language string, to distinguish file locations by language. The software vendor must still arrange for the user's system administrator to install the message catalogs in the correct locations and to ensure that **NLSPATH** is appropriately set in the user's environment.

11.3.5 Images, Pixmaps, and Localization

A pixmap is a screen image that is stored in memory so that it can be recalled and displayed when needed. Motif has a number of pixmap resources that allow the application to supply pixmaps for backgrounds, borders, shadows, label and button faces, drag icons, and other uses. As with text, some pixmaps may be specific to particular language environments; these pixmaps need to be localized.

Motif maintains caches of pixmaps and images. The function **XmGetPixmapByDepth** searches these caches for a requested pixmap. If the requested pixmap is not in the pixmap cache and a corresponding image is not in the image cache, **XmGetPixmapByDepth** searches for an X bitmap file whose name matches the requested image name.

XmGetPixmapByDepth calls **XtResolvePathname** to search for the file. If the requested image name is an absolute pathname, that pathname is the search path for **XtResolvePathname**. Otherwise, **XmGetPixmapByDepth** constructs a search path in the following way:

- If the environment variable **XBMLANGPATH** is set, the value of that variable is the search path.

- If **XBMLANGPATH** is not set but **XAPPLRESDIR** is set, **XmGetPixmapByDepth** uses a default search path with entries that include **$XAPPLRESDIR**, the user's home directory, and vendor-dependent system directories.

- If neither **XBMLANGPATH** nor **XAPPLRESDIR** is set, **XmGetPixmapByDepth** uses a default search path with entries that include the user's home directory and vendor-dependent system directories.

These paths may include the substitution field **%B**. In each call to **XtResolvePathname**, **XmGetPixmapByDepth** substitutes the requested image name for **%B**. The paths may also include other substitution fields accepted by **XtResolvePathname**. In particular, **XtResolvePathname** substitutes the display's language string for **%L**, and it substitutes the components of the display's language string (in a vendor-dependent way) for **%l**, **%t**, and **%c**. The substitution field **%T** is always mapped to **bitmaps**, and **%S** is always mapped to NULL.

As with resource and UID files, the usual mechanism for employing localized X bitmap files is to use a search path that contains one of the substitutions derived from the display's language string. As with resource and UID files, the vendor and system administrator must ensure that the directories where the localized X bitmap files reside match the display's language string (or the appropriate component of the language string).

See Chapter 12 for more information on images and pixmaps.

11.3.6 Comparing Approaches to Localization

The locale approach allows an application to use existing internationalization routines. On the other hand, the application is limited in portability to systems that support the same internationalization standards (XPG3, POSIX, or ANSI). This approach is also only applicable to applications using a single language.

The nonlocale approach only addresses the aspect of isolating information from the application and ensuring that it uses the proper localized version of this information. The disadvantage is that there is more work for the programmer and there may be nonstandard functionality. The advantages are that there is guaranteed portability across all platforms that support Motif, and that it allows handling of multiple character sets for specialized applications that require this functionality.

11.4 Advanced Topics in Internationalization

This section covers some advanced topics dealing with internationalization.

11.4.1 Internationalization and Text Input

An application subject to internationalization presents some unique problems when it deals with text input. The application must be able to correctly interpret and process text input in any language. This section explains how an application accomplishes this.

11.4.1.1 Input Method

Although there are many different keyboards in use, sometimes certain characters in an alphabetic language are not directly available on any keyboard. In this case, the user must type a combination of keys to input the desired character. The number of characters in an ideographic language far exceeds the capability of any keyboard and makes it impossible to have a keyboard with all of the language's symbols. In this case, input is usually accomplished based on the language's phonetics. These cases illustrate the concept of an input method. An input method is simply the mechanism that is used to map between the keys typed by a user and the resulting characters that are input to the application. A common feature of many input methods is that the application user may type combinations of keys to create a single character. Creating characters from keystrokes is called **pre-editing**.

Input methods may require several areas to display the actual keystrokes.

- The **status area** is an output-only window that identifies the style of input (phonetic, numeric, stroke and radial, and so on) and the current status of an input method interaction.

- The **pre-edit area** displays the intermediate text for languages that are composed before the application acts on the data. There are several possible locations for the pre-edit area:

Over-the-spot
> Displays the data in an input method window that is placed over the point of insertion.

Off-the-spot
> Displays the pre-edit window inside the application window (usually at the bottom) but not at the point of insertion.

Root-window
> Uses a pre-edit window that is a child of the root window.

A VendorShell resource, **XmNpreeditType** determines which style is used for a Text or TextField input method. The syntax, possible values, and default value of this resource are implementation dependent.

- The **auxiliary area** is used for popup menus and customizing dialogs that some input methods use.

Input methods are supplied by vendors and are implementation dependent. The VendorShell resource **XmNinputMethod** is an implementation-dependent string that specifies the input method portion of the locale modifiers. If a value is supplied for this resource, Motif uses it to set the locale modifiers before opening an input method for Text or TextField.

The following figure shows one possible program window with a Text widget using over-the-spot interaction for Japanese text input. The status area indicates that phonetic input is in use and insert mode is enabled. The pre-edit area shows that the letter "H" has been entered. Since there is no Hiragana phonetic equivalent, the "H" appears in the pre-edit window.

Figure 11-4. Text Widget Pre-Edit and Status Areas Using Over-the-Spot

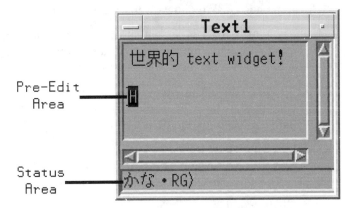

The following figure shows the same window after a "u" has been entered following the "H" shown in the previous figure.

Figure 11-5. Text Widget Pre-Edit Area After Next Character Entry

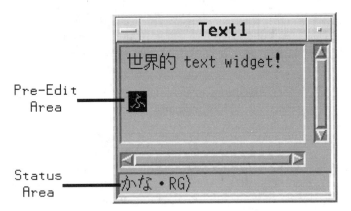

Here the pre-edit area is displaying the phonetic equivalent of the English letters "hu" in Hiragana.

11.4.1.2 Input Context

An **input context** is the mechanism used to provide the state information needed to manage the information flow between the application and the input method. It is a combination of an input method, a locale specifying the encoding of character strings to be returned, an application window, and internal state information. The following figure shows the relationships involved. The input method is determined by the locale specified by the application user.

Figure 11–6. Input Method and Input Contexts

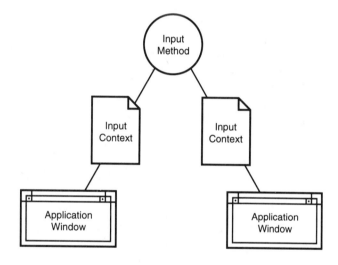

11.4.1.3 Input and the Motif Text Widget

The Motif Text and TextField widgets, when editable, provide a transparent connection to the locale-specific input method for text input. The application programmer specifies an appropriate font set in the Text or TextField **XmNfontList** resource and creates either widget as a descendant of **VendorShell**. VendorShell provides geometry management of the status and pre-edit areas. It also supplies a visual separator between the status area window and the application's top level window.

Setting the **VendorShell** resource **XmNpreeditType** dictates the location of the input method window. With an off-the-spot input method, the pre-edit and status area windows appear at the bottom of the application window.

11.4.1.4 Text Input Using a DrawingArea

An application that needs special text processing may use a DrawingArea for text input and output. For internationalized text input with any widget other than Text or TextField, the application must use the Xlib input method facilities. These allow the application to open an input method and input context and to obtain input from the input method. When using these facilities, an application may also need to handle input method geometry management, focus management, event filtering, and other issues. For more information, see *Xlib—C Language X Interface*.

11.4.1.5 Geometry Management of Pre-Edit and Status Areas

When an off-the-spot input method is used with the Text or TextField widget, the pre-edit and status areas are below the client's main window but inside the VendorShell. VendorShell accomplishes the necessary geometry management. If the application uses either **XtGetValues** or **XtSetValues** to get or set the height (**XmNheight**) of **VendorShell**, the height includes the height of the input method area.

The following figure shows a Text widget using an off-the-spot input method. The distance "h" is the additional height that the input manager needs to display the status and pre-edit areas. Note that in off-the-spot, the pre-edit area is at the bottom of the interaction.

Figure 11–7. Text Widget Pre-Edit and Status Areas Using Off-the-Spot

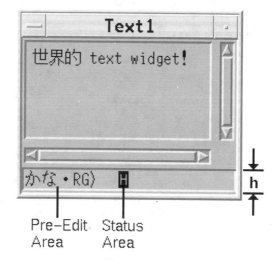

11.4.2 Compound Strings and Compound Text

Compound text is the standard format for exchanging textual data between X window system applications. This is necessary when the user moves text displayed in one codeset to another window with text in a different codeset. For example, the following figure shows two windows, one titled "UJIS" and the other titled "Shift JIS."

Figure 11–8. Reason for Compound Text

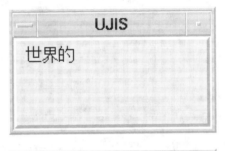

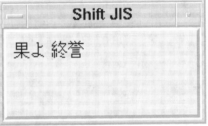

Both windows represent a Motif Text widget, one with some Japanese UJIS characters displayed, and the other with some Shift JIS characters. If the user wants to cut text from one window and paste it in the other window, compound text is used to pass data between the two. The Motif Text widget does this automatically.

If one of the widgets in the previous figure is a Label widget instead of a Text widget, a different situation exists. This is because the Label widget has its text data in compound string format, while the text widget data is a simple character string. In order to pass text data between a Text or TextField widget and any other widget, the application needs to convert the compound string to compound text.

Motif has two functions, **XmCvtXmStringToCT** and **XmCvtCTToXmString**, for converting between compound strings and compound text.

XmCvtXmStringToCT converts a compound string to compound text. The converter uses the font list tag associated with a given compound string segment to select a compound text format for that segment. A registry defines a mapping between font list tags and compound text encoding formats. The converter uses the following algorithm for each compound string segment:

1. If the compound string segment tag is mapped to **XmFONTLIST_DEFAULT_TAG** in the registry, the converter passes the text of the compound string segment to **XmbTextListToTextProperty** with an encoding style of **XCompoundTextStyle** and uses the resulting compound text for that segment.

2. If the compound string segment tag is mapped to an MIT registered charset in the registry, the converter creates the compound text for that segment using the charset (from the registry) and the text of the compound string segment as defined in the X Consortium Standard *Compound Text Encoding*.

3. If the compound string segment tag is mapped to a charset in the registry that is neither **XmFONTLIST_DEFAULT_TAG** nor an MIT registered charset, the converter creates the compound text for that segment using the charset (from the registry) and the text of the compound string segment as an "extended segment" with a variable number of octets per character.

4. If the compound string segment tag is not mapped in the registry, the result is implementation dependent.

An application can use **XmRegisterSegmentEncoding** to map a font list element tag to a compound text encoding format. For example, the application may be using a font list element tag of "BOLD" to identify a compound text segment consisting of localized text to be displayed in a bold font. To ensure that the segment is treated as localized text when converted to compound text, the tag "BOLD" should be mapped to **XmFONTLIST_DEFAULT_TAG** as follows:

```
char *old_encoding = XmRegisterSegmentEncoding("BOLD",
                        XmFONTLIST_DEFAULT_TAG);
XtFree(old_encoding);
```

XmCvtCTToXmString converts compound text to a compound string. This function is implementation dependent.

See Chapter 16 for more information on transferring data between applications. The compound text format is described in the X Consortium Standard *Compound Text Encoding*.

Chapter 12

Color and Pixmaps

Motif uses colors and pixmaps for several general purposes:

- To fill window backgrounds and borders

- To draw text and graphics in window foregrounds

- To generate shadows with a three-dimensional appearance

- To highlight the widget that has keyboard focus

- To indicate that a button is armed or selected

Motif uses other pixmaps for specific purposes:

- As the application's icon for use by the window manager

- For drag icons and drop site animation

- As a CascadeButton symbol indicating that a menu is attached to the CascadeButton

- As a MessageBox symbol indicating the type of message displayed

- As the face of a button when the button is insensitive

All of these colors and pixmaps are represented as resources. The user or application can set the resource values using resource files, and the application can set them using **XtSetValues**.

Motif also uses a number of pixmaps that are not represented as resources. The user and application cannot change these. Among these fixed pixmaps are the following:

- The pixmaps used to stipple insensitive widgets

- The pixmaps used to draw arrows in ScrollBars

- The pixmaps used to create the default source cursor icons in Text, TextField, List, and Label subclasses

12.1 Default Colors and Pixmaps

The following resources determine the colors or pixmaps generally used in Motif:

Borders   Core resources **XmNborderColor** and **XmNborderPixmap**

Backgrounds
> Core resources **XmNbackground** and **XmNbackgroundPixmap**

Foregrounds
> Primitive and Manager resource **XmNforeground**; Label and LabelGadget resources **XmNlabelPixmap** and **XmNlabelInsensitivePixmap**

Shadows   Primitive and Manager resources **XmNbottomShadowColor**, **XmNbottomShadowPixmap**, **XmNtopShadowColor**, and **XmNtopShadowPixmap**

Focus highlights
> Primitive and Manager resources **XmNhighlightColor** and **XmNhighlightPixmap**

Arming and selection
> PushButton and PushButtonGadget resources **XmNarmColor** and **XmNarmPixmap**; ToggleButton and ToggleButtonGadget resources **XmNarmColor**, **XmNselectPixmap**, and **XmNselectInsensitivePixmap**; ScrollBar resource **XmNtroughColor**

The following sections describe these groups of resources and their defaults.

12.1.1 Borders

The border color or border pixmap is used to fill the border of a widget if **XmNborderWidth** is greater than 0. Note that the border is outside the widget; that is, it is not within the area determined by the widget's **XmNheight** and **XmNwidth**. If the user or application supplies a value for **XmNborderPixmap**, that pixmap is used to fill the border; otherwise, **XmNborderColor** is used.

If the application resource **reverseVideo** is False or unspecified, the default for **XmNborderColor** is the black pixel of the widget's screen. If **reverseVideo** is True, the default for **XmNborderColor** is the white pixel of the widget's screen.

12.1.2 Backgrounds

The background color or background pixmap is used to fill a widget before anything else is displayed in it. If the user or application supplies a value for **XmNbackgroundPixmap**, that pixmap is used to fill the background; otherwise, the **XmNbackground** color is used. A gadget inherits the background color and background pixmap of its parent.

The default for **XmNbackground** is implementation dependent.

12.1.3 Foregrounds

The foreground color is used to display text and most graphics in a widget. Most widgets use the **XmNforeground** color for this purpose. Label, LabelGadget, and their subclasses, including buttons, have pixmap resources that are used for the face of the label or button when **XmNlabelType** is set to **XmPIXMAP**. In this case, **XmNlabelPixmap** is used for the face when the widget is sensitive, and **XmNlabelInsensitivePixmap** is used when the widget is insensitive. A gadget inherits the foreground color of its parent.

The default for **XmNforeground** is a color that contrasts with the background color, based on the XmScreen resource **XmNforegroundThreshold**. The value of this resource is an integer between 0 and 100, inclusive, that specifies a level of perceived brightness for a color. If the perceived brightness of the background color is equal to or below this level, Motif treats the background as "dark" when computing the default foreground color. If the perceived brightness of the background color is above this level, Motif treats the background as "light" when computing the default foreground color. When the background is "dark," the default foreground is white; when the background is "light," the default foreground is black.

12.1.4 Shadows

The top shadow color or top shadow pixmap is used to draw the top and left sides of the three-dimensional shadow at the edge of some widgets. If the user or application supplies a value for **XmNtopShadowPixmap**, that pixmap is used for the top and left sides; otherwise, **XmNtopShadowColor** is used.

The bottom shadow color or bottom shadow pixmap is used to draw the bottom and right sides of the three-dimensional shadow. If the user or application supplies a value for **XmNbottomShadowPixmap**, that pixmap is used for the bottom and right sides; otherwise, **XmNbottomShadowColor** is used.

A gadget inherits the top and bottom shadow colors and pixmaps of its parent.

In computing the defaults for **XmNtopShadowColor** and **XmNbottomShadowColor**, Motif uses the XmScreen resources **XmNdarkThreshold** and **XmNlightThreshold**. The value of each resource is an integer between 0 and 100, inclusive, that specifies a level of perceived brightness for a color. If the perceived brightness of the background color is equal to or below the **XmNdarkThreshold**, Motif treats the background as "dark" when computing the default shadow colors. If the perceived brightness of the background color is above the **XmNlightThreshold**, Motif treats the background as "light" when computing the default shadow colors. Otherwise, Motif treats the background as "medium" when computing the defaults.

Motif computes the defaults in the following way, depending on the perceived brightness of the background:

Dark background

The top and bottom shadow colors are interpolated toward white from the background, with the top shadow color shifted more toward white than the bottom shadow color.

Light background

The top and bottom shadow colors are interpolated toward black from the background, with the bottom shadow color shifted more toward black than the top shadow color.

Medium background

The top shadow color is interpolated toward white from the background, and the bottom shadow color is interpolated toward black from the background.

12.1.5 Focus Highlights

The highlight color or highlight pixmap is used to draw the highlighting rectangle around widgets that have keyboard focus. If the user or application supplies a value for **XmNhighlightPixmap**, that pixmap is used for the highlight; otherwise, **XmNhighlightColor** is used. The highlight color is also used to draw the location cursor around List items that have keyboard focus. A gadget inherits the highlight color and highlight pixmap of its parent.

The default highlight color is the same as the default foreground color.

12.1.6 Arming and Selection

In PushButtons and PushButtonGadgets outside menus, **XmNarmColor** is used as the button background when the **XmNfillOnArm** resource is True and the user arms the button. In PushButtons and PushButtonGadgets outside menus, **XmNarmPixmap** is used as the button face (the label area) when **XmNlabelType** is **XmPIXMAP** and the user arms the button.

In ToggleButtons and ToggleButtonGadgets outside menus, **XmNselectColor** is used to fill the toggle indicator when the **XmNindicatorOn** and **XmNfillOnSelect** resources are both True and the user sets the toggle. For sensitive ToggleButtons and ToggleButtonGadgets outside menus, **XmNselectPixmap** is used as the button face (the label area) when **XmNlabelType** is **XmPIXMAP** and the toggle is set. For insensitive ToggleButtons under these conditions, **XmNselectInsensitivePixmap** is used as the button face.

In ScrollBars, **XmNtroughColor** is used to fill the part of the slider area that is not taken up by the slider.

Motif computes a single default, known as the select color, for **XmNarmColor**, **XmNselectColor**, and **XmNtroughColor**. Motif uses the XmScreen resources **XmNdarkThreshold** and **XmNlightThreshold** to determine whether the background is "dark," "light," or "medium" in the same way as for shadow colors. Motif then computes the default in the following way:

Dark background
> The select color is interpolated toward white from the background.

Light background
> The select color is interpolated toward black from the background.

Medium background
> The select color is interpolated toward black from the background.

12.2 Application-Defined Color Generation

Motif generates default colors whenever the application creates a widget that has no specified value for one or more of the color resources. Motif does not regenerate default colors when an application changes the value of **XmNbackground** using **XtSetValues**.

An application can use **XmChangeColor** to recalculate default colors for a widget based on a new background and set the appropriate color resources in the widget. For primitives and managers, **XmChangeColor** sets

XmNbackground, **XmNforeground**, **XmNtopShadowColor**, and **XmNbottomShadowColor**. For widgets and gadgets with select colors, **XmChangeColor** also sets the appropriate resources for those colors.

An application can use **XmGetColors** to produce default colors for a given background color without setting any resources. **XmGetColors** takes as arguments a screen pointer, a colormap, and a background pixel representing a color allocated in the colormap. **XmGetColors** also has return arguments that are pointers to pixel values for the foreground, top shadow, bottom shadow, and select colors. The function generates default colors for the given background. For each of the return arguments that is not NULL, **XmGetColors** allocates a color in the colormap and returns the pixel value at the address specified by the argument.

By default, **XmChangeColor** and **XmGetColors** calculate colors as described in the previous discussion of default colors. An application can use **XmSetColorCalculation** to change the procedure that these routines use and that Motif uses to calculate default colors when the application creates a widget. **XmSetColorCalculation** takes as its only argument a procedure of type **XmColorProc**. It sets Motif's color-calculation procedure to the new **XmColorProc** and returns the color-calculation procedure used previously. **XmSetColorCalculation** does not change the procedure used by **XmChangeColor**, **XmGetColors**, and Motif to calculate default colors for a monochrome screen.

Motif calls the **XmColorProc** when it needs to compute default colors or when the application calls **XmChangeColor** or **XmGetColors**. The **XmColorProc** takes five arguments, all pointers to **XColor** structures. The **red**, **green**, **blue**, and **pixel** members of the first structure are filled in with the background color. The procedure calculates **red**, **green**, and **blue** values for the foreground, select, top shadow, and bottom shadow colors and fills in the other four **XColor** structures with these values.

The procedure should not allocate color cells for any of these colors. Motif caches the returned **XColor** structures and allocates a color when it needs a pixel value. Usually Motif allocates a color when it computes the default value for a resource, when the application calls **XmChangeColor**, or when the application calls **XmGetColors** with a non-NULL value for one of the return pixel values. When allocating colors as a result of widget creation or a call to **XmChangeColor**, Motif uses the colormap of the widget. When allocating colors as a result of a call to **XmGetColors**, Motif uses the colormap passed as an argument to the function.

XmGetColorCalculation returns the color-calculation procedure being used at the time of the call to that routine. Calling **XmSetColorCalculation** with an argument of NULL restores the Motif default color-calculation procedure.

12.3 Colormaps

The colormap used by a widget is the value of the Core resource **XmNcolormap**. An application that does not supply its own colormap does not need to set this resource. The default for a top-level shell is the default colormap of the screen. For other widgets, the default is copied from the parent.

An application that uses its own colormap should not use **XtAppInitialize** to create the top-level shell, because the shell would then use the screen's default colormap. Instead, the application should open the display, create the colormap, and then call **XtAppCreateShell** with the colormap as the **XmNcolormap** argument.

If an application uses different colormaps for some windows in its hierarchy, it must tell the window manager about those colormaps by setting a WM_COLORMAP_WINDOWS property on the top-level window. See Chapter 16 for more information.

For more information about colormaps, see *Xlib—C Language X Interface*.

12.4 Using Pixmaps

Motif uses pixmaps supplied by the application or the user for widget borders, backgrounds, labels, shadows, focus highlights, and button arming or selection indicators. Motif also uses other pixmaps that the application or user can supply for more specific purposes: as application icons, drag icons, CascadeButton menu indicators, MessageBox symbols, and labels for insensitive buttons.

Motif provides facilities for an application to install and cache images and pixmaps. Motif also has string-to-pixmap resource converters that retrieve pixmaps from the cache or install them from files in X bitmap format.

Because of these converters both applications and users can specify pixmaps as resource values from resource files or the command line.

An application can use **XmGetPixmapByDepth** to retrieve or create a pixmap with a specified name, screen, foreground, background, and depth. **XmGetPixmapByDepth** finds or creates a pixmap in the following way:

- It searches the pixmap cache for a pixmap matching the specified name, screen, foreground, background, and depth. If it finds a matching pixmap, it returns the pixmap.

- If it does not find a matching pixmap in the cache, it searches the image cache for an image matching the specified name. If it finds a matching image, it creates and caches a pixmap of the specified depth on the specified screen, transfers the image to the pixmap, and returns the pixmap.

- If it does not find a matching image in the cache, it uses **XtResolvePathname** to search for a file of the specified name. The search path comes from the environment variable **XBMLANGPATH** or, if **XBMLANGPATH** is not set, from a default search path. If it finds such a file, it assumes that the file is in X bitmap format, reads the file, and creates and caches an image in **XYBitmap** format. It then creates and caches a pixmap of the specified depth on the specified screen, transfers the image to the pixmap, and returns the pixmap.

- If it does not find a matching X bitmap file, it returns **XmUNSPECIFIED_PIXMAP**.

Motif preinstalls a number of images in the image cache. The names and characteristics of these images are documented in the **XmInstallImage(3X)** reference page. Motif offers two ways for an application to provide its own image as the source for a pixmap to be created by **XmGetPixmapByDepth**:

- The application can create its own image, usually by using **XCreateImage** or **XGetImage**. The image can be of any depth. The application can then call **XmInstallImage** to install the image in the image cache by name.

- The application or user can create a file in X bitmap format and install the file under an appropriate name in a directory that is in the search path used by **XmGetPixmapByDepth**. For a description of the X bitmap format, see *Xlib—C Language X Interface*.

Both of these mechanisms have advantages and disadvantages. An application using **XmInstallImage** can create an image of any depth.

However, if it intends to use the image name in a resource specification, it must be sure to call **XmInstallImage** before creating any widgets that use the image.

An application using an X bitmap file is limited to creating an image of depth 1. However, the image is always available for use by a resource converter, and the application can use the search path mechanism of **XtResolvePathname** for such purposes as supplying different images for different locales.

XmInstallImage does not make a copy of the image when it caches it. The application must not destroy the image until it removes the image from the cache, using **XmUninstallImage**. An application can use **XmDestroyPixmap** to free a pixmap cached by **XmGetPixmapByDepth**. **XmDestroyPixmap** does not actually destroy the pixmap until all references to it are freed.

Chapter 13

Input, Focus, and Keyboard Navigation

The X server communicates with clients by means of various classes of **events**. Among these are events denoting input from the keyboard and mouse (and, in some X extensions, input from other devices). Each event is associated with a window, and the X server sends the event to any client that has expressed interest in events of that type on that window.

In the simplest case, when a keyboard or pointer event occurs, the X server sends the event to the client that has expressed interest in events of that type on the window that contains the pointer. If no such client exists, the server searches up the window's hierarchy until it finds a client that has expressed interest in events of that type on an ancestor window. In many cases, however, event processing is more complex:

- A client can **grab** a pointer button or key, the pointer or keyboard, or the entire server. The grabbing client then receives the relevant events for the duration of the grab.

- A client can set the **keyboard focus** to some window. Keyboard events that would normally be reported to this window or one of its inferiors are reported as usual, but other events are reported with respect to the focus window. Window managers typically use this technique to implement a "click-to-type" interaction style, in which the user clicks the pointer on some window, and that window retains the keyboard focus regardless of the position of the pointer. Other clients, often in cooperation with the window manager, can set the focus to a particular window within the application hierarchy.

To insulate applications from the complexities of X event handling, Xt and Motif have developed higher-level facilities based on widgets:

- Motif supplies a VendorShell resource, **XmNkeyboardFocusPolicy**, to allow a user or application to control the model of keyboard focus in the VendorShell and its descendants. Keyboard focus can be with the widget the contains the pointer or with the widget in which the user presses **BSelect**.

- In the click-to-type model, the user can also use keys to navigate from widget to widget. Motif provides a model of **tab groups**, which are widgets or sets of widgets to which the user moves using **KNextField** and **KPrevField**. Within a tab group, the user traverses between widgets using **KUp**, **KDown**, **KLeft**, and **KRight**. Motif supplies resources to control whether or not a widget constitutes a tab group and whether or not the user can traverse to it using the keyboard. Motif also has a general routine, **XmProcessTraversal**, for use by the application in moving keyboard focus to a widget or tab group. The Motif menu system has a specialized traversal mechanism.

- Xt provides the basic event-dispatching loop used by most applications. Xt takes events out of the application's queue and dispatches them to the appropriate widget, usually the widget that has input focus. Xt usually invokes an **action** associated with the particular event through a table of **translations** from event specifications to action routines. The action, in turn, often invokes a callback list. An application primarily responds to events by means of its callback routines. At a lower level, it can also provide its own **event handler**, a routine invoked by the Xt dispatching loop when the widget receives events of the specified type.

- Motif and Xt provide **mnemonics** and **accelerators**, which are shortcuts for taking actions associated with a widget when the widget does not have input focus. A **mnemonic** is a keysym for a key that activates a visible button in a menu. An **accelerator** is a description for an event that invokes an action routine through a translation.

13.1 Focus Models

Motif provides two models for determining which widget within an application receives keyboard events. The focus model is determined for all descendants of a VendorShell by the value of the VendorShell resource **XmNkeyboardFocusPolicy**:

- When the value is **XmEXPLICIT**, the widget under the pointer does not necessarily receive keyboard events. The user must take an action other than moving the pointer to transfer keyboard focus to a widget. The user can usually transfer focus to a widget by pressing **BSelect** on that widget or by using a keyboard navigation action to traverse to the widget.

  When the value is **XmEXPLICIT**, a widget must be **traversable** to receive keyboard events. In general, a widget is traversable when its **XmNsensitive**, **XmNancestorSensitive**, and **XmNtraversalOn** resources are True and when the widget and its ancestors are managed, realized, mapped, and viewable. See Section 13.2 for more information.

- When the value is **XmPOINTER**, the widget under the pointer receives keyboard events, unless that widget is insensitive. Keyboard navigation operations are not available. However, the user can still use the keyboard to traverse a menu system. **KMenuBar** moves focus to the MenuBar, and **KMenu** posts a PopupMenu if available. When the user posts a menu using **KMenu** or **BSelect Release**, **KActivate**, or **KSelect** in a CascadeButton, keyboard navigation operations are available in the menu until the menu is unposted. When the user exits the menu system, keyboard focus returns to the widget under the pointer.

MWM provides two parallel focus models for determining which top-level window receives keyboard events. The focus model is determined by the value of the **mwm** resource **keyboardFocusPolicy**:

- When the value is "explicit", the window under the pointer does not necessarily receive keyboard events. The user must take an action other than moving the pointer to transfer keyboard focus to a window. The user can usually transfer focus to a window by pressing **BSelect** on that window or by using **KNextFamilyWindow**, **KPrevFamilyWindow**, **KNextWindow**, or **KPrevWindow** to traverse to the window.

- When the value is "pointer", the widget under the pointer receives keyboard events. Keyboard window navigation operations are not available.

When the focus policy is "explicit", four Boolean **mwm** resources can be set to True to allow a window to receive keyboard focus automatically at specified times:

autoKeyFocus
> When the window with focus is iconified or unmapped (gives focus to the window that last had it)

deiconifyKeyFocus
> When the window is iconified

raiseKeyFocus
> When the window is raised to the top of the stack

startupKeyFocus
> When the window is mapped

13.2 Controlling Keyboard Navigation

In order to receive keyboard focus when the shell's **XmNkeyboardFocusPolicy** is **XmEXPLICIT**, a widget or gadget must meet the following conditions:

- The widget and its ancestors must not be in the process of being destroyed.

- The widget and its ancestors must be **sensitive**. A widget is sensitive when its **XmNsensitive** and **XmNancestorSensitive** resources are both True.

- The **XmNtraversalOn** resource for the widget and its ancestors must be True.

- The widget must be viewable. This means that the widget and its ancestors must be managed, realized, and (except for gadgets) mapped. Furthermore, in general, some part of the widget's rectangular area must be unobscured by the widget's ancestors.

In a ScrolledWindow with an **XmNscrollingPolicy** of **XmAUTOMATIC**, a widget that is obscured because it is not within the clip window may be traversable if some part of the widget is within the work area and if an **XmNtraverseObscuredCallback** routine can make the widget unobscured by scrolling the window.

Most managers cannot receive focus even if they meet all these conditions. In general only primitives and gadgets are eligible to receive focus. A DrawingArea can receive focus if it meets the conditions above and if, in addition, it has no child whose **XmNtraversalOn** resource is True.

XmGetFocusWidget takes a widget argument that identifies a widget hierarchy, up to the nearest shell ancestor. It returns the widget in that hierarchy that has keyboard focus or that last had focus when the user navigated away from that hierarchy.

An application can use **XmIsTraversable** and **XmGetVisibility** to determine whether a widget is eligible to receive focus. **XmIsTraversable** returns True if the widget argument meets all the conditions described in this section. Otherwise, it returns False. This routine generally returns False if the widget argument is a composite, even if it has traversable children.

XmGetVisibility returns a value indicating the visibility of the widget argument:

XmVISIBILITY_FULLY_OBSCURED
> The widget is completely obscured by its ancestors or is not visible for some other reason (such as being unmapped or unrealized).

XmVISIBILITY_PARTIALLY_OBSCURED
> Some part of the widget's rectangular area is obscured by its ancestors.

XmVISIBILITY_UNOBSCURED
> None of the widget's rectangular area is obscured by its ancestors.

Note that a fully obscured widget may be traversable if it is inside the work area of an automatic ScrolledWindow with an **XmNtraverseObscuredCallback** list. See Section 13.2.5 for more information.

13.2.1 Sensitivity

Unless a widget is sensitive, Xt does not dispatch keyboard or pointer events to the widget. An insensitive widget, therefore, cannot receive keyboard focus.

A widget can be sensitive only when all its ancestors are sensitive. Two Boolean resources determine sensitivity: **XmNsensitive** and **XmNancestorSensitive**. **XmNsensitive** indicates whether the widget itself is sensitive, and **XmNancestorSensitive** indicates whether all ancestors are sensitive.

An application uses the function **XtIsSensitive** to find out whether a widget is sensitive. This function returns True when **XmNsensitive** and **XmNancestorSensitive** are both True; otherwise, it returns False.

The function **XtSetSensitive** changes the sensitivity of a widget. With an argument of False, this function sets **XmNsensitive** to False and sets each child's **XmNancestorSensitive** to False. With an argument of True, this function sets **XmNsensitive** to True and, if the widget's **XmNancestorSensitive** is also True, it sets each child's **XmNancestorSensitive** to True. The function then recursively descends the widget tree. For each descendant whose **XmNsensitive** and **XmNancestorSensitive** are both True, it sets **XmNancestorSensitive** to True for that widget's children. Otherwise, it sets **XmNancestorSensitive** to False for the descendant widget's children.

In this way, **XtSetSensitive** ensures that each widget's **XmNancestorSensitive** is True only when the parent's **XmNsensitive** and **XmNancestorSensitive** are both True. In other words, the widget is sensitive only when it and all its ancestors are sensitive. To maintain this relation, an application should always use **XtSetSensitive** to change a widget's sensitivity instead of calling **XtSetValues** on the widget's resources.

Note that **XtSetSensitive** does not modify any resources for pop-up children. If the parent widget is insensitive when a pop-up child is created, the child's **XmNancestorSensitive** will be False. **XtSetSensitive** on the parent widget will not change this value, and the child will remain insensitive. To avoid this problem, an application that creates a DialogShell or a MenuShell should either ensure that the parent is sensitive when the child is created, or specify a value of True for the child's **XmNancestorSensitive**.

One way to do this is in a resource file:

```
*XmMenuShell.ancestorSensitive:    True
*XmDialogShell.ancestorSensitive: True
```

When a widget or gadget is insensitive, Motif indicates the insensitivity to the user by stippling or graying the widget.

13.2.2 XmNtraversalOn

XmNtraversalOn determines whether or not a widget is eligible to receive keyboard focus when **XmNkeyboardFocusPolicy** is **XmEXPLICIT**. When **XmNtraversalOn** is False and **XmNkeyboardFocusPolicy** is **XmEXPLICIT**, it is not possible for the user to give keyboard focus to the widget, even if the widget is sensitive and viewable. **XmNtraversalOn** has no effect when **XmNkeyboardFocusPolicy** is **XmPOINTER**.

The default value for **XmNtraversalOn** is True for most Motif widgets. Following are the exceptions:

- Separator and SeparatorGadget, where **XmNtraversalOn** is forced to False

- ScrollBar, where **XmNtraversalOn** defaults to True when it is the child of a ScrolledWindow whose **XmNscrollingPolicy** is **XmAUTOMATIC** and to False otherwise

- Label and LabelGadget, where **XmNtraversalOn** is forced to False inside menus and defaults to False otherwise

- RowColumn, where **XmNtraversalOn** defaults to True in a WorkArea and is not applicable otherwise

13.2.3 Tab Groups

A tab group is a collection of traversable widgets or a single widget that contains a collection of traversable elements. When the shell's **XmNkeyboardFocusPolicy** is **XmEXPLICIT**, the user traverses to a tab group using **KNextField** and **KPrevField**. Within a tab group, when the focus is on a non-tab-group widget or an element, the user traverses to another non-tab-group widget or another element using **KUp**, **KDown**, **KLeft**, and **KRight**.

A tab group is always represented by a widget or gadget. When the group is a collection of widgets, the tab group is typically the manager that is the parent of the widgets. When the group is a single widget like List or Text, the tab group is that widget itself.

The arrow keys do not traverse to tab groups or to non-tab-group widgets or elements outside the current tab group. To traverse to another tab group using the keyboard, the user must press **KNextField** or **KPrevField**.

To be eligible for traversal, a tab group must meet all the conditions discussed in Section 13.2, except that a manager that is a tab group and meets the other conditions is eligible for traversal as long as it contains a descendant that can receive focus. If the tab group does not meet these conditions, the **KNextField** and **KPrevField** actions ignore the tab group.

Within a tab group, non-tab-group widgets must also meet all the conditions discussed in Section 13.2 to be eligible for traversal. If they do not meet these conditions, the arrow key actions ignore the widgets.

Whether or not a widget is a tab group is determined by the value of the **XmNnavigationType** resource. The two primary values for this resource are **XmTAB_GROUP**, which indicates that the widget is a tab group, and **XmNONE**, which indicates that it is not.

When the user traverses to the next or previous tab group, the direction of the traversal is usually determined by the relative locations of the current and target groups. In a left-to-right language environment, traversal to each subsequent tab group proceeds from left to right and top to bottom. At the bottom right, traversal wraps to the tab group at the top left. Traversal to previous tab groups proceeds in the opposite direction.

The application can control the order of traversal by specifying an **XmNnavigationType** of **XmEXCLUSIVE_TAB_GROUP** for a widget in the hierarchy. When any widget in a hierarchy has an **XmNnavigationType** of **XmEXCLUSIVE_TAB_GROUP**, **KNextField** and **KPrevField** do not move to any widgets in that hierarchy that have been designated tab groups by means of an **XmNnavigationType** of **XmTAB_GROUP**. But **KNextField** and **KPrevField** do move to widgets whose **XmNnavigationType** is **XmSTICKY_TAB_GROUP**, even if some widgets are exclusive tab groups. Thus, an application that uses **XmEXCLUSIVE_TAB_GROUP** to control traversal must be sure that all tab groups have an **XmNnavigationType** of either **XmEXCLUSIVE_TAB_GROUP** or **XmSTICKY_TAB_GROUP**.

When any widget in a hierarchy has an **XmNnavigationType** of **XmEXCLUSIVE_TAB_GROUP**, traversal to subsequent tab groups does not depend on the relative locations of the groups. Instead, it proceeds to widgets in the order in which their **XmNnavigationType** resources were specified as **XmEXCLUSIVE_TAB_GROUP** or **XmSTICKY_TAB_GROUP**, either by creating the widgets with that value or by calling **XtSetValues**. That is, traversal proceeds to the widget whose **XmNnavigationType** was next specified to be **XmEXCLUSIVE_TAB_GROUP** or **XmSTICKY_TAB_GROUP**. Traversal to previous tab groups proceeds in the opposite direction.

Within a tab group whose **XmNnavigationType** is **XmEXCLUSIVE_TAB_GROUP**, the arrow keys do not behave the same way as they would if the **XmNnavigationType** were either **XmTAB_GROUP** or **XmSTICKY_TAB_GROUP**. With **XmTAB_GROUP** or **XmSTICKY_TAB_GROUP**, the direction of traversal using the arrow keys depends on the relative locations of the tab group's children. **KRight** moves to the next traversable child to the right of the child with the focus; **KDown** moves to the next traversable child below the child with the focus; and so on.

With **XmEXCLUSIVE_TAB_GROUP**, traversal using the arrow keys depends on the order of the tab group's list of children, not on the relative locations of the children. **KRight** has the same effect as **KDown**: both move to the next traversable child in the tab group's list of children. **KLeft** has the same effect as **KUp**: both move to the previous traversable child in the tab group's list of children.

There are three principal differences between **XmEXCLUSIVE_TAB_GROUP** and **XmSTICKY_TAB_GROUP**:

- **XmEXCLUSIVE_TAB_GROUP** has the effect of disabling traversal to tab groups that have an **XmNnavigationType** of **XmTAB_GROUP**. **XmSTICKY_TAB_GROUP** does not; it simply ensures that traversal to that tab group is possible, even when some widget in the hierarchy has an **XmNnavigationType** of **XmEXCLUSIVE_TAB_GROUP**.

- **XmEXCLUSIVE_TAB_GROUP** changes the order of traversal of tab groups within the widget hierarchy. **XmSTICKY_TAB_GROUP** does not.

- **XmEXCLUSIVE_TAB_GROUP** changes the order of traversal of widgets inside the tab group. **XmSTICKY_TAB_GROUP** does not.

The function **XmAddTabGroup** has the same effect as calling **XtSetValues** with an **XmNnavigationType** of **XmEXCLUSIVE_TAB_GROUP**. The function **XmRemoveTabGroup** has the same effect as calling **XtSetValues** with an **XmNnavigationType** of **XmNONE**. **XmAddTabGroup** and **XmRemoveTabGroup** are obsolete and exist for compatibility with earlier releases of OSF/Motif.

All Motif managers except RowColumn have a default **XmNnavigationType** of **XmTAB_GROUP**. In RowColumn, **XmNnavigationType** is not applicable for MenuBars, PulldownMenus, and PopupMenus. For a WorkArea the default is **XmTAB_GROUP**, and for an OptionMenu the default is **XmNONE**.

All Motif primitives except List, ScrollBar, Text, and TextField have a default **XmNnavigationType** of **XmNONE**. The default for List, Text, and TextField is **XmTAB_GROUP**, and the default for ScrollBar is **XmSTICKY_TAB_GROUP**. These are all controls that have their own internal navigation.

Motif sets the navigation type of widgets in some situations. In particular:

- The child of a shell always behaves as a tab group, no matter what the value of its **XmNnavigationType**.

- Panes and sashes inside PanedWindows have a default **XmNnavigationType** of **XmTAB_GROUP**. If the **XmNnavigationType** of a pane is **XmNONE** when the pane is created, Motif sets the value of that resource to **XmTAB_GROUP**.

- SelectionBox and its subclasses set the **XmNnavigationType** of their automatically created List and Text children to **XmSTICKY_TAB_GROUP**.

The function **XmGetTabGroup** returns the tab group that contains a widget. If the widget itself is a tab group or a shell, it returns that widget. If neither the widget nor any ancestor up to the nearest shell is a tab group, it returns the nearest ancestor that is a shell. Otherwise, it returns the nearest ancestor that is a tab group.

13.2.3.1 Controlling Tab Group Traversal Order

By default, **KNextField** and **KPrevField** traverse to successive tab groups in order of layout, from left to right and top to bottom, within a parent tab group, before proceeding in layout order to the next tab group that is a sibling of the parent. Traversal order changes when any widget in a shell hierarchy has an **XmNnavigationType** of **XmEXCLUSIVE_TAB_GROUP**. In this case, **KNextField** and **KPrevField** traverse only to widgets in the hierarchy whose **XmNnavigationType** is either **XmEXCLUSIVE_TAB_GROUP** or **XmSTICKY_TAB_GROUP**. The traversal order is the order in which the widgets' **XmNnavigationType** was specified to be either **XmEXCLUSIVE_TAB_GROUP** or **XmSTICKY_TAB_GROUP**.

This mechanism gives an application the means to control tab group traversal order. An application must do the following:

- Ensure that at least one widget in the shell hierarchy has an **XmNnavigationType** of **XmEXCLUSIVE_TAB_GROUP**

- Ensure that all widgets that the application wants to be tab groups have an **XmNnavigationType** of either **XmEXCLUSIVE_TAB_GROUP** or **XmSTICKY_TAB_GROUP**

- Specify values for the tab groups' **XmNnavigationType**, using either creation argument lists or **XtSetValues**, in the order in which the tab groups are to be traversed

Note that, when a tab group has an **XmNnavigationType** of **XmEXCLUSIVE_TAB_GROUP**, traversal to non-tab-group widgets inside that tab group proceeds in the order in which the children appear in their parents' **XmNchildren** lists. If the application wants to specify the order of tab group traversal but still wants traversal of non-tab-group widgets to proceed according to layout, it should select one widget in the hierarchy to have an **XmNnavigationType** of **XmEXCLUSIVE_TAB_GROUP**. This tab group should contain no non-tab-group widgets. For example, it could be the MainWindow if the MainWindow contains only tab groups, or it could be a primitive tab group, such as List or Text. The application should then specify an **XmNnavigationType** of **XmSTICKY_TAB_GROUP** for all other tab groups in the hierarchy.

13.2.4 Initial Focus

A tab group may contain any combination of tab group and non-tab-group widgets. A tab group that contains other widgets cannot receive focus itself. When the user traverses to a composite tab group, Motif gives focus to some widget within the tab group.

Motif uses the Manager resource **XmNinitialFocus** in determining which widget receives focus. The value of **XmNinitialFocus** is a widget that meets the following conditions:

- The widget must be either a tab group or a non-tab-group widget that can receive keyboard focus. In general, a widget can receive keyboard focus when it is a primitive, a gadget, or a manager (such as a DrawingArea with no traversable children) that acts as a primitive.

- The widget must not be a descendant of a tab group that is itself a descendant of the manager. That is, the widget cannot be contained within a tab group that is nested inside the manager.

- The widget and its ancestors must have a value of True for their **XmNtraversalOn** resources.

If the widget does not meet these conditions, **XmNinitialFocus** is treated as if the value were NULL.

Motif uses **XmNinitialFocus** to determine which widget receives focus in these situations:

- When the manager is the child of a shell and the shell hierarchy receives focus for the first time

- When focus is inside the shell hierarchy, the manager is a composite tab group, and the user traverses to the manager using the keyboard

Motif then determines focus as follows:

- If **XmNinitialFocus** is a traversable non-tab-group widget, that widget receives focus.

- If **XmNinitialFocus** is a traversable tab group, that tab group receives focus. If that tab group is a composite with descendant tab groups or traversable non-tab-group widgets, these procedures are used recursively to assign focus to a descendant of that tab group.

- If **XmNinitialFocus** is NULL, the first traversable non-tab-group widget that is not contained within a nested tab group receives focus.

- If **XmNinitialFocus** is NULL and no traversable non-tab-group widget exists, the first traversable tab group that is not contained within a nested tab group receives focus. If that tab group is a composite with descendant tab groups or traversable non-tab-group widgets, these procedures are used recursively to assign focus to a descendant of that tab group.

If a shell hierarchy regains focus after losing it, focus returns to the widget that had the focus at the time it left the hierarchy.

The use of **XmNinitialFocus** is undefined if the manager is a MenuBar, PulldownMenu, PopupMenu, or OptionMenu.

13.2.5 Traversing to Obscured Widgets

In general, a widget is not eligible to receive focus unless some part of its rectangular area is unobscured by its ancestors. However, it may be possible to traverse to a widget that is a descendant of a ScrolledWindow whose **XmNscrollingPolicy** is **XmAUTOMATIC**, even if that widget is not within the ScrolledWindow's clip window. Traversal to such a widget is possible under the following conditions:

- Some part of the widget's rectangular area is within the bounds of the ScrolledWindow's work window.

- The ScrolledWindow's clip window is completely unobscured by its ancestors. If the ScrolledWindow is a descendant of another ScrolledWindow, it must be unobscured by the ancestor's work window but may be outside the ancestor's clip window.

- The ScrolledWindow has a procedure on its **XmNtraverseObscuredCallback** list that can bring some part of the widget's rectangular area into the clip window.

- The widget meets the other conditions for receiving focus described in Section 13.2.

Whenever the user attempts to traverse to such a widget and the widget is partially or fully obscured by the clip window, Motif calls the ScrolledWindow's **XmNtraverseObscuredCallback** procedures. If the ScrolledWindow has one or more ancestor ScrolledWindows, Motif calls the **XmNtraverseObscuredCallback** list for each ScrolledWindow whose clip window obscures the traversal target, from the lowest level of the hierarchy to the highest. The **XmNtraverseObscuredCallback** procedure can try to bring the widget into the clip window if necessary, usually by calling **XmScrollVisible**. If the target widget is traversable after the **XmNtraverseObscuredCallback** procedures are invoked, that widget receives focus.

A procedure can determine the visibility of a widget by calling **XmGetVisibility**.

13.2.6 XmProcessTraversal

The principal routine for traversing to a widget is **XmProcessTraversal**. Motif uses this routine to effect traversal when the user presses an arrow key, **KNextField**, or **KPrevField**. An application can use **XmProcessTraversal** to implement its own traversal actions.

XmProcessTraversal takes two arguments, a widget and a constant specifying a traversal action. The routine uses the widget argument to identify the hierarchy that contains the widget and that has its root at the nearest shell. If that shell does not currently have the focus, any changes to the element with focus within that shell will not occur until the next time the shell receives focus.

The traversal action argument identifies one of three kinds of action to take. The following descriptions of these actions refer to traversable non-tab-group widgets and traversable tab groups. A traversable non-tab-group widget is a widget that is not a tab group and that meets all the conditions for receiving focus discussed in Section 13.2. A traversable tab group is a tab group widget that meets the same conditions, except that a manager that is a tab group and meets the other conditions is also traversable as long as it contains a descendant that can receive focus.

The routine begins the traversal action from the widget in the hierarchy that currently has keyboard focus or that last had focus when the user traversed away from the shell hierarchy.

- Traversal to a non-tab-group widget. This kind of traversal is possible only when the widget that currently has focus is not a tab group. Also, these actions do not move focus from one tab group to another. The actions first determine the containing tab group. This is the tab group containing the widget that currently has focus. The actions traverse only to a non-tab-group widget within the containing tab group.

XmTRAVERSE_RIGHT

If the **XmNnavigationType** of the containing tab group is not **XmEXCLUSIVE_TAB_GROUP**, focus moves to the next traversable non-tab-group widget to the right of the widget that currently has focus. At the right side of the tab group, this action wraps to the non-tab-group widget at the left side and next toward the bottom. At the lower right corner of the tab group, this action wraps to the non-tab-group widget at the upper left.

If the **XmNnavigationType** of the containing tab group is **XmEXCLUSIVE_TAB_GROUP**, focus moves to the next traversable non-tab-group widget in the tab group, proceeding in the order in which the widgets appear in their parents' **XmNchildren** lists. After the last widget in the tab group, this action wraps to the first non-tab-group widget.

XmTRAVERSE_LEFT

If the **XmNnavigationType** of the containing tab group is not **XmEXCLUSIVE_TAB_GROUP**, focus moves to the next traversable non-tab-group widget to the left of the widget that currently has focus. At the left side of the tab group, this action wraps to the non-tab-group widget at the right side and next toward the top. At the upper left corner of the tab group, this action wraps to the non-tab-group widget at the lower right.

If the **XmNnavigationType** of the containing tab group is **XmEXCLUSIVE_TAB_GROUP**, focus moves to the previous traversable non-tab-group widget in the tab group, proceeding in the reverse order in which the widgets appear in their parents' **XmNchildren** lists. After the first widget in the tab group, this action wraps to the last non-tab-group widget.

XmTRAVERSE_DOWN

If the **XmNnavigationType** of the containing tab group is not **XmEXCLUSIVE_TAB_GROUP**, focus moves to the next traversable non-tab-group widget below the widget that currently has focus. At the bottom of the tab group, this action wraps to the non-tab-group widget at the top and next toward the right. At the lower right corner of the tab group, this action wraps to the non-tab-group widget at the upper left.

If the **XmNnavigationType** of the containing tab group is **XmEXCLUSIVE_TAB_GROUP**, focus moves to the next traversable non-tab-group widget in the tab group, proceeding in the order in which the widgets appear in their parents' **XmNchildren** lists. After the last widget in the tab group, this action wraps to the first non-tab-group widget.

XmTRAVERSE_UP

If the **XmNnavigationType** of the containing tab group is not **XmEXCLUSIVE_TAB_GROUP**, focus moves to the next traversable non-tab-group widget above the widget that currently has focus. At the top of the tab group, this action wraps to the non-tab-group widget at the bottom and next toward the left. At the upper left corner of the tab group, this action wraps to the non-tab-group widget at the lower right.

If the **XmNnavigationType** of the containing tab group is **XmEXCLUSIVE_TAB_GROUP**, focus moves to the previous traversable non-tab-group widget in the tab group, proceeding in the reverse order in which the widgets appear in their parents' **XmNchildren** lists. After the first widget in the tab group, this action wraps to the last non-tab-group widget.

XmTRAVERSE_NEXT

Focus moves to the next traversable non-tab-group widget in the tab group, proceeding in the order in which the widgets appear in their parents' **XmNchildren** lists. After the last widget in the tab group, this action wraps to the first non-tab-group widget.

XmTRAVERSE_PREV

Focus moves to the previous traversable non-tab-group widget in the tab group, proceeding in the reverse order in which the widgets appear in their parents' **XmNchildren** lists. After the first widget in the tab group, this action wraps to the last non-tab-group widget.

XmTRAVERSE_HOME

If the **XmNnavigationType** of the containing tab group is not **XmEXCLUSIVE_TAB_GROUP**, focus moves to the first traversable non-tab-group widget at the top left corner of the tab group.

If the **XmNnavigationType** of the containing tab group is **XmEXCLUSIVE_TAB_GROUP**, focus moves to the first traversable non-tab-group widget in the tab group, according to the order in which the widgets appear in their parents' **XmNchildren** lists.

- Traversal to a tab group. These actions first determine the current widget hierarchy and the containing tab group. The current widget hierarchy is the widget hierarchy whose root is the nearest shell ancestor of the widget that currently has focus. The containing tab group is the tab group containing the widget that currently has focus.

XmTRAVERSE_NEXT_TAB_GROUP

If no tab group in the current widget hierarchy has a value of **XmEXCLUSIVE_TAB_GROUP** for **XmNnavigationType**, focus goes to the next traversable tab group that is to the right of the widget with current focus and is within the containing tab group. At the right side of the containing tab group, this action wraps to the tab group at the left side and next toward the bottom. At the lower right corner of the containing tab group, this action recursively moves up one level in the hierarchy. Focus then goes to the next traversable tab group that is to the right of the original containing tab group and is within the tab group that contains that one. At the lower right corner of the topmost tab group in the hierarchy, this action wraps to the first traversable tab group at the upper left corner of the topmost tab group.

If any tab group in the current widget hierarchy has a value of **XmEXCLUSIVE_TAB_GROUP** for **XmNnavigationType**, focus goes to the next traversable tab group in the hierarchy, in the order in which the **XmNnavigationType** resources of the tab groups were set to **XmEXCLUSIVE_TAB_GROUP** or **XmSTICKY_TAB_GROUP**. After the last tab group in the hierarchy, this action wraps to the first tab group.

XmTRAVERSE_PREV_TAB_GROUP

If no tab group in the current widget hierarchy has a value of **XmEXCLUSIVE_TAB_GROUP** for **XmNnavigationType**, focus goes to the next traversable tab group that is to the left of the widget with current focus and is within the containing tab group. At the left side of the containing tab group, this action wraps to the tab group at the right side and next toward the top. At the upper left corner of the containing tab group, this action recursively moves up one level in the hierarchy. Focus then goes to the next traversable tab group that is to the left of the original containing tab group and is within the tab group that contains that one. At the upper left corner of the topmost tab group in the hierarchy, this action wraps to the first traversable tab group at the lower right corner of the topmost tab group.

If any tab group in the current widget hierarchy has a value of **XmEXCLUSIVE_TAB_GROUP** for **XmNnavigationType**, focus goes to the previous traversable tab group in the hierarchy, in the reverse order in which the **XmNnavigationType** resources of the tab groups were set to either **XmEXCLUSIVE_TAB_GROUP** or **XmSTICKY_TAB_GROUP**. After the first tab group in the hierarchy, this action wraps to the last tab group.

- Traversal to any widget. In this case, the widget argument is the widget to which **XmProcessTraversal** tries to give focus.

XmTRAVERSE_CURRENT

Focus goes to the widget argument if that widget is a traversable non-tab-group widget or tab group.

Note that **XmProcessTraversal** cannot be called recursively. In particular, an application cannot call this routine from an **XmNfocusCallback** or **XmNlosingFocusCallback** procedure.

13.2.7 Focus Callbacks

BulletinBoard, Text, and TextField have **XmNfocusMovedCallback** callback lists. Motif invokes the procedures on these lists when these widgets receive keyboard focus. A callback procedure may change the widget's state to reflect the new focus, but it should not try to change the focus and, in particular, must not call **XmProcessTraversal**.

Text and TextField also have **XmNlosingFocusCallback** callback lists. The Text and TextField traversal actions invoke these procedures before traversing to another widget. The third argument to each procedure is a pointer to an **XmTextVerifyCallbackStruct** structure whose **reason** member is **XmCR_LOSING_FOCUS**. If a callback procedure sets the **doit** member of this structure to False, the traversal action does not carry out the traversal. In this way the application can prevent a user from traversing out of the widget by means of these actions.

Motif also invokes the **XmNlosingFocusCallback** procedures when the widget loses focus by some other means. For example, the user might click **BSelect** in another traversable widget, or when the shell's **XmNkeyboardFocusPolicy** is **XmPOINTER** the user might move the pointer into another widget. In such cases, setting the **doit** member of the callback structure has no effect.

13.3 Translations and Actions

In Xt, the primary means of associating an input event with a widget-specific procedure is the combination of translations and actions. Each widget (but not gadget) instance contains a table of translations that maps event descriptions to procedure names. Each widget instance also has a table of actions that maps these procedure names to actual procedures. When a widget receives an input event, the Xt event-dispatching facility looks up the event in the translation table, looks up the associated procedure in the action table, and invokes the action procedure itself. This procedure usually takes some action to change the widget state and often invokes callback procedures.

13.3.1 Translation Table Format

An application or user specifies a translation table as a string whose format is defined in *X Toolkit Intrinsics—C Language Interface*. In general, the table consists of individual translations separated by "\n". Each translation consists of an event description sequence, a colon, and one or more associated procedure names. Each procedure name also has a list of parameters within parentheses to be passed to the procedure when it is invoked as a result of that translation.

An event description in general consists of an optional list of modifiers, an event type within angle brackets (< and >), an optional repeat count within parentheses, and an optional event detail. Modifiers apply only to key, button, motion, enter, and leave events. If an exclamation point (!) precedes the modifiers, then the modifiers in the list and no others must be asserted for the action to be invoked. Otherwise, the modifiers in the list must be asserted, but others may be as well. A tilde (˜) before any modifier means that that modifier must not be asserted. If the modifier list is empty, any modifiers may be asserted.

The detail field varies depending on the event type. The most common use is to identify the keysym for a **KeyPress** or **KeyRelease** event.

Event descriptions in a sequence are separated by commas. Mouse motion is discarded if it occurs between events in a sequence that does not include explicit motion events. This allows the following sort of translation to invoke an action even if the mouse moves between button press and release:

```
<Btn1Down>,<Btn1Up> : action()
```

Following are some important considerations in using translations:

- More specific events should always precede less specific events in the table:

```
Ctrl<Key>space : action_1()
<Key>space    : action_2()
```

- Translations with event sequences that are noninitial subsequences of other translations are not invoked when the events occur as part of the longer sequence. For instance, **up_action()** in the following example would not be invoked on a button release that followed a button press:

```
<Btn1Down>,<Btn1Up> : click_action()
<Btn1Up>            : up_action()
```

- Event descriptions that use a repeat count expand into longer sequences. For example, the following descriptions are more or less equivalent:

```
<Btn1Up>(2)                     : double_click()
<Btn1Up>,<Btn1Down>,<Btn1Up> : double_click()
```

This result, combined with the implicit insertion of motion events between any two other events, means that motion translations cannot exist in a table with multiclick translations.

See *X Toolkit Intrinsics—C Language Interface* for more information on the format of translation tables.

13.3.2 Using Translations

One translation table frequently needs to be merged with another. For example, a user may want to add one or more translations to a widget's default translations. A translation table may begin with one of three directives that specifies how the table is to be merged with an existing table:

#replace   The new translation table should completely replace any existing table. This is the default if no directive is specified.

#augment   The new translation table should be added to any existing table. If the two tables contain duplicate event descriptions, the translations in the existing table are used.

#override   The new translation table should be added to any existing table. If the two tables contain duplicate event descriptions, the translations in the new table are used.

A widget's translation table is the value of the Core **XmNtranslations** resource. The initial value is determined in the following way:

- If a non-NULL value is specified for **XmNtranslations** in the widget creation argument list, the widget class translations are merged with that value, in order, and the resulting table is used.

- Otherwise, the following tables are merged, in order, and the resulting table is used:

  — The widget class translations

  — The value of the **baseTranslations** resource from the resource database

  — The value of the **XmNtranslations** resource from the resource database or, if no value was specified, the default value for the widget's **XmNtranslations**

To take advantage of this initialization ordering, an application should usually provide any translations of its own by specifying a value for **baseTranslations** rather than **XmNtranslations** in an application class defaults file or a fallback resource list. This essentially reserves **XmNtranslations** to the user. The application can change the widget class translations by specifying **baseTranslations**, and the user can change the application's translations by specifying **XmNtranslations**.

As the value of a widget's **XmNtranslations**, a translation table must be in a parsed format rather than a string. The string-to-translation-table converter parses a resource string into a translation table. An application can also use **XtParseTranslationTable** to compile a translation table string into the parsed format. The application can then merge the parsed table with a widget's **XmNtranslations** in three ways:

- **XtAugmentTranslations** merges the parsed table in **#augment** mode

- **XtOverrideTranslations** merges the parsed table in **#override** mode

- **XtSetValues** of **XmNtranslations** replaces the existing value with the parsed table

Some Motif widgets merge additional translations in their **initialize** and **set_values** methods. This process may make it impossible for an application or user to override some translations by means of resource files. For example, for some widgets it may not be possible to change traversal translations in this way.

13.3.3 Actions

Each widget instance has a table that maps action procedure names, as they appear in translation tables, to actual action procedures. When an action is invoked through a translation, Xt looks up the action procedure name in this table and calls the associated procedure.

Each widget class may have its own action table. In addition, an application can use **XtAppAddActions** to add entries to an action table associated with the application context. Only one such table exists per application context. If a call to **XtAppAddActions** contains an action name that is already in the table, the action name becomes associated with the action procedure supplied in the call to **XtAppAddActions**, overriding the existing action.

Xt creates a widget's action table when the widget is realized. It uses actions from the following action tables, those listed first having highest precedence:

- The action tables for the widget's class and its superclasses, in subclass-to-superclass order

- The action tables for the parent's class and its superclasses, in subclass-to-superclass order, and so on up the widget hierarchy

- The application context action table (created by calls to **XtAppAddActions**)

This ordering means that an application cannot use **XtAppAddActions** to provide a new action procedure for an action name that is already registered by a widget class. To do that, the application must supply a translation that maps the event to an action name that is not registered by the class. The application must then call **XtAppAddActions** to supply a procedure for the action name.

An action procedure is a function of type **XtActionProc**. This function receives four arguments:

- The widget

- The event, or the last event of a sequence, that caused the procedure to be invoked

- A list of strings representing the parameters specified for this action in the translation table

- An integer representing the number of parameters in the parameter list

An application can use the parameter list to perform a number of related actions in a single action routine. For example, a widget might have the following translations:

```
c <Key> osfLeft    : move-object(left) \n\
c <Key> osfRight   : move-object(right) \n\
c <Key> osfUp      : move-object(up) \n\
c <Key> osfDown    : move-object(down)
```

The routine implementing the **move-object**() action is passed one of the strings "left", "right", "up", and "down" as the only item in the parameter list, depending on which key event invoked the action. The routine performs the action appropriate for this parameter.

13.3.4 Bindings for osf Keysyms

Motif maintains a client-side mechanism for mapping one set of keysyms to another set. This mapping allows Motif widgets and applications to use a single set of keysyms in translation tables and also allows applications and users to customize the keysyms used in the translations for the particular keyboard used with the display.

The names of keysyms eligible for use in translations in this way begin with the prefix "osf" and are referred to as *osf keysyms*. Motif maintains a mapping between these "virtual" keysyms and the "actual" keysyms that correspond to keys on a particular keyboard. When Xt receives a keyboard event, the function **XmTranslateKey** translates the keycode of the event to the appropriate osf keysym if a mapping exists for that keysym. Xt then dispatches the event to the appropriate action routine if a translation exists for that osf keysym.

The mapping between osf and actual keysyms is determined at application startup based on information obtained from one of the following sources, listed in order of precedence:

- A **defaultVirtualBindings** application resource in the resource database.

- A property on the root window, which can be set by **mwm** on startup, by the **xmbind** client, or on prior startup of a Motif application.

- A **.motifbind** file in the user's home directory.

- A default binding based on the vendor string and optionally the vendor release of the X server. Motif searches the file **xmbind.alias** in the user's home directory, the directory specified by the environment variable **XMBINDDIR**, or the directory **/usr/lib/Xm/bindings**.

The file **xmbind.alias** maps combinations of vendor strings and vendor release numbers to pathnames. Each pathname represents a file that contains keysym bindings for a particular vendor string and optional vendor release number. If Motif fails to find a bindings file for the current display, it uses a set of hard-coded fallback bindings.

The format of the **defaultVirtualBindings** resource is similar to that of a string specifying translations. Each binding consists of an osf keysym, a colon, a key event description (with optional modifiers) for the actual keysym, and "\n". The format of a **.motifbind** file or a file containing vendor bindings is the same, except that each binding is on a separate line.

Following is an example of a specification for the **defaultVirtualBindings** resource in a resource file:

```
*defaultVirtualBindings: \
    osfBackSpace      :       <Key>BackSpace\n\
    osfInsert         :       <Key>InsertChar\n\
...
    osfDelete         :       <Key>DeleteChar
```

The example specification above appears as follows in a **.motifbind** or vendor bindings file:

```
osfBackSpace      :       <Key>BackSpace
osfInsert         :       <Key>InsertChar
...
osfDelete         :       <Key>DeleteChar
```

For more information, see the **VirtualBindings(3X)** and **xmbind(1X)** reference pages in the *OSF/Motif Programmer's Reference*.

13.4 Mnemonics and Accelerators

Sometimes it is desirable for an event received by one widget to activate an action in another. For example, the application may establish a shortcut for activating a button in a menu; the user can activate the menu item even when focus is not in the menu. Motif has two facilities, mnemonics and accelerators, for allowing events in one widget to invoke actions in another.

A mnemonic is a keysym that identifies a key the user can press to activate a menu item when the menu is posted. A button in a MenuBar, PulldownMenu, or PopupMenu can have a mnemonic. When the button is in a PulldownMenu or PopupMenu that is the most recently posted menu, the user activates the button by pressing the key associated with the mnemonic. When the button is in a MenuBar, the MenuBar must have focus for the mnemonic to activate the button. However, the user can activate the button from within the hierarchy that contains the MenuBar, even if the MenuBar does not have focus, by pressing the key while holding the **MAlt** modifier.

An application or user supplies a mnemonic for a button by specifying a value for the Label or LabelGadget resource **XmNmnemonic**. When the button is displayed, Motif underlines the first character in the label string that exactly matches the mnemonic in the character set specified by **XmNmnemonicCharSet**. Although the mnemonic must match a character in the label string exactly in order to be underlined, the user can activate the mnemonic by pressing either the shifted or the unshifted key.

An accelerator allows the user to activate a menu item when focus is anywhere in the hierarchy containing the menu even if the menu is not posted. Accelerators are supported only for PushButtons and ToggleButtons (or their gadget equivalents) in PulldownMenus and PopupMenus.

An application or user supplies an accelerator for a button by specifying a value for the Label or LabelGadget resource **XmNaccelerator**. The value is a string in the same format as an event description in a translation table, except that only **KeyPress** events are allowed. Thus, an accelerator can have a modifier like **MCtrl** or **MAlt**. **XmNacceleratorText** is a compound string that describes the accelerator event, for example, "Ctrl+A". Motif displays the accelerator text to the side of the button's label string or pixmap.

The following example creates a button with a mnemonic and an accelerator:

```
n = 0;
XtSetArg(args[n], XmNmnemonic, XStringToKeysym("A")); n++;
XtSetArg(args[n], XmNaccelerator, "Ctrl<Key>A"); n++;
XtSetArg(args[n], XmNacceleratorText,
        XmStringCreateLocalized("Ctrl+A"); n++;
button1 = XmCreatePushButton(file_pane, "Answer", args, n);
```

Motif's button accelerators and mnemonics are supported only for buttons in certain menus. Xt has a more general facility, also called accelerators, for allowing events in one widget to invoke actions in another.

Xt accelerators are mappings of event descriptions to actions, in the same format as a translation table. An application or user supplies accelerators for a widget as the value of the Core resource **XmNaccelerators**. The accelerators map events to actions of this widget, called the source widget. The application must then install the accelerators on a destination widget, using **XtInstallAccelerators**. This routine takes two arguments: the source widget, whose **XmNaccelerators** resource contains the accelerator table; and the destination widget, where the accelerators are to be installed. When the user produces an event in the destination widget that maps to an accelerator in the table, the event invokes the corresponding action *in the source widget*.

XtInstallAccelerators merges the accelerators with the destination widget's existing translations (the value of **XmNtranslations**). Accelerators can be merged in either **#augment** mode, the default, or **#override** mode. An accelerator table may begin with an **#augment** directive or a **#override** directive. The **#replace** directive is ignored.

As with translations, accelerators must be in an internal format when they are the value of **XmNaccelerators**. A string-to-accelerator-table converter parses an accelerator table string from a resource file. An application can use **XtParseAcceleratorTable** to compile an acclerator table string explicitly.

Accelerators are often defined for a parent source widget and installed on one or more child destination widgets. The SelectionBox and FileSelectionBox widgets install accelerators, the value of **XmNtextAccelerators**, on their text children. The default accelerators bind **KUp**, **KDown**, **KBeginLine**, **KEndLine**, and **KRestore** events in the Text widget to SelectionBox or FileSelectionBox actions that select an item in the List and replace the Text widget value with that List item.

13.5 Event Handlers

Many applications can implement their entire input processing by adding procedures to widget callback lists and by adding mnemonics and accelerators for menu buttons. Some applications change translations, accelerators, or actions. More rarely, an application needs finer control over event processing. Such an application can register an event handler with the Xt event dispatcher.

An event handler is a procedure that the Xt event dispatcher calls when the application receives events of one or more types. An event handler procedure is of type **XtEventHandler**. It receives four arguments: the widget for which the event arrived; any client data registered with the event handler; a pointer to the event; and a Boolean return argument telling the Xt dispatch facility whether or not to call the remaining event handlers registered for this event. This argument is initialized to True and should rarely be changed.

An application usually registers an event handler using the function **XtAddEventHandler**. The arguments are the widget, an event mask, an indication whether or not the hander should be called for nonmaskable events, the procedure itself, and any client data to be passed to the event handler when it is called. The order in which event handlers are called is undefined when more than one handler exists for a given widget and event type. However, if the application registers the event handler using **XtInsertEventHandler**, it can specify that the procedure is to be called either before or after all currently registered event handlers.

Motif requires an application to provide an event handler if it wants to post a PopupMenu on a button press. The call to **XtAddEventHandler** should specify **ButtonPressMask** as the event mask and the popup RowColumn as the client data. The event handler should use **XmMenuPosition** to position the menu at the x and y location of the button press event. It should then manage the RowColumn. If the button press matches the event specified by the RowColumn's **XmNmenuPost** resource, Motif posts the PopupMenu. See Chapter 6 for more information.

Chapter 14

Graphics and Text in a DrawingArea

Most Motif widgets have specific functions. A PushButton activates an action; a ScrollBar moves a scroll with respect to a viewport; a RowColumn contains a menu, a RadioBox or CheckBox, or a collection of widgets laid out in rows and columns. In contrast, DrawingArea does not have a specific function. It is useful for implementing a canvas, a specialized text editor, or other customized portions of an application.

14.1 DrawingArea: A General-Purpose Widget

DrawingArea is a manager with little specific behavior of its own. It provides basic geometry management for widget and gadget children. It also has callback lists that provide the application with low-level event handling. An application can use these features to implement a canvas or a more specialized widget.

By default a DrawingArea attempts to adjust its size to contain all its children just inside its margins. The DrawingArea resource **XmNresizePolicy** determines how the DrawingArea responds to geometry requests from its children.

This resource has three possible values:

XmRESIZE_ANY

> The DrawingArea tries to accept requests that would cause the DrawingArea to grow or shrink to enclose all its children. This is the default.

XmRESIZE_GROW

> If its parent approves, the DrawingArea accepts requests from its children that would cause the DrawingArea to grow. It may accept requests that would cause it to shrink, but it does not reduce its size.

XmRESIZE_NONE

> The DrawingArea has a fixed size determined by its **XmNheight** and **XmNwidth** resources. It rejects geometry requests from its children that would cause the DrawingArea to grow. It may accept requests that would cause it to shrink, but it does not reduce its size.

The DrawingArea resources **XmNmarginHeight** and **XmNmarginWidth** also affect geometry management. When the value of **XmNmarginHeight** is greater than 0, the DrawingArea ensures that the top edges of all children are inside the top margin. When the value of **XmNmarginWidth** is greater than 0, the DrawingArea ensures that the left edges of all children are inside the left margin.

See Chapter 10 for more information on DrawingArea's geometry management.

14.2 Event Handling and Callbacks

DrawingArea has callbacks, translations, and actions that inform the application when the DrawingArea is resized or when it receives an exposure event or one of many input events. DrawingArea has the following callbacks:

XmNexposeCallback

> DrawingArea invokes these callbacks whenever its **expose** widget class procedure is called. The callback reason is **XmCR_EXPOSE**.

XmNinputCallback

> DrawingArea invokes these callbacks from the **DrawingAreaInput()** action. With the default translations, this action is called when the DrawingArea receives a key press, key release, button press, or button release event. The callback reason is **XmCR_INPUT**.

XmNresizeCallback

> DrawingArea invokes these callbacks whenever its **resize** widget class procedure is called. The callback reason is **XmCR_RESIZE**.

Each callback procedure is passed a pointer to an **XmDrawingAreaCallbackStruct**, which includes the reason, the event (NULL for **XmNresizeCallback**), and the DrawingArea's window.

14.2.1 Handling Resize Events

A widget's **resize** procedure is invoked when the widget is resized by its parent or when the widget's width or height changes as a result of **XtSetValues**. DrawingArea also invokes its own **resize** procedure when it has made a successful geometry request of its parent to change its width or height.

For most widgets, the **resize** procedure recomputes the widget's layout to take account of the new size. DrawingArea's **resize** procedure does no layout of its own. It simply invokes the **XmNresizeCallback** callbacks. It is the responsibility of these callback procedures to resize or reposition children or to recompute other contents of the DrawingArea. The callback procedures essentially take the place of the DrawingArea's **resize** procedure.

Note that a **resize** procedure can be called when the widget is not realized.

14.2.1.1 Moving and Resizing Children

An **XmNresizeCallback** procedure should reposition or resize children by calling **XtMoveWidget**, **XtResizeWidget**, or **XtConfigureWidget**. Use of these functions is usually restricted to widget class methods, but for DrawingArea, the **XmNresizeCallback** procedures act as part of the widget class **resize** procedure.

A callback procedure could also resize or reposition a child by invoking **XtSetValues** on one or more of the child's geometry resources (**XmNx**, **XmNy**, **XmNheight**, **XmNwidth**, and **XmNborderWidth**). This causes **XtSetValues** to generate a geometry request on behalf of the child. This request in turn might cause the DrawingArea to make a geometry request of its own parent. In particular, when a child's request would cause the DrawingArea to change size and when the **XmNresizePolicy** of the DrawingArea is **XmRESIZE_GROW** or **XmRESIZE_ANY**, the DrawingArea is likely to make a geometry request.

However, the Intrinsics forbid a widget's **resize** procedure from making geometry requests. Therefore, an **XmNresizeCallback** procedure must take care not to reposition or resize a child in such a way that the DrawingArea makes a geometry request. The easiest way to avoid this problem is to use **XtMoveWidget**, **XtResizeWidget**, and **XtConfigureWidget**, which are guaranteed not to make geometry requests.

An **XmNresizeCallback** procedure must take care not to call the **resize** procedure for a child that is in the midst of making a geometry request. This situation can arise when a child makes a geometry request, perhaps as a result of **XtSetValues**, that would cause the DrawingArea to change size. If the DrawingArea's **geometry_manager** procedure issues a successful geometry request, it invokes its own **resize** procedure, which in turn calls the **XmNresizeCallback** procedures.

When this situation arises, the **XmNresizeCallback** procedure must not call the requesting child's **resize** procedure, whether it does this directly, as a result of calling **XtResizeWidget** or **XtConfigureWidget**, or as a result of a call to **XtSetValues** that changes the child's width or height. If an application causes a DrawingArea child to make a geometry request—for example, by calling **XtSetValues** for one of the child's geometry resources—it should store information in an internal data structure that identifies that child as making a geometry request. The **XmNresizeCallback** procedure should check this information and take care not to call that child's **resize** procedure.

14.2.1.2 Resizing and Redisplay

A **resize** procedure often recomputes the layout of the widget but does not actually perform the redisplay. In many cases, the act of resizing the widget generates one or more subsequent exposure events, and these in turn cause Xt to invoke the widget's **expose** procedure. In general, the **expose** procedure is responsible for redisplay.

However, resizing a widget does not always generate exposure events, particularly when the widget is made smaller. This is not a problem when the widget's contents consist solely of child widgets or gadgets. The **resize** procedure can reposition or resize the children, and these actions generate the appropriate exposure events for both the children and the parent.

A resizing without an exposure event presents a problem when the contents of the widget include graphics, text, or other decoration outside child widgets. For example, if the widget displays a shadow or other decoration around its inside edge, it must redisplay that decoration when the widget becomes smaller. An application using a DrawingArea in this way must arrange to redisplay the window contents when the DrawingArea becomes smaller. Following are two possible approaches:

- In an **XmNresizeCallback** procedure, compare the DrawingArea's width and height with their previous values. If either width or height has decreased, redisplay the appropriate portions of the DrawingArea's contents. In an internal data structure, store the width and height as the previous width and height for use by the next invocation of the **XmNresizeCallback** procedure.

- In an **XmNexposeCallback** procedure, when the procedure is first invoked, set the window's bit gravity to **ForgetGravity**. This causes the window's contents to be lost and an exposure event to be generated anytime the window is resized. If the application does not set the bit gravity of the DrawingArea's window, the default set by the toolkit is **NorthWestGravity**. This usually causes the server not to generate an exposure event when the window is made smaller.

DrawingArea itself does not draw shadows, and the default **XmNshadowThickness** is 0. It is not practical for an application to draw OSF/Motif shadows itself in a DrawingArea, because the Motif shadow-drawing interface is not public. An application that wants shadows with a DrawingArea should place the DrawingArea inside a Frame.

14.2.1.3 Example of a Resize Procedure

Following is an **XmNresizeCallback** procedure for a DrawingArea that contains button children and lines connecting them. The procedure spreads or contracts the layout of children and lines in proportion to the increase or decrease in size of the DrawingArea. It uses an internal data structure to hold information about the end points of the lines and the previous width and height of the DrawingArea. It assumes that an **XmNexposeCallback** procedure redisplays the lines.

```
void ReSize (
Widget          w,              /*  widget id              */
XtPointer       client_data,    /*  data from application   */
XtPointer       call_data )     /*  data from widget class  */
{
  Graphic * graph = (Graphic *) client_data ;
  Dimension width, height ;
  Cardinal i,j ;
  Arg args[5];
  int n ;
  Widget * children ;
  Cardinal num_children ;
  Position x,y ;
  n = 0;
  XtSetArg (args[n], XmNwidth, &width);   n++;
  XtSetArg (args[n], XmNheight, &height);   n++;
  XtGetValues (w, args, n);
  float xratio = (float) width / graph->old_width,
  yratio = (float) height / graph->old_height ;

  /* reposition and resize the graphic units */
  for (i=0; i < graph->num_graphics; i++) {
    for (j=0; j < graph->graphics[i].num_points; j++) {
      graph->graphics[i].points[j].x *= xratio ;
      graph->graphics[i].points[j].y *= yratio ;
    }
  }

  /* reposition the pushbutton children */
  n = 0;
  XtSetArg (args[n], XmNnumChildren, &num_children);   n++;
```

```
XtSetArg (args[n], XmNchildren, &children);  n++;
XtGetValues (w, args, n);
for (i=0; i < num_children; i++) {
  n = 0;
  XtSetArg (args[n], XmNx, &x);  n++;
  XtSetArg (args[n], XmNy, &y);  n++;
  XtGetValues (children[i], args, n);
  XtMoveWidget (children[i], (Position) (x * xratio),
            (Position) (y * yratio));
}

/* save width and height for next time */
graph->old_width = width ;
graph->old_height = height ;
}
```

14.2.2 Handling Exposure Events

Xt calls a widget's **expose** procedure when the widget receives an exposure event. The precise types of events that cause Xt to invoke the **expose** procedure are determined by the widget class **compress_exposure** field. For **XmDrawingArea**, the value of this field is **XtExposeNoCompress**. This means that Xt invokes the **expose** procedure when the widget receives an **Expose** event.

When the **expose** procedure is called, some part of the contents of the widget's window has been lost, and the window needs to be redisplayed. Xt redisplays the contents of widget children by calling their **expose** procedures. DrawingArea's **expose** procedure calls the **XmNexposeCallback** procedures. These callbacks are responsible for redisplaying any contents of the DrawingArea that are outside the DrawingArea's children. DrawingArea's **expose** procedure then redisplays the contents of gadget children by calling their **expose** procedures.

The X server generates **Expose** events when parts of a window are exposed for a variety of reasons, as when the window is raised or resized. The server determines which portions of the window are exposed and decomposes these into a series of rectangles. The server generates a series of **Expose** events, one for each rectangle.

DrawingArea does not compress exposure events. The **expose** procedure, and therefore the **XmNexposeCallback** list, is called for each rectangle in an exposure series. A simple callback procedure may redisplay the entire window on each exposure series. Such a procedure should examine the **count** member of the **XExposeEvent** structure for the event. A nonzero **count** indicates that more events are to follow in the exposure series. The callback procedure should ignore these events and redisplay the entire window when **count** reaches 0.

A more complex procedure may redisplay only the exposed rectangles. Such a procedure should extract the bounds of each rectangle from the **x**, **y**, **width**, and **height** members of each **XExposeEvent** structure. The procedure can either redisplay each rectangle immediately or accumulate all the rectangles in an exposure series into a region, using **XtAddExposureToRegion**, and then redisplay the region.

An application that draws directly into the DrawingArea must be sure to regenerate the window contents correctly when the DrawingArea becomes smaller. Making the DrawingArea smaller does not always generate **Expose** events. The application can either perform the redisplay in an **XmNresizeCallback** procedure or, on the first invocation of the **XmNexposeCallback** list, set the window's bit gravity to **ForgetGravity**. This ensures that each resizing of the DrawingArea generates an **Expose** event, so the application can safely leave all redisplay to the **XmNexposeCallback** procedure. However, it also means that application must regenerate the entire contents of the window every time the window is resized.

14.2.2.1 Example of an Expose Procedure

Following is an **XmNexposeCallback** procedure for a DrawingArea that contains button children and lines connecting them. The first time the procedure is invoked, it sets the window's bit gravity to **ForgetGravity** so that resizing the window generates **Expose** events. On the last of each series of exposure events, the procedure redraws all lines. It uses an internal data structure to hold information about the end points of the lines.

```
void Redisplay (
Widget          w,              /*  widget id          */
XtPointer       client_data,    /*  data from application  */
XtPointer       call_data )     /*  data from widget class  */
{

  XmDrawingAreaCallbackStruct * dacs =
    (XmDrawingAreaCallbackStruct *) call_data ;
  Graphic * graph = (Graphic *) client_data ;
  XExposeEvent * event = (XExposeEvent *) dacs->event;
  XSetWindowAttributes xswa;

  static Boolean first_time = True ;

  if (first_time) {
    /* Change once the bit gravity of the Drawing Area; default
       is NorthWest and we want Forget, so that resize
       always generates exposure events */
    first_time = False ;
    xswa.bit_gravity = ForgetGravity ;
    XChangeWindowAttributes(XtDisplay(w), XtWindow(w),
                      CWBitGravity, &xswa);
  }

  /* Redisplay only on last event of the series */
  if (! event->count) {
    for (i=0; i < graph->num_graphics; i++) {
      if (graph->graphics[i].type == POLYLINE)
        XDrawLines(XtDisplay(w), XtWindow(w),
                   XDefaultGCOfScreen(XtScreen(w)),
                   graph->graphics[i].points,
                   graph->graphics[i].num_points,
                   CoordModeOrigin);
    }
  }
}
```

14.2.3 Handling Input Events

As with any manager, DrawingArea may have three general kinds of input events within its borders:

- Events that belong to a widget child
- Events that belong to a gadget child
- Events that belong to no child

Xt dispatches events to widget children when appropriate, and the DrawingArea does not process these. DrawingArea inherits Manager's translations for dispatching events to gadget children. Before calling any Manager action as a result of a button press or release or a key press or release, DrawingArea calls its own **DrawingAreaInput()** action. DrawingArea also calls this action whenever it receives a button press or release or a key press or release that does not have an associated Manager action.

The **DrawingAreaInput()** action simply returns if the input event is not of type **KeyPress**, **KeyRelease**, **ButtonPress**, **ButtonRelease**, or **MotionNotify**. If the event is of one of these types, and if the event does not take place within a gadget child of the DrawingArea, the action calls the **XmNinputCallback** callbacks.

With the default translations, the result is that the **XmNinputCallback** procedures are invoked whenever the DrawingArea receives a **KeyPress**, **KeyRelease**, **ButtonPress**, or **ButtonRelease** event that does not occur within a child.

The default translations do not invoke the **DrawingAreaInput()** action, and therefore the **XmNinputCallback** procedures, when the DrawingArea receives a **MotionNotify** event. An application that wants its **XmNinputCallback** procedures invoked on pointer motion events must install the appropriate translations. When installing a translation for **BtnMotion**, the application must override the existing translations. The following translations cause a motion event to be sent to any gadget child in which it takes place. If the event does not take place within a child, the **XmNinputCallback** procedures are invoked:

```
<BtnMotion>:DrawingAreaInput() ManagerGadgetButtonMotion()\n\
<Motion>:DrawingAreaInput()
```

There is one problem with these translations: because DrawingArea has translations for **BSelect** click and double click, the **BtnMotion** actions are not invoked when the user moves the pointer while pressing **BSelect**. In order to receive these events, the application must replace the DrawingArea translations, omitting the translations for **BSelect** click and double click.

14.2.3.1 Example of an Input Procedure

Following is an **XmNinputCallback** procedure for a DrawingArea that contains button children and lines connecting them. The procedure takes action on **ButtonPress** and **MotionNotify** events. When the user presses a mouse button, the procedure retrieves the text from a TextField elsewhere in the application. If the user has entered text here, the input procedure creates a PushButton with the text as the label and places it at the point of the click. If the TextField contains no text and the user has pressed a button over a line or PushButton while holding the Shift key, the procedure deletes the line or PushButton.

If the TextField is empty and the user presses a button without holding the Shift key, the procedure either starts or finishes drawing a line. The application uses a rubber-banding effect for line drawing. When it starts a line the procedure sets a flag indicating it is drawing a line; when it finishes the line, the procedure clears this flag. When the procedure receives a MotionNotify event and is in the process of drawing a line, it erases the previous line (using XOR) and draws a new line from the anchor point to the current pointer position.

```
void HandleInput (
Widget          w,              /*  widget id            */
XtPointer       client_data,    /*  data from application  */
XtPointer       call_data )     /*  data from widget class  */
{

  XmDrawingAreaCallbackStruct * dacs =
    (XmDrawingAreaCallbackStruct *) call_data ;
  Graphic * graph = (Graphic *) client_data ;
  Arg args[5];
  int   n ;
  String name ;
  Widget newpush ;
```

```
if (dacs->event->type == ButtonPress) {
  name = XmTextFieldGetString(graph->textf); /* textfield */
  if (strcmp ("", name) != 0) {
    n = 0;
    XtSetArg (args[n], XmNx, dacs->event->xbutton.x);   n++;
    XtSetArg (args[n], XmNy, dacs->event->xbutton.y);   n++;
    newpush = XmCreatePushButton(w, name, args, n);
    XtAddCallback (newpush, XmNactivateCallback, PushCB,
                      NULL);
    XtManageChild (newpush);
  } else
    if ((dacs->event->xbutton.state & ShiftMask) &&
        (!graph->in_drag)) {
      DeleteUnit (graph, dacs->event->xbutton.x,
                    dacs->event->xbutton.y);
    } else {
      if (!graph->in_drag) {
        StartUnit(graph, dacs->event->xbutton.x,
                    dacs->event->xbutton.y);
      } else {
        EndUnit(graph, dacs->event->xbutton.x,
                    dacs->event->xbutton.y);
      }
    }
  XtFree(name);
} else  /* need to get motion events here: app_default
            should modify DrawingArea translation with
            both Motion and BtnMotion additions */
  if (dacs->event->type == MotionNotify) {
    /* this one just exits if in_drag is False */
    DragUnit(graph, dacs->event->xbutton.x,
                dacs->event->xbutton.y);
  }
}
```

14.3 Using a DrawingArea in a ScrolledWindow

The ScrolledWindow widget provides a viewport onto a virtual scroll and allows the user to move the scroll with respect to the viewport by manipulating ScrollBars. ScrolledWindow offers two scrolling policies: automatic and application-defined. In automatic scrolling, the application provides the scroll widget; ScrolledWindow creates a fixed-size viewport and handles user interaction with the ScrollBars. In application-defined scrolling, the application provides the scroll widget and, if necessary, the viewport, and it handles all user interaction with the ScrollBars.

When using separate viewport and scroll widgets with either scrolling policy, an application can use a default DrawingArea as the scroll widget. When the **XmNresizePolicy** is **XmRESIZE_ANY**, the application can use **XtSetValues** of **XmNx** and **XmNy** to place children within the DrawingArea. The DrawingArea adjusts its size as necessary to enclose all the children. The application can also use **XtSetValues** of the DrawingArea's **XmNwidth** and **XmNheight** to change the size of the scroll widget.

An application can also use a DrawingArea as the viewport widget in application-defined scrolling. One approach is not to use a separate scroll widget but to maintain a virtual scroll, keeping the contents in internal data structures and displaying as much of the contents as will fit into the viewport. The application can use a default DrawingArea as the viewport widget.

Another approach to application-defined scrolling is to create one widget as a viewport and another, a child of the viewport, as the scroll. The application can expand the scroll widget as necessary to contain all the data. In response to user manipulation of the ScrollBars, the application can reposition the scroll widget with respect to the viewport. The viewport acts as a clipping region for its child, the scroll.

In this approach the application can use a DrawingArea as the viewport, the scroll widget, or both. When using a DrawingArea as the viewport, the application must position and resize the scroll child using **XtMoveWidget**, **XtResizeWidget**, or **XtConfigureWidget**. Using **XtSetValues** for the child's geometry resources does not work, because the parent's geometry manager does not permit the child to move or grow beyond the bounds of the parent.

When a DrawingArea is the viewport widget in a ScrolledWindow with application-defined scrolling, the **XmNresizeCallback** procedure must recompute the ScrollBars' **XmNsliderSize** and **XmNpageIncrement** and possibly other resources to reflect the new relation between the viewport and the scroll. It may also need to reposition and resize the scroll with respect to the viewport.

See Chapter 9 for more information on ScrolledWindow, including examples using DrawingAreas as scrolls in both automatic and application-defined scrolling.

14.4 Using a DrawingArea for Graphics

DrawingArea is an appropriate widget to use as a canvas or as a manager that requires graphics operations in addition to children. An application can use Xlib graphics facilities to draw into a DrawingArea. See *Xlib—C Language X Interface* for more information on Xlib graphics operations.

An interactive graphics application can use the **XmNinputCallback** procedure to respond to user input. For example, when the user presses a mouse button, drags, and then releases the button, this procedure might draw a line from the point of the button press to the point of the button release. The **XmNinputCallback** procedures are invoked on button press and release events and on key press and release events. To receive pointer motion events, the application can provide translations that invoke the **DrawingAreaInput**() action.

An application that needs to produce graphics but does not require children or interaction with the user in the canvas might use a DrawnButton instead of a DrawingArea. DrawnButton has no input callbacks, but it does provide exposure and resize callbacks.

Following is some of the drawing code from the earlier example (in Section 14.2.3.1) of a DrawingArea containing button children and lines connecting them. This example implements the rubber-band effect in which a line starts at an anchor point and follows the pointer as the user moves it.

The example maintains an internal data structure with information about the DrawingArea and its graphic objects. The application initially stores a GC for use in drawing and erasing the rubber-band lines. This GC uses a foreground color that results from combining the DrawingArea's foreground and background using XOR. The GC also uses the **GXxor** function.

The remainder of the example code updates the internal data structures and draws lines as appropriate when the user starts a line, moves the pointer, and ends a line.

```
/* Initialize data structures */
void InitDraw (
Graphic          * graph,
ApplicationData  * app_data )
{
  XGCValues val ;
  Arg args[5];
  int   n ;
  Cardinal i ;

  /* create the gc used for the rubber banding effect */
  n = 0;
  XtSetArg (args[n], XmNforeground, &val.foreground);  n++;
  XtSetArg (args[n], XmNbackground, &val.background);  n++;
  XtGetValues (graph->work_area, args, n);

  val.foreground = val.foreground ^ val.background ;
  val.function = GXxor ;
  graph->drag_gc =
      XtGetGC(graph->work_area,
            GCForeground | GCBackground | GCFunction, &val);

  graph->in_drag = False ;

  graph->num_graphics = 0 ;
  for (i=0; i < MAX_GRAPH; i++) {
    graph->graphics[i].num_points = 0 ;
  }
}

/* Start a line */
void StartUnit (
Graphic          * graph,
Position          x,
Position          y )
{
```

```
    Widget w = graph->work_area ;

    graph->drag_point.x = graph->anchor_point.x = x ;
    graph->drag_point.y = graph->anchor_point.y = y ;
    graph->in_drag = True ;
    XDrawLine(XtDisplay(w), XtWindow(w),
            graph->drag_gc,
            graph->anchor_point.x, graph->anchor_point.y,
            graph->drag_point.x, graph->drag_point.y);
}

/* Pointer moved: if drawing a line, erase the last line
 * and draw a new line from the anchor to the pointer
 * position */
void DragUnit (
Graphic             * graph,
Position              x,
Position              y )
{
  Widget w = graph->work_area ;

  if (!graph->in_drag) return ;

  XDrawLine(XtDisplay(w), XtWindow(w),
          graph->drag_gc,
          graph->anchor_point.x, graph->anchor_point.y,
          graph->drag_point.x, graph->drag_point.y);

  graph->drag_point.x = x ;
  graph->drag_point.y = y ;

  XDrawLine(XtDisplay(w), XtWindow(w),
          graph->drag_gc,
          graph->anchor_point.x, graph->anchor_point.y,
          graph->drag_point.x, graph->drag_point.y);
}

/* Utility routine */
static Boolean NearPoint (
XPoint                point,
Position              x,
```

```
Position          y )
{
#define ERROR 5
  if ((point.x > x - ERROR) &&
      (point.x < x + ERROR) &&
      (point.y > y - ERROR) &&
      (point.y < y + ERROR)) return True ;
  else return False ;
}

/* End a line */
void EndUnit (
Graphic           * graph,
Position          x,
Position          y )
{
  Widget w = graph->work_area ;
  Cardinal num_points ;

  /* no matter what happens, we need to remove the current
   * rubber band */
  XDrawLine(XtDisplay(w), XtWindow(w),
          graph->drag_gc,
          graph->anchor_point.x, graph->anchor_point.y,
          graph->drag_point.x, graph->drag_point.y);

  /* if the given point if the same as the anchor, we're
     done with this polyline, exit drag mode and be ready
     for the next graphic unit (increment num_graphics) */

  if (NearPoint(graph->anchor_point, x, y)) {
    graph->in_drag = False ;
    /* now see if a new unit needs to be created */
    if (graph->graphics[graph->num_graphics].num_points) {
      graph->graphics[graph->num_graphics].type = POLYLINE ;
      if (graph->num_graphics < MAX_GRAPH)
        graph->num_graphics ++ ;
      else BufferFullError() ;
    }
  } else {
```

```
/* draw the real line and store it in the structure */
XDrawLine(XtDisplay(w), XtWindow(w),
        XDefaultGCOfScreen(XtScreen(w)),
        graph->anchor_point.x, graph->anchor_point.y,
        x, y);

/* first point in a unit is actually special */
num_points =
    graph->graphics[graph->num_graphics].num_points ;
if (num_points == 0) {
  graph->graphics[graph->num_graphics].points[num_points].x =
    graph->anchor_point.x ;
  graph->graphics[graph->num_graphics].points[num_points].y =
    graph->anchor_point.y ;
  graph->graphics[graph->num_graphics].num_points ++ ;
  num_points ++ ;
}
graph->graphics[graph->num_graphics].points[num_points].x = x;
graph->graphics[graph->num_graphics].points[num_points].y = y;
if (graph->graphics[graph->num_graphics].num_points
    < MAX_POINT)
  graph->graphics[graph->num_graphics].num_points ++ ;
else BufferFullError() ;

/* now start the new unit */
graph->drag_point.x = graph->anchor_point.x = x ;
graph->drag_point.y = graph->anchor_point.y = y ;
XDrawLine(XtDisplay(w), XtWindow(w),
        graph->drag_gc,
        graph->anchor_point.x, graph->anchor_point.y,
        graph->drag_point.x, graph->drag_point.y);
  }
}
```

14.5 DrawingArea and Advanced Text Editing

Some applications may need text-editing capabilities beyond those provided by the Motif Text widget. For example, the application may want to display text using different fonts or colors within the same editor. Such an application might use a DrawingArea to implement a text editor based on compound strings.

14.5.1 Text Output

An application that uses compound strings can use **XmStringDraw** or **XmStringDrawImage** to display the compound string text in a DrawingArea. These functions use different Xlib routines to display compound string segments, depending on whether the segments are associated with font sets or font structs in the font list. **XmStringDraw** uses **XmbDrawString** to display segments associated with font sets. It uses **XDrawString** or **XDrawString16** to display segments associated with font structs. **XmStringDrawImage** uses **XmbDrawImageString** to display segments associated with font sets. It uses **XDrawImageString** or **XDrawImageString16** to display segments associated with font structs.

An application that does not use compound strings may call the Xlib text-drawing routines directly. In addition to those mentioned previously, these include **XDrawText** for text associated with a font and **XmbDrawText** for text associated with a font set. Wide-character versions exist for all the **Xmb** routines.

An application that draws text must determine where to place the text, what the width and height of the text will be, and how to move to the origin of the next text it will draw. For compound strings, an application can use **XmStringExtent**, **XmStringHeight**, **XmStringWidth**, and **XmStringBaseline** to determine the extents of the text.

An application that does not use compound strings may call Xlib routines. To determine the extents of a font struct, the application can examine the **ascent**, **descent**, **max_bounds**, and **min_bounds** members of the **XFontStruct**. To determine the width and extents of text, the application can call **XStringWidth**, **XTextExtents**, and **XTextExtents16**.

To determine the extents of a font set, the application can call **XExtentsOfFontSet**. To determine the width and extents of text, the application can call **XmbTextEscapement**, **XmbTextExtents**, and **XmbTextPerCharExtents**. Wide-character versions exist for all the **Xmb** routines.

For more information about the Xlib text facilities, see *Xlib—C Language X Interface*.

14.5.2 Text Input

To obtain text input in a DrawingArea, an application should use the Xlib input method facilities. These facilities allow the application to open an input method and an input context and to obtain input from the input method. For more information, see Chapter 11 and *Xlib—C Language X Interface*.

Chapter 15

Drag and Drop

Drag and drop allows the user to "pick up" objects on the screen, "drag" them around the display, and "drop" them at a new location, possibly in another application.

With drag and drop the user can

- Move text or other information between windows.

- Cause application-specific actions to occur.

- Obtain help information about drop sites.

This chapter first provides an overview of the drag and drop process and concepts from both the user's and the application developer's perspectives, then explains the actions of both initiator and receiver clients during the drag and at the drop, giving code samples.

15.1 User Overview of Drag and Drop

This section describes what the user does and sees during a drag and drop transaction.

15.1.1 Overview of User Interaction

A drag and drop transaction consists of the following actions:

1. A user presses and holds **BTransfer**, usually mouse button 2, over a source object starting a drag transaction. The application owning that object is the initiator of the drag. The current pointer is replaced by a drag icon—a picture representing the item being dragged.

2. The user moves the pointer. From now until a drop occurs, the drag icon replaces the mouse pointer.

3. The user drops the object, usually by releasing the mouse button.

    Locations on the screen that can accept drops are drop sites, and the application owning that drop site is the destination or receiver.

    The drag icon can be dropped anywhere on the screen. However, only certain widgets have registered themselves as drop sites and are able to process the drop.

    The receiver application usually performs some action on the information represented by the dragged icon. The initiator application may also perform some action based on the results of a drag transaction.

A drop can be between applications or within the same application. An application can be both source and destination of a drop, source only, destination only, or not participate in drag and drop at all.

The user can request help about a drop site, if available, by dragging to the drop site, and pressing **KHelp** (usually **F1**).

The user can cancel the drag at any time by pressing **KCancel**, usually **Escape**.

15.1.2 Overview of Drag-Over Effects

The drag icon consists of three parts:

- The source icon is a picture representing the type of the source object, such as text.

- The state icon can be used to show whether or not the object being dragged can be dropped at its current location on the screen.

- The operation icon can be used to show what action should happen when the drop takes place.

In the following illustration, the running figure is the source icon, the arrow in the upper left is the state icon, and the rectangles with the corner folded over indicate a Copy is desired.

Figure 15–1. A Drag Icon

These parts can be combined (blended) and attached to each other in different ways. The default blending and attachment are shown in the previous illustration.

Parts of the drag icon may change shape or color as it is being dragged through potential drop sites, providing visual feedback about possible drop sites to the user. These changes are drag-over effects.

Applications can use the default drag icon effects, or provide more sophisticated or custom drag icons. The application or user can customize these drag-over effects in resource files.

15.1.2.1 Drag States

During a drag, there are three states that describe the relationship of a drag icon to what is under it at the time:

Valid drop site

        The drag icon is over a drop site on which it can potentially be dropped (this is only a hint; when the drop is actually attempted, further processing may show that the drop cannot actually be done).

Invalid drop site
> The drag icon is over a drop site, but it cannot be dropped there.

No drop site
> The drag icon is not over a registered drop site.

The default state icon for all three states is the same: an arrow in the upper left corner of the drag icon. Because the icon is the same for all three states, it appears not to change during the drag. The application or the user can provide custom state icons or colors in a resource file.

15.1.2.2 Drag Operations

The user specifies what action is to take place when the drop occurs by pressing certain keys when the drag starts or while the drag is in process:

Shift only   Force a move from the initiator to the receiver client (Move)

Ctrl only   Force a copy from the initiator to the receiver client (Copy)

Shift and Ctrl
> Force a link between the initiator and receiver clients (Link)

The operation chosen by the user must be valid for both the drag source and the drop site, or the drop site will be considered invalid.

If the user does not specify an operation, one is chosen by the toolkit. It choses an operation that is valid for both the drag source and drop site. Move is the first choice, Copy is the second, and Link is the third. If the system cannot find a valid operation, the drop site is considered invalid.

The operation icon reflects the operation chosen by the user or by the system. If the operation is changed by the user during the drag, the operation icon changes also.

The operation icon may change as the drag icon moves to different drop sites if the drop sites accept different operations.

15.1.3 Overview of Drag-Under Effects

A widget registered as a drop site may change visually as a drag icon passes over it. These visual cues are drag-under effects. The sensitive area of the widget is the part that responds to drag and drop. By default it is the whole widget, but applications can specify that only parts of the widget respond to drag and drop.

Various highlighting styles are possible:

- A border around the sensitive area of the drop site widget. This is the default value.

- The sensitive area of the drop site widget looks pushed out.

- The sensitive area of the drop site widget looks pushed in.

- A special pixmap is displayed within the sensitive area of the drop site widget, overwriting what is normally there.

- No drag-under effects are used for the drop site widget.

Applications can use the default drag-under visual effects, or create more sophisticated or custom effects, such as special animation or sound effects.

15.1.4 Overview of Drop Effects

Visual effects also take place during the drop:

- The drag icon appears to sit over the drop site while the processing for the drop is finishing, but the standard cursor is restored and can be used normally.

- The source icon appears to melt into the drop site if the drop is successful.

- The source icon appears to snap back to the source if the drop is unsuccessful.

- A dialog window containing information about a drop site should appear if the user has requested help and the receiver client provides help, otherwise nothing happens.

- The source icon appears to snap back to the source and the previous X cursor returns if Cancel is requested. All drag-under and drag-over effects are removed.

These drop effects cannot be changed by the application or the user.

15.2 Technical Overview of Drag and Drop

This section explains some drag and drop concepts, and provides a general view of the initiator and receiver duties during the drag and at the drop.

The Motif toolkit for drag and drop consists of

- Widgets and widget classes that provide resources containing details about the source and destination of the drag

- Functions that applications use to manage the widgets and widget classes

- Protocols that specify how interactions between source and destination clients are to take place

- Functions that manage messages, call callbacks, decide on the valid operations for a potential drop, and keep the drop site status updated

If the initiator and receiver are in the same client, they share the same toolkit. If the initiator and receiver are different clients, each client has a version of the toolkit.

An application can allow any widget to be a drag source or initiator by specifying a translation for **BTransfer Press** in that widget. The corresponding action creates a DragContext which starts the drag and drop transaction. The toolkit on the initiator side in charge during the drag and manages all drag messages and callbacks.

An application can register any widget as a drop site. The drop site widget may change visually as a drag icon moves in and out of it, providing drag-under visual clues to the status of the drag. The application controlling the current drop site is known as the receiver. The toolkit on the receiver side is in charge of the drop operation, and manages all drop messages and callbacks.

Each drag source and drop site specifies the types of data it is prepared to handle and what operations it can perform on that data.

The state of the drag indicates whether the drag icon is over a valid drop site, an invalid drop site, or no drop site. For a drop site to be valid, there must be at least one target type and one operation in common between the drag source and drop site.

15.2.1 Complexity of Drag and Drop Programs

Applications can use drag and drop functionality on any of several levels:

- Text, List, Label, and Button widgets are already defined as drag sources. Text and TextField widgets are registered as drop sites. Therefore, at the simplest, an application can compile with the Motif libraries, and have those widgets participate in drag and drop. For example, text could be selected from one application and moved into a text area in another application.

- On a slightly more advanced level, applications can let the toolkit do most of the work, but provide some customization. For example, an application could register a pushbutton as a drop site, but still use default visual effects. In this case, the application would register a widget as a DropSite and provide code to handle drop and transfer duties. The example programs **DNDlabel.c** in Section 15.2.1.1 and **DNDscroll.c** in Section 15.2.1.2 are at this level.

- A complex application can take much of the control of the drag and drop itself. It can provide custom visuals for both drag icon and drop site. It can manage overlapping drop sites and can include complex transfers of information. The example program **DNDdemo** in Appendix B contains extensive customization.

15.2.1.1 A Simple Drag Receiver

This sample program displays a Label widget and registers it as a drop site. It accepts compound text, and supports only the Copy operation (that is, it does not support Move or Link).

When a valid drop is made on the Label widget, its HandleDrop routine changes the Label widget's label to compound text passed from the initiator.

The appropriate include files, the **DropTransferCallback** routine, the **HandleDrop** routine, and a few lines in the main routine to register the drop site are all that is needed to customize a Label widget to accept a drop and change its label in response. The details of this additional code are covered in later sections of this chapter.

Figure 15–2. A Label Widget Receiver Before and After Drag

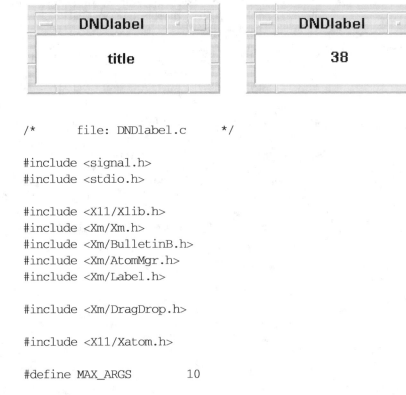

```
/*      file: DNDlabel.c      */

#include <signal.h>
#include <stdio.h>

#include <X11/Xlib.h>
#include <Xm/Xm.h>
#include <Xm/BulletinB.h>
#include <Xm/AtomMgr.h>
#include <Xm/Label.h>

#include <Xm/DragDrop.h>

#include <X11/Xatom.h>

#define MAX_ARGS        10
```

```
/* global variables */
Widget    myDC;
Atom      COMPOUND_TEXT;

/* This routine transfers information from the initiator */
static void TransferProc(w, closure, seltype, type, value,
                              length, format)
Widget            w;
XtPointer         closure;
Atom              *seltype;
Atom              *type;
XtPointer         value;
unsigned long     *length;
int               format;
{
    int           n;
    Arg           args[MAX_ARGS];

    /* information from the drag initiator is passed in
     * compound compound text format.  Convert it to compound
     * string and replace the  Label label. */

    if (*type = COMPOUND_TEXT) {
       n = 0;
       XtSetArg(args[n], XmNlabelString,
               XmCvtCTToXmString(value));
       n++;
       XtSetValues(closure, args, n);
       }
}

/* This routine is performed when a drop is made.  It decides
what information it wants and uses TransferProc to transfer
the data from the initiator */

static void HandleDrop(w, client_data, call_data)
Widget            w;
XtPointer         client_data, call_data;
{

   XmDropProcCallback        DropData;
```

```
XmDropTransferEntryRec   transferEntries[2];
XmDropTransferEntry      transferList;
Arg                      args[MAX_ARGS];
int                      n;

DropData = (XmDropProcCallback)call_data;

/* set the transfer resources */
n = 0;

/* if the action is not Drop or the operation is not Copy,
 * cancel the drop */
if ((DropData->dropAction != XmDROP) ||
    (DropData->operation != XmDROP_COPY))
   XtSetArg(args[n], XmNtransferStatus, XmTRANSFER_FAILURE);
     n++;
else {
    /* the drop can continue.  Establish the transfer list
     * and start the transfer */
    transferEntries[0].target = COMPOUND_TEXT;
    transferEntries[0].client_data = (XtPointer)w;
    transferList = transferEntries;
    XtSetArg(args[n], XmNdropTransfers, transferList); n++;
    XtSetArg(args[n], XmNnumDropTransfers, 1); n++;
    XtSetArg(args[n], XmNtransferProc, TransferProc); n++;
    }

/* start the transfer or cancel */
XmDropTransferStart(DropData->dragContext, args, n);
}

/* This program creates a Label widget, which is
 * registered as a drop site.  The label changes when compound
 * text is dropped on it.  */

void main (argc, argv)
unsigned int argc;
char **argv;
{

    Arg                      args[MAX_ARGS];
```

```
    int                     n;
    Widget                  topLevel, BulletinB, Label;
    XtAppContext            app_context;
    Atom                    importList[1];

    /* make supporting widget structure for the Label widget */
    topLevel = XtAppInitialize(&app_context, "XMTest", NULL, 0,
                        &argc, argv, NULL, NULL, 0);

    n = 0;
    BulletinB = XmCreateBulletinBoard(topLevel, "BulletinB",
                                args, n);
    XtManageChild(BulletinB);

    COMPOUND_TEXT = XmInternAtom(XtDisplay(topLevel),
                            "COMPOUND_TEXT", False);

    /* create a Label widget */
    n = 0;
    Label = XmCreateLabel(BulletinB, "title", args, n);
    XtManageChild(Label);

    /* register the label as a drop site */
    importList[0] = COMPOUND_TEXT;
    n = 0;
    XtSetArg(args[n], XmNimportTargets, importList); n++;
    XtSetArg(args[n], XmNnumImportTargets, 1); n++;
    XtSetArg(args[n], XmNdropSiteOperations, XmDROP_COPY); n++;
    XtSetArg(args[n], XmNdropProc, HandleDrop); n++;
    XmDropSiteRegister(Label, args, n);

    XtRealizeWidget(topLevel);
    XtAppMainLoop(app_context);
}
```

15.2.1.2 A Simple Drag Source

This program creates a ScrollBar widget which is to be used as a drag source. The normal action for Button 2 Press has been overridden to cause it to call the **StartDrag** routine, which causes the drag to begin. The program allows only the Copy operation, and will reply to requests for compound text.

When a drag is started on the ScrollBar, the default drag icons are used.

When a transfer request is received by the **DragConvertProc** routine, it returns the value of the scrollbar slider converted into compound text.

The code necessary to make a normal ScrollBar widget into a source for drag and drop is the appropriate include files, the **DragConvertProc** routine, the StartDrag routine, and translation and action commands. The details of this additional code are covered in later sections of this chapter.

Figure 15–3. A ScrollBar Widget as Drag Source

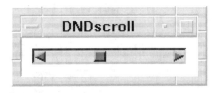

```
/*       file: DNDscroll.c        */

#include <signal.h>
#include <stdio.h>

#include <X11/Xlib.h>
#include <Xm/Xm.h>
#include <Xm/BulletinB.h>
#include <Xm/ScrollBar.h>
#include <Xm/AtomMgr.h>

#include <Xm/DragDrop.h>

#include <X11/Xatom.h>
```

```
#define MAX_ARGS          10

/* global variables */
Widget                   scrollbar;
Atom                     COMPOUND_TEXT;

/* this routine returns the value of the scrollbar slider,
 * converted into compound text. */

static
Boolean DragConvertProc(w, selection, target, typeRtn,
                        valueRtn, lengthRtn, formatRtn,
                        max_lengthRtn, client_data,
                        request_id)
Widget              w;
Atom                *selection;
Atom                *target;
Atom                *typeRtn;
XtPointer           *valueRtn;
unsigned long       *lengthRtn;
int                 *formatRtn;
unsigned long       *max_lengthRtn;
XtPointer           client_data;
XtRequestId         *request_id;
{
    Widget      dc;
    XmString    cstring;
    static char tmpstring[100];
    int         *value;
    int         n;
    Arg         args[MAX_ARGS];
    char            *ctext;
    char        *passtext;

    /* this routine processes only compound text */
    if (*target != COMPOUND_TEXT)
       return(False);

    /* get the value of the scrollbar slider */
    n = 0;
```

```
      XtSetArg(args[n], XmNvalue, &value); n++;
      XtGetValues(scrollbar, args, n);

      /* convert the slider value to compound text */
      sprintf(tmpstring, "%d", value);
      cstring = XmStringCreateLocalized(tmpstring);
      ctext = XmCvtXmStringToCT(cstring);

      passtext = XtMalloc(strlen(ctext)+1);
      memcpy(passtext, ctext, strlen(ctext)+1);

      /* format the value for transfer.  convert the value from
       * compound string to compound text for the transfer */
      *typeRtn = COMPOUND_TEXT;
      *valueRtn = (XtPointer) passtext;
      *lengthRtn = strlen(passtext);
      *formatRtn = 8;
      return(True);
}

/* This routine is performed by the initiator when a drag
 * starts  (in this case, when mouse button 2 was pressed).
 * It starts  the drag processing, and establishes a drag
 * context. */

static void StartDrag(w, event)
Widget  w;
XEvent  *event;
{
    Arg             args[MAX_ARGS];
    Cardinal        n;
    Atom            exportList[1];

    /* establish the list of valid target types */
    exportList[0] = COMPOUND_TEXT;

    n = 0;
    XtSetArg(args[n], XmNexportTargets, exportList); n++;
    XtSetArg(args[n], XmNnumExportTargets, 1); n++;
    XtSetArg(args[n], XmNdragOperations, XmDROP_COPY); n++;
    XtSetArg(args[n], XmNconvertProc, DragConvertProc); n++;
```

```
    XmDragStart(w, event, args, n);
}


/* translations and actions.  Pressing mouse button 2
 * overrides  the normal scrollbar action and calls StartDrag
 * to start a drag transaction */

static char dragTranslations[] =
    "#override <Btn2Down>: StartDrag()";
static XtActionsRec dragActions[] =
    { {"StartDrag", (XtActionProc)StartDrag} };

/* This routine creates a window with a scrollbar in it. */

void main (argc, argv)
unsigned int argc;
char **argv;
{

    Arg                     args[MAX_ARGS];
    int                     n;
    Widget                  topLevel, BulletinB;
    XtAppContext            app_context;
    Atom                    importList[1];
    XtTranslations          parsed_xlations;

    /* create widget structure for scrollbar widget */
    topLevel = XtAppInitialize(&app_context, "DNDscroll", NULL,
                        0, &argc, argv, NULL, NULL, 0);

    COMPOUND_TEXT = XmInternAtom(XtDisplay(topLevel),
                        "COMPOUND_TEXT", False);

    n = 0;
    BulletinB = XmCreateBulletinBoard(topLevel, "BBoard",
                                args, n);
    XtManageChild(BulletinB);

    /* override button two press to start a drag */
    parsed_xlations = XtParseTranslationTable(dragTranslations);
```

```
XtAppAddActions(app_context, dragActions,
                XtNumber(dragActions));

/* create a scroll bar widget */
n = 0;
XtSetArg(args[n], XmNtranslations, parsed_xlations); n++;
XtSetArg(args[n], XmNorientation, XmHORIZONTAL); n++;
XtSetArg(args[n], XmNwidth, 150); n++;
scrollbar = XmCreateScrollBar(BulletinB, "testscroll",
                             args, n);
XtManageChild(scrollbar);

XtRealizeWidget(topLevel);
XtAppMainLoop(app_context);
}
```

15.2.2 Drag Sources and Drop Sites

Text, List, Label, and Button widgets are automatically drag sources. Applications need do nothing further to use them. An application can allow any widget to be a drag source by establishing a callback when **BTransfer** is pressed within that widget. The application that owns the widget in which the drop was started is the initiator.

A drag icon, which is a pictorial representation of the data being dragged, replaces the normal cursor while the drag is in effect. The icon may change as it moves around the screen. The actual data is not being dragged, only a representation of it. The data is transferred to a new location only when the drop is made, through the drop transfer protocol.

Any widget can be registered as a drop site. Text and TextField widgets are automatically registered as drop sites. If an application wants to use these as drop sites, it does not need to register them separately.

The DropSite registry contains information about widgets that have been registered as drop sites. Although the drag icon can be dropped anywhere on the screen, only widgets that have been registered as drop sites can accept information from the initiator. The receiver is the application controlling the current drop site.

The "sensitive area" is the part of the widget that responds to drag and drop. By default, the sensitive area is the whole widget. However, the application can specify that only part of the widget is sensitive.

Widgets that are drop sites can be stacked on each other, with one widget partially or completely within the boundary of another. The sensitive areas of lower drop sites are clipped if they are covered by a higher widget.

The stacking order of the widgets with drop sites can be changed by the application.

15.2.3 Protocols

The protocol describes how the initiator and receiver clients interact through the toolkit with each other.

15.2.3.1 Drag Protocols

There are two types of drag protocol:

Preregister   Does not require messaging

Dynamic   Requires messaging

Applications can support either, both, or neither. If possible, clients should support both to allow the most flexibility for users. The Motif toolkit automatically supports both unless a user or client sets resources to force the use of one or the other.

The user can specify which drag protocol to use when the client is the initiator or receiver. The application can specify drag protocol in an application-class defaults file. If neither the application nor the user specifies a protocol, the preregister drag protocol is used.

The toolkit uses the requested protocols and the protocols allowed by the initiator and receiver clients to arrive at the protocol actually being used. Therefore, the protocol can change as the drag icon moves from window to window, depending on which protocols each window supports. If the initiator and receiver cannot agree on a protocol, no drag-over or drag-under visual effects are shown.

Even if no drag-over or drag-under visual effects are shown, a drop can still occur with the drop protocol, unless a client has specified that that window does not participate in drag and drop.

15.2.3.2 Drop Protocol

The drop protocol is based on the Xt Selection transfer protocol. The transfer between either client and the toolkit can be incremental or nonincremental, regardless of how the other client is transferring. Each client has a procedure to process transfers: **XmNconvertProc** for the initiator, and **XmNtransferProc** for the receiver. Incremental transfer is indicated by a resource value.

The receiver creates a list of information and target types desired from the initiator, along with an **XmNtransferProc** to handle any processing needed during the transfer. It then calls **XmDropTransferStart** to start the transfer process. Even if there is no transfer, the receiver should call this routine, so that the status can be updated correctly for the initiator.

For each item in the transfer list, the initiator's **XmNconvertProc** is called. This procedure reads and processes the request and returns the information.

When the transfer has finished, the toolkit on the receiver side updates the **XmNtransferStatus** DropTransfer resource to indicate if the transfer was successful. The receiver's **XmNtransferProc** routine can also update this resource.

15.2.4 Drag and Drop Widget Classes

Motif provides a number of Xt objects and widgets to encapsulate the underlying protocol; however, these are not mapped onto the screen:

XmDisplay

> An object that contains display-specific information, such as the initiator and receiver protocol styles.

XmScreen

> An object that describes screen-specific information, such as font and default drag-over icons.

XmDragIcon

A widget that describes the pixmap, mask, and attachment of an icon. The source icon, state icon, operation icon, and the resulting blended drag icon are all Drag Icons.

XmDragContext

A widget that describes the resources specified by each drag initiator, such as target type, custom icons, custom colors, blending model, permitted operations, and callback routines for various situations encountered during the drag and drop transaction.

XmDropSite

A drop site database that maintains a registry of the resources unique to each drop site, such as animation for drag-under effects, valid target types and operations, and callback routines for situations encountered during a drag and drop transaction. It is not an Xt object, although it acts like one with respect to resource fetching.

XmDropTransfer

A widget that describes the information desired from the initiator client and the procedure used to process the results.

15.2.5 Drag and Drop Functions

Motif provides the following functions to support drag and drop processing:

XmCreateDragIcon

Creates any of the parts of a drag icon (status icon, operation icon, or source icon) from a cursor or pixmap. This allows custom icons for all or part of the drag icon, rather than the default icons.

XmDragCancel

Cancels a drag that is in progress. This function is called when the user presses **KCancel**.

XmDragStart

This function is called in the routine that is performed when the user starts a drag. Resources describing the initiator are established. This function creates a DragContext object, which is referenced by other functions whenever information about the drag initiator is needed.

XmDropSiteConfigureStackingOrder

Sets the order of overlapping drop sites. The default order is with the first-registered drop site on the bottom and the last-declared drop site on top.

XmDropSiteEndUpdate

Causes the **XmDropSiteUpdate** requests made after **XmDropSiteStartUpdate** to take place.

XmDropSiteQueryStackingOrder

Provides information about the stacking order of overlapping drop sites. The order can be changed with **XmDropSiteConfigureStackingOrder**.

XmDropSiteRegister

Registers a drop site. Resources describing the drop site are defined.

XmDropSiteRetrieve

Retrieves the values of drop site resources.

XmDropSiteStartUpdate

Signals the toolkit to wait until **XmDropSiteEndUpdate** is called to process drop site changes requested by **XmDropSiteUpdate**. This provides a more efficient way to update several drop sites than changing them one at a time.

XmDropSiteUpdate

Updates drop site resources for a single drop site. If a series of **XmDropSiteUpdate** requests are surrounded by **XmDropSiteStartUpdate** and **XmDropSiteEndUpdate**, then the changes will be made all at once after the end update request.

XmDropSiteUnregister

Removes a drop site. After a drop site has been unregistered, it is unavailable as a destination for a drag.

XmDropTransferAdd

Adds additional transfer requests once a transfer has started.

XmDropTransferStart

Specifies what information should be requested from the drag initiator, and starts the process to get the information.

XmGetDragContext

Returns the DragContext ID associated with a particular time stamp.

XmGetXmDisplay

Returns the ID for the specified display.

XmGetXmScreen

Returns the ID for a specified screen. Some resources, such as the drag icons, are screen-specific.

XmTargetsAreCompatible

Checks if there are any matching targets between the initiator and destination to help determine the correct drag state.

15.2.6 Targets

Each drag source and drop site specifies what kinds of data types it can process, called targets. These targets are atoms, such as **XA_STRING**.

The DragContext resources **XmNexportTargets** and **XmNnumExportTargets** provide a list and number of the data types provided by the drag source. These are export targets.

The DropSite resources **XmNimportTargets** and **XmNnumImportTargets** provide a list and number of the data types accepted by the drop site. These are known as import targets.

Any number of targets may be listed for each source and site. A drop site is considered valid for a particular drag if at least one of its targets matches any of the source's targets and if the source and drop site operations are compatible.

An application can define anything it wants as a target. Be aware, however, that other applications might not recognize that target.

15.2.7 Operations

There are three ways that the initiator and receiver can interact with each other:

- Data can be moved from the initiator to the receiver (Move).

- Data can be copied from the initiator to the receiver (Copy).

- Data can be linked from the receiver to the initiator (Link).

When a drag is started, the initiator provides a list of valid operations in the DragContext **XmNdragOperations** resource. When a drop site is registered, the receiver provides a list of operations it supports in the DropSite **XmNdropSiteOperations** resource. These lists are the values **XmDROP_MOVE**, **XmDROP_COPY**, or **XmDROP_LINK**, connected by the bitwise OR operator (|). For example, the following value means that Move and Copy are valid operations, but Link is not:

XmDROP_MOVE | XmDROP_COPY

The value **XmDROP_NOOP** indicates that there are no operations possible for a drop at the current site.

Callback structures for both DragContext and DropSite have **operation** and **operations** fields. The **operations** field lists all valid operations if a drop were to occur at this point. The **operation** field shows the operations that would happen if a drop occurred at this point. As the drag icon moves over different potential drop sites, the values in its callback structures change in response to what operations the drop sites allow. If there are no common operations between a drag source and a drop site, the **operation** and **operations** fields are set to **XmDROP_NOOP**, and the **dropSiteStatus** field is set to **XmDROP_SITE_INVALID**.

The user can specify an operation using key combinations discussed earlier in this chapter. The user can also change the operation at any time until the drop starts.

The initiator and the receiver need to be able to handle all the operations their application supports. If the operation is Move, the receiver first gets a copy of the data, then tells the initiator that it can delete the data. If the operation is Copy, both applications have the data, making two copies of it. If the operation is Link, there is only one copy of the data, and the receiver establishes a link to that copy.

15.2.7.1 Drop Site Status

The drag and drop callbacks for both receiver and initiator contain a **dropSiteStatus** field. This field is initialized and maintained by the receiver through the toolkit, although the receiver's drag and drop procedures can update it if they wish. This field is used by the toolkit to determine what drag-over and drag-under visual effects to use.

The **dropSiteStatus** field indicates the relationship of the drag source to the drop site over which the drag icon is located:

XmDROP_SITE_VALID

> A drop can take place. There is at least one matching target and operation between the drag source and the drop site.

XmDROP_SITE_INVALID

> A drop cannot take place. Either there were no matching targets, no matching operations, or the receiver's **XmNdragProc** or **XmNdropProc** discovered some other problem that would make a drop impossible.

XmNO_DROP_SITE

> The drag icon is not over a drop site.

If the toolkit on the receiver's side has set either the **operation** or the **operations** field to **XmDROP_NOOP**, it also sets the **dropSiteStatus** field to **XmDROP_SITE_INVALID**.

15.2.8 Overview of Programmer Responsibilities

This section provides an overview of the actions of the initiator client and the receiver client while a drag and drop transaction is in progress. The actions are covered in more detail later in the chapter.

Before a drag starts

- The user or client uses the protocol resources to indicate the type of protocol and visual effects to be used for the initiator and receiver if possible.

- The initiator client creates any special icons it wants to use for drag-over effects, using **XmCreateDragIcon**.

The initiator establishes translation or event handlers to react to **BTransfer Press**.

- The receiver client registers widgets as potential drop sites using **XmDropSiteRegister**, providing information about

  — The shape of the area of the widget sensitive to drag and drop, if it is not the whole widget

  — Valid targets

  — Optional drag-under visual effects

  — An optional **XmNdragProc** to receive messages during the drag

  — An **XmNdropProc** to be performed at the drop

  The receiver can check and change the stacking order of overlapping drop sites with **XmDropSiteQueryStackingOrder** and **XmDropSiteConfigureStackingOrder**.

  The receiver can update drop site information using the functions **XmDropSiteUpdate**, **XmDropSiteStartUpdate**, and **XmDropSiteEndUpdate**.

  The receiver can unregister a drop site with **XmDropSiteUnregister**.

When the drag starts (typically a **BTransfer Press** event)

- The toolkit on the initiator's side is in charge during the drag until a drop is made. The initiator client

  — Receives an indication that the user has started a drag

  — Creates a DragContext using **XmDragStart**, specifying:

    — Valid targets

    — Optional callbacks to be performed during the drag

    — An **XmNconvertProc** to process transfer requests from the receiver

    — Optional custom drag-over visuals

    — Optional drop callbacks to be performed when a drop occurs

- The receiver client does nothing.

During a drag

- The user can cancel the drag or change operation.

- The receiver is not involved unless the pointer is within one of its registered drop sites.

  The toolkit on the receiver's side initializes the **dropSiteStatus**, **operation**, and **operations** fields in the callback structure .

  The receiver's **XmNdragProc** routine (if one was registered) is notified of drag source actions within the drop site: drop site enter, drop site leave, drag icon motion, or change of operation. This **XmNdragProc** routine is called only if the drag protocol is dynamic. It handles any special processing and drag-under visuals.

  If the protocol is preregister, drag-under visuals are handled by the toolkit on the initiator side.

- By default, the initiator needs to do nothing during a drag.

  If the initiator client has registered the appropriate callback routines, it is notified after the receiver's **XmNdragProc** when the drag is entering or leaving a top-level window, entering or leaving a drop site, is in motion, or the user has changed the desired operation. The values of **dropSiteStatus**, **operation**, and **operations** in the drag callbacks are initialized by the toolkit on the receiver side, by the **XmNdragProc**, or by the toolkit on the initiator side if the pointer is not over a registered drop site.

  The initiator can activate custom drag-over effects or other special processing.

  The initiator can cancel the drag in progress by using **XmDragCancel**.

- Either client can check the compatibility of export and import targets with **XmTargetsAreCompatible**.

  Either client can obtain information about the drop site that the drag icon is over (if any) with **XmDropSiteRetrieve**.

When the drop occurs

- The toolkit on the receiver side is in charge during the drop and transfer.

  The receiver's **XmNdropProc** routine makes a final check that a drop is possible and updates the **dropSiteStatus**, **operations**, and **operation** fields in the **XmNdropProc** callback structure for the initiator to read in its **XmNdropStartCallback** callback structure.

If the drop was the result of the user requesting help, the receiver's **XmNdropProc** displays information in a dialog and waits for a response from the user before either continuing or cancelling the drop.

If the drop is valid, the receiver requests transfer information from the initiator.

Only the receiver can cancel a drop.

- The initiator's **XmNdropStartCallback** callback routine is called after the receiver's **XmNdropProc** has finished. The values of the **dropSiteStatus**, **operation**, and **operations** fields in the callback structure were set by the toolkit on the receiver side or **XmNdropProc**.

When data is transferred between initiator and receiver

- The receiver's **XmNdropProc** establishes a list of data and target formats it wants to receive, and calls the **XmDropTransferStart** function. The list can be updated with **XmDropTransferAdd** during the transfer.

  The receiver registers an **XmNtransferProc** to process each transfer from the initiator.

  The receiver can cancel the drop while the transfer is in progress.

  If there is no information to be transferred, or if the drop is cancelled, the receiver must still call **XmDropTransferStart**. The initiator is unable to proceed until it is notified that a transfer has ended. Only the receiver can cancel a drop

- The initiator's **XmNconvertProc** routine is executed in response to a request from the **XmDropTransferStart** function called by the receiver. It returns the information formatted according to the requested target to the receiver's **XmNtransferProc**.

After the drop has finished

- The initiator's **XmNdropFinishCallback** is called when the transfer is complete. The initiator's **XmNdragDropFinishCallback** is called after the whole drag and drop transaction has finished.

15.3 Drag and Drop Protocols

The protocols refer to how the initiator and receiver clients use the toolkit to communicate with each other. There are two drag protocol styles that are available. The drop protocol is based on the Xt selection protocol.

15.3.1 Drag Protocols

The toolkit on the initiator side is in charge during the drag. The protocol in effect determines how it will find the information about drop sites that it needs to manage visuals, and how extensively the initiator and receiver clients are involved during the drag.

There are two kinds of drag protocol styles:

Preregister   Stores drop site information in a database when the drop site is registered. The receiver is not involved in the drag until a drop occurs. All drag-over and drag-under visual effects are managed by the toolkit on the initiator side.

Dynamic   Uses messages from the toolkit to the receiver to find out drop site information. The toolkit on the receiver side can reply to the messages, or the application can take action based on these messages. The receiver manages the drag-under effects.

The code for the initiator is the same regardless of the protocol. The code for the receiver applications is the same except that in the dynamic mode, the receiver's **XmNdragProc** is called.

The drag protocol in use can change during the course of a drag. When the drag icon enters or leaves a top-level window, the source and potential drop receiver negotiate a mutually acceptable drag protocol, as described in Section 15.3.2.

15.3.1.1 The Preregister Drag Protocol

When a receiver supports the preregister protocol, the toolkit on the receiver side stores drop site information in a database. The toolkit on the initiator side manages all drag-under effects based on the information in the drop site database. By setting some DropSite resources appropriately, the receiver can have the toolkit use different highlighting or pixmaps, but the receiver does not participate directly in the drag-under effects.

With the preregister protocol

- The toolkit uses pixmap source icons if the client provides them. If not, it uses bitmap source icons if the client provides them. If the client provides neither, the toolkit uses **XmScreen** icons. The **XmScreen** icons can be either the default icons or ones provided by the client or user.

- The server is grabbed.

- The only customization a receiver can perform is providing custom values for the DropSite visual resources.

- The drag icon can be any size supported by the system on which the application is running.

15.3.1.2 The Dynamic Drag Protocol

With the dynamic drag protocol, the initiator and receiver communicate with messages through the toolkit.

As the drag icon moves within the receiver's window, messages are sent from the toolkit on the initiator side to the toolkit on the receiver side. Based on these messages, the receiver determines whether the drag icon is entering, within, or leaving a drop site. Although the toolkit on the receiver side initializes state and operation information, the receiver can check and update this information further if it registers a **XmNdragProc** for the drop site. The initiator receives the updated message in one of its drag-related callbacks (described later in this chapter), and can take action accordingly.

The dynamic drag protocol allows the receiver to provide more sophisticated visual effects using the **XmNdragProc** than the toolkit can provide alone.

With the dynamic drag procotol

- The receiver can provide custom drag processing and drag-under visual effects.

- The drag icon must fit in the largest cursor size supported by the system running the application. If it is too large, it will be truncated to fit.

15.3.2 Choosing the Protocol and Visual Style

The user can specify which drag protocol to use or the application can specify the drag protocol in resource file.

The preregister drag protocol can be used with a minimum of additional coding in an application, because the toolkit manages the drag-over visual effects using the default drag icons specified in the **XmScreen** object. Or the application can override the default **XmScreen** icons with custom icons, but still allow the toolkit to manage the effects.

The dynamic drag protocol requires more work for the application program, but allows a receiver application to provide visual effects beyond the capabilities of the toolkit.

The drag protocol in use has an effect on the system performance as described later in this section.

15.3.2.1 Specifying Drag Protocols

Two Display resources specify which protocol the toolkit should try to use when a client is an initiator or receiver. These resources can be set by the client in a resource file or by the user.

- **XmNdragInitiatorProtocolStyle**

- **XmNdragReceiverProtocolStyle**

These resources can take the following values (the letter in brackets following the value is used in Table 15-1):

XmDRAG_NONE [N]
> Does not participate in drag and drop. There are no drag-under effects. The drag-over effects depend on the value of **XmNdragInitiatorProtocolStyle**.

XmDRAG_DROP_ONLY [X]
> Does not support either the preregister mode or the dynamic mode, but does data transfer after the drop occurs. There are no drag-over or drag-under visual effects.

XmDRAG_PREREGISTER [P]
> Supports the preregister mode only. The visual effects are managed by the toolkit.

XmDRAG_PREFER_PREREGISTER [PP]
> Supports both protocols, but prefers the preregister protocol. This is the default for receivers. The visual effects are determined by the protocol actually used.

XmDRAG_PREFER_RECEIVER [R]
> Used by initiators only. Uses the protocol that the receiver specifies. This is the default for initiators. The visual effects are determined by the protocol actually used.

XmDRAG_PREFER_DYNAMIC [PD]
> Supports both protocols, but prefers the dynamic mode. The visual effects are determined by the protocol actually used.

XmDRAG_DYNAMIC [D]
> Supports the dynamic protocol only. The drag-over and drag-under visual effects are managed by the clients.

For example:

```
myclient*dragInitiatorProtocolStyle: DRAG_PREFER_DYNAMIC
myclient*dragReceiverProtocolStyle:  DRAG_PREFER_DYNAMIC
```

If the initiator and receiver have specified the same protocol, that protocol is used. If they specify different protocols, the protocol that is used is shown in the following table.

Table 15–1. Initiator and Receiver Protocols

Initiator Protocol	Receiver Protocol					
	P	PP	PD	D	X	N
P	P	P	P	X	X	N
PP	P	P	P	D	X	N
R	P	P	D	D	X	N
PD	P	D	D	D	X	N
D	X	D	D	D	X	N
X	X	X	X	X	X	N
N	N	N	N	N	N	N

The **XmGetXmDisplay** function returns the Display object ID associated with a specific display. **XtGetValues** can be used to check the protocol style resources.

If an **XmNdragProc** is specified for a drop site, it will be performed only if the protocol is dynamic. In this case, the application should set the **XmNdragReceiverProtocolStyle** resource to the value **XmDRAG_PREFER_DYNAMIC** in the application-class defaults file rather than use the default value.

15.3.2.2 Protocols and Visuals

When the resulting protocol is preregister, a preregister visual style is used, and the server is grabbed. The drag-over visual can be a pixmap with an arbitrary size whose depth and colormap are the same as those of the widget associated with the drag source. The pixmap is specified in the DragContext **XmNsourcePixmapIcon** resource.

When the resulting protocol is dynamic, a dynamic visual style is always used. The drag-over visual is implemented with the X cursor, which must be a bitmap, and often has limited size (use **XQueryBestSize** to find out the largest size available per screen). The cursor is specified using **XmNsourceCursorIcon**.

Users will specify one of the preregister values for **XmNdragInitiatorProtocolStyle** because they want good performance when network loading or context switching are problems, or because they want better drag-over visuals rather than more sophisticated drag-under visuals.

Users will specify one of the dynamic values for **XmNdragInitiatorProtocolStyle** because there are clients that use use the dynamic effects, and for visual consistency, they want to use a dynamic visual style whenever possible.

Consequently, when the resulting protocol is **XmDRAG_NONE** or **XmDRAG_DROP_ONLY**, the visual style depends upon the value of **XmNdragInitiatorProtocolStyle**. When it is **XmDRAG_DYNAMIC** or **XmDRAG_PREFER_DYNAMIC**, the dynamic visual style is used; otherwise, the preregister visual style is used.

15.3.3 Drop Protocol

When a drop is made, the receiver checks what action should happen:

- If the user requested help, the receiver should display a dialog explaining the consequences of a drop on the site and determine if the user wants to continue or cancel the drop.

- If the user requests a cancel from the help dialog or presses **KCancel**, or if the receiver determines that the drop cannot continue, the receiver sets the number of transfers to zero and the status to failed to cancel the drop.

- If the drop can continue normally, the receiver starts a transfer.

The drop protocol is a superset of the Xt incremental and nonincremental protocol, with two main differences:

- The receiver and initiator need only one **XmNtransferProc** and **XmNconvertProc** (the Xt selection process requires separate procedures for incremental and nonincremental transfer). They each specify whether the transfer is incremental or not from their side of the transfer with DropTransfer and DragContext resources. If the initiator and receiver use the same incremental or nonincremental protocol, the toolkit deals with each in the requested protocol.

- The initiator and receiver are both notified of the completion of the entire transfer, regardless of how many subtransfers were involved.

The drop protocol is handled by a DropTransfer widget created by **XmDropTransferStart** in the receiver client. The receiver creates a list of information and target types desired from the initiator, along with an **XmNtransferProc** to handle any processing needed during the transfer. The toolkit processes the requests one at a time, until it has finished with the list.

The receiver must call **XmDropTransferStart**, even if the number of transfer requests is zero. Otherwise, the initiator will keep waiting for a transfer request.

For each transfer request, the initiator's **XmNconvertProc** is called. This procedure reads and processes the request and returns the information.

15.4 Drop Receiver Responsibilities for Dragging

The drop receiver responsibilities are covered first in this chapter, because in the dynamic protocol, motion messages go first to the receiver client. The receiver evaluates the state of the drag and sends an updated message to the initiator, which then manages its drag-over visuals based on the results.

The drag receiver has some responsibilities before a drag even starts:

- It registers widgets as drop sites, providing information about valid operations, target types accepted, and drag-under effects (animation style). The application can use the default values for this information, or provide its own values.

- It registers an **XmNdropProc** that is called when a drop occurs and which starts the transfer of information from the initiator. This **XmNdropProc** also processes any Help information the application provides about a drop site.

- It optionally registers an **XmNdragProc** for use with the dynamic protocol that is called for events while a drag is within the widget's boundaries.

If the drag protocol in effect is preregister, the drop site information is put in the database as the drop sites are registered and the receiver client does nothing until a drop is made. All visual effects are handled by the toolkit.

If the drag protocol is dynamic, messaging begins when the pointer enters the window containing the drop site. The receiver is given the opportunity to provide additional processing in its **XmNdragProc**. The **XmNdragProc**

- Receives messages when the drag icon enters or leaves the drop site, the operation changes, the drag icon is in motion, or the drag is cancelled.

- Provides information back to the toolkit about the state of the drag (valid drop site, invalid drop site, no drop site) and the operation to be performed when a drop is made.

- Manages any custom drag-under visual effects.

15.4.1 Establishing a Drop Site

Text and TextField widgets register themselves as drop sites. An application must register any other widgets it wants to use for drop sites. A widget may be registered as only one drop site.

XmDropSiteRegister registers a widget as a drop site, establishes callbacks to be used when a drag is made through the drop site or a drop is made in the drop site, and provides target and operation information. If the protocol is preregister, the information is stored in a database, which is read by the toolkit during the drag. If the drag protocol is dynamic, messaging is used to check for possible drop sites within a widget.

The application must register an **XmNdropProc** routine to establish a list of transfer requests and start the transfer. The other resources can be left at their default values if those values are acceptable to the application.

The optional **XmNdragProc** routine is executed only if the drag protocol is dynamic. It is called in response to events during the drag, and allows the receiver to provide additional drag-under effects or additional drag processing.

The **XmNdropSiteOperations** resource lists all operations that the drop site will support, combined by the bitwise OR operations (|). For example, the default value

> **XmDROP_COPY | XmDROP_MOVE**

means that Copy and Move are valid operations, but Link is not. During a drag, the toolkit on the receiver side compares this list with the DragContext's **XmNdragOperations** list and the user-selected operation to arrive at the operation that will be performed if a drop occurs on this site, along with a list of all operations possible between the initiator and the current drop site.

If an application wants to use only one operation, such as Copy, it should set the **XmNdropSiteOperations** field to just that operation to ensure that the toolkit chooses the correct operation and drag icon during the drag and drop transaction.

Drop sites that represent copying devices, such as printers, or transformation devices, such as compilers, should perform a Copy rather than a Move if both are possible.

The **XmNdropSiteActivity** resource indicates whether the drop site is available for use:

XmDROP_SITE_ACTIVE

> The drop site is available for use. This is the default value.

XmDROP_SITE_INACTIVE

> The drop site is not available for use. If the drag icon is moved over the drop site, both the icon and drop site act as if the icon were not over a drop site.

The **XmDropSiteUnregister** function removes a widget from the DropSite registry. Once a widget is unregistered, it displays no drag-under visual effects and cannot accept a drop.

The difference between an unregistered drop site and an inactive drop site is that the inactive drop site is still registered; it still uses memory, but does not engage in any drag and drop transactions. One use for inactive drop sites is to provide the correct clipping on overlapping drop sites. An unregistered drop site is no longer involved in the drag and drop system. It is the same as a widget that was never registered.

The following code from the main routine in **DNDlabel.c** in Section 15.2.1.1 generates a simple drop site on a Label widget. The only target type it recognizes is compound text. The only operation it will accept is Copy. The other resources, including drag-under effects, are left at their default values.

Figure 15–4. A Label Widget

```
Label = XmCreateLabel(BulletinB, "title", args, n);
XtManageChild(Label);

/* register the label as a drop site */
importList[0] = COMPOUND_TEXT;
n = 0;
XtSetArg(args[n], XmNimportTargets, importList); n++;
XtSetArg(args[n], XmNnumImportTargets, 1); n++;
XtSetArg(args[n], XmNdropSiteOperations, XmDROP_COPY); n++;
XtSetArg(args[n], XmNdropProc, HandleDrop); n++;
XmDropSiteRegister(Label, args, n);

XtRealizeWidget(topLevel);
XtAppMainLoop(app_context);
```

15.4.1.1 Changing a Drop Site

The **XmDropSiteUpdate** function is used to change drop site resources for a single drop site. For multiple requests, **XmDropSiteStartUpdate** signals that a series of **XmDropSiteUpdate** requests will follow, and **XmDropSiteEndUpdate** ends the series and processes the requests at one time.

XmDropSiteUpdate can also be used to change the resource values of the widgets that register themselves as drop sites (Text and TextField). For instance, an application can change Text's **XmNdropProc** to call a procedure in the application.

15.4.1.2 Specially Shaped Drop Sites

The shape of a simple drop site can be specified as the union of a set of specified rectangles clipped by the associated widget.

If only part of the widget is to be sensitive to a drop, it is defined by a list of rectangles in the **XmNdropRectangles** resource. If the resource is NULL, the drop site is the smallest enclosing widget and the shape of the drop site is the shape of the widget.

The rectangles that make up the drop site do not need to be contiguous. All the noncontiguous segments of the drop site act as one; they are all highlighted the same way at the same time. A drop on one segment is the same as a drop on any of the other segments. This might look to the user as if there were several drop sites on a single widget, but the application handles nested drop sites differently from drop sites made of noncontiguous segments. Nested drop sites, whether simulated or real, may have different drag-under effects, targets, operations, or callback procedures.

The following example establishes a sensitive area shaped like a plus sign on a DrawnButton widget named Button2. Even if the drag icon is within the Button2 widget, no drag-under effects are shown until the drag icon is within the sensitive area. The area is visible only when a drag icon enters it and highlighting occurs. The sensitive area is the only part of the widget that accepts a drop. This code is not in one of the three example programs included in Section 15.2.1 and Appendix B.

Figure 15–5. Specially Shaped Drop Site

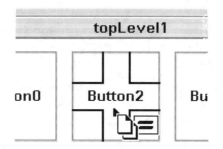

```
XRectangle plus[] = {
    {30, 0, 30, 30},
    {0, 30, 90, 30},
    {30, 60, 30, 30},
    };
        .
        .
        .
n = 0;
XtSetArg(args[n], XmNimportTargets, importList); n++;
XtSetArg(args[n], XmNnumImportTargets, 1); n++;
XtSetArg(args[n], XmNdropProc, HandleDrop); n++;
XtSetArg(args[n], XmNdropRectangles, plus); n++;
XtSetArg(args[n], XmNnumDropRectangles, 3); n++;
XmDropSiteRegister(Button2, args, n);
```

15.4.1.3 Nested Drop Sites

A widget can be registered as only one drop site. However, widgets that are registered as drop sites can be nested within each other, providing nested drop sites.

The **XmNdropSiteType** indicates the complexity of the drop site:

XmDROP_SITE_SIMPLE
> The drop site contains no other drop sites.

XmDROP_SITE_COMPOSITE
> The drop site contains other drop sites. This value is generally associated with a Manager.

A composite drop site must be registered before any of its children are registered. If a composite drop site is inactive, so are all of its children.

The composite and children drop sites do not need to have the same operations or targets.

A manager that contains a number of widgets with their associated drop sites does not need to be a composite drop site unless it is possible to drop in the background of the manager.

It is possible for an application to simulate nested drop sites on a single widget, for example, a DrawingArea. The process is described as part of the discussion of the duties of the optional **XmNdragProc** routine in Section 15.4.2.

15.4.1.4 Overlapping Drop Sites

Drop sites can overlap. Their stacking order is assumed to correspond to the order in which they are registered, with the first-registered one on top. **XmDropSiteQueryStackingOrder** checks the stacking order, whereas **XmDropSiteConfigureStackingOrder** changes it.

When a drop site is overlapped by another drop site, the drag-under effects of the drop site underneath are clipped as appropriate by the obscuring drop site.

A widget or gadget that is not a drop site can overlap and partially obscure a drop site. To ensure that the drop-site's drag-under visuals are appropriately clipped by the obscuring widget, such sibling widgets should be registered as inactive drop sites. Parent widgets, whether drop sites or not, will clip their children's drop site visuals. If a parent has some active and some inactive drop site children, it should be registered as an active drop site.

15.4.1.5 Drag-Under Visual Effects

Drag-under visual effects are displayed only when the pointer is within the sensitive area of the drop site widget. Various drag-under styles can be chosen in the **XmNanimationStyle** DropSite resource:

XmDRAG_UNDER_HIGHLIGHT
> A solid border around the sensitive area of the drop site is used to show the drop site is valid. This is the default value.

XmDRAG_UNDER_SHADOW_OUT
> The sensitive area of the drop site looks pushed out when it is valid.

XmDRAG_UNDER_SHADOW_IN
> The sensitive are of the drop site looks pushed in when it is valid.

XmDRAG_UNDER_PIXMAP
> A custom pixmap is used to indicate the drop site is valid. The pixmap is specified in **XmNanimationPixmap**.

XmDRAG_UNDER_NONE
> No indication is given that the drop site is valid.

The following illustration shows the default drag-under animation around the Label widget drop site.

Figure 15–6. Default Drag-Under Animation

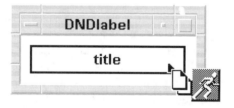

If the value of **XmNanimationStyle** is **XmDRAG_UNDER_PIXMAP**, the resources **XmNanimationPixmap**, **XmNanimationMask**, and **XmNanimationPixmapDepth** are used to provide more information about the pixmap. If the depth does not match the depth of the window controlling the drop site widget, no animation occurs. Except for

XmDRAG_UNDER_PIXMAP, the colors used for the visual effects are based on the colors of the widget associated with the drop site.

The dynamic protocol provides the most control over the drop site animation. It is the only way to get visual effects that do not remain the same for the duration of the drag icon's stay in the drop site, for example, a background that flashes.

15.4.2 XmNdragProc

The procedure registered in the DropSite's **XmNdragProc** resource is called only when the dynamic protocol is in effect. This procedure is optional. Applications that need to provide special drag-under effects or other special processing during a drag can do so with this procedure.

The **XmNdragProc** procedure is called in response to messages from the toolkit, before the initiator's equivalent drag callback. Fields in the callback structure provide information to the receiver about the drag.

The **reason** field in the callback structure indicates why the procedure was called.

XmCR_DROP_SITE_ENTER_MESSAGE
> The drag icon hotspot has entered the drop site.

XmCR_DROP_SITE_LEAVE_MESSAGE
> The drag icon hotspot has left the drop site.

XmCR_DRAG_MOTION_MESSAGE
> The drag icon hotspot has moved.

XmCR_OPERATION_CHANGED_MESSAGE
> The operation has changed.

The **operations** field lists all the operations that are valid for the drop site with the current drag source. The **operations** field is initialized by the toolkit as follows:

- If the user has selected an operation, the value of **operations** is initialized to that operation if it is in the DragContext's **XmNdragOperations** list.

- Otherwise, the **operations** field is initialized to the list in the DragContext's **XmNdragOperations** list.

The **operation** field indicates the type of action a successful drop will perform. The toolkit initializes the **operation** field by taking the following steps, in order of precedence from highest to lowest:

1. If Move is a valid operation (in both the **operations** field and the DropSite's **XmNdropSiteOperations** list), **operation** is initialized to **XmDROP_MOVE**.

2. If Copy is a valid operation, **operation** is initialized to **XmDROP_COPY**.

3. If Link is a valid operation, **operation** is initialized to **XmDROP_LINK**.

4. Otherwise, **operation** is initialized to **XmDROP_NOOP**.

The **dropSiteStatus** field provides an indication of whether a transfer between the initiator and this drop site could occur. The value that the toolkit selects for the **dropSiteStatus** field depends on the reason the **XmNdragProc** procedure was entered:

- If the reason is motion or drop site leave, and the drop site is the same as in the last call to **XmNdragProc**, the **dropSiteStatus** field is the same as at the end of the previous call.

- Otherwise, if there is at least one target in common and at least one operation in common, the value is initialized to **XmDROP_SITE_VALID**. If not, the value is initialized to **XmDROP_SITE_INVALID**.

- If the **operation** field is **XmDROP_NOOP**, the **dropSiteStatus** field is initialized to **XmDROP_SITE_INVALID**.

The **XmNdragProc** procedure can update **operation**, **operations**, or **dropSiteStatus** further during its execution. The final values for these fields are available to the initiator in its drag callback structures. If the receiver's **XmNdragProc** procedure is called more than once while the drag icon is within the drop site (for example, because of motion events), the values used by the toolkit when it initializes the drag callback **operations**, **operation**, and **dropSiteStatus** fields are the ones at the end of the previous call to **XmNdragProc**.

The **animate** field tells the toolkit who should provide the drag-under visual effects. It is initially set to True, but the **XmNdragProc** routine can set it to False.

True   The toolkit provides the drag-under visuals as if the protocol were preregister.

False   The receiver provides the drag-under visuals. The application can provide special visual effects, such as a blinking background, that are not possible with the toolkit.

The **DragProcCallback** routine in the **DNDDemo.c** program in Appendix B is an example of a **DragProc** routine. It can process every drag message, changes the **operations**, **operation**, and **dropSiteStatus** as necessary, and sets the **animate** field to **True**, allowing the toolkit to manage the drag-under effects. The **DragProcCallback** routine is shown in the next section of this chapter.

15.4.2.1 Simulating Nested Drop Sites

A widget can be registered as only a single drop site. However, if the application needs one or more drop sites entirely enclosed within another drop site, there are two ways to accomplish this:

- Widgets that contain other widgets that are drop sites should be registered as composite drop sites as described earlier in this chapter.

  This method allows the toolkit to manage drop site messages and drag-under effects for each nested drop site.

- An application can simulate multiple drop sites on a single widget in the **XmNdragProc** and **XmNdropProc** routines. Because the **XmNdragProc** routine is executed only in the dynamic drag protocol mode, this method would not work if the drag procotol chosen is preregister.

  This method requires that the application manage all drag-under effects, because the toolkit is not aware of the simulated nesting.

To simulate nested drop sites on a single widget:

1. Register the widget as a single active drop site. Set **XmNdropSiteOperations** to all the operations possible for any of the nested drop sites. Set **XmNimportTargets** to all the targets possible for any of the nested drop sites. Register an **XmNdragProc** routine to provide any special drag-under effects for the simulated drop sites.

The **operations**, **operation**, and **dropSiteStatus** fields are initialized by the toolkit only when this outer drop site is entered or left. The simulated drop sites must be managed by the application.

2. When either **XmNdragProc** or **XmNdropProc** is called, check the **x** and **y** fields in the callback structure to determine which of the nested drop sites contains the pointer.

3. If the pointer is within a simulated nested drop site, update the callback fields as follows:

   - When the pointer enters the simulated nested drop site, save the value of the **operations** and **operation** fields.

   - Remove any operations from the **operations** field that do not apply to the simulated drop site.

   - Set **operation** to the valid operation preferred by the simulated drop site, or to **XmDROP_NOOP** if the **operations** list does not contain the preferred operation.

   - The **dropSiteStatus** field must reflect the status of the simulated drop site so that the initiator can manage drag-over effects correctly:

     — Set the **dropSiteStatus** to **XmDROP_SITE_VALID** if the **operation** is allowed in the simulated drop site and if there is at least one target in common between the simulated drop site and the initiator. (Use the **XmTargetsAreCompatible** routine to check the targets.)

     — Set the **dropSiteStatus** to **XmDROP_SITE_INVALID** if the **operation** is not allowed in the simulated drop site, if there are no targets in common, or if the **operation** is **XmDROP_NOOP**.

   - Display appropriate drag-under visual effects.

   - When the pointer leaves the simulated drop site, restore the original values of **operations** and **operation** that apply to the outer drop site.

4. If the pointer is not within a simulated drop site, but drops are allowed in the outer drop site, update the fields as described in the previous step.

5. If the pointer is not within a simulated drop site, and drops are not allowed in the outer drop site, set the **dropSiteStatus** field to **XmDROP_SITE_INVALID**.

If the preregister protocol is in effect, the simulated drop sites cannot be managed during the move, because **XmNdragProc** is not performed; but they can be managed at the drop with **XmNdropProc**.

In the following example, only the top-level window, **DNDDemo**, is registered as a drop site. The user can create rectangles within the window that then act like drop sites themselves. The user can drag and drop colors from one of the six buttons in the lower part of the window onto the rectangles to change the color of the rectangle. However, these rectangles are not registered drop sites, they are simulated.

The user can also drag these rectangles to new locations.

Figure 15–7. Simulated Drop Sites

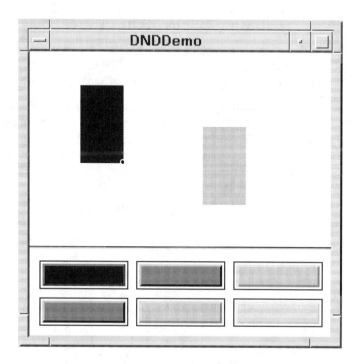

The **RegisterDropSite** routine registers the DrawingArea widget as a drop site. The list of operations and targets may not be valid for each simulated drop site, but are valid for other simulated drop sites.

```
RegisterDropSite(w)
Widget w;
{

    Display *display = XtDisplay(w);
    Atom    targets[3];
    Arg     args[5];
    int     n = 0;

    /* Only accept moves or copies */
    XtSetArg(args[n], XmNdragOperations,
            XmDROP_COPY | XmDROP_MOVE);
    n++;
```

```
/* set all possible targets for any of the
 * nested drop sites
 */
targets[0] = XmInternAtom(display, "_MY_RECTANGLE", False);
targets[1] = XmInternAtom(display, "BACKGROUND", False);
targets[2] = XmInternAtom(display, "PIXMAP", False);
XtSetArg(args[n], XmNimportTargets, targets); n++;
XtSetArg(args[n], XmNnumImportTargets, 3); n++;

/* register a dragProc - necessary for simulating nested
 * drop sites
 */
XtSetArg(args[n], XmNdragProc, DragProcCallback); n++;

/* register a dropProc */
XtSetArg(args[n], XmNdropProc, DropProcCallback); n++;
XmDropSiteRegister(w, args, n);

}
```

The **XmNdragProc** routine, **DragProcCallback**, is called whenever a drag icon enters the registered drop site (the top level window). The **RectFind** routine from **DNDDraw.c** in Appendix B determines if the pointer is in a simulated drop site. The **CheckTargets** routine determines if the object being dragged is one of the six colors (**bgFound**) or one of the created rectangles (**rectFound**). (The value **pixFound** to represent a pixmap being dragged is coded in this routine, but not in the rest of the program.)

The only drag-under visual is displayed when a color is dragged to a rectangle. The outline of the rectangle is highlighted.

The entire **DragProcCallback** routine is too long to be listed in its entirety here. The section dealing with the drop site enter message is used as an example.

```
static void DragProcCallback(w, client, call)
Widget w;
XtPointer client;
XtPointer call;
{

    XmDragProcCallbackStruct *cb =
```

```
                                (XmDragProcCallbackStruct *) call;
Display                         *display = XtDisplay(w);
Boolean                         rectFound, bgFound, pixFound;
static unsigned char            initial_operations;
static unsigned char            initial_operation;
RectPtr                         rect;

CheckTargets(cb->dragContext, display, &rectFound,
    &bgFound, &pixFound);

switch(cb->reason) {

    case XmCR_DROP_SITE_ENTER_MESSAGE:

        /* save the value of the operations and operation
         * fields
         */
        initial_operations = cb->operations;
        initial_operation = cb->operation;

        rect = RectFind(cb->x, cb->y);

        /* Remove any operations for the operations field
         * which do not apply to the simulated drop site.
         */
        if (rect) {

            if (bgFound || pixFound) {
                cb->operations = XmDROP_COPY;
                RectHighlight(w, rect);
            }
            else if (rectFound) {
                cb->operations = cb->operations &
                            (XmDROP_COPY | XmDROP_MOVE);
                RectUnhighlight(w);
            }

        }
        else {
            cb->operations = initial_operations &
                            (XmDROP_COPY | XmDROP_MOVE);
```

```
        RectUnhighlight(w);
}

/* Set operation to the valid operation preferred
 * by the simulated drop site or to XmDROP_NOOP
 * if the operations list does not contain the
 * preferred operation.
 */
if (rect) {

    if (bgFound || pixFound) {

        if (cb->operations & XmDROP_COPY)
            cb->operation = XmDROP_COPY;
        else
            cb->operation = XmDROP_NOOP;

    }
    else if (rectFound) {

        if (cb->operations & XmDROP_MOVE)
            cb->operation = XmDROP_MOVE;
        else if (cb->operations & XmDROP_COPY)
            cb->operation = XmDROP_COPY;
        else
            cb->operation = XmDROP_NOOP;

    }

}
else {

    if (rectFound) {

        if (cb->operations & XmDROP_MOVE)
            cb->operation = XmDROP_MOVE;
        else if (cb->operations & XmDROP_COPY)
            cb->operation = XmDROP_COPY;
        else
            cb->operation = XmDROP_NOOP;
```

```
        }
        else
            cb->operation = initial_operation;

    }

    /*
     * Set dropSiteStatus to XmDROP_SITE_INVALID if
     * the operation field is XmDROP_NOOP, or if there
     * are no  common targets between the source and
     * the nested  drop site.  Otherwise, set
     * dropSiteStatus to  XmDROP_SITE_VALID.
     */
    if (cb->operation == XmDROP_NOOP ||
        (rect && (!rectFound && !bgFound && !pixFound))
        || (!rect && !rectFound))
        cb->dropSiteStatus = XmINVALID_DROP_SITE;
    else
        cb->dropSiteStatus = XmVALID_DROP_SITE;

    /*
     * Display appropriate drag-under visuals.  Only
     * highlight the rectangle if we are changing
     * rectangle attributes.
     */
    if (rect && bgFound || pixFound &&
        cb->dropSiteStatus == XmVALID_DROP_SITE)
        RectHighlight(w, rect);
    break;

case XmCR_DROP_SITE_LEAVE_MESSAGE:
    .
    .
    .
```

15.5 Drag Initiator Responsibilities for Dragging

The application in which the user initiates the drag is considered the drag initiator.

The drag initiator

- Recognizes the start of a drag (**BTransfer Press**) within a widget controlled by the application.

- Establishes a DragContext for the widget, providing information about operations, targets, and drag-over visuals, using the **XmDragStart** function.

- Optionally, provides special drag-over effects.

These steps are described in the following sections.

15.5.1 Recognizing a Drag Has Started

The initiator client must be able to recognize the **BTransfer Press** event within a widget it allows to be a drag source. It may have to override an already-assigned translation for the widget.

The following example from the main routine of **DNDscroll.c** in Section 15.2.1.2 overrides the existing mouse button 2 translation for the ScrollBar widget, and maps it to the **StartDrag** routine, which will start the drag transaction.

```
static char dragTranslations[] =
    "#override <Btn2Down>: StartDrag()";
static XtActionsRec dragActions[] =
    { {"StartDrag", (XtActionProc)StartDrag}, };
        .
        .
XtTranslations parsed_xlations;
        .
        .
/* override button two press to start a drag */
parsed_xlations = XtParseTranslationTable(dragTranslations);
XtAppAddActions(app_context, dragActions,
```

```
                    XtNumber(dragActions));

/* create a scroll bar widget */
n = 0;
XtSetArg(args[n], XmNtranslations, parsed_xlations); n++;
scrollbar = XmCreateScrollBar(BulletinB, "testscroll",
                              args, n);
XtManageChild(scrollbar);
```

Translation may be more complicated in some editable widgets, in which
BTransfer Click is used for primary transfer, and **BTransfer Motion** is
used for drag and drop.

15.5.2 Starting a Drag With XmDragStart

Not every widget in an application can be a drag source. Text, Label,
Button, and List widgets are automatically defined as drag sources. Other
widgets must have a translation for **BTransfer** assigned to them, establish
DragContext resources for the widget, and call the **XmDragStart** routine to
become drag sources. If the user tries to drag objects from a widget that is
not recognized as a drag source by either the toolkit or the source
application, nothing happens.

The **XmDragStart** function initiates a drag and creates a DragContext
widget. At a minimum, the **XmNconvertProc** DragContext resource, must
be specified. Other resources are optional, for example, those specifying
drag-over visual effects.

The **XmNdragOperations** resource lists all the operations that the initiator
will support for this drag source, combined by the bitwise OR operation (|).
During a drag, the toolkit compares this list with the receiver's
XmNdropSiteOperations list and the user-selected operation to arrive at
the operation that will be performed if a drop occurs on this site.

If an application wants to use only one operation, it should set the
XmNdragOperations resource to just that operation to ensure that the
correct operation and drag icon are chosen by the toolkit during the drag and
drop transaction.

The following example from **DNDscroll.c** in Section 15.2.1.2 establishes a
target type of compound text and an operation of Copy, then establishes a

DragContext for this transaction with **XmDragStart**. This drag source does not have any custom drag icons or any drag callbacks.

```
static void StartDrag(w, event)
Widget   w;
XEvent   *event;
{
    Arg             args[MAX_ARGS];
    Cardinal        n;
    Atom            exportList[1];

    /* establish the list of valid target types */
    exportList[0] = COMPOUND_TEXT;

    n = 0;
    XtSetArg(args[n], XmNexportTargets, exportList); n++;
    XtSetArg(args[n], XmNnumExportTargets, 1); n++;
    XtSetArg(args[n], XmNdragOperations, XmDROP_COPY); n++;
    XtSetArg(args[n], XmNconvertProc, DragConvertProc); n++;
    XmDragStart(w, event, args, n);
}
```

If drag or drop callbacks are desired, they are added to the DragContext's callback resources. For example, a callback procedure named **EnterCallBack** that is performed when the pointer enters an active drop site could be added as follows:

```
Widget          dc;
    .
    .
    .
    dc = XmDragStart(w, event, args, n);
    XtAddCallback(dc, XmNdropSiteEnterCallback, EnterCallBack,
                  NULL);
```

15.5.3 Overriding Existing Drag Sources

XtGetValues is used to check the values of widgets resources established as drag sources earlier in the application, and **XtSetValues** is used to update these values. The widget ID used is the DragContext, not the source widget ID, so that the change applies only to the widget during the drag.

If the widget is a predefined drag source (Text, Label, Button, or List), overriding the default behavior becomes more complex. The widget calls **XmDragStart** when the drag starts, and the application cannot call **XmDragStart** again for the widget. Instead, it must update the existing DragContext. First it must find the DragContext for the widget, then establish the new behavior. One possible means to accomplish this is as follows:

- Override the existing Btn2Down translation with a new translation that calls the widget's action and also an action supplied by the application. For the Text widget, this new translation might look as follows:

```
<Btn2Down> : process-bdrag() my-drag-start()
```

- Register the new action, using **XtAppAddActions**.

- In the new action procedure, call **XmGetDragContext** to get the DragContext, and then call **XtSetValues** to change resource values. The timestamp argument to **XmGetDragContext** can be the timestamp from the event passed to the action routine.

For instance, Text allows the Copy and Move operations. If an application can support only Copy, it must update the DragContext's **XmNdragOperations** resource.

15.5.4 Drag-Over Visual Effects

When the user moves the mouse, a drag icon representing the object being dragged moves around the screen instead of the usual pointer. As the icon is dragged over portions of the screen, the icon may change to show the status of a possible drop. These drag-over visual effects help the user know how to proceed with the drag.

There are four ways to provide drag-over visual effects:

- Use the default drag-over visuals, specified in the **XmScreen** object. The toolkit manages all the drag-over effects.

- Put custom icons and pixmaps in the **XmScreen** visual resources to be used as default icons for all drag and drop transactions running on that **XmScreen**. The toolkit manages all the drag-over effects using these new icons. These resources can be modified by the application or the user in a resource file.

- Put custom icons and pixmaps in the DragContext visual resources for source, state, or operation icons. The application must monitor the state of the drag using the drag callbacks and update the DragContext icon values as necessary. The default icons specified in the **XmScreen** object are used only if the value for the equivalent DragContext visual resource is NULL.

- Manage the drag-over effects entirely in the application by drawing directly to the screen. The toolkit is not used, nor are the **XmScreen** and DragContext visual resources.

If the application provides custom icons and they are unsuitable for some reason, the toolkit defaults to the **XmScreen** drag-over visuals.

The drag icon consists of a source icon, optionally combined with a state icon and an operation icon.

Each drag icon has a hotspot. Since a drag icon could be quite large, the hotspot provides a single pixel that is used in providing drag-over and drag-under effects. For example, if the drag icon moves into the area of a valid drop site, neither the drag icon or the drop site will provide visual clues until the hotspot has moved into the area. By default, the hotspot is the upper left corner of the state icon.

In the following illustration, the running figure is the source icon, the state icon is the arrow in the corner, and the operation icon shows a Copy will happen if a drop is made. The default blending and attachment values are used.

Figure 15–8. A Drag Icon

15.5.4.1 Source Icon

The source icon is a picture representing the object being dragged. It can be either a pixmap or cursor. The client can specify a custom pixmap in the DragContext resource **XmNsourcePixmapIcon** or a custom cursor in the **XmNsourceCursorIcon** resource. If these resources are NULL or not usable (too large, not a bitmap, or created on a different screen, for example), the default cursor given in the **XmScreen** resource **XmNdefaultSourceCursorIcon** is used.

The pixmap icon is used with the preregister visual style. The colormap is based on the source widget. The cursor icon is used for the dynamic visual style.

The following illustration shows the default source icons for general purpose, List, Label, and Text widgets.

Figure 15–9. Source Icons

15.5.4.2 State Icon

The state icon is a cursor that indicates if the drag is over a valid drop site, invalid drop site, or no drop site. The default state icons are in the **XmScreen** resources **XmNdefaultValidCursorIcon**, **XmNdefaultInvalidCursorIcon**, and **XmNdefaultNoneCursorIcon**.

A custom state icon can be specified in the DragContext resource **XmNstateCursorIcon**. This icon must be changed appropriately as the state of the drag changes, using the drag callbacks. If

XmNstateCursorIcon is NULL, not a bitmap, or not defined on the same screen as **XmScreen**, the default **XmScreen** icons are used.

The default state icon for all three states is an arrow, usually shown at the upper left corner of the operation icon.

Three DragContext resources can be used to change the color of the drag icon based on the state of the drag: **XmNvalidCursorForeground**, **XmNinvalidCursorForeground**, **XmNnoneCursorForeground**. This allows visual feedback about the drag to the user, without changing the icon shape. For example, the following lines in a resource file would make the drag icon green when it was over a valid drop site, red when it was over an invalid drop site, and yellow when it was not over any drop site:

```
*.validCursorIcon:        green
*.invalidCursorIcon:      red
*.noneCursorIcon:         yellow
```

15.5.4.3 Operation Icon

The operation icon is a cursor that indicates what operation is to happen when the drop is made. The default operation icons are the values of the **XmScreen** resources **XmNdefaultMoveCursorIcon**, **XmNdefaultCopyCursorIcon**, and **XmNdefaultLinkCursorIcon**.

A custom operation icon can be specified in the DragContext resource **XmNoperationCursorIcon**. The icon should be changed as the operation changes, using the drag callbacks. If this resource is NULL, not a bitmap, or not defined on the same screen as **XmScreen**, the default **XmScreen** icons are used.

The following illustration shows the default Copy, Link, and Move operation icons.

Figure 15–10. Operation Icons

If the operation in effect is **XmDROP_NOOP**, meaning that no operation is possible, then the operation icon is left blank, as shown in the following illustration. This condition also sets the **dropSiteStatus** to **XmDROP_SITE_INVALID**.

Figure 15–11. Copy and Noop Drag Icons

15.5.4.4 Drag Icon Blending and Attachment

The client can specify which of the three icons to mix together to form the drag icon with the **XmNblendModel** DragContext resource:

XmBLEND_ALL
> Use the source icon, state icon, and operation icon. The hotspot comes from the state icon. This is the default value. The order listed is also the order of the blend.

XmBLEND_STATE_SOURCE
> Use only the source icon and state icon. The hotspot comes from the state icon.

XmBLEND_JUST_SOURCE
> Use only the source icon. The hotspot comes from the source icon.

XmBLEND_NONE
> Do not display any drag icon. The client handles all drag-over effects.

The **XmNattachment** DragIcon resource specifies where the state and operation icons will be placed on the source icon. The default placement is both the state and operation icons at the attachment point of the source icon, with the operation icon on top. The default value is **XmATTACH_NORTH_WEST**.

XmNoffsetX and **XmNoffsetY** are used to place the icon relative to the attachment point.

If the attachment point is **XmATTACH_HOT**, the state and operation icons are attached to the source icon at a point the same x and y distance from the upper left corner of the source icon as the pointer is from the upper left corner of the widget containing the source. This attachment style is particularly useful when the application makes a custom source icon that exactly reflects the source widget at the time the drag starts.

In the following illustration, the custom source icon is an outline of the scrollbar. When the drag was started, the pointer was on the slider. The operation and state icons are placed at the same location on the source icon.

Figure 15–12. An Attach_Hot Icon

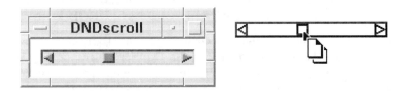

When the state or operation icon is blended with a source icon, a specified point of the icon's **XmNpixmap** is aligned with the upper left corner of the source icon. The resulting **XmNpixmap** is large enough to include both, and the resulting **XmNmask** has 1 bits wherever either the source icon or source mask did.

If a dynamic cursor style is being used, and the resulting blended cursor is too large for the screen, the blending is done with the **XmScreen XmNdefaultSourceCursorIcon** instead of the DragContext's **XmNsourceCursorIcon**. If it is still too large, it is clipped relative to the hotspot (that is, if the hotspot is at an edge, the other edge is clipped; if the hotspot is in the center, opposite edges are clipped equally).

15.5.4.5 Visual Style Notes

If **XmNsourcePixmapIcon** is used, the colormap used for rendering is that of the DragContext's reference widget.

If the DragContext **XmNblendModel** is **XmBLEND_NONE**, and the dynamic cursor style is in use, the application must use **XChangeActivePointerGrab** to change the cursor. If **XmBLEND_NONE** is specified, and the preregister cursor style is in use, the application can render the cursor directly onto the screen, saving and restoring the image underneath.

The cursor style can change as the pointer moves from window to window. An application can tell which style is in use by looking at the **dragProtocolStyle** field in the **XmNtopLevelEnterCallback** structure, or looking at the **XmNdragInitiatorProtocolStyle** Display resource in the case of **XmDRAG_NONE** or **XmDRAG_DROP_ONLY**.

The resolution and best cursor size can vary from screen to screen. This is why the default cursor icons are **XmScreen** resources. An application that wants its source cursor or pixmap to be screen dependent can look for changes in the **screen** field in the **XmNtopLevelEnterCallback** struct, and update the various icon DragContext resources appropriately.

15.5.4.6 Creating a Drag Icon

Any of the three parts of a drag icon can be customized: the source icon, the state icon, and the operation icon.

Use the **XmCreateDragIcon** function to create any of these parts. The **XmNattachment** resource is not used for the source icon. The other resources specify pixmap, size, and hotspot details. The DragContext **XmNblendModel** resource indicates which hotspot is used for the entire drag icon.

The following example from **DNDDemo.c** in Appendix B creates a source icon from a bitmap. The source icon is the palette and the state icon is the paintbrush. (Actually, the state icon is not shown when the drag starts, because the blend style is **XmBLEND_JUST_SOURCE**. It is shown here as if the blend style were **XmBLEND_ALL**.)

Figure 15–13. Custom Source Icon

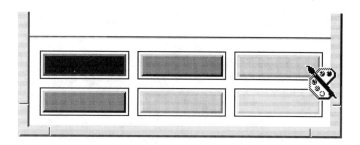

The **ColorRect** function is called when a drag starts from one of the color rectangles in the lower portion of the window. Among its other duties, it establishes the drag icon from source bits from the **DNDDraw.c** file in Appendix B.

```
/* If the server will handle a large icon, create
   one */
if (appInfo->maxCursorWidth >= ICON_WIDTH &&
    appInfo->maxCursorHeight >= ICON_HEIGHT) {

    source_bits = SOURCE_ICON_BITS;
    source_mask = SOURCE_ICON_MASK;
    state_bits = STATE_ICON_BITS;
    state_mask = STATE_ICON_MASK;
    width = ICON_WIDTH;
    height = ICON_HEIGHT;

}
else {

    /* If the server will handle a small icon, create
       one */
    source_bits = SMALL_SOURCE_ICON_BITS;
    source_mask = SMALL_SOURCE_ICON_MASK;
    state_bits = SMALL_STATE_ICON_BITS;
    state_mask = SMALL_STATE_ICON_MASK;
    width = SMALL_ICON_WIDTH;
    height = SMALL_ICON_HEIGHT;

}
```

```
/* Create the drag cursor icons */
sourceIcon = GetDragIconFromBits(w, source_bits,
            source_mask, width, height, background,
            foreground);

stateIcon = GetDragIconFromBits(w, state_bits,
            state_mask, width, height, background,
            foreground);

/* Setup the arglist for the drag context that is
 * created at drag start */
n = 0;
    .

    .

    .

XtSetArg(args[n], XmNsourceCursorIcon, sourceIcon); n++;
XtSetArg(args[n], XmNstateCursorIcon, stateIcon); n++;
    .

    .

    .


/* start the drag.  This creates a drag context. */
myDC = XmDragStart(w, event, args, n);

}
```

The **GetDragIconFromBits** function turns the bits into a bitmap.

```
static Widget GetDragIconFromBits(w, bits, mask, width,
                        height, background, foreground)
Widget w;
char *bits;
char *mask;
Dimension width;
Dimension height;
Pixel background;
Pixel foreground;
{

    Pixmap      icon, iconMask;
    Display     *display = XtDisplay(w);
```

```
icon = XCreateBitmapFromData(display,
        DefaultRootWindow(display), bits, width,
        height);

iconMask = XCreateBitmapFromData(display,
            DefaultRootWindow(display), mask,
            width, height);

return(GetDragIcon(w, icon, iconMask, width, height,
                background, foreground));

}
```

The **GetDragIcon** function uses the bitmap created by the **GetDragIconFromBits** function to create a drag icon.

```
static Widget GetDragIcon(w, icon, iconMask, width, height,
                          background, foreground)
Widget w;
Pixmap icon;
Pixmap iconMask;
Dimension width;
Dimension height;
Pixel background;
Pixel foreground;
{

    Widget   dragIcon;
    Arg      args[10];
    int      n = 0;

    XtSetArg(args[n], XmNhotX, ICON_X_HOT); n++;
    XtSetArg(args[n], XmNhotY, ICON_Y_HOT); n++;
    XtSetArg(args[n], XmNwidth, width); n++;
    XtSetArg(args[n], XmNheight, height); n++;
    XtSetArg(args[n], XmNmaxWidth, appInfo->maxCursorWidth);
       n++;
    XtSetArg(args[n], XmNmaxHeight, appInfo->maxCursorHeight);
       n++;
    XtSetArg(args[n], XmNbackground, background); n++;
    XtSetArg(args[n], XmNforeground, foreground); n++;
```

```
XtSetArg(args[n], XmNpixmap, icon); n++;
XtSetArg(args[n], XmNmask, iconMask); n++;
dragIcon = XmCreateDragIcon(w, "dragIcon", args, n);

return(dragIcon);

}
```

15.5.5 Drag Callbacks

Callbacks notify the initiator of how the drag is proceeding. The receiver's **XmNdragProc** (if any) is first notified of the action and given a chance to update the **operation**, **operations**, and **dropSiteStatus** fields in its callback structure. The new values are available to the initiator's drag callback in the appropriate callback structure.

These drag callbacks are all optional. They enable the initiator to monitor the progress of the drag and manage its visual effects accordingly. Otherwise, the toolkit on the initiator side handles the drag-over effects.

XmNdragMotionCallback
> Called when the drag icon is in motion

XmNoperationChangedCallback
> Called when the user requests a different operation be performed on the drop than was previously in effect

XmNdropSiteEnterCallback
> Called when the drag icon enters a drop site

XmNdropSiteLeaveCallback
> Called when the drag icon leaves a drop site

XmNtopLevelEnterCallback
> Called when the drag icon enters a top-level window or root window (when changing screens)

XmNtopLevelLeaveCallback
> Called when the drag icon leaves a top-level window or root window (when changing screens)

Callback structures for these routines contain information about the drag. The callback structures for **XmNdragMotionCallback**, **XmNoperationChangedCallback**, and **XmNdropSiteEnterCallback** contain the **operations**, **operation**, and **dropSiteStatus** fields (among others), which are initialized by the toolkit before the callback is called.

The **operations** field lists all operations possible for a drop on the current site, whether the site is registered as a DropSite or not. The toolkit initializes the **operations** field as follows:

- If the receiver's **XmNdragProc** was called, the value of **operations** is the list of operations common to the value of the **XmNdragProc**'s **operations** field at the end of **XmNdragProc** and the DropSite's **XmNdropSiteOperations** list.

- If the **XmNdragProc** routine was not called but the user selected an operation, **operations** is set to that operation if it is in the **XmNdragOperations** list. If it is not in the list, **operations** is set to **XmDROP_NOOP**.

- Otherwise, the **operations** field is initialized to the list in the DragContext's **XmNdragOperations** resource.

The **operation** field shows the operation that will occur if a drop happens at the current cursor location. It is initialized as follows:

- If the receiver's **XmNdragProc** was called, **operation** is initialized to the value of **operation** at the end of the **XmNdragProc**.

- If the **XmNdragProc** routine was not called but the pointer is in or entering an active drop site, the toolkit initializes **operation** by taking the following steps, in order of precedence from highest to lowest:

  1. If Move is in both the **operations** field and the DropSite's **XmNdropSiteOperations** list, **operation** is set to **XmDROP_MOVE**.

  2. If Copy is in both the **operations** field and the DropSite's **XmNdropSiteOperations** list, **operation** is set to **XmDROP_COPY**.

  3. If Link is in both the **operations** field and the DropSite's **XmNdropSiteOperations** list, **operation** is set to **XmDROP_LINK**.

  4. Otherwise, **operation** is set to **XmDROP_NOOP**.

- Otherwise, the toolkit initializes **operation** by taking the following steps, in order of precedence from highest to lowest:

  1. If Move is in the **operations** field, **operation** is set to **XmDROP_MOVE**.

  2. If Copy is in the **operations** field, **operation** is set to **XmDROP_COPY**.

  3. If Link is in the **operations** field, **operation** is set to **XmDROP_LINK**.

  4. Otherwise, **operation** is set to **XmDROP_NOOP**.

The **dropSiteStatus** field in the callback structure indicates if the drag icon is over a valid drop site, an invalid drop site, or no drop site. The callback procedure can use this information to display the appropriate drag-over visuals. The toolkit initializes the **dropSiteStatus** field as follows:

- If the pointer is over an active drop site:

  — If the receiver's **XmNdragProc** was called, **dropSiteStatus** is initialized to the value of **dropSiteStatus** at the end of the **XmNdragProc** procedure.

  — If the **XmNdragProc** routine was not called but the initiator and receiver have at least one target and one operation in common, **dropSiteStatus** is initialized to **XmDROP_SITE_VALID**.

  — Otherwise, **dropSiteStatus** is initialized to **XmDROP_SITE_INVALID**.

- If the pointer is not over an active drop site, **dropSiteStatus** is initialized to **XmNO_DROP_SITE**.

- If the **operation** field is **XmDROP_NOOP**, **dropSiteStatus** is initialized to **XmDROP_SITE_INVALID**.

If the application has not stored the DragContext ID in a global location, these callbacks can find the DragContext ID by passing the **timeStamp** field from the callback structure to the **XmGetDragContext** function.

This example shows a callback that is called when a new drop site is entered. It checks the validity of the drop site, and uses one of three custom source icons, depending on the status.

```
static void EnterCB(w, client_data, call_data)
Widget          w;
```

```
XtPointer          client_data, call_data;
{

    XmDragContext                    dc;
    XmDropSiteEnterCallback          EnterData;
    Cardinal                         n;
    Arg                              args[MAX_ARGS];

    dc = (XmDragContext)w;
    EnterData = (XmDropSiteEnterCallback )call_data;

    n = 0;

    if (EnterData->dropSiteStatus == XmVALID_DROP_SITE) {
       XtSetArg(args[n], XmNsourceCursorIcon,
                 GetValidIcon(w)); n++;
       XtSetValues(dc, args, n);
       }
    if (EnterData->dropSiteStatus == XmINVALID_DROP_SITE) {
       XtSetArg(args[n], XmNsourceCursorIcon,
                 GetInvalidIcon(w)); n++;
       XtSetValues(dc, args, n);
       }
    if (EnterData->dropSiteStatus == XmNO_DROP_SITE) {
       XtSetArg(args[n], XmNsourceCursorIcon,
                 GetNeutralIcon(w)); n++;
       XtSetValues(dc, args, n);
       }
}
```

If a drag callback is desired, it is added to the DragContext's callback resources.The following example adds a callback named **EnterCB** that is performed when the pointer enters an active drop site:

```
Widget      dc;

    dc = XmDragStart(w, event, args, n);
    XtAddCallback(dc, XmNdropSiteEnterCallback, EnterCB,
                  NULL);
```

15.5.6 Getting Data about the Current Drop Site

The initiator can find information about the current drop site with the **XmDropSiteRetrieve** function. It must pass in the DragContext, so that the toolkit knows what drop site the request is for. The initiator can find the value of any drop site resource except the callback routines.

The following example gets the number and list of import targets for a drop site. The example shows a drop site enter callback, but it could be in any of the initiator's drag callbacks.

```
XmDropSiteEnterCallback      DragData;
        .
        .
        .
n = 0;
XtSetArg(args[n], XmNimportTargets, &importTargets); n++;
XtSetArg(args[n], XmNnumImportTargets,
            &numImportTargets); n++;
XmDropSiteRetrieve(DragData->DragContext, args, n);
```

15.5.7 Cancelling the Drag

The drag in progress can be cancelled in either of two ways. Both ways are treated the same by the toolkit.

- The user can press **KCancel**.

- The initiator can call the **XmDragCancel** function if it decides the drag should not continue for some reason.

The initiator is notified of the cancel by the **XmNdropStartCallback** with a **dropAction** field value of **XmDROP_CANCEL**.

The receiver is notified by a **XmCR_DROP_SITE_LEAVE_MESSAGE** message. This message is processed by the **XmNdragProc** in the dynamic protocol mode. This allows any drag-under effects to be undone.

15.6 Drop Receiver Responsibilities for Dropping

When the user releases the drag to start a drop, the toolkit sends a message to the receiver. The receiver's **XmNdropProc** routine processes it by checking that the proposed targets and actions are valid, and updates the status and operations fields accordingly. This information is sent back to the initiator's **XmNdropStartCallback** routine.

The application receiving a drop must

- Have registered an **XmNdropProc** routine to be processed when a drop is made on the site. This is done as part of registering a widget as a drop site.

- Make a list of transfer requests. If the drop is cancelled, the number of transfer requests is set to zero.

- Register a DropTransfer **XmNtransferProc** to process transfers from the initiator if the number of transfers is not zero.

- Call **XmDropTransferStart** at least once, to either cancel the drop or start the transfer process.

The receiving application may also do the following:

- Provide drop site Help information

- Cancel a drop

15.6.1 XmNdropProc

When a drop occurs (except for a Cancel), a message is sent from the toolkit on the initiator side to the receiver, and the receiver's **XmNdropProc** is called. Fields in its callback structure provide information about the drop to the receiver.

The **operations**, **operation**, and **dropSiteStatus** fields are initialized by the toolkit in a similar manner to that described for the receiver's **XmNdragProc** earlier in this chapter.

The **XmNdropProc** routine can update the **operations**, **operation**, and **dropSiteStatus** fields further. The final values are available to the initiator in its drop callback structures.

The **dropAction** field indicates if a normal drop is requested, or if the user requested help. For information about processing a help request, refer to Section 15.6.4.

If the receiver takes too long before ending the **XmNdropProc** routine, the toolkit will cause the drag to time out. Therefore, if the receiver needs to do any processing before the transfer other than verifying that a transfer can take place, it should start a new process and end the **XmNdropProc** routine.

Either the **XmNdropProc** routine or one of its subprocedures must start a transfer by calling **XmDropTransferStart**. The initiator waits for a transfer request to finish its part in the drop. If a drop is not possible, the drop is cancelled as described below. If a drop is possible, the **XmNdropProc** routine provides the appropriate details to start the transfer.

The **XmNdropProc** procedure creates a list of DropTransfer entries containing target and client-specific information for each transfer desired. There is a separate entry for each data-target type combination. For example, if the data is desired in both TEXT and COMPOUND_TEXT forms, there would be two entries on the list. This list and the number of items in the list are used by **XmDropTransferStart** to start the transfer.

The receiver establishes the values of the DropTransfer resources before calling **XmDropTransferStart**. Following are the DropTransfer resources:

XmNdropTransfers
> The list of drag transfer entries.

XmNincremental
> Whether to use the incremental transfer mechanism.

XmNnumDropTransfers
> The number of transfer entries in the list. This number is decremented each time a transfer is made.

XmNtransferProc
> The procedure to process transferred information. This procedure is an **XtSelectionCallbackProc** procedure. For more information about **XtSelectionCallbackProc**, see *X Toolkit Intrinsics—C Language Interface*.

XmNtransferStatus
> Whether the transfer failed or not. The default value is **XmTRANSFER_SUCCESS**.

The following example from **DNDlabel.c** in Section 15.2.1.1 creates a transfer request list of one transfer entry, asking that the initiator send its data in compound text format. Copy is the only action it accepts; the rest result in a cancelled drop. The **DropTransferCallback** routine receives and processes the data from the initiator.

```
static void HandleDrop(w, client_data, call_data)
Widget          w;
XtPointer       client_data, call_data;
{
    XmDropProcCallback      DropData;
    XmDropTransferEntryRec  transferEntries[2];
    XmDropTransferEntry     transferList;
    Arg                     args[MAX_ARGS];
    int                     n;

    DropData = (XmDropProcCallback)call_data;

    /* set the transfer resources */
    n = 0;

    /* if the action is Help, or the operation is not Copy,
     *cancel the drop */
    if ((DropData->dropAction != XmDROP) ||
        (DropData->operation != XmDROP_COPY))
        XtSetArg(args[n], XmNtransferStatus,
                    XmTRANSFER_FAILURE); n++;
    else {
        /* the drop can continue.  Establish the transfer list
         * and start the transfer */
        transferEntries[0].target = COMPOUND_TEXT;
        transferEntries[0].client_data = (XtPointer)w;
        transferList = transferEntries;
        XtSetArg(args[n], XmNdropTransfers, transferList); n++;
        XtSetArg(args[n], XmNnumDropTransfers, 1); n++;
        XtSetArg(args[n], XmNtransferProc,
                    DropTransferCallback); n++;
    }

    /* start the transfer or cancel */
    XmDropTransferStart(DropData->dragContext, args, n);
```

```
}
```

If the program could accept transfers in more than one target type, for example, TEXT and COMPOUND_TEXT, then a separate transfer entry is needed for each request:

```
transferEntries[0].target = COMPOUND_TEXT;
transferEntries[1].target = TEXT;
        .
        .
        .
XtSetArg(args[n], XmNnumDropTransfers, 2); n++;
```

15.6.2 XmDropTransfer

The toolkit on the receiver side is in charge of the transfer procedure. Information about the transfer is stored in a DropTransfer widget, which is created by the **XmDropTransferStart** routine.

Before calling **XmDropTransferStart**, the receiver stores a list of DropTransfer transfer entries in the **XmNdropTransfers** resource. Each entry contains target and client-specific information for each transfer desired. It also registers a procedure to receive transfers from the initiator in the **XmNtransferProc** resource. These resources, along with the other DropTransfer resources, are used by the **XmDropTransferStart** function.

The toolkit processes the items on the list, one at a time, decrementing **XmNnumDropTransfers** each time. When the **XmNnumDropTransfers** value is zero, the drop is finished. The toolkit on the receiver side sends a message to the initiator, whose **XmNdropFinishCallback** is then called.

If **XmNincremental** is True, the Xt selection incremental transfer protocol is used between the toolkit and the receiver, regardless of what the initiator sent. Refer to the Xt documentation for details of how to use incremental transfer. If the value is False, the transfer between the toolkit and the receiver is made in one pass, regardless of how the initiator sent it.

The **XmNtransferProc** routine receives each transfer from the initiator. If more than one target type is acceptable to the receiver, this procedure needs to check which target type was used in this transfer, and process the transferred data accordingly.

The **XmNtransferProc** routine can examine and update the DropTransfer resources during the transfer with **XtGetValues** and **XtSetValues**.

The **XmDropTransferAdd** routine is used to add to the transfer list after the transfer has begun. For example, this routine is used when a Move operation is performed, to add a new transfer entry record telling the initiator to delete the data. It can be used in other situations where the entire transfer list is not known when **XmDropTransferStart** is called.

If there are problems with the drop, it can be cancelled as described later in the chapter.

The following example from **DNDlabel.c** in Section 15.2.1.1 receives compound string data from the initiator, and uses it to replace the label of the Label widget.

```
static void TransferProc(w, closure, seltype, type,
                         value, length, format)
Widget          w;
XtPointer       closure;
Atom            *seltype;
Atom            *type;
XtPointer       value;
unsigned long   *length;
int             format;
{
    int         n;
    Arg         args[MAX_ARGS];

    /* information from the drag initiator is passed in
     * compound  text format.  Convert it to compound string
     * and replace the Label label. */

    if (*type = COMPOUND_TEXT) {
        n = 0;
        XtSetArg(args[n], XmNlabelString,
                XmCvtCTToXmString(value));
        n++;
        XtSetValues(closure, args, n);
    }
}
```

If the program is able to handle more than one target type, this routine needs to check for them all. For instance:

```
if (*type = COMPOUND_TEXT) {
    /* code to change the label to the compound text
       passed */
}
else if (*type = TEXT) {
    /* code to change the label to the text passed */
}
```

15.6.2.1 Processing Each Operation

The **XmNtransferProc** routine must be able to process the data from the initiator correctly for each operation listed in the DropSite **XmNdropSiteOperations** resource:

- If the operation is Copy, the **value** field contains a pointer to the data from the initiator. It is used to assign the value to some element in the receiver's program. The example in the previous section shows a Copy in effect. When the transfer is finished, both the initiator and receiver have the data in each of their applications.

- If the operation is Move, data is first copied to the receiver, then deleted from the initiator. It is important that the initiator not delete the data before the receiver has it. Therefore, a Move is a two-step process:

  — The first transfer is processed by the initiator like a Copy. It returns a pointer to the data in the **value** field.

  — When the **XmNtransferProc** routine has the data, it uses **XmDropTransferAdd** to make a new transfer entry for that data, setting the **target** to DELETE. The initiator will not delete the data until the receiver has issued this second transfer request.

  At the end of the transfer, the receiver has the only copy of the data.

- If the operation is Link, the pointer is used to link an element in the receiver to the data. At the end of the operation, there is only one copy of the data, belonging to the initiator, but both applications have access to it.

15.6.3 Cancelling a Drop

A drop can be cancelled only by the receiver, from the **XmNdropProc** procedure or any subroutine it calls, such as **XmNtransferProc**. To cancel a drop:

- Set the **XmNnumDropTransfers** DropTransfer resource to zero. This tells the toolkit that there are no more transfers to make and the drop is complete.

- Set the **XmNtransferStatus** to **XmTRANSFER_FAILURE**. This information is passed to the initiator in the **XmNdropFinishedCallback** structure.

- Call the **XmDropTransferStart** function from the **XmNdropProc** routine, or exit a subroutine called by the **XmNdropProc** procedure.

The transfer will be cancelled at the next transfer request. The drop is over, and the initiator's **XmNdropFinishCallback** and **XmNdragDropFinishCallback** routines are called.

The following example is from a program's **XmNdropProc** routine:

```
XtSetArg(args[n], XmNtransferStatus,
         XmTRANSFER_FAILURE); n++;
XtSetArg(args[n], XmNnumDropTransfers, 0); n++;
XmDropTransferStart(DropData->dragContext, args, n);
```

15.6.4 Providing Help

It might not always be obvious to the user what the result of dropping a particular source on a drop site might be. The user can request more information about the drop site by pressing **KHelp** while the drag icon is over the drop site.

When the user presses **KHelp**, the receiver's **XmNdropProc** routine is called with a value of **XmDROP_HELP** in the **dropAction** field of its callback structure. If the receiver supports help, it should post a dialog, providing information about the type of drop this site expects, and what it will do when a successful drop occurs.

The receiver should then exit the **XmNdropProc** routine without waiting for a response from the user. When the **XmNdropProc** routine has finished, the initiator's **XmNdropStartCallback** is called with a **dropAction** of **XmDROP_HELP** if the initiator has registered that callback. The initiator is not expected to do anything at this point, but it could provide special processing such as changing the drag icon.

Typically, the help dialog allows the user the opportunity to continue the drop or to cancel the drop. If more than one operation is possible, the dialog should explain the consequences of each operation and let the user select one. The dialog procedure may change the operation based on the user's selection:

- If the user indicates that the drop should be cancelled, the receiver's help procedure should cancel the drop by requesting no transfers, as described in the previous section.

- If the user indicates that the drop should continue, the help procedure should call **XmDropTransferStart** to begin the transfer of information from the initiator.

In either case, the help procedure must call **XmDropTranferStart** before it ends to either start the transfers or notify the initiator that no transfers will be requested.

The receiver may want to issue help information if a drop is considered invalid, even if the user has not requested it. If so, the receiver's **XmNdropProc** sets the **dropAction** field to **XmDROP_HELP**, and displays the help dialog as if help had been requested.

The following example taken from **DNDDemo.c** in Appendix B shows how the help dialog shown in the illustration was created.

Figure 15–14. Help Dialog

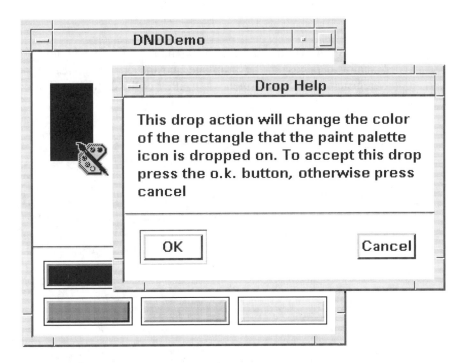

The **XmDropProc DropProcCallback** routine checks if the drop is normal
or if there is a request for help.

```
static void DropProcCallback(w, client, call)
Widget w;
XtPointer client;
XtPointer call;
{

    XmDropProcCallbackStruct *cb =
                (XmDropProcCallbackStruct *)call;

    if (appInfo->highlightRect != NULL)
        RectUnhighlight(w);

    if (cb->dropAction != XmDROP_HELP)
        HandleDrop(w, call);
    else
```

```
        HandleHelp(w, call);

}
```

The **HandleHelp** routine displays the help dialog. The text presented in the
dialog depends on the drop site and the operation. Callback routines are
registered to be performed when either of the dialog pushbuttons is pressed.

```
static void HandleHelp(w, call)
Widget w;
XtPointer call;
{

    XmDropProcCallbackStruct *cb =
                    (XmDropProcCallbackStruct *)call;
    static XmDropProcCallbackStruct client;
    Boolean                 rectFound, bgFound, pixFound;
    XmString                helpStr;
    RectPtr                 rect;
    Arg                     args[5];
    XmString                tempStr, buttonArray[2];
    int                     n = 0;

    /* the drop is valid until it is determined invalid */
    cb->dropSiteStatus = XmVALID_DROP_SITE;

    /* if we haven't created a help dialog, create one now */
    if (helpDialog == NULL) {

        XtSetArg(args[n], XmNdialogStyle,
            XmDIALOG_FULL_APPLICATION_MODAL); n++;
        XtSetArg(args[n], XmNtitle, "Drop Help"); n++;
        helpDialog = XmCreateMessageDialog(topLevel, "Help",
            args, n);

        n = 0;
        buttonArray[0] = XmStringCreateSimple("Move");
        buttonArray[1] = XmStringCreateSimple("Copy");
        XtSetArg(args[n], XmNbuttons, buttonArray); n++;
        XtSetArg(args[n], XmNbuttonCount, 2); n++;
        XtSetArg(args[n], XmNbuttonSet, 0); n++;
```

```
            XtSetArg(args[n], XmNsimpleCallback,
                    ChangeOperation); n++;
        tempStr = XmStringCreateSimple("Operations:");
        XtSetArg(args[n], XmNoptionLabel, tempStr); n++;
        helpMenu = XmCreateSimpleOptionMenu(helpDialog,
                        "helpMenu", args, n);
        XmStringFree(tempStr);
        XmStringFree(buttonArray[0]);
        XmStringFree(buttonArray[1]);

        XtAddCallback(helpDialog, XmNokCallback,
            (XtCallbackProc) HandleOK, (XtPointer) &client);
        XtAddCallback(helpDialog, XmNcancelCallback,
            (XtCallbackProc) CancelDrop,
            (XtPointer) &client);

        XtUnmanageChild(XmMessageBoxGetChild(helpDialog,
            XmDIALOG_HELP_BUTTON));

        XtRealizeWidget(helpDialog);

    }

    /* pass the necessary callback information along */
    client.dragContext = cb->dragContext;
    client.x = cb->x;
    client.y = cb->y;
    client.dropSiteStatus = cb->dropSiteStatus;
    client.operation = cb->operation;
    client.operations = cb->operations;

    /* find the valid targets */
    CheckTargets(cb->dragContext, XtDisplay(w),
                &rectFound, &bgFound, &pixFound);

    /* determine the appropriate help message */
    if (rectFound) {

        if (cb->operations == XmDROP_MOVE | XmDROP_COPY) {
            XtManageChild(helpMenu);
            helpStr = XmStringCreateLtoR(HELP_MSG4,
```

```
                    XmFONTLIST_DEFAULT_TAG);
                XtManageChild(XmMessageBoxGetChild(helpDialog,
                    XmDIALOG_OK_BUTTON));
            }
            else if (cb->operation == XmDROP_MOVE) {
                XtUnmanageChild(helpMenu);
                helpStr = XmStringCreateLtoR(HELP_MSG2,
                    XmFONTLIST_DEFAULT_TAG);
                XtManageChild(XmMessageBoxGetChild(helpDialog,
                    XmDIALOG_OK_BUTTON));
            }
            else if (cb->operation == XmDROP_COPY) {
                XtUnmanageChild(helpMenu);
                helpStr = XmStringCreateLtoR(HELP_MSG3,
                    XmFONTLIST_DEFAULT_TAG);
                XtManageChild(XmMessageBoxGetChild(helpDialog,
                    XmDIALOG_OK_BUTTON));
            }

        }
        else if (bgFound ||
                pixFound && cb->operation == XmDROP_COPY) {

            XtUnmanageChild(helpMenu);
            rect = RectFind(cb->x, cb->y);
            if (rect) {
                helpStr = XmStringCreateLtoR(HELP_MSG1,
                    XmFONTLIST_DEFAULT_TAG);
                XtManageChild(XmMessageBoxGetChild(helpDialog,
                    XmDIALOG_OK_BUTTON));
            }
            else {
                helpStr = XmStringCreateLtoR(HELP_MSG5,
                    XmFONTLIST_DEFAULT_TAG);
                XtUnmanageChild(XmMessageBoxGetChild(helpDialog,
                    XmDIALOG_OK_BUTTON));
            }

        }
        else {
            XtUnmanageChild(helpMenu);
```

```
    helpStr = XmStringCreateLtoR(HELP_MSG5,
        XmFONTLIST_DEFAULT_TAG);
    XtUnmanageChild(XmMessageBoxGetChild(helpDialog,
        XmDIALOG_OK_BUTTON));
}

/* set the help message into the dialog */
XtSetArg(args[0], XmNmessageString, helpStr);
XtSetValues(helpDialog, args, 1);

/* Free the XmString */
XmStringFree(helpStr);

/* map the help dialog */
XtManageChild(helpDialog);

}
```

The **HandleOK** callback routine is performed when the user selects the OK button. It allows the drop to continue normally by calling the **HandleDrop** routine.

```
static void HandleOK(w, client, call)
Widget w;
XtPointer client;
XtPointer call;
{

    XmDropProcCallbackStruct *cb =
            (XmDropProcCallbackStruct *)client;

    cb->operation = appInfo->operation;
    HandleDrop(w, (XtPointer) cb);

}
```

The **CancelDrop** callback routine is performed when the user selects the Cancel button. It cancels the drop by calling **XmDropTransferStart** with indicators that the drop failed.

```
static void CancelDrop(w, client, call)
Widget w;
XtPointer client;
XtPointer call;
{

    XmDropProcCallbackStruct *cb =
                    (XmDropProcCallbackStruct *)client;
    Arg                args[2];

    /* On help, we need to cancel the drop transfer */
    XtSetArg(args[0], XmNtransferStatus,
            XmTRANSFER_FAILURE);
    XtSetArg(args[1], XmNnumDropTransfers, 0);

    /* we need to start the drop transfer to cancel
       the transfer */
    XmDropTransferStart(cb->dragContext, args, 2);

}
```

15.7 Drag Initiator Responsibilities for Dropping

The drag initiator

- Registers an **XmNconvertProc** procedure to format data and send the formatted data to the receiver.

- Optionally, registers an **XmNdropStartCallback** to be performed at the drop.

- Optionally, registers an **XmNdropFinishCallback** to be performed after the drop and transfer have finished.

- Optionally, registers an **XmNdragDropFinishCallback** to be performed after the entire drag and drop transaction has finished.

15.7.1 XmNdropStartCallback

The receiver's **XmNdropProc** routine receives the drop message first if the drop occurred over a widget that was registered as a drop site. It verifies that a drop is possible, and updates fields in its callback structure. These fields become available to the initiator in its **XmNdropStartCallback** callback structure. The initiator can perform any actions necessary before the information is transferred, for example, providing a new drag icon.

The toolkit initializes the **operation**, **operations**, and **dropSiteStatus** fields as described in Section 15.5.5, with one difference: the initialization for the drag callbacks uses the values at the end of the receiver's **XmNdragProc**, while the initialization for the drop callbacks uses the values at the end of the receiver's **XmNdropProc**.

The **dropAction** field indicates the action that the receiver has taken. **XmDROP** shows that a normal drop is in progress. **XmDROP_CANCEL** shows that the receiver has cancelled the drop. If the action is **XmDROP_HELP**, the initiator is not expected to do anything, although this callback provides the opportunity to do so if desired (for example, changing the drag icon to reflect the Help request).

This procedure will not know the resolution of the help dialog. However, if the user chooses to continue, the initiator's **XmNconvertProc** routine is called as part of the transfer process, and if the user chooses to cancel, the receiver's **XmNdropFinishCallback** is called with a **dropAction** of **XmDROP_CANCEL**.

15.7.2 Dealing with Requests for Transfer

The drag initiator must register a callback to process transfers in the **XmNconvertProc** DragContext resource. This routine is called when the receiver client invokes **XmDropTransferStart**. Before calling **XmDropTransferStart**, the receiver makes a list of the target formats it wants.

The initiator's **XmNconvertProc** callback routine processes transfer requests from the receiver. The routine should be able to return information about each object being dragged in each possible target format for that item.

If the DropTransfer **XmNincremental** resource is True, information is transferred between the initiator and the toolkit using the Xt selection incremental protocol. If the value is False, the information is transferred between the initiator and the toolkit in one pass. The initiator and receiver need not be using the same incremental or nonincremental protocol.

The **XmNconvertProc** routine is called for each target type desired by the receiver, a single target type for each request. The **XmNconvertProc** routine should be able to perform any of the operations listed in the DragContext's **XmNdragOperations** resource on data in any of the target types listed in the **XmNexportTargets** resource:

- If the operation is Copy or Link, the **XmNconvertProc** returns a pointer to the data. The receiver will use this pointer to copy this data into its own storage, or establish a link using this pointer.

- If the operation is Move, the first transfer request has a normal **target** type. The **XmNconvertProc** routine should return a pointer to the data, as it would for a Copy.

  A second transfer request for the data has a **target** type of DELETE. The receiver does not issue this request until it has received the data and handled it appropriately (such as storing it in a file). Only then should the initiator delete the data.

In the following example from **DNDscroll.c** in Section 15.2.1.2, the routine returns the value of the scrollbar slider in only one target type, compound text. This information is passed to the receiver's **XmNtransferProc** routine. This routine is called once for each item in the receiver's **XmNdropTransfers** list. Copy is the only operation allowed by the application, so this routine need not process any delete requests from the receiver.

```
static
Boolean DragConvertProc(w, selection, target, typeRtn,
                        valueRtn, lengthRtn, formatRtn,
                        max_lengthRtn, client_data,
                        request_id)
Widget              w;
Atom                *selection;
Atom                *target;
Atom                *typeRtn;
XtPointer           *valueRtn;
unsigned long       *lengthRtn;
```

```
int             *formatRtn;
unsigned long   *max_lengthRtn;
XtPointer       client_data;
XtRequestId     *request_id;
{

    XmString    cstring;
    static char tmpstring[100];
    int         *value;
    int         n;
    Arg         args[MAX_ARGS];
    char        *ctext;
    char        *passtext;

    /* this routine processes only compound text */
    if (*target != COMPOUND_TEXT)
        return(False);

    /* get the value of the scrollbar slider */
    n = 0;
    XtSetArg(args[n], XmNvalue, &value); n++;
    XtGetValues(scrollbar, args, n);

    /* convert the slider value to compound text */
    sprintf(tmpstring, "%d", value);
    cstring = XmStringCreateLocalized(tmpstring);
    ctext = XmCvtXmStringToCT(cstring);

    passtext = XtMalloc(strlen(ctext)+1);
    memcpy(passtext, ctext, strlen(ctext)+1);

    /* Format the value for transfer.  Convert the value
     * from compound string to compound text for the
     * transfer */
    *typeRtn = COMPOUND_TEXT;
    *valueRtn = (XtPointer) passtext;
    *lengthRtn = strlen(passtext);
    *formatRtn = 8;
    return(True);
}
```

If the **DNDscroll.c** program in Section 15.2.1.2 processed more than one target, such as text and compound text, then this routine would have to handle both types. For example:

```
if (*target = COMPOUND_TEXT) {
    /* processing to convert the slider to compound string
       format */
    }
else if (*target = TEXT) {
    /* processing to convert the slider to text format */
    }
else
    return(False);
```

15.7.3 XmNdropFinishCallback

The **XmNdropFinishCallback** is called when the receiver's **XmNtransferProc** routine has finished processing all the transfers desired by the receiver.

The **completionStatus** field indicates whether the entire drop was successful or not.

The **operations**, **operation**, **dropSiteStatus**, and **dropAction** fields are initialized as for the **XmNdropStartCallback** procedure.

15.7.4 XmNdragDropFinishCallback

The **XmNdragDropFinishCallback** routine is performed when the complete drag and drop transaction has finished. This routine is called immediately after the initiator's **XmNdropFinishCallback** has finished. The initiator frees any remaining structures it has allocated during the drag.

The following sample code destroys any cursor icons that were created during the drag:

```
static void DnDFinishCallback(w, client_data, call_data)
Widget          w;
XtPointer       client_data, call_data;
{

    XmDragContext   dc;
    Widget          source_icon, state_icon, op_icon;
    Arg             args[MAX_ARGS];
    int             n;

    dc = (XmDragContext)w;
    source_icon = state_icon = op_icon = NULL;

    n = 0;
    XtSetArg(args[n], XmNsourceCursorIcon,
            &source_icon); n++;
    XtSetArg(args[n], XmNstateCursorIcon,
            &state_icon); n++;
    XtSetArg(args[n], XmNoperationCursorIcon,
            &op_icon); n++;
    XtGetValues(dc, args, n);

    if (source_icon != NULL)
       XtDestroyWidget(source_icon);
       if (state_icon != NULL)
          XtDestroyWidget(state_icon);
       if (op_icon != NULL)
          XtDestroyWidget(op_icon);
}
```

Chapter 16

Interclient Communication

A Motif application can communicate with another application in a variety of circumstances:

- When negotiating with a window manager such as MWM

- When the user makes or transfers a primary, secondary, or clipboard selection

- When the user drags data from one application and drops it in another

- When the application deals with a resource that is shared with other clients on the display, such as input focus, the pointer, grabs, and colormaps

The X Consortium Standard *Inter-Client Communication Conventions Manual* (ICCCM) defines standards by which X clients should communicate with each other. The Motif toolkit and MWM comply with ICCCM. Applications may define private protocols for communicating with other applications that share those protocols. If they do so, they should also conform to ICCCM standards.

16.1 Window Managers, ICCCM, and Shells

ICCCM defines protocols for communication between clients and window managers. Most of the communication takes place through properties on an application's top-level windows. The window manager can also generate events that are available to the application.

In Motif and Xt, shells handle most communication between an application and a window manager. An application seldom has to deal directly with properties or events. The application can usually specify properties by setting resources of a shell. Shells also select for and handle most events from the window manager.

This section discusses the relations between some shell resources, properties, and events concerned with communication between an application and any window manager. The following section discusses resources, properties, and events that apply to MWM in particular.

16.1.1 Application Startup

When a top-level window is mapped, the window manager may search the resource database for information about the window. The resource name and class come from the WM_CLASS property for the window. This property contains two consecutive strings that identify the instance and class names.

Xt sets the WM_CLASS property when a shell that is a subclass of **WMShell** is realized. The instance name is the name of the shell. For an ApplicationShell, this is generally the name of the application passed to **XtDisplayInitialize**. The class name is the application class from the highest-level widget in the hierarchy. For an ApplicationShell, this is generally the application class passed to **XtDisplayInitialize**. If the root widget is not an ApplicationShell, the class name is the widget's class name.

Most window managers display a name for a top-level window, often in a title bar. The window name comes from the WM_NAME property. This property is a string whose encoding is identified by the type of the property.

A Motif application specifies a window name using the WMShell resources **XmNtitle** and **XmNtitleEncoding**. If the shell is a TopLevelShell subclass and the **XmNiconName** resource is not NULL, the value of that resource is the default for **XmNtitle**. Otherwise, the default title is the name of the shell. For a dialog, an application can supply a title as the value of the BulletinBoard resource **XmNdialogTitle**.

XmNtitleEncoding is an atom representing the encoding of the name. The default title encoding depends on whether or not a language procedure has been set. If no language procedure has been set, the default is STRING. If a language procedure has been set, the title is assumed to be in the encoding of the locale and is passed to **XmbTextListToTextProperty** with an encoding style of **XStdICCTextStyle**. The returned property is used as the WM_NAME property. If the title is fully convertible to type STRING, the encoding is STRING; otherwise, the encoding is COMPOUND_TEXT.

16.1.2 Window Configuration

A window manager can assign any position and size to a window. The user and application can supply preferred positions and sizes, but the window manager is free to use or ignore these as it wishes.

The user generally specifies position and size using the **-geometry** option when invoking the command that starts the application. In Motif, the value specified for **-geometry** becomes the value of the Shell **XmNgeometry** resource. An application should never set this resource itself; it should reserve it for the user. An application specifies size and position by supplying values for the Core resources **XmNx**, **XmNy**, **XmNheight**, **XmNwidth**, and **XmNborderWidth**. When an x, y, width, or height value is specified for both **XmNgeometry** and one of the specific geometry resources, the value from **XmNgeometry** takes precedence.

The MWM **positionIsFrame** resource determines whether MWM interprets x and y values as referring to the upper left corner of the client window itself or the upper left corner of the frame that MWM puts around the client window. By default x and y values refer to the frame.

When a top-level window is mapped, MWM uses the following order of precedence in determining size and position:

- If the user specifies position and size using the **-geometry** option, MWM uses those values.

- If the MWM **interactivePlacement** resource is True, MWM waits for the user to select a position using a button press for the upper left corner of the window. If the user drags the pointer down and to the right with the mouse button pressed, the user can then determine the size of the window by releasing the mouse button. If the user does not determine a size in this way, MWM uses the window's **XmNwidth** and **XmNheight**.

- If the MWM **usePPosition** resource is True, or if **usePPosition** is **nonzero** and the window's **XmNx** or **XmNy** is nonzero, MWM uses the window's **XmNx** and **XmNy** to position the window. MWM uses the window's **XmNwidth** and **XmNheight** for the window's size. If the MWM **positionOnScreen** resource is True and if the window would be completely off the screen, MWM alters the window position so that at least part of the window is on the screen.

- If the MWM **clientAutoPlace** resource is True, MWM positions the window with its top left corner offset horizontally and vertically from the last client mapped. MWM uses the window's **XmNwidth** and **XmNheight** for the window's size.

- MWM positions the window in the upper left corner of the screen and uses the window's **XmNwidth** and **XmNheight** for the window's size.

Before a window is mapped, the application communicates additional position and size information to the window manager through the WM_NORMAL_HINTS property on the window. This property is of type WM_SIZE_HINTS and contains a number of fields derived from WMShell resources:

XmNminHeight, XmNminWidth

Specifies the minimum height and width that the application wants the widget's window to have. If an initial value is supplied for one of these resources but not for the other, the value of the unspecified resource is set to 1 when the widget is realized. If no value is specified for either resource, MWM uses the values from **XmNbaseHeight** and **XmNbaseWidth** if specified. Otherwise, MWM uses a minimum height and width of at least 1.

XmNmaxHeight, **XmNmaxWidth**

Specifies the maximum height and width that the application wants the widget's window to have. If an initial value is supplied for one of these resources but not for the other, the value of the unspecified resource is set to 32767 when the widget is realized. If the MWM resource **maximumClientSize** is specified, MWM uses that value to determine the maximum window size. Otherwise, MWM uses the maximum height and width from the WM_NORMAL_HINTS property, except that the window size may not exceed the height and width specified by the MWM **maximumMaximumSize** resource.

XmNbaseHeight, **XmNbaseWidth**

Specifies the base for a progression of preferred heights and widths for the window manager to use in sizing the widget. The preferred heights are **XmNbaseHeight** plus integral multiples of **XmNheightInc**, with a minimum of **XmNminHeight** and a maximum of **XmNmaxHeight**. The preferred widths are **XmNbaseWidth** plus integral multiples of **XmNwidthInc**, with a minimum of **XmNminWidth** and a maximum of **XmNmaxWidth**. If an initial value is supplied for one of these resources but not for the other, the value of the unspecified resource is set to 0 when the widget is realized. If no value is specified for either resource, MWM uses the values from **XmNminHeight** and **XmNminWidth** if specified. Otherwise, MWM uses a base height and width of at least 1.

XmNheightInc, **XmNwidthInc**

Specifies the increment for a progression of preferred heights and widths for the window manager to use in sizing the widget. The preferred heights are **XmNbaseHeight** plus integral multiples of **XmNheightInc**, with a minimum of **XmNminHeight** and a maximum of **XmNmaxHeight**. The preferred widths are **XmNbaseWidth** plus integral multiples of **XmNwidthInc**, with a minimum of **XmNminWidth** and a maximum of **XmNmaxWidth**. If an initial value is supplied for one of these resources but not for the other, the value of the unspecified resource is set to 1 when the widget is realized. If no value is specified for either resource, MWM uses an increment of 1.

XmNminAspectX, **XmNminAspectY**

> Specifies the numerator and denominator of the minimum aspect ratio (X/Y) that the application wants the widget's window to have. If no value is specified for either resource, MWM imposes no minimum aspect ratio.

XmNmaxAspectX, **XmNmaxAspectY**

> Specifies the numerator and denominator of the maximum aspect ratio (X/Y) that the application wants the widget's window to have. If no value is specified for either resource, MWM imposes no maximum aspect ratio.

XmNwinGravity

> Specifies the window gravity for use by the window manager in positioning the widget. If no initial value is specified, the value is set when the widget is realized. If **XmNgeometry** is not NULL, **XmNwinGravity** is set to the window gravity returned by **XWMGeometry**. Otherwise, **XmNwinGravity** is set to **NorthWestGravity**.

After a window is mapped, an application can request changes to window size or position by calling **XtSetValues** for one or more of the Core geometry resources. A user can generally employ window manager facilities to move or resize a top-level window.

Calling **XtSetValues** for a geometry resource generates a geometry request that may propagate up the widget hierarchy to the shell. This may cause the shell to make its own geometry request, and this invokes the shell's **root_geometry_manager** procedure. This procedure uses **XConfigureWindow** to ask the window manager to change the window's size or position.

If a window manager responds to a configuration request by denying it or by moving the window without resizing it, the window manager sends a synthetic **ConfigureNotify** event. If the window is resized, the window receives a real **ConfigureNotify** event.

These events may be handled by either the **root_geometry_manager** procedure or a Shell event handler. If the VendorShell resource **XmNuseAsyncGeometry** is True, the **root_geometry_manager** procedure does not wait for the window manager to respond to the configuration request, but instead returns **XtGeometryYes**. If the WMShell resource **XmNwaitForWm** is True and if the window manager grants the configuration request within the **XmNwmTimeout** interval, the

root_geometry_manager procedure updates the widget's geometry resources and returns **XtGeometryYes**. Otherwise, the **root_geometry_manager** procedure returns **XtGeometryNo** and relies on the event handler to reconfigure the widget when it receives a subsequent **ConfigureNotify** event.

The shell's **ConfigureNotify** event handler is invoked when the user reconfigures a top-level window or when the application reconfigures a window and this reconfiguration is not handled by the **root_geometry_manager** procedure. The event handler updates the shell's core geometry fields with the values allowed by the window manager. If the size of the shell changes, the event handler calls the shell's **resize** procedure. This procedure calls **XtResizeWidget** to change the height, width, and border width of the child to be the same as those of the shell.

16.1.3 Icons

An application uses several properties to communicate with the window manager about icons associated with top-level windows. A Motif application can use resources of several Shell subclasses to specify values for these properties.

When a window is first mapped, it can appear in either its normal state or iconic state. An application uses a field in the WM_HINTS property to tell the window manager which initial state it prefers. A Motif application specifies the initial state by setting the WMShell resource **XmNinitialState** or the TopLevelShell resource **XmNiconic**. **XmNiconic** takes precedence over **XmNinitialState**. After a window is realized, an application can use **XtSetValues** for **XmNiconic** to either iconify or deiconify the window.

An application can supply a name, a bitmap, or a window for the window manager to use as an icon. When a top-level window is in iconic state, the window manager usually displays the icon window if one is supplied, or else the icon pixmap if one is supplied, or else the icon name. MWM uses the **iconDecoration** resource in determining what aspects of an icon to display.

The icon name comes from the WM_ICON_NAME property. Like WM_NAME, this property is a string whose encoding is identified by the type of the property.

A Motif application specifies an icon name using the TopLevelShell resources **XmNiconName** and **XmNiconNameEncoding**. The default icon name is the name of the shell. **XmNiconNameEncoding** is an atom representing the encoding of the name. The default encoding depends on whether or not a language procedure has been set. If no language procedure has been set, the default is STRING. If a language procedure has been set, the icon name is assumed to be in the encoding of the locale and is passed to **XmbTextListToTextProperty** with an encoding style of **XStdICCTextStyle**. The returned property is used as the WM_ICON_NAME property. If the icon name is fully convertible to type STRING, the encoding is STRING; otherwise, the encoding is COMPOUND_TEXT.

An application uses fields in the WM_HINTS property to supply an icon bitmap and an optional mask for displaying the bitmap in a nonrectangular shape. A Motif application specifies an icon bitmap as the value of the WMShell resource **XmNiconPixmap**, and it specifies the mask as the value of the WMShell resource **XmNiconMask**.

An application uses a field in the WM_HINTS property to supply an icon window. A Motif application specifies an icon window as the value of the WMShell resource **XmNiconWindow**. The icon window must be an InputOutput child of the root window. It must also use the root visual and the default colormap of the screen. The application must not map, unmap, or configure this window. It must, however, select for Expose events on the window and redisplay the contents when it receives these events.

The window manager may specify preferred maximum and minimum sizes and size increments for icon bitmaps and windows. To do this it puts a WM_ICON_SIZE property on the root window. MWM uses the **iconImageMaximum** and **iconImageMinimum** resources, with increments of 1, in setting this property. Before an application specifies an icon bitmap or window, it should use the Xlib routine **XGetIconSizes** to check these constraints and then supply a bitmap or window that is of one of the preferred sizes.

An application can use two fields of the WM_HINTS property to supply preferred x and y root coordinates for the icon location. A Motif application specifies these coordinates as the values of the WMShell resources **XmNiconX** and **XmNiconY**. The window manager may ignore these values. MWM uses the **useIconBox**, **iconPlacement**, and **iconPlacementMargin** resources in determining where to place icons.

16.1.4 Window Groups

An application can use a field of the WM_HINTS property to supply the window ID of a window to serve as the "leader" for a group of windows. The window manager may treat all windows in this group as a whole for certain purposes, such as showing a single icon when the entire group is iconified.

A Motif application specifies a window group leader as the value of the WMShell resource **XmNwindowGroup**. For VendorShell and its subclasses, if the shell has a parent, Motif sets the **XmNwindowGroup** to the parent's window at the time that the shell and its parent are both realized. Otherwise, the default value is **XtUnspecifiedWindowGroup**, which means that no window group is set.

16.1.5 Menus and Dialogs

A window manager may treat dialogs differently from other top-level windows, and it must not interfere with menus at all.

An application tells a window manager not to decorate or otherwise interfere with a window by setting the **override_redirect** attribute of the window to True. A Motif application does this by setting the **Shell** resource **XmNoverrideRedirect** to True, or by using an **OverrideShell**, which has a default value of True for this resource. **XmMenuShell** is a subclass of **OverrideShell**, and MenuShells are the only widgets that should have a value of True for **XmNoverrideRedirect**. An application normally does not supply a value other than the default for this resource.

An application tells a window manager to treat a window as transient or secondary by setting the window's WM_TRANSIENT_FOR property. This property contains the window ID of another top-level window, usually the window from which the transient window was popped up. A Motif application generally specifies this property by creating a DialogShell, a subclass of TransientShell, which has an **XmNtransientFor** resource. The value is a widget, and the default is set to the shell's parent at the time that both the shell and its parent are realized. The window of the **XmNtransientFor** widget is used for the WM_TRANSIENT_FOR property. For a shell that is not a subclass of TransientShell, an application can set the WMShell **XmNtransient** resource to True. The

XmNwindowGroup is then used for the WM_TRANSIENT_FOR property. An application normally does not supply a value other than the default for **XmNtransient** or **XmNtransientFor**.

MWM treats transient windows differently from other top-level windows. By default it keeps transient windows stacked on top of their primary windows and does not allow transient windows to be iconified separately from their primary windows. The MWM **transientDecoration** and **transientFunctions** resources determine which decorations and functions apply to transient windows. An application can further specify these decorations and functions by using the VendorShell **XmNmwmDecorations** and **XmNmwmFunctions** resources, explained in Section 16.2.

16.1.6 Input Focus

ICCCM recognizes four models for the relationship between clients and window managers in setting input focus:

No input   The client does not expect keyboard input and does not want the window manager to set focus to any of its windows.

Passive input

The client expects keyboard input and wants the window manager to set focus to its top-level window. It does not set focus itself.

Locally active input

The client expects keyboard input and wants the window manager to set focus to its top-level window. It may also set focus to one of its subwindows when one of its windows already has the focus. It does not set focus itself when the current focus is in a window that the client does not own.

Globally active input

The client expects keyboard input but does not want the window manager to set focus to any of its windows. Instead, it sets focus itself, even when the current focus is in a window that the client does not own.

An application tells the window which model it prefers by using two properties:

- If the **input** field of the WM_HINTS property is True, the application wants the window manager to set focus to its top-level window. If this field is False, the application does not want the window manager to set focus.

- If the WM_PROTOCOLS property contains a WM_TAKE_FOCUS atom, the application sometimes sets focus itself. If the WM_PROTOCOLS property does not contain a WM_TAKE_FOCUS atom, the application does not set focus itself.

These combinations are summarized in the following table:

Table 16–1. Input Models

Input Model	Input field	WM_TAKE_FOCUS
No input	False	Absent
Passive	True	Absent
Locally active	True	Present
Globally active	False	Present

A window manager generally does not set input focus to a window when the WM_HINTS **input** field is False. A window with a WM_TAKE_FOCUS protocol may receive a ClientMessage when the window manager wants the window to accept keyboard focus. The window may respond by setting the input focus or by ignoring the message.

A Motif application can set the **input** field of the WM_HINTS property by specifying a value for the WMShell resource **XmNinput**. The application can install the WM_TAKE_FOCUS atom on the WM_PROTOCOLS property by calling **XmAddWMProtocols** or **XmAddWMProtocolCallback**, explained in Section 16.3.

A Motif application normally should avoid setting input focus itself. The application can control the location of focus within its subwindows by using the VendorShell resource **XmNkeyboardFocusPolicy**, the Gadget, Primitive, and Manager resource **XmNtraversalOn**, and the **XmProcessTraversal** routine. If the application wants a widget to receive no input at all, it can use **XtSetSensitive** to make the widget insensitive. If the application needs to set focus directly, it should usually use

XtSetKeyboardFocus and avoid using **XSetInputFocus**. For more information, see Chapter 13.

A number of MWM resources influence keyboard focus. When **keyboardFocusPolicy** is "explicit" (the default), the user must press **BSelect** on a window or its decoration to give it focus. When **keyboardFocusPolicy** is "pointer", the window that contains the pointer has the focus. With an explicit policy, other resources determine whether a window has focus when it is first mapped (**startupKeyFocus**), deiconified (**deiconifyKeyFocus**), or raised (**raiseKeyFocus**). When **autoKeyFocus** is True, and the window with focus is iconified or withdrawn, focus passes to the window that last had focus. When **enforceKeyFocus** is True, MWM sets focus to globally active windows.

16.1.7 Colormaps

An application can create and set colormaps for its windows, but only the window manager should install colormaps. Each window manager has a colormap focus policy that determines which top-level window has the colormap focus at a given time. When a window has colormap focus, the window manager installs one or more colormaps associated with that window.

If all windows in an application use the same colormap, the application need take no special action to tell the window manager to use that colormap. The window manager keeps track of the colormap attribute for each top-level window and installs that colormap when the window has colormap focus.

If an application uses different colormaps for some windows in its hierarchy, it must tell the window manager about those colormaps by setting a WM_COLORMAP_WINDOWS property on the top-level window. This property is a list of windows whose colormaps the window manager should install when the top-level window has colormap focus. The list should be in order of priority, with the windows whose colormaps the application would most like to have installed listed first. The application can use **XSetWMColormapWindows** to set this property.

On many servers, only one hardware colormap can be installed at a time. This may cause colors in windows that use different colormaps to be displayed incorrectly when their own colormaps are not installed. To reduce contention for colormaps, applications should use the facilities for standard colormaps described in *Xlib—C Language X Interface*.

The MWM **colormapFocusPolicy** resource determines the colormap focus policy. When the value is "keyboard", the window with keyboard focus has the colormap focus. When the value is "pointer", the window under the pointer has the colormap focus, regardless of whether that window also has keyboard focus. When the value is "explicit", the colormap focus changes only when the user invokes the **f.focus_color** function.

When a window with colormap focus has a WM_COLORMAP_WINDOWS property, the user can install the next and previous colormaps on the list by invoking the **f.next_cmap** and **f.prev_cmap** functions.

16.1.8 Application Shutdown and Restart

An application may run under a session manager with facilities for saving and restoring the state of the application. An application communicates with a session manager by placing WM_COMMAND and WM_CLIENT_MACHINE properties on its top-level windows. WM_COMMAND contains a string that would restart the client in its current state.

A Motif application should have only one non-NULL WM_COMMAND property for each logical application (that is, for each ApplicationShell hierarchy). Xt sets the WM_COMMAND property for an ApplicationShell when the shell is realized, using the command that started the application. Note that if an application is using an unrealized ApplicationShell with multiple TopLevelShell popup children, Xt will not place a WM_COMMAND property on any window, and the application must put this property on some (possibly unmapped) window in the application.

WM_CLIENT_MACHINE contains a string that represents the name of the host on which the application is running. Xt sets the WM_CLIENT_MACHINE for a WMShell or subclass when the shell is realized.

A session manager can inform an application when a top-level window is about to be deleted or when the application should try to save its state. An application expresses interest in these notifications by adding a WM_DELETE_WINDOW atom or a WM_SAVE_YOURSELF atom to the WM_PROTOCOLS property.

If a WM_DELETE_WINDOW protocol exists, the session manager sends a ClientMessage when it wants to delete a top-level window. The application may ask for user confirmation and may decide to comply or not comply with the request. If it decides to comply, the application can either unmap or destroy the window.

If a WM_SAVE_YOURSELF protocol exists, the session manager sends a ClientMessage when it wants the application to save its current state in such a way that it could be restored. The application should do whatever is necessary to save its internal state and then update the non-NULL WM_COMMAND property with a command that will restart the application in its current state. Finally, the application updates the WM_COMMAND property on the window that has the WM_SAVE_YOURSELF protocol if it has not already done so. This informs the session manager that the application has finished saving its state.

Motif installs a WM_DELETE_WINDOW protocol for VendorShell and its subclasses. It also installs a procedure to be called after any application-supplied WM_DELETE_WINDOW handlers are invoked. This procedure destroys the widget, unmaps the window, or does nothing, depending on the value of the VendorShell resource **XmNdeleteResponse**. If the procedure destroys an ApplicationShell, it then exits the application.

An application can add its own WM_DELETE_WINDOW and WM_SAVE_YOURSELF protocols by using **XmAddWMProtocols** or **XmAddWMProtocolCallback**.

When the user invokes the **f.kill** command, MWM sends a ClientMessage if an application has a WM_DELETE_WINDOW protocol and a separate ClientMessage if an application has a WM_SAVE_YOURSELF protocol. If the application has no WM_DELETE_WINLOW protocol, the **f.kill** command kills the client. In this case, if a WM_SAVE_YOURSELF protocol exists, MWM sends the ClientMessage and then waits for the time specified by the **quitTimeout** resource before killing the client.

16.2 MWM Properties and Resources

In addition to the properties and protocols described in ICCCM, Motif uses properties and protocols of its own. A Motif application usually specifies these properties using VendorShell and BulletinBoard resources.

16.2.1 Decorations

An application expresses preferences for MWM window decorations by supplying a value for the **decorations** field of the _MOTIF_WM_HINTS property on the window. A Motif application does this by supplying a value for the VendorShell resource **XmNmwmDecorations**. The value is the bitwise inclusive OR of one or more flag bit constants, each of which indicates a preference for or against a particular decoration. If a value has been supplied for this resource, MWM displays only those decorations specified by both **XmNmwmDecorations** and the MWM **clientDecoration** resource (for primary windows) or specified by both **XmNmwmDecorations** and the MWM **transientDecoration** resource (for transient windows). If no value has been supplied for **XmNmwmDecorations**, MWM displays the decorations specified by the **clientDecoration** or **transientDecoration** resource.

16.2.2 Functions

An application expresses preferences for MWM window functions by supplying a value for the **functions** field of the _MOTIF_WM_HINTS property on the window. A Motif application does this by supplying a value for the VendorShell resource **XmNmwmFunctions**. The value is the bitwise inclusive OR of one or more flag bit constants, each of which indicates a preference for or against a particular function. If a value has been supplied for this resource, MWM displays only those functions specified by both **XmNmwmFunctions** and the MWM **clientFunctions** resource (for primary windows) or specified by both **XmNmwmFunctions** and the MWM **transientFunctions** resource (for transient windows). If no value has been supplied for **XmNmwmFunctions**, MWM displays the functions specified by the **clientFunctions** or **transientFunctions** resource.

BulletinBoard may change the initial value of **XmNmwmFunctions** if its parent is a subclass of VendorShell. The BulletinBoard resource **XmNnoResize** determines whether the decorations of the VendorShell parent include resize controls.

16.2.3 Input Mode

An application can inform MWM that it should impose constraints on which windows can obtain input. It does so by setting the **input_mode** field of the _MOTIF_WM_HINTS property on a window. A Motif application does this by supplying a value for the VendorShell resource **XmNmwmInputMode**. For a BulletinBoard whose parent is a DialogShell, the application can set **XmNmwmInputMode** indirectly by specifying a value for the BulletinBoard resource **XmNdialogStyle**.

The possible modes are as follows:

Modeless   Input goes to any window.

Primary application modal
>   Input does not go to ancestors of this window or their descendants.

Full application modal
>   Input goes to this window or its descendants and to other applications but not to other windows in this application.

System modal
>   Input goes only to this window or it: descendants.

16.2.4 Window Menu

An application can supply items for MWM to add to the end of the window menu for a window by specifying a value for the _MOTIF_WM_MENU property. A Motif application does this by supplying a value for the VendorShell resource **XmNmwmMenu**. The window menu itself is the value of the MWM **windowMenu** resource.

16.2.5 MWM Messages

An application can specify a message for MWM to send the application when the user invokes the **f.send_msg** function. The application places a _MOTIF_WM_MESSAGES atom on the WM_PROTOCOLS property for the window. The application also places an atom on the _MOTIF_WM_MESSAGES property. When the **f.send_msg** function is invoked with this atom as the argument, MWM sends the application a ClientMessage. The application can use **XmAddWMProtocols** to place a _MOTIF_WM_MESSAGES atom on the WM_PROTOCOLS property, and it can use **XmAddProtocolCallback** to place an atom on the _MOTIF_WM_MESSAGES property and associate it with a routine to be called when MWM sends the ClientMessage.

16.2.6 MWM Information

MWM maintains a _MOTIF_WM_INFO property on the root window of each screen it manages. This property is available for applications to inspect but not to change. The **XmIsMotifWMRunning** routine examines this property when determining whether or not MWM is running.

16.3 Atom and Protocol Management

Motif has two routines that can reduce overhead for applications that use atoms. **XmInternAtom** returns an existing atom or (if the third argument is False) creates and returns an atom that matches the given string. **XmGetAtomName** returns the string that matches the given atom. These functions parallel **XInternAtom** and **XGetAtomName**, but they cache the atoms and names on the client side and avoid unnecessary trips to the server.

Motif has a number of routines to help an application install protocol atoms and handle ClientMessages sent when the protocols are invoked. These routines maintain an internal registry of properties, protocol atoms associated with the properties, and callback routines associated with the protocol atoms. The application can use these routines with shells that are subclasses of VendorShell.

XmAddProtocols associates one or more protocol atoms with a property for a given shell. If the shell is realized, it adds those protocols to the property for the shell's window. If the shell is not realized, it arranges for the protocols to be added to the property and for a ClientMessage event handler to be added at the time the shell is realized. **XmAddWMProtocols** is a specialized version that adds protocols for the WM_PROTOCOLS property.

XmAddProtocolCallback adds a callback routine to a callback list associated with a protocol. It calls **XmAddProtocols** if the protocol has not yet been registered. When the protocol manager's ClientMessage event handler receives a ClientMessage for the protocol, it invokes the procedures on the associated callback list. The first argument to each callback procedure is the shell associated with the protocol. The second argument is the client data, if any, specified in the call to **XmAddProtocolCallback**. The third argument is a pointer to an **XmAnyCallbackStruct** structure whose **reason** member is **XmCR_PROTOCOLS** and whose **event** member is a pointer to the ClientMessage event. In the ClientMessage event, the **message_type** member is the property that contains the protocol, the **format** member is 32, and the **data.l[0]** member is the protocol atom. **XmAddWMProtocolCallback** is a specialized version of **XmAddProtocolCallback** that adds a callback for a protocol on the WM_PROTOCOLS property.

An application can also use **XmSetProtocolHooks** to specify a routine to be called before or after a callback list is invoked for a protocol. **XmSetWMProtocolHooks** is a specialized version that adds prehooks and posthooks for a protocol on the WM_PROTOCOLS property.

Once an application has registered a protocol and optional callback routines, it can make the protocol active or inactive. A protocol is active if it has been added to the associated property for the window. A protocol is inactive if it has been removed from the associated property. **XmActivateProtocol** makes a registered protocol active, and **XmDeactivateProtocol** makes a protocol inactive. **XmActivateWMProtocol** and **XmDeactivateWMProtocol** are specialized versions that activate or inactivate a protocol on the WM_PROTOCOLS property.

XmRemoveProtocolCallback removes a callback routine from the callback list associated with the protocol. **XmRemoveProtocols** removes one or more protocols and all callbacks associated with those protocols from the internal registry. If the shell is realized, it removes those protocols from the associated property. **XmRemoveWMProtocolCallback** and

XmRemoveWMProtocols are specialized versions that remove callbacks or protocols for the WM_PROTOCOLS property.

16.4 Selections

Selections are the standard ICCCM mechanism for transferring data from one application to another on the same display. Each selection is represented by an atom. The display contains only one selection of each type. It is owned by a client or by no one and, if owned, is attached to a window of the owning client. Any client may assert or remove ownership of a selection.

The data represented by the selection is internal to the client that owns the selection. If another client wants to obtain the data in the selection, it asks the owner to convert the selection to some target type. Each target type is represented by an atom. The owner may or may not be able to convert the selection to the requested type or to some other type. If it can convert the selection, the owner places the converted data into a property on the requesting client's window, using the actual target as the type of the property. The owner sends the requestor a SelectionNotify event when the conversion (whether successful or not) is complete. For a successful transfer, this event includes the property on the requestor's window that contains the converted selection. When the requestor receives a SelectionNotify event for a successful conversion, it retrieves the contents of the specified property from its window and then deletes the property.

16.4.1 Selection Types

ICCCM defines three selections that all clients should support, although clients may support other selections as well:

PRIMARY   The principal selection.

SECONDARY

> A means of exchanging data without disturbing the primary selection.

CLIPBOARD

The selection often used to "cut" or "copy" data from one client and "paste" it into another. A client transfers data to the clipboard by asserting ownership of this selection. A client transfers data from the clipboard by requesting conversion of the selection.

A separate client may also represent the clipboard. This client can notice when it loses the selection (because another client wants to transfer data to the clipboard), then request a conversion of the selection and finally reassert ownership.

The Motif Text and TextField widgets support all three of these selections. The List widget supports only copying of selected items to the clipboard. Motif also makes use of other selections, notably for the destination widget and for drag and drop. For more information on drag and drop selections, see Chapter 15.

16.4.2 Targets

ICCCM lists a number of suggested target atoms that clients may support. Clients are free to request and perform conversion to these and to other targets as well. Clients that follow ICCCM must support only three targets:

TARGETS   When a selection owner is asked to convert the selection to this type, it returns a list of the target types to which it can convert the selection. By first requesting a conversion to TARGETS, a client can determi e whether a conversion request of a particular type is likely to succeed or fail.

MULTIPLE   This target signifies a request for a series of conversions. The requestor places in its specified window property a list of pairs of atoms. Each pair names a target and a property. The selection owner processes each pair in order, converting the selection to the specified target and placing the results in the specified property. It sends the requestor a SelectionNotify event when all conversions are complete.

TIMESTAMP

The owner returns the timestamp it used to obtain ownership of the selection.

Some targets have side-effects for the owner. Among these targets are the following:

DELETE   The owner deletes the selection and, if successful, returns a zero-length property of type NULL.

INSERT_SELECTION
           The requestor places in its specified window property a pair of atoms that names a selection and a target. The owner requests conversion of the specified selection to the specified target and places the result at the location of the selection named in the INSERT_SELECTION request. The owner then returns a zero-length property of type NULL. The Motif Text widget uses this target with the destination selection when it asks the owner of the destination selection to insert the secondary selection at the destination.

INSERT_PROPERTY
           The requestor places in its specified window property some data to be inserted at the location of the selection named in the request. The owner then returns a zero-length property of type NULL.

16.4.3 Text Conversion

Conversion of textual selections raises problems, because the requesting client and the selection owner may be in different locales. A requestor may specify a target type of TEXT, but the owner may then convert the selection into any encoding that is convenient. The type of the returned property indicates what this encoding is; the type will never be TEXT. The requestor may or may not be able to convert the value into a useful form.

Converted text is generally of one of three types:

STRING   The text includes only characters in ISO8859-1 plus TAB and NEWLINE.

COMPOUND_TEXT
           The text is in compound text format as specified by the X Consortium Standard *Compound Text Encoding*.

locale encoding
> The text is in the encoding of the selection owner's locale. The encoding is represented by the atom used as the type of the returned property.

A selection owner can use **XmbTextListToTextProperty** or **XwcTextListToTextProperty** to convert text in its own locale to a text property. The type of the property is determined by the composition of the text and by the encoding style passed to **XmbTextListToTextProperty**. Encoding styles exist for converting text to STRING, COMPOUND_TEXT, and the encoding of the locale. Another encoding style specifies conversion to STRING if all the characters in the text can be so converted, or otherwise to COMPOUND_TEXT.

A Motif application that has text in compound strings can use **XmCvtXmStringToCT** to convert a compound string to compound text. The application can then place the compound text in the requestor's property using type COMPOUND_TEXT.

STRING, COMPOUND_TEXT, and the locale encoding can also be selection targets. To obtain a text selection in its own locale, an application can request conversion to one of these targets and can then call **XmbTextPropertyToTextList** or **XwcTextPropertyToTextList** to convert the returned property to text in the current locale. An application can also request conversion to TEXT, but there is no guarantee that it can convert the returned property to text in the current locale.

One possible strategy is first to request conversion to TARGETS. If one of the returned targets is the encoding of the current locale (as determined by a call to **XmbTextListToTextProperty** with an encoding style of **XTextStyle**), the application can request conversion to that target. Otherwise, if one of the returned targets is COMPOUND_TEXT, the application can request conversion to that target. If neither the locale encoding nor COMPOUND_TEXT is one of the returned targets, the application can request conversion to STRING or TEXT if the selection owner supports one of those targets.

A Motif application that has text in compound strings can request conversion of a selection to COMPOUND_TEXT and can then use **XmCvtCTToXmString** to convert the returned property to a compound string.

16.4.4 Incremental Transfers

When a selection contains a large quantity of data, the selection owner may place converted data into the returned property incrementally. It signals the requestor that it intends to do this by setting the type of the returned property to INCR and placing into the property an integer that represents the minimum number of bytes of data to be transferred. The owner and requestor must then cooperate in transferring the data.

The requestor starts the interaction by deleting the returned property. The owner then appends the first chunk of data to the same property, giving the property the type of the converted data. The requestor receives a PropertyNotify event for the new value of the property, retrieves the data in the property, and deletes the property. The owner receives a PropertyNotify event for the deletion of the property and then appends the next chunk of data to the property. This interaction continues until all that data has been transferred. The owner then writes zero-length data to the property, and the requestor deletes the property to terminate the interaction.

16.4.5 The Xt Selection Interface

Xlib provides routines to set the owner of a selection (**XSetSelectionOwner**, get the owner of a selection (**XGetSelectionOwner**), and convert a selection (**XConvertSelection**). Applications that use only the Xlib interface must do additional work to support selections, such as providing a handler for SelectionRequest events to convert selections that the application owns.

Xt provides a richer interface for handling selections. This interface consists of two parallel sets of routines, one for transferring data atomically and the other for transferring data incrementally. In an atomic data transfer, the owner converts all data for one selection request before responding to another request to convert the same selection. In an incremental data transfer, the owner may need to start a second conversion before finishing the first conversion for a given selection. The selection owner and the requestor need not use the same (atomic or incremental) interface. This distinction is independent of whether the actual transfer uses the ICCCM incremental (INCR) protocol. For an atomic transfer of a large amount of data, Xt automatically uses the ICCCM incremental protocol when necessary.

An application asserts ownership of a selection by calling **XtOwnSelection** for atomic transfers or **XtOwnSelectionIncremental** for incremental transfers. In this call, the application can supply a procedure to convert the selection and procedures to be called when the requestor has retrieved the data and when the application loses ownership of the selection. For an incremental transfer, the conversion routine can be called multiple times for the same request and can be called to begin a new conversion before it has transferred all data for the first request. The conversion routine can obtain the SelectionRequest event by calling **XtGetSelectionRequest**. When calling **XtOwnSelectionIncremental** the application can also provide a routine to be called to cancel a conversion in progress. With either atomic or incremental transfer, an application relinquishes ownership of the selection by calling **XtDisownSelection**.

An application requests conversion of a selection by calling **XtGetSelectionValue** or **XtGetSelectionValues** for atomic transfers, or **XtGetSelectionValueIncremental** or **XtGetSelectionValuesIncremental** for incremental transfers. The difference between the "Value" and "Values" form of each routine is that the "Values" form allows multiple conversions while guaranteeing that the selection owner does not change during the call. When invoking one of these routines, the requestor supplies a routine to be called to deliver the data from the returned property.

Xt provides a timeout for the period in which a requestor and a selection owner must respond to each other. The initial value comes from the **selectionTimeout** application resource. An application can use **XtAppSetSelectionTimeout** to set a new value, and it can use **XtAppGetSelectionTimeout** to retrieve the value.

The Motif drag and drop interface uses the Xt selection mechanism. A drag source supplies a single procedure to convert the selection, and a drop site supplies a procedure to receive the transferred data. The drag source and the receiver can determine independently whether or not to use atomic or incremental transfer. The drag source does this by specifying a value for the DragContext resource **XmNincremental**, and the receiver does this by specifying a value for the DropTransfer resource **XmNincremental**. When the drag source uses atomic transfer, it ignores the arguments to the conversion routine that pertain to incremental transfers.

16.5 The Motif Clipboard

Motif provides a set of routines for dealing with the CLIPBOARD selection. The Motif clipboard interface allows an application to assert ownership of the selection and request conversion of the selection. The interface stores the data in the selection and other information about the selection on the server. The owner can place the selection value in these server data structures either at the time it asserts ownership or at the time a client requests conversion.

By copying the selection value at the time it asserts ownership, an application can simplify conversion and make the data available for retrieval even if the owner is killed. By copying the selection value when a client requests it, an application can avoid converting data that no client may request. However, in this case, the application may need to make a copy of the data to be transferred. With either copying mechanism, the data is stored in the Motif clipboard's server data structures the first time a client requests the data.

16.5.1 Copying Data to the Clipboard

To assert ownership and copy data to the clipboard, an application takes these steps:

- It calls **XmClipboardStartCopy** to begin the interaction

- It makes one or more calls to **XmClipboardCopy** to place data on the clipboard

- It terminates the interaction by calling **XmClipboardEndCopy** or **XmClipboardCancelCopy**

An application begins an interaction to copy data to the clipboard by calling **XmClipboardStartCopy**. The application passes the following: a display pointer and timestamp; the ID of a window in the application; a compound string that could be used to label the data; and, if the application intends to delay copying the data until it is requested, a widget ID and a function to be called to convert the data. **XmClipboardStartCopy** returns in one of the arguments a data ID that the application must later pass to **XmClipboardEndCopy** or **XmClipboardCancelCopy**. The application must also pass the same window ID to subsequent clipboard calls in this sequence that it uses in the call to **XmClipboardStartCopy**.

After calling **XmClipboardStartCopy**, the application makes one or more calls to **XmClipboardCopy** to place data on the clipboard. Each call associates the data with a single target (called a format in the clipboard interface). The application can associate the same data or different data with more than one target, but it must do so by making separate calls to **XmClipboardCopy**.

If the application passes a NULL data buffer to **XmClipboardCopy**, it asserts that it intends to transfer the actual data for that target when a client requests it. Otherwise, **XmClipboardCopy** transfers data to be stored on the clipboard by **XmClipboardEndCopy**. If the application makes more than one call to **XmClipboardCopy** for the same target, the data is appended to the previously transferred data for that target.

XmClipboardCopy returns in one of its arguments a data ID that identifies the data and target specified in this call. An application that provides actual data at the time a client requests it uses this ID in its conversion routine to identify the data and target to be converted. Such an application must store a mapping of the data ID to the data and target after **XmClipboardCopy** returns.

The application terminates the interaction by calling either **XmClipboardEndCopy** or **XmClipboardCancelCopy**. **XmClipboardEndCopy** stores in the server data structures the data transferred by the calls to **XmClipboardCopy** during this interaction sequence. It also asserts ownership of the CLIPBOARD selection. If the application calls **XmClipboardCancelCopy** instead of **XmClipboardEndCopy**, the interaction is terminated without storing any of the transferred data or asserting ownership of the selection.

If a client later requests data that the owner has declared it would provide at the time of the request, the clipboard interface invokes the conversion routine that the owner registered in the call to **XmClipboardStartCopy**. This routine receives the following as arguments: the widget ID passed to **XmClipboardStartCopy**; the data ID for this data and target returned by **XmClipboardCopy**; a private ID the application may have supplied in the call to **XmClipboardCopy**; and a reason for invoking the routine.

The conversion routine is responsible for converting the data to the requested target. In order to do this it must consult the mapping it established between the data ID or the private ID and the data and target when it called **XmClipboardCopy**. Once the conversion routine has determined the proper target, it copies the data to the clipboard. To do this it calls **XmClipboardCopyByName**, using the data ID passed to the conversion routine. The application can call **XmClipboardCopyByName** more than once, if necessary, to convert all the data for this target.

Once an application has copied data to the clipboard in this way, it no longer asserts that it will convert the same data to the same target in the future. It can remove the data ID from its mapping of data IDs to data and targets, and it can free any data it has associated with this ID if it is not needed for any other purpose.

The clipboard interface calls the conversion routine when a data item intended for later conversion has been removed from the clipboard and is no longer needed. For example, another application may have copied new data to the clipboard. In this case, the conversion routine can remove the data ID from its mapping of data IDs to data and targets, and it can free any data it has associated with this ID if it is not needed for any other purpose. If the conversion routine is being called because an item has been removed from the clipboard, the *reason* argument to the conversion routine is **XmCR_CLIPBOARD_DATA_DELETE**. If the conversion routine is being called because a client has requested data conversion, the *reason* argument is **XmCR_CLIPBOARD_DATA_REQUEST**.

An application can use **XmClipboardWithdrawFormat** to rescind its assertion that it will convert data to a particular target on request.

XmClipboardUndoCopy removes the last item placed on the clipboard by an application using the same *display* and *window* arguments. This function also restores to the clipboard the item that was on the clipboard before the cancelled copy was done. If the application calls **XmClipboardUndoCopy** a second time, the function restores to the clipboard the item that was removed by the first call to **XmClipboardUndoCopy**.

16.5.2 Retrieving Data from the Clipboard

To retrieve data from the clipboard, an application takes these steps:

- It calls **XmClipboardStartRetrieve** to begin the interaction.

- It makes one or more calls to **XmClipboardRetrieve** to retrieve data from the clipboard.

- It terminates the interaction by calling **XmClipboardEndRetrieve**.

An application begins an interaction to retrieve data from the clipboard by calling **XmClipboardStartRetrieve**. The application passes a display pointer, a timestamp, and the ID of a window in the application. The application must pass the same window ID to subsequent clipboard calls in this sequence that it uses in the call to **XmClipboardStartRetrieve**. **XmClipboardStartRetrieve** locks the clipboard.

After calling **XmClipboardStartRetrieve**, the application makes one or more calls to **XmClipboardRetrieve** to retrieve data from the clipboard, converted to a given target. The application passes **XmClipboardRetrieve** a buffer to receive the data. If this buffer is not large enough to contain all the data for the given target, **XmClipboardRetrieve** returns **XmClipboardTruncate**. The application can make repeated calls to **XmClipboardRetrieve** to retrieve the remainder of the data. The function **XmClipboardInquireLength** returns the length of the data on the clipboard for the given target. This allows the application to allocate a buffer of the correct size.

XmClipboardEndRetrieve unlocks the clipboard and ends the interaction.

16.5.3 Utility Routines

The Motif clipboard interface has routines to lock and unlock the clipboard, to make inquiries about its contents, and to register new targets.

XmClipboardLock prevents another application from gaining access to the Motif clipboard. **XmClipboardUnlock** allows other applications to gain access. The clipboard interface automatically locks the clipboard during calls to **XmClipboardStartRetrieve** and **XmClipboardEndRetrieve**. At other times, an application can use **XmClipboardLock** and **XmClipboardUnlock** to lock the clipboard explicitly.

The clipboard interface includes four routines for making inquiries about the clipboard contents:

- **XmClipboardInquireCount** returns the number of targets for which data exists on the clipboard.

- **XmClipboardInquireFormat** returns the name of the target for a given index of targets on the clipboard. An application could retrieve the names of all the targets associated with data on the clipboard by first calling **XmClipboardInquireCount** to find out how many such targets exist and then calling **XmClipboardInquireFormat** with indices from 1 to the number of targets, inclusive. Note that the first index for **XmClipboardInquireFormat** is 1, not 0.

- **XmClipboardInquireLength** returns the number of bytes of data associated with a given target on the clipboard.

- **XmClipboardInquirePendingItems** returns a list of pairs of data ID and private ID for a given target if that target exists on the clipboard and if the owner has asserted that it will supply the actual data on request (but has not yet done so).

An application that makes more than one call to an inquiry function at a time should use **XmClipboardLock** and **XmClipboardUnlock** to lock the clipboard for the duration of the interaction.

XmClipboardRegisterFormat registers a new target with the clipboard interface. The application supplies the length of the data in bits along with the name of the target so that the correct byte order will be maintained when transferring data across platforms. All targets defined in ICCCM are preregistered; the application does not have to call **XmClipboardRegisterFormat** for these.

Appendix A

The Widget Meta-Language Facility

The Widget Meta-Language (WML) facility generates the components of the User Interface Language (UIL) compiler that can change depending on the widget set. WML adds support in UIL for additional widgets that are not in the OSF/Motif widget set or for a totally new widget set.

UIL is made up of the following:

- Static syntax
- Dynamic syntax
- Data types

The static syntax elements are the basic syntax and keywords of UIL. These elements do not change when the widget set is modified. The static syntax elements of UIL are defined in the file **Uil.y** in the WML source directory.

The dynamic syntax elements are the parts of UIL that change with the widget set. These elements describe the widget and gadget classes supported by UIL, including their resources and hierarchy. The dynamic elements of UIL are defined in WML files. For the OSF/Motif widget set, these elements are defined in the file **motif.wml** in the WML source directory.

The data type elements describe the allowable data types for each widget and gadget resource. Although the data types do not change, the resources that they are assigned to change with the widget set. The allowable data types for each resource are defined in the same file as the dynamic syntax elements.

The WML facility combines the static syntax, dynamic syntax, and data type elements to produce new source code for UIL. This allows a developer to modify the dynamic elements of UIL, adding resources, widgets, gadgets, or even new widget sets.

A developer can use WML files to modify UIL in two ways:

- Build a new UIL compiler by running the WML facility with a customized WML file.

- Compile a customized WML file into a Widget Meta-Language Database (WMD) file. The UIL compiler reads this file at run time and processes the new or modified widget definitions dynamically.

A.1 Using WML

When Motif is built, the WML facility uses the file **motif.wml** to produce UIL source files. The **motif.wml** file contains definitions for the OSF/Motif widget set. A developer can create a new WML file in the directory **tools/wml** to use in place of **motif.wml**. By convention, WML files have a suffix of **.wml**. For information on the syntax of WML files, see the **WML(5X)** reference page in the *OSF/Motif Programmer's Reference*.

A developer uses a customized WML file to build UIL in a four-step process:

1. Build WML

2. Run WML with the customized WML file

3. Install the UIL source files

4. Build UIL

All four steps are done as needed each time Motif is built. By default, UIL is built using the **motif.wml** file from the **tools/wml** directory.

The command-line **make** variable **TABLE** specifies the WML file to use in building UIL:

make TABLE=*anyfile.wml*

where *anyfile.wml* is the name of a WML file in the **tools/wml** directory of the Motif build tree.

When Motif is built, a default WMD file named **motif.wmd** is created. By convention, WMD files use the suffix **.wmd**. WMD files provide a method for including new widget definitions into the UIL compiler without rebuilding the compiler. Rebuilding this file or building a new WMD file is a two-step process that closely parallels the first two steps of creating a new UIL compiler:

1. Build WML

2. Run WML with the customized WML file

The following **make** command line rebuilds **motif.wmd** based on a given WML file:

make TABLE=*anyfile.wml* **motif.wmd**

The following **make** command line creates a new WMD file based on a given WML file:

make TABLE=*anyfile.wml* **WMDTABLE=***anyfile.wmd anyfile.wmd*

where *anyfile.wmd* is the name of the WMD file to create. In both of the preceding **make** commands, the **make** variable **TABLE** specifies the WML file to use as the source for the WMD file.

A developer of a UIL application specifies a WMD file for the UIL compiler in one of two ways:

- By using the **-wmd** option to the **uil** command

- By supplying values for the **database** and **database_flag** members of the **Uil_command_type** structure whose address is the first argument to the **Uil** function

See the *OSF/Motif Release Notes* for more information about building Motif.

The following sections describe how to do each of the four steps involved in rebuilding UIL independently.

A.1.1 Building WML

Building Motif builds WML by default, but a developer can also build WML separately. A developer must build WML in order to build the UIL compiler or new WMD files. The WML source is located in the subdirectory **tools/wml**. Before WML is built, the directory should contain the following files:

Imakefile	**wml.h**	**wmlparse.y**
Makefile	**wmldbcreate.c**	**wmlresolve.c**
README	**wmllex.l**	**wmlsynbld.c**
Uil.y	**wmlouth.c**	**wmluiltok.l**
UilDBDef.h	**wmloutkey.c**	**wmlutils.c**
motif.wml	**wmloutmm.c**	
wml.c	**wmloutp1.c**	

The files **Imakefile** and **Makefile** are used to build and run the WML facility. The **README** file contains instructions for building and using WML. The files **Uil.y** and **motif.wml** are the data files for the static syntax, dynamic syntax, and data type elements of UIL. The files with the **wml** prefix are the source files for the WML facility.

The following commands change to the directory **tools/wml**, build the makefile, and build WML:

cd tools/wml
make Makefile
make depend
make wmltools

The **make Makefile** and **make depend** commands build the makefile using the Imake facility. The **make Makefile** command produces a machine-dependent makefile. The **make depend** command adds include file dependencies to the new makefile.

After WML is built, the **tools/wml** directory should contain the following additional files:

lex.yy.c	**wmloutkey.o**	**wmlresolve.o**
libwml.a	**wmloutmm.o**	**wmlsynbld.o**
wml	**wmloutp1.o**	**wmluiltok**
wml.o	**wmlparse.c**	**wmlutils.o**
wmllex.c	**wmlparse.h**	
wmlouth.o	**wmlparse.o**	

A.1.2 Running WML

Building Motif runs WML, installs the resulting files in the UIL source directory, and builds the UIL compiler. A developer who does not want to install or build UIL can also run WML separately. Running WML automatically builds the WML source files if necessary.

The **make motif.wmd** command from the **tools/wml** directory runs the WML facility. The **make** variable **TABLE** specifies the WML file to use, as in the following example:

make motif.wmd TABLE=_anyfile.wml_

where _anyfile.wml_ is a WML file in the **tools/wml** directory. The default WML file is **motif.wml**.

Running WML produces the following files:

UIL source files

WML produces the following files, which **make copy** copies to the **clients/uil** directory to be used in building UIL:

UilConst.h	**UilSymArTy.h**	**UilSymRArg.h**
UilDBDef.h	**UilSymCSet.h**	**UilSymReas.h**
UilKeyTab.h	**UilSymCtl.h**	**UilTokName.h**
UilLexPars.c	**UilSymEnum.h**	**UilUrmClas.h**
UilLexPars.h	**UilSymGen.h**	
UilSymArTa.h	**UilSymNam.h**	

wml.report   This report describes the widget set supported by the newly created UIL sources. It is intended to help validate the WML source file. It is organized as follows:

- Class names are ordered alphabetically by name.

- Resources are ordered by ancestor, from the top down.

- Resources are listed alphabetically within ancestor, along with data types and default values.

- Reasons are ordered alphabetically within ancestor.

- Controls are ordered alphabetically.

- Automatically created children are ordered alphabetically.

wml-uil.mm

This file contains the information in Appendix B of the *OSF/Motif Programmer's Reference*. This file can be processed by **tbl**, **troff,** and the **mm** macro package to produce three tables for each supported widget class:

- Controls and reasons supported by the class

- Resources for the class, including their types and default values

- Automatically created children of the class

motif.wmd   This is the default WMD file.

These files overwrite any existing WML output files in the **tools/wml** directory.

A.1.3 Installing UIL

A developer can use the **make** command from the **tools/wml** directory to install the UIL source files in the **clients/uil** directory without rebuilding UIL. The **make all** and **make copy** commands are synonyms for the **make** command. This command automatically builds the WML source files and runs WML if necessary. It overwrites the existing source files in the **clients/uil** directory.

See the previous section for more information on using the **make** command in the **tools/wml** directory.

A.1.4 Building UIL

A developer can use the **make** command from the **clients/uil** directory to build UIL, as in the following example:

cd clients/uil
make

See the *OSF/Motif Release Notes* for more information about building UIL.

Appendix B

Drag and Drop Example Program

The **DNDDemo** program is a complex drag and drop application. It uses many of the features covered in Chapter 15. The application uses both drag source and drop sites.

The window, shown in Figure B-1, consists of an array of 6 colors in the lower section, with an empty drawing area in the upper section. The user can create a black box within the drawing area by pressing and holding mouse button 1 while moving the mouse until the desired size rectangle is outlined, then releasing the button. There can be as many rectangles as desired and they can overlap each other. A rectangle can be raised to the top by clicking mouse button 1 on it.

The user can change the color of a particular rectangle by moving the pointer to one of the six color choices, pressing button 2, and moving the pointer to the rectangle. A palette in that color becomes the drag icon. The state icon does not appear while the drag icon is in the lower section. It shows as a slashed circle in the background of the upper section, and as a paintbrush in the rectangles. When the mouse button is released to make a drop, the rectangle changes to the color chosen. If the rectangle is overlapped by another, the whole rectangle is changed, but only the unobscured part is shown in the new color.

The user can move the rectangles around the drawing area by pressing button 2 when the pointer is over the rectangle, holding it, and moving the mouse until the new location is reached. If the rectangle is small enough, it is used to create a pixmap for the source drag icon; otherwise, a similarly shaped, smaller pixmap is used for the source icon.

The program demonstrates the following drag and drop features:

- Drag Source

  — Establishes translations

  — Establishes custom drag source targets

  — Starts a drag and creates a drag context

  — Creates custom drag icons

  — Transfers information to the receiver (about color or location)

- Drop Site

  — Establishes simulated drop sites

  — Establishes custom drop site targets

  — Follows the progress of the drag with an **XmNdragProc** routine.

  — Requests transfer of information from the source (about color or location)

The demonstration program consists of three files:

- **DNDDemo.h** contains header information, global constants, and forward declarations of procedures.

- **DNDDemo.c** creates the windows and manages the drag and drop functions.

- **DNDDraw.c** does not have any drag and drop specific code in it. It manages creating, coloring, and destroying the rectangles and bitmaps within the window.

Figure B–1. Drag and Drop Demonstration

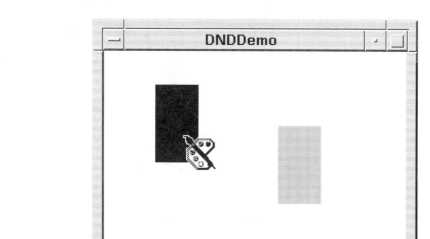

B.1 DNDDemo.h

```
/*
 *      file: DNDDemo.h
 *
 *          Header file for the program DNDDemo.
 */

#include <stdio.h>
#include <X11/Xatom.h>
#include <X11/Intrinsic.h>
#include <Xm/Xm.h>
#include <Xm/AtomMgr.h>
#include <Xm/MainW.h>
```

```
#include <Xm/DrawingA.h>
#include <Xm/SeparatoG.h>
#include <Xm/Form.h>
#include <Xm/RowColumn.h>
#include <Xm/PushB.h>
#include <Xm/MessageB.h>
#include <Xm/DragDrop.h>
#include <Xm/Screen.h>


/* The following is used to layout the color labels */
#define BOX_WIDTH          85
#define BOX_HEIGHT         25
#define BOX_X_OFFSET       95
#define BOX_Y_OFFSET       35
#define BOX_X_MARGIN       10
#define BOX_Y_MARGIN       10


/* The following are used in setting up the drag icons */
#define ICON_WIDTH         32
#define ICON_HEIGHT        32
#define SMALL_ICON_WIDTH   16
#define SMALL_ICON_HEIGHT  16
#define ICON_X_HOT         0
#define ICON_Y_HOT         0


/* Some scales or text entry field could be added to change
 * this value */
#define RECT_WIDTH  20
#define RECT_HEIGHT 50


/* The following defines could be setup as application resources */
#define RECT_START_COLOR     "black"
#define HIGHLIGHT_THICKNESS 3
#define HIGHLIGHT_COLOR      "Black"    /* this is equivalent to
                                          gray60 in the R5 rgb.txt */
#define DRAW_AREA_BG_COLOR "white"
#define DRAW_AREA_FG_COLOR "white"
#define LABEL1_COLOR         "#ff5026"    /* a soft shade of red */
#define LABEL2_COLOR     "orange"
#define LABEL3_COLOR     "yellow"
```

```
#define LABEL4_COLOR      "violet"
#define LABEL5_COLOR      "#00C3ff"              /* a blue green color */
#define LABEL6_COLOR      "green"

#define VALID_CURSOR_FG_COLOR    "black"
#define INVALID_CURSOR_FG_COLOR  "maroon"
#define NONE_CURSOR_FG_COLOR     "maroon"


/*
 * This struct is used to contain information about each rectangle
 * to use in the dislay routines
 */
typedef struct _RectStruct {
    Position x;
    Position y;
    Dimension width;
    Dimension height;
    Pixel color;
    Pixmap pixmap;   /* currently not in use */
} RectStruct, *RectPtr;

/* This struct is used to hold global application information */
typedef struct _AppInfoRec {
    GC rectGC;                  /* graphic context used to draw the
                                   rectangles */
    Pixel currentColor;      /* color that is currently in the GC */
    RectPtr *rectDpyTable;   /* the rectangle display table */
    int rectsAllocd;         /* keeps track of how much the above
                                table has been alloc'd */
    int numRects;            /* number of rects that are visible */
    RectPtr highlightRect;   /* the current highlighted rectangle */
    RectPtr clearRect;       /* the rectangle that is being moved */
    Boolean doMove;          /* indicates that a move is being
                                performed */
    Boolean creatingRect;    /* indicates that a rect create is being
                                performed */
    unsigned char operation;/* indicates the drop help operation */
    unsigned int maxCursorWidth;  /* the maximum allowable cursor
                                     width */
    unsigned int maxCursorHeight; /* the maximum allowable cursor
```

```
                                            height */
    Position rectX;
    Position rectY;
    Position rectX2;
    Position rectY2;
} AppInfoRec, *AppInfo;


/*
 * This struct is used to pass information
 * from the dropProc to the transferProc
 */
typedef struct _DropTransferRec {
    Widget widget;
    Position x;
    Position y;
} DropTransferRec, *DropTransfer;


/*
 * This struct is used to pass information
 * from the rectangle dragStart proc to it's associated
 * callback procs.
 */
typedef struct _DragConvertRec {
    Widget widget;
    RectPtr rect;
} DragConvertRec, *DragConvertPtr;



#ifdef _NO_PROTO

extern void     InitializeAppInfo();
extern void     StartRect();
extern void     ExtendRect();
extern void     EndRect();
extern RectPtr  RectCreate();
extern RectPtr  RectFind();
extern void     RectSetColor();
extern Pixel    RectGetColor();
extern Pixmap   GetBitmapFromRect();
extern void     RectHide();
extern void     RectFree();
```

```
extern void        RedrawRectangles();
extern void        RectDrawStippled();
extern void        RectHighlight();
extern void        RectUnhighlight();
extern void        RectSetPixmap();
extern void        RectRegister();
extern void        InitializeRectDpyTable();
extern void        CreateLayout();
extern void        CreateRectGC();
extern Pixel       GetColor();
extern void        ColorRect();

#else

extern void        InitializeAppInfo(void);
extern void        StartRect(Widget, XEvent *, String *, Cardinal *);
extern void        ExtendRect(Widget, XEvent *, String *, Cardinal *);
extern void        EndRect(Widget, XEvent *, String *, Cardinal *);
extern RectPtr     RectCreate(Position, Position, Dimension,
                             Dimension, Pixel, Pixmap);
extern RectPtr     RectFind(Position, Position);
extern void        RectSetColor(RectPtr, Display *, Window, Pixel);
extern Pixel       RectGetColor(RectPtr);
extern Pixmap      GetBitmapFromRect(Widget, RectPtr, Pixel, Pixel,
                                    Dimension *, Dimension *);
extern void        RectHide(Display *, Window, RectPtr);
extern void        RectFree(RectPtr);
extern void        RedrawRectangles(Widget);
extern void        RectDrawStippled(Display *, Window, RectPtr);
extern void        RectHighlight(Widget, RectPtr);
extern void        RectUnhighlight(Widget);
extern void        RectSetPixmap(RectPtr, Display *, Window, Pixmap);
extern void        RectRegister(RectPtr, Position, Position);
extern void        InitializeRectDpyTable(void);
extern void        CreateLayout(void);
extern void        CreateRectGC(void);
extern Pixel       GetColor(char *);
extern void        ColorRect(Widget, XEvent *, String *, Cardinal *);

#endif     /* _NO_PROTO */
```

B-7

```
/* The following character arrays hold the bits for the source and
 * state icons for both 32x32 and 16x16 drag icons.  The source is
 * a color palette icon and the state is a paint brush icon.
 */
extern char SOURCE_ICON_BITS[];
extern char SOURCE_ICON_MASK[];
extern char STATE_ICON_BITS[];
extern char STATE_ICON_MASK[];
extern char INVALID_ICON_BITS[];
extern char SMALL_SOURCE_ICON_BITS[];
extern char SMALL_SOURCE_ICON_MASK[];
extern char SMALL_STATE_ICON_BITS[];
extern char SMALL_STATE_ICON_MASK[];
extern char SMALL_INVALID_ICON_BITS[];

/* The folowing character arrays are for use with the drop help
 * dialogs.  For internationalization, message catalogs should
 * replace these static declarations.
 */
extern char HELP_MSG1[];
extern char HELP_MSG2[];
extern char HELP_MSG3[];
extern char HELP_MSG4[];
extern char HELP_MSG5[];


/* Globals variables */
extern AppInfo       appInfo;
extern Widget        topLevel;
extern Widget        drawingArea;
extern Widget        helpDialog;
extern Widget        helpLabel, helpMenu;
extern XtAppContext appContext;
```

B.2 DNDDemo.c

```
/*
 *      file: DNDDemo.c
 *
 *      A demo program showing the basic Drag And Drop operations.
 */

#include "DNDDemo.h"


/*
 * The folowing character arrays are for use with the drop help
 * dialogs.  For internationalization, message catalogs should
 * replace these static declarations.
 */
char HELP_MSG1[] =
"This drop action will change the color\n\
of the rectangle that the paint palette\n\
icon is dropped on. To accept this drop\n\
press the o.k. button, otherwise press\n\
cancel";

char HELP_MSG2[] =
"This drop action will move the rectangle\n\
to the new position.  To accept this drop\n\
press the o.k. button, otherwise press\n\
cancel";

char HELP_MSG3[] =
"This drop action will copy the rectangle\n\
to the new position.  To accept this drop\n\
press the o.k. button, otherwise press\n\
cancel";

char HELP_MSG4[] =
"This drop action can either copy or\n\
move the rectangle to the new position.\n\
Select the operation that you desire.\n\
```

In the future, use Ctrl with Btn2 to\n\
perform copy operations. The default\n\
operation is move. To accept this drop\n\
press the o.k. button, otherwise press\n\
cancel";

char HELP_MSG5[] =
"This drop action is at an Invalid drop\n\
position. Please cancel this drop \n\
by pressing the cancel button.";


```
/* Globals variables */
Widget          topLevel;
Widget          drawingArea;
Widget          helpDialog = NULL;
Widget          helpLabel, helpMenu;
Widget          myDC;
XtAppContext    appContext;


/* This function creates the Drag Icon. */
static Widget
#ifdef _NO_PROTO
GetDragIcon(w, icon, iconMask, width, height, background,
            foreground)
Widget w;
Pixmap icon;
Pixmap iconMask;
Dimension width;
Dimension height;
Pixel background;
Pixel foreground;
#else
GetDragIcon(Widget w, Pixmap icon, Pixmap iconMask, Dimension width,
Dimension height, Pixel background, Pixel foreground)
#endif /* _NO_PROTO */
{

    Widget  dragIcon;
    Arg     args[10];
```

```
    int      n = 0;

    XtSetArg(args[n], XmNhotX, ICON_X_HOT); n++;
    XtSetArg(args[n], XmNhotY, ICON_Y_HOT); n++;
    XtSetArg(args[n], XmNwidth, width); n++;
    XtSetArg(args[n], XmNheight, height); n++;
    XtSetArg(args[n], XmNmaxWidth, appInfo->maxCursorWidth); n++;
    XtSetArg(args[n], XmNmaxHeight, appInfo->maxCursorHeight); n++;
    XtSetArg(args[n], XmNbackground, background); n++;
    XtSetArg(args[n], XmNforeground, foreground); n++;
    XtSetArg(args[n], XmNpixmap, icon); n++;
    XtSetArg(args[n], XmNmask, iconMask); n++;
    dragIcon = XmCreateDragIcon(w, "dragIcon", args, n);

    return(dragIcon);

}


/* This function creates the bitmaps for the icon and the mask
 * and then calls GetDragIcon() to  create the drag icon.
 */
static Widget
#ifdef _NO_PROTO
GetDragIconFromBits(w, bits, mask, width, height, background,
                    foreground)
Widget w;
char *bits;
char *mask;
Dimension width;
Dimension height;
Pixel background;
Pixel foreground;
#else
GetDragIconFromBits(Widget w, char *bits, char *mask,
                    Dimension width, Dimension height,
                    Pixel background, Pixel foreground)
#endif /* _NO_PROTO */
{

    Pixmap      icon, iconMask;
```

```
    Display    *display = XtDisplay(w);

    icon = XCreateBitmapFromData(display,
              DefaultRootWindow(display), bits, width, height);

    iconMask = XCreateBitmapFromData(display,
              DefaultRootWindow(display), mask, width, height);

    return(GetDragIcon(w, icon, iconMask, width, height,
                  background, foreground));

}


/* This function creates the rectangle bitmaps for the icon and
 * the mask based on the maximum server allowable cursor size
 * and then calls GetDragIcon() to create the drag icon.
 */
static Widget
#ifdef _NO_PROTO
GetDragIconFromRect(w, rect, background)
Widget w;
RectPtr rect;
Pixel background;
#else
GetDragIconFromRect(Widget w, RectPtr rect, Pixel background)
#endif /* _NO_PROTO */
{

    Pixmap     icon, icon_mask;
    Pixel      foreground = RectGetColor(rect);
    Dimension  width, height;

    /* Create a depth 1 pixmap (bitmap) for use with the drag
       icon */
    icon = icon_mask = GetBitmapFromRect(w, rect, background,
                        foreground, &width, &height);

    /* use bitmap for both the bitmap and mask */
    return(GetDragIcon(w, icon, icon_mask, width, height,
                  background, foreground));
```

```
}


/* This is a selection conversion function that is used in
 * converting drag/drop export background color targets.
 * The return types follow ICCC standards.
 */
/* ARGSUSED */
Boolean
#ifdef _NO_PROTO
ColorConvert(w, selection, target, type, value, length, format)
Widget w ;
Atom *selection ;
Atom *target ;
Atom *type ;
XtPointer *value ;
unsigned long *length ;
int *format ;
#else
ColorConvert(Widget w, Atom *selection, Atom *target, Atom *type,
XtPointer *value, unsigned long *length, int *format)
#endif /* _NO_PROTO */
{

    Display      *display = XtDisplay(w);
    Atom         BACKGROUND = XmInternAtom(display, "BACKGROUND",
                                            False);
    Atom         PIXEL = XmInternAtom(display, "PIXEL", False);
    Atom         TARGETS = XmInternAtom(display, "TARGETS", False);
    Atom         MULTIPLE = XmInternAtom(display, "MULTIPLE", False);
    Atom         TIMESTAMP = XmInternAtom(display, "TIMESTAMP",
                                            False);
    int          MAX_TARGS = 5;
    Widget       widget;
    XtPointer    client;
    Arg          args[1];

    /* get the widget that initiated the drag */
    XtSetArg(args[0], XmNclientData, &client);
    XtGetValues(w, args, 1);
    widget = (Widget) client;
```

```
    /* Make sure we are doing a motif drag by checking if the
     * widget that is passed in is a drag context. Make sure the
     * widget in the client data is not NULL.
     */
    if (!XmIsDragContext(w) || widget == NULL)
        return False;

    if (*target == BACKGROUND) {

        /* Get widget's background */
        Pixel *background;

        background = (Pixel *) XtMalloc(sizeof(Pixel));
        XtSetArg(args[0], XmNbackground, background);
        XtGetValues(widget, args, 1);

        /* value, type, length, and format must be set */
        *value = (XtPointer) background;
        *type = PIXEL;
        *length = sizeof(Pixel);
        *format = 32;

    }
    else if (*target == TARGETS) {

        /* This target is required by ICCC */
        Atom *targs = (Atom *)XtMalloc((unsigned)
                                (MAX_TARGS * sizeof(Atom)));
        int target_count = 0;

        *value = (XtPointer) targs;
        *targs++ = BACKGROUND;
        target_count++;
        *targs++ = TARGETS;
        target_count++;
        *targs++ = MULTIPLE;
        target_count++;   /* supported in the Intrinsics */
        *targs++ = TIMESTAMP;
        target_count++; /* supported in the Intrinsics */
        *type = XA_ATOM;
        *length = (target_count * sizeof(Atom)) >> 2;
```

```
        *format = 32;

    }
    else
        return False;

    return True;

}


/* This callback procedure resets the drag icon cursor to show
 * when the drag is in a valid region .  It cause the
 * state icon to become visible when a drop is at a valid
 * position for drag over effects.
 */
static void
#ifdef _NO_PROTO
DragMotionCallback(w, client, call)
Widget w;
XtPointer client;
XtPointer call;
#else
DragMotionCallback(Widget w, XtPointer client, XtPointer call)
#endif /* _NO_PROTO */
{

    XmDragMotionCallback    cb = (XmDragMotionCallback) call;
    Arg                     args[2];
    Widget                  stateIcon, invalidIcon;

    if (cb->dropSiteStatus == XmVALID_DROP_SITE) {

        stateIcon = (Widget) client;

        XtSetArg(args[0], XmNblendModel, XmBLEND_STATE_SOURCE);
        XtSetArg(args[1], XmNstateCursorIcon, stateIcon);
        XtSetValues(w, args, 2);

    }
    else if (cb->dropSiteStatus == XmINVALID_DROP_SITE) {
```

```
        XtSetArg(args[0], XmNdefaultInvalidCursorIcon,
              &invalidIcon);
        XtGetValues(XmGetXmScreen(XtScreen(w)), args, 1);
        XtSetArg(args[0], XmNblendModel, XmBLEND_STATE_SOURCE);
        XtSetArg(args[1], XmNstateCursorIcon, invalidIcon);
        XtSetValues(w, args, 2);

    }
    else {
        XtSetArg(args[0], XmNblendModel, XmBLEND_JUST_SOURCE);
        XtSetValues(w, args, 1);
    }

}


/* This callback procedure resets the drag icon cursor to show
 * when the drag is in a valid region .  It cause the
 * state icon to become visible when a drop is at a valid
 * position for drag over effects.
 */
/* ARGSUSED */
static void
#ifdef _NO_PROTO
DropSiteLeaveCallback(w, client, call)
Widget w;
XtPointer client;
XtPointer call;
#else
DropSiteLeaveCallback(Widget w, XtPointer client, XtPointer call)
#endif /* _NO_PROTO */
{

    Arg     args[1];

    XtSetArg(args[0], XmNblendModel, XmBLEND_JUST_SOURCE);
    XtSetValues(w, args, 1);

}
```

```
/* This callback procedure removes the icons when the drop is
 * complete */
/* ARGSUSED */
static void
#ifdef _NO_PROTO
ColorDragDropFinishCB(w, client, call)
Widget w;
XtPointer client;
XtPointer call;
#else
ColorDragDropFinishCB(Widget w, XtPointer client, XtPointer call)
#endif /* _NO_PROTO */
{

    Widget   sourceIcon;
    Widget   stateIcon = (Widget) client;
    Arg      args[1];

    XtSetArg(args[0], XmNsourceCursorIcon, &sourceIcon);
    XtGetValues(w, args, 1);

    XtDestroyWidget(sourceIcon);
    XtDestroyWidget(stateIcon);

}


/* This action procedure sets up the drag data and begins the drag
 * operation */
/* ARGSUSED */
void
#ifdef _NO_PROTO
ColorRect(w, event, params, num_params)
Widget w;
XEvent *event;
String *params;
Cardinal *num_params;
#else
ColorRect(Widget w, XEvent *event, String *params,
          Cardinal *num_params)
#endif /* _NO_PROTO */
```

```
{
    static XtCallbackRec dragDropFinishCB[] = {
        {ColorDragDropFinishCB, NULL},
        {NULL, NULL}
    };

    static XtCallbackRec dragMotionCB[] = {
        {DragMotionCallback, NULL},
        {NULL, NULL}
    };

    static XtCallbackRec dropSiteLeaveCB[] = {
        {DropSiteLeaveCallback, NULL},
        {NULL, NULL}
    };

    Atom        targets[1];
    Widget      sourceIcon, stateIcon;
    Pixel       background, foreground;
    char        *source_bits, *source_mask;
    char        *state_bits, *state_mask;
    Dimension   width, height;
    Arg         args[16];
    int         n = 0;

    n = 0;
    XtSetArg(args[n], XmNbackground, &background); n++;
    XtSetArg(args[n], XmNforeground, &foreground); n++;
    XtGetValues(w, args, n);

    /* If the server will handle a large icon, create one */
    if (appInfo->maxCursorWidth >= ICON_WIDTH &&
        appInfo->maxCursorHeight >= ICON_HEIGHT) {

        source_bits = SOURCE_ICON_BITS;
        source_mask = SOURCE_ICON_MASK;
        state_bits = STATE_ICON_BITS;
        state_mask = STATE_ICON_MASK;
        width = ICON_WIDTH;
        height = ICON_HEIGHT;
```

```
}
else {

    /* If the server will handle a small icon, create one */
    source_bits = SMALL_SOURCE_ICON_BITS;
    source_mask = SMALL_SOURCE_ICON_MASK;
    state_bits = SMALL_STATE_ICON_BITS;
    state_mask = SMALL_STATE_ICON_MASK;
    width = SMALL_ICON_WIDTH;
    height = SMALL_ICON_HEIGHT;

}

/* Create the drag cursor icons */
sourceIcon = GetDragIconFromBits(w, source_bits, source_mask,
                width, height, background, foreground);

stateIcon = GetDragIconFromBits(w, state_bits, state_mask,
                width, height, background, foreground);

/* Setup the arglist for the drag context that is created at
 * drag start */
n = 0;
/* initially only show the source icon */
XtSetArg(args[n], XmNblendModel, XmBLEND_JUST_SOURCE); n++;

/* set cursor colors for the drag states */
XtSetArg(args[n], XmNvalidCursorForeground,
        GetColor(VALID_CURSOR_FG_COLOR)); n++;
XtSetArg(args[n], XmNinvalidCursorForeground,
        GetColor(INVALID_CURSOR_FG_COLOR)); n++;
XtSetArg(args[n], XmNnoneCursorForeground,
        GetColor(NONE_CURSOR_FG_COLOR)); n++;

/* set args for the drag cursor icons */
XtSetArg(args[n], XmNcursorBackground, background); n++;
XtSetArg(args[n], XmNcursorForeground, foreground); n++;
XtSetArg(args[n], XmNsourceCursorIcon, sourceIcon); n++;
XtSetArg(args[n], XmNstateCursorIcon, stateIcon); n++;

/*
```

```
 * set up the available export targets.  These are targets that
 * we wish to provide data on
 */
targets[0] = XmInternAtom(XtDisplay(w), "BACKGROUND", False);
XtSetArg(args[n], XmNexportTargets, targets); n++;
XtSetArg(args[n], XmNnumExportTargets, 1); n++;

/*
 * identify the conversion procedure and
 * the client data passed to the procedure
 */
XtSetArg(args[n], XmNclientData, w); n++;
XtSetArg(args[n], XmNconvertProc, ColorConvert); n++;

/* identify the necessary callbacks */
dragDropFinishCB[0].closure = (XtPointer) stateIcon;
XtSetArg(args[n], XmNdragDropFinishCallback, dragDropFinishCB);
n++;
dragMotionCB[0].closure = (XtPointer) stateIcon;
XtSetArg(args[n], XmNdragMotionCallback, dragMotionCB); n++;
XtSetArg(args[n], XmNdropSiteLeaveCallback, dragMotionCB); n++;

/* set the drag operations that are supported */
XtSetArg(args[n], XmNdragOperations, XmDROP_COPY); n++;

/* start the drag.  This creates a drag context. */
myDC = XmDragStart(w, event, args, n);

}



/*
 * This is a selection conversion function that is used in
 * converting requests for rectangle targets.  The return types
 * follow ICCC standards.
 */
/* ARGSUSED */
Boolean
#ifdef _NO_PROTO
RectConvert( w, selection, target, type, value, length, format)
Widget w ;
```

```
Atom *selection ;
Atom *target ;
Atom *type ;
XtPointer *value ;
unsigned long *length ;
int *format ;
#else
RectConvert(Widget w, Atom *selection, Atom *target, Atom *type,
XtPointer *value, unsigned long *length, int *format)
#endif /* _NO_PROTO */
{

    Display    *display = XtDisplay(w);
    Atom       MY_RECT = XmInternAtom(display, "_MY_RECTANGLE", False);
    Atom       RECT_INFO = XmInternAtom(display, "RECT_INFO", False);
    Atom       DELETE = XmInternAtom(display, "DELETE", False);
    Atom       TARGETS = XmInternAtom(display, "TARGETS", False);
    Atom       MULTIPLE = XmInternAtom(display, "MULTIPLE", False);
    Atom       TIMESTAMP = XmInternAtom(display, "TIMESTAMP", False);
    Atom       *targs;
    int        MAX_TARGS = 6;
    int        target_count;
    DragConvertPtr  conv;
    Widget     widget;
    Arg        args[1];
    RectPtr    rect, oldRect;

    /* get the widget that initiated the drag */
    XtSetArg(args[0], XmNclientData, &conv);
    XtGetValues(w, args, 1);
    widget = (Widget) conv->widget;

    /* Make sure we are doing a motif drag by checking if the
     * widget that is passed in is a drag context. Make sure the
     * widget in the client data is not NULL.
     */
    if (!XmIsDragContext(w) || widget == NULL)
        return False;

    if (*target == MY_RECT) {
```

```
    /* Create a new rectangle using information from the old
       retangle */
    oldRect = conv->rect;

    /* We create create a new rectangle and wait for a delete
     * target on the old rectangle instead of just moving the
     * old rectangle because the rectangle movement might be an
     * interclient move.
     */
    rect = RectCreate(oldRect->x, oldRect->y, oldRect->width,
        oldRect->height, oldRect->color, oldRect->pixmap);
    /* value, type, length, and format must be assigned values */
    *value = (XtPointer) rect;
    *type = RECT_INFO;
    *length = sizeof(Pixel);
    *format = 32;

}
else if (*target == DELETE) {

    /* delete the old rectangle */
    RectHide(XtDisplay(widget), XtWindow(widget), conv->rect);
    RectFree(conv->rect);

    conv->rect = NULL;
    /*
     * DELETE target return parameters MUST be assigned as
     * follows to ICCC compliant.
     */
    *value = NULL;
    *type = XmInternAtom(XtDisplay(w), "NULL", False);
    *length = 0;
    *format = 8;

}
else if (*target == TARGETS) {

    /* This target is required by ICCC */
    targs = (Atom *)XtMalloc((unsigned)
                            (MAX_TARGS * sizeof(Atom)));
    target_count = 0;
```

```
        *value = (XtPointer) targs;
        *targs++ = MY_RECT;
        target_count++;
        *targs++ = DELETE;
        target_count++;
        *targs++ = TARGETS;
        target_count++;
        *targs++ = MULTIPLE;
        target_count++;   /* supported in the Intrinsics */
        *targs++ = TIMESTAMP;
        target_count++; /* supported in the Intrinsics */
        *type = XA_ATOM;
        *length = (target_count * sizeof(Atom)) >> 2;
        *format = 32;

    }
    else
        return False;

    return True;

}


/* This callback procedure removes the old cursor icon */
/* ARGSUSED */
static void
#ifdef _NO_PROTO
RectDragDropFinishCB(w, client, call)
Widget w;
XtPointer client;
XtPointer call;
#else
RectDragDropFinishCB(Widget w, XtPointer client, XtPointer call)
#endif /* _NO_PROTO */
{

    DragConvertPtr  conv = (DragConvertPtr) client;
    Widget          sourceCursorIcon;
    Arg             args[1];
```

```
        XtSetArg(args[0], XmNsourceCursorIcon, &sourceCursorIcon);
        XtGetValues(w, args, 1);

        XtFree((char *) conv);

        XtDestroyWidget(sourceCursorIcon);

}


/* This callback procedure redraws the rectangles once the drop
 * is completed */
/* ARGSUSED */
static void
#ifdef _NO_PROTO
RectDropFinishCB(w, client, call)
Widget w;
XtPointer client;
XtPointer call;
#else
RectDropFinishCB(Widget w, XtPointer client, XtPointer call)
#endif /* _NO_PROTO */
{

    DragConvertPtr    conv = (DragConvertPtr) client;

    appInfo->clearRect = NULL;
    appInfo->doMove = True;
    RedrawRectangles(conv->widget);

}


/* This callback procedure handle the drawing of the target
 * rectangle depending of the dropSiteStatus for drag over
 * effects.
 */
/* ARGSUSED */
static void
#ifdef _NO_PROTO
RectDragMotionCB(w, client, call)
```

```
Widget w;
XtPointer client;
XtPointer call;
#else
RectDragMotionCB(Widget w, XtPointer client, XtPointer call)
#endif /* _NO_PROTO */
{

    XmDragMotionCallback    cb = (XmDragMotionCallback) call;
    DragConvertPtr          conv = (DragConvertPtr) client;
    Display                 *display;
    Window                  window;
    RectPtr                 rect;

    if (cb->dropSiteStatus == XmVALID_DROP_SITE) {

        /* re-stipple the rectangle when the pointer is inside the
         * drop site */
        if ( appInfo->clearRect == NULL && appInfo->doMove) {

            display = XtDisplay(conv->widget);
            window = XtWindow(conv->widget);
            rect = conv->rect;

            RectHide(display, window, rect);
            RectDrawStippled(display, window, rect);

        }

    }
    else {

        /* re-fill the rectangle when the pointer is outside the
         * drop site */
        if (appInfo->clearRect != NULL && appInfo->doMove) {
            appInfo->clearRect = NULL;
            RedrawRectangles(conv->widget);
        }

    }
```

```
}


/* This callback procedure handle the drawing of the target
 * rectangle When the operation changes.
 */
/* ARGSUSED */
static void
#ifdef _NO_PROTO
RectOperationChangedCB(w, client, call)
Widget w;
XtPointer client;
XtPointer call;
#else
RectOperationChangedCB(Widget w, XtPointer client, XtPointer call)
#endif /* _NO_PROTO */
{

    XmDragMotionCallback    cb = (XmDragMotionCallback) call;
    DragConvertPtr          conv = (DragConvertPtr) client;
    Display                 *display;
    Window                  window;
    RectPtr                 rect;

    /* re-stipple the rectangle when the pointer is inside the drop
     * site */
    if ( appInfo->clearRect == NULL && appInfo->doMove) {

        display = XtDisplay(conv->widget);
        window = XtWindow(conv->widget);
        rect = conv->rect;

        RectHide(display, window, rect);
        RectDrawStippled(display, window, rect);

    }

    /* re-fill the rectangle when the operation changes to copy */
    if (appInfo->clearRect != NULL && !appInfo->doMove) {
        appInfo->clearRect = NULL;
        RedrawRectangles(conv->widget);
```

```
        }

}


/* This action procedure sets up the drag data and begins the drag
 * operation */
/* ARGSUSED */
static void
#ifdef _NO_PROTO
StartMove(w, event, params, num_params)
Widget w;
XEvent *event;
String *params;
Cardinal *num_params;
#else
StartMove(Widget w, XEvent *event, String *params,
          Cardinal *num_params)
#endif /* _NO_PROTO */
{

    RectPtr     rect;
    Position    x = event->xbutton.x;
    Position    y = event->xbutton.y;
    static XtCallbackRec dragDropFinishCB[] = {
        {RectDragDropFinishCB, NULL},
        {NULL, NULL}
    };

    static XtCallbackRec dropFinishCB[] = {
        {RectDropFinishCB, NULL},
        {NULL, NULL}
    };

    static XtCallbackRec dragMotionCB[] = {
        {RectDragMotionCB, NULL},
        {NULL, NULL}
    };

    static XtCallbackRec operationChangedCB[] = {
        {RectOperationChangedCB, NULL},
```

```
        {NULL, NULL}
};

Atom              targets[1];
Display           *display = XtDisplay(w);
Widget            sourceCursorIcon;
DragConvertPtr    conv;
Pixel             background, foreground;
Arg               args[16];
int               n = 0;

/* find a rectangle at the given x,y position */
rect = RectFind(x, y);

/* start move only if it begins on a rectangle */
if (rect) {

    XtSetArg(args[0], XmNbackground, &background);
    XtGetValues(w, args, 1);

    foreground = RectGetColor(rect);
    sourceCursorIcon = GetDragIconFromRect(w, rect, background);

    /*
     * Set up information to pass to the convert
     * function and callback procs.
     */
    conv = (DragConvertPtr) XtMalloc(sizeof(DragConvertRec));
    conv->widget = w;
    conv->rect = rect;

    /* On a move operation, draw the current
     * rectangle as a stippled outline.
     */
    if (!(event->xbutton.state & ControlMask)) {
        RectHide(display, XtWindow(w), rect);
        RectDrawStippled(display, XtWindow(w), rect);
    }
    else
        appInfo->doMove = False;
```

```
/* Setup arglist for the drag context that is created at
 * drag start */
n = 0;
/* initially only show the source icon */
XtSetArg(args[n], XmNblendModel, XmBLEND_JUST_SOURCE); n++;

/* set args for the drag cursor icons */
XtSetArg(args[n], XmNcursorBackground, background); n++;
XtSetArg(args[n], XmNcursorForeground, foreground); n++;
XtSetArg(args[n], XmNsourceCursorIcon, sourceCursorIcon);
n++;

/*
 * set up the available export targets.  These are targets
 * that we wish to provide data on
 */
targets[0] = XmInternAtom(display, "_MY_RECTANGLE", False);
XtSetArg(args[n], XmNexportTargets, targets); n++;
XtSetArg(args[n], XmNnumExportTargets, 1); n++;

/*
 * identify the conversion procedure and
 * the client data passed to the procedure
 */
XtSetArg(args[n], XmNclientData, conv); n++;
XtSetArg(args[n], XmNconvertProc, RectConvert); n++;

/* identify the necessary callbacks and the client data to
 * be passed */
dragDropFinishCB[0].closure = (XtPointer) conv;
XtSetArg(args[n], XmNdragDropFinishCallback,
                            dragDropFinishCB); n++;
dropFinishCB[0].closure = (XtPointer) conv;
XtSetArg(args[n], XmNdropFinishCallback, dropFinishCB); n++;
dragMotionCB[0].closure = (XtPointer) conv;
XtSetArg(args[n], XmNdragMotionCallback, dragMotionCB); n++;
operationChangedCB[0].closure = (XtPointer) conv;
XtSetArg(args[n], XmNoperationChangedCallback,
                            operationChangedCB); n++;

/* set the drag operations that are supported */
```

B–29

```
        XtSetArg(args[n], XmNdragOperations,
                                XmDROP_COPY | XmDROP_MOVE); n++;

        /* start the drag. This creates a drag context. */
        myDC = XmDragStart(w, event, args, n);


    }


}


/* This procedure searches through the export targets and
 * returns flags to indicate which targets were found
 */
/* ARGSUSED */
static void
#ifdef _NO_PROTO
CheckTargets(w, display, rectFound, bgFound, pixFound)
Widget w;
Display *display;
Boolean *rectFound;
Boolean *bgFound;
Boolean *pixFound;
#else
CheckTargets(Widget w, Display *display, Boolean *rectFound,
Boolean *bgFound, Boolean *pixFound)
#endif /* _NO_PROTO */
{

    Atom        MY_RECT = XmInternAtom(display, "_MY_RECTANGLE",
                                False);
    Atom        BACKGROUND = XmInternAtom(display, "BACKGROUND",
                                False);
    Atom        PIXMAP = XmInternAtom(display, "PIXMAP", False);
    Atom        *exportTargets;
    Cardinal    numExportTargets;
    Arg         args[2];
    int         n;

    /* Get list of transfer targets */
    n = 0;
```

```
    XtSetArg(args[0], XmNexportTargets, &exportTargets);
    XtSetArg(args[1], XmNnumExportTargets, &numExportTargets);
    XtGetValues(w, args, 2);

    /* initialize targets found flags */
    *rectFound = *bgFound = *pixFound = False;

    /* search through the export targets */
    for (n = 0; n < numExportTargets; n++) {

        if (exportTargets[n] == MY_RECT)
            *rectFound = True;
        else if (exportTargets[n] == BACKGROUND)
            *bgFound = True;
        else if (exportTargets[n] == PIXMAP)
            *pixFound = True;

    }

}


/* This procedure handles drop site messages and performs the
 * appropriate drag under effects.
 */
/* ARGSUSED */
static void
#ifdef _NO_PROTO
DragProcCallback(w, client, call)
Widget w;
XtPointer client;
XtPointer call;
#else
DragProcCallback(Widget w, XtPointer client, XtPointer call)
#endif /* _NO_PROTO */
{

    XmDragProcCallbackStruct    *cb = (XmDragProcCallbackStruct *)
                                        call;
    Display                     *display = XtDisplay(w);
    Boolean                     rectFound, bgFound, pixFound;
```

```
static unsigned char        initial_operations;
static unsigned char        initial_operation;
RectPtr                     rect;

CheckTargets(cb->dragContext, display, &rectFound, &bgFound,
            &pixFound);

switch(cb->reason) {

    case XmCR_DROP_SITE_ENTER_MESSAGE:

        /* save the value of the operations and operation
         * fields */
        initial_operations = cb->operations;
        initial_operation = cb->operation;

        rect = RectFind(cb->x, cb->y);

        /* Remove any operations for the operations field
         * which do not apply to the simulated drop site.
         */
        if (rect) {

            if (bgFound || pixFound) {
                cb->operations = XmDROP_COPY;
                RectHighlight(w, rect);
            }
            else if (rectFound) {
                cb->operations = cb->operations &
                                (XmDROP_COPY | XmDROP_MOVE);
                RectUnhighlight(w);
            }

        }
        else {
            cb->operations = initial_operations &
                            (XmDROP_COPY | XmDROP_MOVE);
            RectUnhighlight(w);
        }

        /* Set operation to the valid operation preferred by
```

```
 * the simulated drop site or to XmDROP_NOOP if the
 * operations list does not * contain the preferred
 * operation.
 */
if (rect) {

    if (bgFound || pixFound) {

        if (cb->operations & XmDROP_COPY)
            cb->operation = XmDROP_COPY;
        else
            cb->operation = XmDROP_NOOP;

    }
    else if (rectFound) {

        if (cb->operations & XmDROP_MOVE)
            cb->operation = XmDROP_MOVE;
        else if (cb->operations & XmDROP_COPY)
            cb->operation = XmDROP_COPY;
        else
            cb->operation = XmDROP_NOOP;

    }

}
else {

    if (rectFound) {

        if (cb->operations & XmDROP_MOVE)
            cb->operation = XmDROP_MOVE;
        else if (cb->operations & XmDROP_COPY)
            cb->operation = XmDROP_COPY;
        else
            cb->operation = XmDROP_NOOP;

    }
    else
        cb->operation = initial_operation;
```

```
    }

    /*
     * Set dropSiteStatus to XmDROP_SITE_INVALID if the
     * operation field is XmDROP_NOOP, or if there are no
     * common targets between the source and the nested
     * drop site.  Otherwise, set * dropSiteStatus to
     * XmDROP_SITE_VALID.
     */
    if (cb->operation == XmDROP_NOOP ||
        (rect && (!rectFound && !bgFound && !pixFound)) ||
        (!rect && !rectFound))
        cb->dropSiteStatus = XmINVALID_DROP_SITE;
    else
        cb->dropSiteStatus = XmVALID_DROP_SITE;

    /*
     * Display appropriate drag under visuals.  Only
     * highlight the rectangle if we are changing rectangle
     * attributes.
     */
    if (rect && bgFound || pixFound &&
        cb->dropSiteStatus == XmVALID_DROP_SITE)
        RectHighlight(w, rect);
    break;

case XmCR_DROP_SITE_LEAVE_MESSAGE:

    /* Only unhighlight the rectangle if previously
     * highlighted */
    if (appInfo->highlightRect != NULL)
        RectUnhighlight(w);
    break;

case XmCR_DROP_SITE_MOTION_MESSAGE:

    rect = RectFind(cb->x, cb->y);

    /*
     * Remove any operations for the operations field
     * which do not
```

```
 * apply to the simulated drop site.
 */
if (rect) {

    if (bgFound || pixFound) {
        cb->operations = XmDROP_COPY;
        RectHighlight(w, rect);
    }
    else if (rectFound) {
        cb->operations = cb->operations &
                        (XmDROP_COPY | XmDROP_MOVE);
        RectUnhighlight(w);
    }

}
else {
    cb->operations = initial_operations &
                    (XmDROP_COPY | XmDROP_MOVE);
    RectUnhighlight(w);
}

/*
 * Set operation to the valid operation preferred by
 * the simulated drop site or to XmDROP_NOOP if the
 * operations list does not * contain the preferred
 * operation.
 */
if (rect) {

    if (bgFound || pixFound) {

        if (cb->operations & XmDROP_COPY)
            cb->operation = XmDROP_COPY;
        else
            cb->operation = XmDROP_NOOP;

    }
    else if (rectFound) {

        if (cb->operations & XmDROP_MOVE)
            cb->operation = XmDROP_MOVE;
```

```
            else if (cb->operations & XmDROP_COPY)
                cb->operation = XmDROP_COPY;
            else
                cb->operation = XmDROP_NOOP;


        }
    }
    else {

        if (rectFound) {
            if (cb->operations & XmDROP_MOVE)
                cb->operation = XmDROP_MOVE;
            else if (cb->operations & XmDROP_COPY)
                cb->operation = XmDROP_COPY;
            else
                cb->operation = XmDROP_NOOP;

        }
        else
            cb->operation = initial_operation;

    }

    /*
     * Set dropSiteStatus to XmDROP_SITE_INVALID if the
     * operation field is XmDROP_NOOP, or if there are no
     * common targets between the source and the nested
     * drop site.  Otherwise, set dropSiteStatus to
     * XmDROP_SITE_VALID.
     */
    if (cb->operation == XmDROP_NOOP ||
        (rect && (!rectFound && !bgFound && !pixFound)) ||
        (!rect && !rectFound))
        cb->dropSiteStatus = XmINVALID_DROP_SITE;
    else
        cb->dropSiteStatus = XmVALID_DROP_SITE;

    /*
     * Display appropriate drag under visuals.  Only
     * highlight the rectangle if we are changing rectangle
     * attributes.
```

```
            */
          if (rect && bgFound || pixFound &&
              cb->dropSiteStatus == XmVALID_DROP_SITE)
              RectHighlight(w, rect);
          break;

      case XmCR_OPERATION_CHANGED:

          if (rectFound) {

              if (cb->operation == XmDROP_MOVE)
                  appInfo->doMove = True;
              else
                  appInfo->doMove = False;

          }
          break;

      default:

          /* other messages we consider invalid */
          cb->dropSiteStatus = XmINVALID_DROP_SITE;
          break;

    }

    /* allow animation to be performed */
    cb->animate = True;

}


/* This procedure handles the data that is being transfer */
/* ARGSUSED */
static void
#ifdef _NO_PROTO
TransferProcCallback(w, closure, seltype, type, value, length,
                  format)
Widget w;
XtPointer closure ;
Atom *seltype ;
```

```
Atom *type ;
XtPointer value ;
unsigned long *length ;
int *format ;
#else
TransferProcCallback(Widget w, XtPointer closure, Atom *seltype,
Atom *type, XtPointer value, unsigned long *length, int *format)
#endif /* _NO_PROTO */
{

    DropTransfer    transferRec = (DropTransfer) closure;
    Widget          wid = transferRec->widget;
    Display         *display = XtDisplay(wid);
    Atom    RECT_INFO = XmInternAtom(display, "RECT_INFO", False);
    Atom    PIXEL = XmInternAtom(display, "PIXEL", False);
    Atom    NULL_ATOM = XmInternAtom(display, "NULL", False);
    Arg             args[10];
    RectPtr         rect;
    int             n;

    /*
     * The delete target returns a NULL_ATOM type and value equal
     * to NULL so it isn't a failure.  Otherwise, check for NULL
     * value or targets that we don't support and set transfer
     * failure.
     */
    if (*type != NULL_ATOM && (!value ||
        (*type != RECT_INFO && *type != PIXEL &&
            *type != XA_DRAWABLE))) {

      n = 0;
      /*
       * On failures set both transferStatus to
       * XmTRANSFER_FAILURE and numDropTransfers to 0.
       */
      XtSetArg(args[n], XmNtransferStatus, XmTRANSFER_FAILURE);
      n++;
      XtSetArg(args[n], XmNnumDropTransfers, 0); n++;
      XtSetValues(w, args, n);
      /* Free the value if there is one, or we would have a
       * memory leak */
```

```
        if (value)
            XtFree(value);

        return;

    }

    /* Handle pixel type (i.e. change in background) */
    if (*type == PIXEL) {
        rect = RectFind(transferRec->x, transferRec->y);
        RectSetColor(rect, display, XtWindow(wid),
                    *((Pixel*)value));
    }
    /* Handle drawable type (i.e. change in pixmap) */
    else if (*type == XA_DRAWABLE) {
        rect = RectFind(transferRec->x, transferRec->y);
        RectSetPixmap(rect, display, XtWindow(wid),
                    *((Pixmap *)value));
    }
    /* Handle rect_info type (i.e. new rectangle) */
    else if (*type == RECT_INFO) {
        rect = (RectPtr) value;
        RectRegister(rect, transferRec->x, transferRec->y);
        value = NULL;
        /* No need to free, it is being stored in RecTable */
    }

    /* Free the value if there is one, or we would have a memory
     * leak */
    if (value)
        XtFree(value);

}


/* This procedure frees the data used the data transfer proc that
 * was passed from the drop procedure.
 */
/* ARGSUSED */
static void
#ifdef _NO_PROTO
```

```
DropDestroyCB(w, clientData, callData)
Widget      w;
XtPointer    clientData;
XtPointer    callData;
#else
DropDestroyCB(Widget w, XtPointer clientData, XtPointer callData)
#endif /* NO_PROTO */
{
    XtFree((char *)clientData);
}


/* This procedure initiates the drop transfer. */
/* ARGSUSED */
static void
#ifdef _NO_PROTO
HandleDrop(w, call)
Widget w;
XtPointer call;
#else
HandleDrop(Widget w, XtPointer call)
#endif /* _NO_PROTO */
{
    static XtCallbackRec dropDestroyCB[] = {
        {DropDestroyCB, NULL},
        {NULL, NULL}
    };

    XmDropProcCallbackStruct *cb = (XmDropProcCallbackStruct *)call;
    Display                  *display = XtDisplay(w);
    Arg                      args[10];
    int                      n;
    Boolean                  rectFound, bgFound, pixFound;
    DropTransfer             transferRec;
    XmDropTransferEntryRec   transferEntries[2];
    XmDropTransferEntryRec   *transferList = NULL;
    Cardinal                 numTransfers = 0;
    Boolean                  transferValid = False;
    RectPtr                  rect;

    /* Cancel the drop on invalid drop operations */
```

```
if (!(cb->operations & XmDROP_MOVE || cb->operations
    & XmDROP_COPY)) {

    n = 0;
    cb->operation = XmDROP_NOOP;
    cb->dropSiteStatus = XmINVALID_DROP_SITE;
    XtSetArg(args[n], XmNtransferStatus, XmTRANSFER_FAILURE);
    n++;
    XtSetArg(args[n], XmNnumDropTransfers, 0); n++;
}
else {

    /* Find out which nested dropsite contains the pointer */
    rect = RectFind(cb->x, cb->y);

    CheckTargets(cb->dragContext, display, &rectFound, &bgFound,
                &pixFound);

    /* rect !NULL indicates we are within a nested dropsite */
    if (rect) {

        /* MY_RECT is a possible target, support it first */
        if (rectFound)
            transferValid = True;
        else if (bgFound || pixFound) {
            /* support only copy with the BACKGROUND and PIXMAP
             * targets */
            if (cb->operation != XmDROP_COPY)
                cb->operation = XmDROP_COPY;
            transferValid = True;
        }

    }
    else {
        if (rectFound)
            transferValid = True;
    }

    if (transferValid) {

        /* initialize data to send to drop transfer callback */
```

```
transferRec = (DropTransfer)
            XtMalloc(sizeof(DropTransferRec));
transferRec->widget = w;
transferRec->x = cb->x;
transferRec->y = cb->y;

/* order of support is MY_RECT, then BACKGROUND, then
 * PIXMAP */
if (rectFound)
    transferEntries[0].target = XmInternAtom(display,
        "_MY_RECTANGLE", False);
else if (bgFound)
    transferEntries[0].target = XmInternAtom(display,
        "BACKGROUND", False);
else if (pixFound)
    transferEntries[0].target = XmInternAtom(display,
        "PIXMAP", False);

transferEntries[0].client_data =
    (XtPointer) transferRec;

/* Set up move targets */
if (cb->operation == XmDROP_MOVE) {

    transferEntries[1].client_data =
        (XtPointer) transferRec;
    transferEntries[1].target = XmInternAtom(display,
        "DELETE", False);
    numTransfers = 2;

}
else if (cb->operation == XmDROP_COPY)
    numTransfers = 1;

transferList = transferEntries;

/* Setup transfer list */
n = 0;
cb->dropSiteStatus = XmVALID_DROP_SITE;
XtSetArg(args[n], XmNdropTransfers, transferList); n++;
XtSetArg(args[n], XmNnumDropTransfers, numTransfers);
```

```
            n++;

            /* Setup destroy callback to free transferRec */
            dropDestroyCB[0].closure = (XtPointer) transferRec;
            XtSetArg(args[n], XmNdestroyCallback, dropDestroyCB);
            n++;

            /* Setup transfer proc to accept the drop transfer data */
            XtSetArg(args[n], XmNtransferProc, TransferProcCallback);
            n++;

        }
        else {

            n = 0;
            cb->operation = XmDROP_NOOP;
            cb->dropSiteStatus = XmINVALID_DROP_SITE;
            XtSetArg(args[n], XmNtransferStatus,
                XmTRANSFER_FAILURE); n++;
            XtSetArg(args[n], XmNnumDropTransfers, 0); n++;

        }

    }

    XmDropTransferStart(cb->dragContext, args, n);

}


/* This procedure is used with the drop help dialog to continue
 * with the drop */
/* ARGSUSED */
static void
#ifdef _NO_PROTO
HandleOK(w, client, call)
Widget w;
XtPointer client;
XtPointer call;
#else
HandleOK(Widget w, XtPointer client, XtPointer call)
```

```
#endif /* _NO_PROTO */
{

    XmDropProcCallbackStruct *cb = (XmDropProcCallbackStruct *)client;

    cb->operation = appInfo->operation;
    HandleDrop(w, (XtPointer) cb);

}


/* This procedure is used with the drop help dialog to cancel the
 * drop */
/* ARGSUSED */
static void
#ifdef _NO_PROTO
CancelDrop(w, client, call)
Widget w;
XtPointer client;
XtPointer call;
#else
CancelDrop(Widget w, XtPointer client, XtPointer call)
#endif /* _NO_PROTO */
{

    XmDropProcCallbackStruct *cb = (XmDropProcCallbackStruct *)client;
    Arg                       args[2];

    /* On help, we need to cancel the drop transfer */
    XtSetArg(args[0], XmNtransferStatus, XmTRANSFER_FAILURE);
    XtSetArg(args[1], XmNnumDropTransfers, 0);

    /* we need to start the drop transfer to cancel the transfer */
    XmDropTransferStart(cb->dragContext, args, 2);

}


#ifdef _NO_PROTO
XtCallbackProc ChangeOperation(widget, client_data, call_data)
Widget widget;
```

```
caddr_t client_data;
XmAnyCallbackStruct *call_data;
#else
XtCallbackProc ChangeOperation(Widget widget, caddr_t client_data,
XmAnyCallbackStruct *call_data)
#endif
{

    if (client_data == 0)
        appInfo->operation = XmDROP_MOVE;
    else
        appInfo->operation = XmDROP_COPY;

}



/* This procedure manages the help dialog and determines which
 * message is displayed in the dialog depending on the position
 * and the type of drop.
 */
/* ARGSUSED */
static void
#ifdef _NO_PROTO
HandleHelp(w, call)
Widget w;
XtPointer call;
#else
HandleHelp(Widget w, XtPointer call)
#endif /* _NO_PROTO */
{

    XmDropProcCallbackStruct *cb = (XmDropProcCallbackStruct *)call;
    static XmDropProcCallbackStruct client;
    Boolean                  rectFound, bgFound, pixFound;
    XmString                 helpStr;
    RectPtr                  rect;
    Arg                      args[5];
    XmString                 tempStr, buttonArray[2];
    int                      n = 0;

    /* the drop is valid until it is determined invalid */
```

```
cb->dropSiteStatus = XmVALID_DROP_SITE;

/* if we haven't created a help dialog, create one now */
if (helpDialog == NULL) {

    XtSetArg(args[n], XmNdialogStyle,
        XmDIALOG_FULL_APPLICATION_MODAL); n++;
    XtSetArg(args[n], XmNtitle, "Drop Help"); n++;
    helpDialog = XmCreateMessageDialog(topLevel, "Help",
        args, n);

    n = 0;
    buttonArray[0] = XmStringCreateSimple("Move");
    buttonArray[1] = XmStringCreateSimple("Copy");
    XtSetArg(args[n], XmNbuttons, buttonArray); n++;
    XtSetArg(args[n], XmNbuttonCount, 2); n++;
    XtSetArg(args[n], XmNbuttonSet, 0); n++;
    XtSetArg(args[n], XmNsimpleCallback, ChangeOperation); n++;
    tempStr = XmStringCreateSimple("Operations:");
    XtSetArg(args[n], XmNoptionLabel, tempStr); n++;
    helpMenu = XmCreateSimpleOptionMenu(helpDialog, "helpMenu",
        args, n);
    XmStringFree(tempStr);
    XmStringFree(buttonArray[0]);
    XmStringFree(buttonArray[1]);

    XtAddCallback(helpDialog, XmNokCallback,
        (XtCallbackProc) HandleOK, (XtPointer) &client);
    XtAddCallback(helpDialog, XmNcancelCallback,
        (XtCallbackProc) CancelDrop, (XtPointer) &client);

    XtUnmanageChild(XmMessageBoxGetChild(helpDialog,
        XmDIALOG_HELP_BUTTON));

    XtRealizeWidget(helpDialog);

}

/* pass the necessary callback information along */
client.dragContext = cb->dragContext;
client.x = cb->x;
```

```
client.y = cb->y;
client.dropSiteStatus = cb->dropSiteStatus;
client.operation = cb->operation;
client.operations = cb->operations;

/* find the valid targets */
CheckTargets(cb->dragContext, XtDisplay(w), &rectFound,
            &bgFound, &pixFound);

/* determine the appropriate help message */
if (rectFound) {

    if (cb->operations == XmDROP_MOVE | XmDROP_COPY) {
        XtManageChild(helpMenu);
        helpStr = XmStringCreateLtoR(HELP_MSG4,
                                     XmFONTLIST_DEFAULT_TAG);
        XtManageChild(XmMessageBoxGetChild(helpDialog,
                      XmDIALOG_OK_BUTTON));
    }
    else if (cb->operation == XmDROP_MOVE) {
        XtUnmanageChild(helpMenu);
        helpStr = XmStringCreateLtoR(HELP_MSG2,
                                     XmFONTLIST_DEFAULT_TAG);
        XtManageChild(XmMessageBoxGetChild(helpDialog,
                      XmDIALOG_OK_BUTTON));
    }
    else if (cb->operation == XmDROP_COPY) {
        XtUnmanageChild(helpMenu);
        helpStr = XmStringCreateLtoR(HELP_MSG3,
                                     XmFONTLIST_DEFAULT_TAG);
        XtManageChild(XmMessageBoxGetChild(helpDialog,
                      XmDIALOG_OK_BUTTON));
    }

}
else if (bgFound || pixFound && cb->operation == XmDROP_COPY) {

    XtUnmanageChild(helpMenu);
    rect = RectFind(cb->x, cb->y);
    if (rect) {
        helpStr = XmStringCreateLtoR(HELP_MSG1,
```

```
                                        XmFONTLIST_DEFAULT_TAG);
        XtManageChild(XmMessageBoxGetChild(helpDialog,
                    XmDIALOG_OK_BUTTON));
    }
    else {
        helpStr = XmStringCreateLtoR(HELP_MSG5,
                                    XmFONTLIST_DEFAULT_TAG);
        XtUnmanageChild(XmMessageBoxGetChild(helpDialog,
                    XmDIALOG_OK_BUTTON));
    }

}
else {
    XtUnmanageChild(helpMenu);
    helpStr = XmStringCreateLtoR(HELP_MSG5,
                                XmFONTLIST_DEFAULT_TAG);
    XtUnmanageChild(XmMessageBoxGetChild(helpDialog,
                XmDIALOG_OK_BUTTON));
}

/* set the help message into the dialog */
XtSetArg(args[0], XmNmessageString, helpStr);
XtSetValues(helpDialog, args, 1);

/* Free the XmString */
XmStringFree(helpStr);

/* map the help dialog */
XtManageChild(helpDialog);

}


/* The procedure either begins the drop of initiates the help
 * dialog depending on the dropAction.
 */
/* ARGSUSED */
static void
#ifdef _NO_PROTO
DropProcCallback(w, client, call)
Widget w;
```

```
XtPointer client;
XtPointer call;
#else
DropProcCallback(Widget w, XtPointer client, XtPointer call)
#endif /* _NO_PROTO */
{

    XmDropProcCallbackStruct *cb = (XmDropProcCallbackStruct *)call;

    if (appInfo->highlightRect != NULL)
        RectUnhighlight(w);

    if (cb->dropAction != XmDROP_HELP)
        HandleDrop(w, call);
    else
        HandleHelp(w, call);

}


/* This procedure registers the drop targets and the drop site */
static void
#ifdef _NO_PROTO
RegisterDropSite(w)
Widget w;
#else
RegisterDropSite(Widget w)
#endif /* _NO_PROTO */
{

    Display *display = XtDisplay(w);
    Atom    targets[3];
    Arg     args[5];
    int     n = 0;

    /* Only accept moves or copies */
    XtSetArg(args[n], XmNdragOperations, XmDROP_COPY | XmDROP_MOVE);
    n++;

    /* set all possible targets for any of the nested drop sites */
    targets[0] = XmInternAtom(display, "_MY_RECTANGLE", False);
```

```
    targets[1] = XmInternAtom(display, "BACKGROUND", False);
    targets[2] = XmInternAtom(display, "PIXMAP", False);
    XtSetArg(args[n], XmNimportTargets, targets); n++;
    XtSetArg(args[n], XmNnumImportTargets, 3); n++;

    /* register a dragProc - necessary for simulating nested drop
     * sites */
    XtSetArg(args[n], XmNdragProc, DragProcCallback); n++;

    /* register a dropProc */
    XtSetArg(args[n], XmNdropProc, DropProcCallback); n++;
    XmDropSiteRegister(w, args, n);

}


static void
#ifdef _NO_PROTO
SetInvalidIcon(w)
Widget w;
#else
SetInvalidIcon(Widget w)
#endif /* _NO_PROTO */
{

    Widget      invalidIcon;
    char        *invalid_bits;
    Dimension   width, height;
    Arg         args[1];

    if (appInfo->maxCursorWidth >= ICON_WIDTH &&
        appInfo->maxCursorHeight >= ICON_HEIGHT) {
        invalid_bits = INVALID_ICON_BITS;
        width = ICON_WIDTH;
        height = ICON_HEIGHT;
    } else {
        /* If the server will handle a small icon, create one */
        invalid_bits = SMALL_INVALID_ICON_BITS;
        width = SMALL_ICON_WIDTH;
        height = SMALL_ICON_HEIGHT;
    }
```

```
    invalidIcon = GetDragIconFromBits(w, invalid_bits, invalid_bits,
                    width, height, GetColor(DRAW_AREA_FG_COLOR),
                    GetColor(DRAW_AREA_BG_COLOR));

    XtSetArg(args[0], XmNdefaultInvalidCursorIcon, invalidIcon);
    XtSetValues(XmGetXmScreen(XtScreen(w)), args, 1);

}


/* This procedure initializes the toolkit and other application
 * information */
static void
#ifdef _NO_PROTO
InitializeApplication(argc, argv)
int *argc;
String *argv;
#else
InitializeApplication(int *argc, String *argv)
#endif /* _NO_PROTO */
{

    static XtActionsRec new_actions[] = {
        {"StartRect", StartRect},
        {"ExtendRect", ExtendRect},
        {"EndRect", EndRect},
        {"StartMove", StartMove},
        {"ColorRect", ColorRect},
    };
    Arg         args[5];
    Cardinal    n = 0;

    /* Ininialize struct that hold global information */
    InitializeAppInfo();

    /* Initialize Toolkit and create shell */
    XtSetArg(args[n], XmNwidth, 295); n++;
    XtSetArg(args[n], XmNheight, 270); n++;
    topLevel = XtAppInitialize(&appContext, "DNDDemo", NULL, 0,
                        argc, argv, NULL, args, n);
```

```
    /* Set drag protocol styles */
    n = 0;
    XtSetArg(args[n], XmNdragInitiatorProtocolStyle,
            XmDRAG_PREFER_RECEIVER); n++;
    XtSetArg(args[n], XmNdragReceiverProtocolStyle, XmDRAG_DYNAMIC);
    n++;
    XtSetValues(XmGetXmDisplay(XtDisplay(topLevel)), args, n);

    /* Initialize tables for holding rectangle information */
    InitializeRectDpyTable();

    /* Add new actions for use with translation tables */
    XtAppAddActions(appContext, new_actions, 5);

    /* Get the display server's best cursor size */
    XQueryBestCursor(XtDisplay(topLevel),
        RootWindowOfScreen(XtScreen(topLevel)), 64, 64,
        &appInfo->maxCursorWidth, &appInfo->maxCursorHeight);

}


/* This the program start procedure */
void
#ifdef _NO_PROTO
main (argc, argv)
int argc;
String *argv;
#else
main (int argc, String *argv)
#endif /* _NO_PROTO */
{

    /* Initialize toolkit and application global values */
    InitializeApplication(&argc, argv);

    /* Create main window, drawing area, and color labels */
    CreateLayout();

    /* Register the drawing area as a drop site */
    RegisterDropSite(drawingArea);
```

```
SetInvalidIcon(drawingArea);

/* Realize and map widget hiearchy */
XtRealizeWidget(topLevel);

/* Create GC for drawing rectangles */
CreateRectGC();

/* Begin event loop processing */
XtAppMainLoop(appContext);

}
```

B.3 DNDDraw.c

```
/*
 *      file: DNDDraw.c
 *
 *      File containing all the drawing routines needed to run
 *      DNDDemo program.
 *
 */

#include "DNDDemo.h"


/* The following character arrays hold the bits for
 * the source and state icons for both 32x32 and 16x16 drag icons.
 * The source is a color palette icon and the state is a paint
 * brush icon.
 */
char SOURCE_ICON_BITS[] = {
    0x00, 0x00, 0x00, 0x00, 0x00, 0x00, 0x00, 0x00, 0x00, 0xa0,
    0xaa, 0x02, 0x00, 0x50, 0x55, 0x07, 0x00, 0x28, 0x00, 0x0c,
    0x00, 0x94, 0x42, 0x19, 0x00, 0xca, 0xe5, 0x33, 0x00, 0x85,
    0xc6, 0x33, 0x80, 0x42, 0xe7, 0x33, 0x40, 0x81, 0xc3, 0x31,
    0xa0, 0x00, 0x00, 0x38, 0x50, 0x00, 0x00, 0x1c, 0x28, 0x00,
```

```
    0x00, 0x0e, 0x90, 0x02, 0x00, 0x07, 0xc8, 0x05, 0x80, 0x03,
    0x90, 0x07, 0xc0, 0x01, 0x48, 0x05, 0xe0, 0x00, 0x90, 0x03,
    0x70, 0x00, 0x08, 0x00, 0x30, 0x00, 0x10, 0x14, 0x30, 0x00,
    0x08, 0x2a, 0x30, 0x00, 0x10, 0x34, 0x30, 0x00, 0x28, 0x2a,
    0x60, 0x00, 0x50, 0x9c, 0xe2, 0x00, 0xa0, 0x40, 0xc4, 0x01,
    0x40, 0x01, 0x84, 0x01, 0x80, 0x42, 0x84, 0x03, 0x00, 0x85,
    0x03, 0x03, 0x00, 0x0a, 0x00, 0x03, 0x00, 0xf4, 0xff, 0x03,
    0x00, 0xf8, 0xff, 0x01, 0x00, 0x00, 0x00, 0x00};

char SOURCE_ICON_MASK[] = {
    0x00, 0x00, 0x00, 0x00, 0x00, 0xf0, 0xff, 0x07, 0x00, 0xf8,
    0xff, 0x0f, 0x00, 0xfc, 0xff, 0x1f, 0x00, 0xfe, 0xff, 0x3f,
    0x00, 0xff, 0xff, 0x7f, 0x80, 0xff, 0xff, 0x7f, 0xc0, 0xff,
    0xff, 0x7f, 0xe0, 0xff, 0xff, 0x7f, 0xf0, 0xff, 0xff, 0x7f,
    0xf8, 0xff, 0xff, 0x7f, 0xfc, 0xff, 0xff, 0x7f, 0xfc, 0xff,
    0xff, 0x3f, 0xfc, 0xff, 0xff, 0x1f, 0xfc, 0xff, 0xff, 0x0f,
    0xfc, 0xff, 0xff, 0x07, 0xfc, 0xff, 0xff, 0x03, 0xfc, 0xff,
    0xff, 0x01, 0xfc, 0xff, 0xff, 0x00, 0xfc, 0xff, 0x7f, 0x00,
    0xfc, 0xff, 0x7f, 0x00, 0xfc, 0xff, 0xff, 0x00, 0xfc, 0xff,
    0xff, 0x01, 0xfc, 0xff, 0xff, 0x03, 0xf8, 0xff, 0xff, 0x03,
    0xf0, 0xff, 0xff, 0x07, 0xe0, 0xff, 0xff, 0x07, 0xc0, 0xff,
    0xff, 0x07, 0x80, 0xff, 0xff, 0x07, 0x00, 0xff, 0xff, 0x07,
    0x00, 0xfe, 0xff, 0x07, 0x00, 0xfc, 0xff, 0x03};

char STATE_ICON_BITS[] = {
    0x00, 0x00, 0x00, 0x00, 0x1e, 0x00, 0x00, 0x00, 0x78, 0x00,
    0x00, 0x00, 0xf8, 0x01, 0x00, 0x00, 0xf8, 0x01, 0x00, 0x00,
    0xf8, 0x03, 0x00, 0x00, 0xf0, 0x03, 0x00, 0x00, 0xf0, 0x07,
    0x00, 0x00, 0xc0, 0x0d, 0x00, 0x00, 0x00, 0x1b, 0x00, 0x00,
    0x00, 0x3e, 0x00, 0x00, 0x00, 0x7e, 0x00, 0x00, 0x00, 0xfc,
    0x00, 0x00, 0x00, 0xf8, 0x01, 0x00, 0x00, 0xf0, 0x03, 0x00,
    0x00, 0xe0, 0x07, 0x00, 0x00, 0xc0, 0x0f, 0x00, 0x00, 0x80,
    0x1f, 0x00, 0x00, 0x00, 0x3f, 0x00, 0x00, 0x00, 0x7e, 0x00,
    0x00, 0x00, 0xfc, 0x00, 0x00, 0x00, 0xf8, 0x01, 0x00, 0x00,
    0xf0, 0x01, 0x00, 0x00, 0xe0, 0x03, 0x00, 0x00, 0xc0, 0x07,
    0x00, 0x00, 0x80, 0x0f, 0x00, 0x00, 0x00, 0x1f, 0x00, 0x00,
    0x00, 0x1e, 0x00, 0x00, 0x00, 0x3c, 0x00, 0x00, 0x00, 0x38,
    0x00, 0x00, 0x00, 0x60, 0x00, 0x00, 0x00, 0xc0};

char STATE_ICON_MASK[] = {
    0x3f, 0x00, 0x00, 0x00, 0xff, 0x00, 0x00, 0x00, 0xff, 0x03,
```

```
      0x00, 0x00, 0xfc, 0x03, 0x00, 0x00, 0xfc, 0x07, 0x00, 0x00,
      0xfc, 0x07, 0x00, 0x00, 0xfc, 0x07, 0x00, 0x00, 0xf8, 0x07,
      0x00, 0x00, 0xf8, 0x0f, 0x00, 0x00, 0xe0, 0x1f, 0x00, 0x00,
      0x00, 0x3e, 0x00, 0x00, 0x00, 0x7e, 0x00, 0x00, 0x00, 0xfc,
      0x00, 0x00, 0x00, 0xf8, 0x01, 0x00, 0x00, 0xf0, 0x03, 0x00,
      0x00, 0xe0, 0x07, 0x00, 0x00, 0xc0, 0x0f, 0x00, 0x00, 0x80,
      0x1f, 0x00, 0x00, 0x00, 0x3f, 0x00, 0x00, 0x00, 0xfe, 0x01,
      0x00, 0x00, 0xfc, 0x03, 0x00, 0x00, 0xf8, 0x03, 0x00, 0x00,
      0xf0, 0x07, 0x00, 0x00, 0xe0, 0x0f, 0x00, 0x00, 0xc0, 0x1f,
      0x00, 0x00, 0x80, 0x3f, 0x00, 0x00, 0x00, 0x7f, 0x00, 0x00,
      0x00, 0x7e, 0x00, 0x00, 0x00, 0x7e, 0x00, 0x00, 0x00, 0xfe,
      0x00, 0x00, 0x00, 0xfc, 0x00, 0x00, 0x00, 0xf0};

char INVALID_ICON_BITS[] = {
      0x00, 0xe0, 0x0f, 0x00, 0x00, 0xfc, 0x7f, 0x00, 0x00, 0xff,
      0xff, 0x01, 0x80, 0xff, 0xff, 0x03, 0xc0, 0x1f, 0xf0, 0x07,
      0xe0, 0x07, 0xc0, 0x0f, 0xf0, 0x07, 0x00, 0x1f, 0xf8, 0x0f,
      0x00, 0x3e, 0xf8, 0x1f, 0x00, 0x3c, 0xfc, 0x3f, 0x00, 0x7c,
      0x3c, 0x7f, 0x00, 0x78, 0x3c, 0xfe, 0x00, 0x78, 0x1e, 0xfc,
      0x01, 0xf0, 0x1e, 0xf8, 0x03, 0xf0, 0x1e, 0xf0, 0x07, 0xf0,
      0x1e, 0xe0, 0x0f, 0xf0, 0x1e, 0xc0, 0x1f, 0xf0, 0x1e, 0x80,
      0x3f, 0xf0, 0x1e, 0x00, 0x7f, 0xf0, 0x3c, 0x00, 0xfe, 0x78,
      0x3c, 0x00, 0xfc, 0x79, 0x7c, 0x00, 0xf8, 0x7f, 0x78, 0x00,
      0xf0, 0x3f, 0xf8, 0x00, 0xe0, 0x3f, 0xf0, 0x01, 0xc0, 0x1f,
      0xe0, 0x07, 0xc0, 0x0f, 0xc0, 0x1f, 0xf0, 0x07, 0x80, 0xff,
      0xff, 0x03, 0x00, 0xff, 0xff, 0x01, 0x00, 0xfc, 0x7f, 0x00,
      0x00, 0xe0, 0x0f, 0x00, 0x00, 0x00, 0x00, 0x00};

char SMALL_SOURCE_ICON_BITS[] = {
      0x80, 0x1f, 0x40, 0x60, 0x20, 0x91, 0x90, 0xaa, 0x08, 0x91,
      0x08, 0x40, 0x08, 0x20, 0x08, 0x10, 0x28, 0x10, 0x78, 0x10,
      0x28, 0x20, 0x08, 0x41, 0x90, 0x43, 0x20, 0x21, 0x40, 0x10,
      0x80, 0x0f};

char SMALL_SOURCE_ICON_MASK[] = {
      0x80, 0x1f, 0xc0, 0x7f, 0xe0, 0xff, 0xf0, 0xff, 0xf8, 0xff,
      0xf8, 0x7f, 0xf8, 0x3f, 0xf8, 0x1f, 0xf8, 0x1f, 0xf8, 0x1f,
      0xf8, 0x3f, 0xf8, 0x7f, 0xf0, 0x7f, 0xe0, 0x3f, 0xc0, 0x1f,
      0x80, 0x0f};

char SMALL_STATE_ICON_BITS[] = {
```

```
    0x0f, 0x00, 0x1e, 0x00, 0x1e, 0x00, 0x3c, 0x00, 0x50, 0x00,
    0xe0, 0x00, 0xc0, 0x01, 0x80, 0x03, 0x00, 0x07, 0x00, 0x0e,
    0x00, 0x1c, 0x00, 0x18, 0x00, 0x20, 0x00, 0x40, 0x00, 0x80,
    0x00, 0x00};

char SMALL_STATE_ICON_MASK[] = {
    0x0f, 0x00, 0x1e, 0x00, 0x1e, 0x00, 0x3c, 0x00, 0x70, 0x00,
    0xe0, 0x00, 0xc0, 0x01, 0x80, 0x03, 0x00, 0x07, 0x00, 0x0e,
    0x00, 0x1c, 0x00, 0x18, 0x00, 0x20, 0x00, 0x40, 0x00, 0x80,
    0x00, 0x00};

char SMALL_INVALID_ICON_BITS[] = {
    0xe0, 0x03, 0xf8, 0x0f, 0x1c, 0x1c, 0x1e, 0x30, 0x3e, 0x30,
    0x73, 0x60, 0xe3, 0x60, 0xc3, 0x61, 0x83, 0x63, 0x03, 0x67,
    0x06, 0x3e, 0x06, 0x3c, 0x1c, 0x1c, 0xf8, 0x0f, 0xe0, 0x03,
    0x00, 0x00};


/* Globals variables */
AppInfo appInfo;


/* This is a string to pixel conversion function. */
Pixel
#ifdef _NO_PROTO
GetColor(colorstr)
char *colorstr;
#else
GetColor(char *colorstr)
#endif /* _NO_PROTO */
{

    XrmValue    from, to;

    from.size = strlen(colorstr) +1;
    if (from.size < sizeof(String))
        from.size = sizeof(String);
    from.addr = colorstr;
    to.addr = NULL;
    XtConvert(topLevel, XmRString, &from, XmRPixel, &to);
```

```
    if (to.addr != NULL)
        return ((Pixel) *((Pixel *) to.addr));
    else
        return ( (XtArgVal) NULL);


}



/* This procedure is used to initialize the application information
 * structure */
void
#ifdef _NO_PROTO
InitializeAppInfo()
#else /* _NO_PROTO */
InitializeAppInfo(void)
#endif /* _NO_PROTO */
{

    if (!appInfo) {

        appInfo = (AppInfo) XtMalloc(sizeof(AppInfoRec));
        appInfo->rectGC = NULL;
        appInfo->currentColor = 0;
        appInfo->rectDpyTable = NULL;
        appInfo->rectsAllocd = 0;
        appInfo->numRects = 0;
        appInfo->highlightRect = NULL;
        appInfo->clearRect = NULL;
        appInfo->doMove = True;
        appInfo->creatingRect = True;
        appInfo->operation = XmDROP_MOVE;
        appInfo->maxCursorWidth = 64;
        appInfo->maxCursorHeight = 64;
        appInfo->rectX = 0;
        appInfo->rectY = 0;
        appInfo->rectX2 = 0;
        appInfo->rectY2 = 0;

    }


}
```

```
/* This procedure sets the color in the GC for drawing the
 * rectangles in a new color.
 */
void
#ifdef _NO_PROTO
SetColor(display, color)
Display *display;
Pixel color;
#else
SetColor(Display *display, Pixel color)
#endif /* _NO_PROTO */
{

    /*
     * if the GC already has a foreground of this color,
     * it would be wasteful to reset the color
     */
    if (color != appInfo->currentColor) {
        XSetForeground(display, appInfo->rectGC,
                        (unsigned long) color);
        appInfo->currentColor = color;
    }

}


/* This function draws the rectangle in the color provided */
static int
#ifdef _NO_PROTO
RectDraw(display, window, rect)
Display *display;
Window window;
RectPtr rect;
#else
RectDraw(Display *display, Window window, RectPtr rect)
#endif /* _NO_PROTO */
{

    SetColor(display, rect->color);
    XFillRectangle(display, window, appInfo->rectGC, rect->x,
                    rect->y, rect->width, rect->height);
```

```
}


/* This procedure draws the rectangle highlight in a specified
 * color */
static void
#ifdef _NO_PROTO
RectDrawHighlight(w, rect, color )
Widget w;
RectPtr rect;
Pixel color;
#else
RectDrawHighlight( Widget w, RectPtr rect, Pixel color )
#endif /* _NO_PROTO */
{

    Display *display = XtDisplay(w);
    Window window = XtWindow(w);
    Pixel currentColor = rect->color;
    XGCValues values;

    values.foreground = color;
    XChangeGC(display, appInfo->rectGC, GCForeground, &values);

    XDrawRectangle(display, window, appInfo->rectGC,
                rect->x + 1, rect->y + 1,
                rect->width - HIGHLIGHT_THICKNESS,
                rect->height - HIGHLIGHT_THICKNESS);

    /* Return the GC to it's previous state */
    values.foreground = appInfo->currentColor = currentColor;
    XChangeGC(display, appInfo->rectGC, GCForeground, &values);

}


/* This procedure handles redrawing the rectangles.  It draws
 * them according to the order in the rectangle display table.
 * The rectangles at the top of the table are drawn first.
 */
void
```

```
#ifdef _NO_PROTO
RedrawRectangles(w)
Widget w;
#else
RedrawRectangles(Widget w)
#endif /* _NO_PROTO */
{

    Display *display = XtDisplay(w);
    RectPtr rect;
    Window window = XtWindow(w);
    int i;

    for (i = 0; i < appInfo->numRects; i++) {

        rect = appInfo->rectDpyTable[i];
        /* Only draw the rectangles that haven't been cleared */
        if (rect != appInfo->clearRect) {
            RectDraw(display, window, rect);
        }
        /* Draw the rectangle highlight of the highlight
         * rectangle */
        if (rect == appInfo->highlightRect) {
            RectDrawHighlight(w, rect, GetColor(HIGHLIGHT_COLOR));
        }

    }

}


/* This procedure will clear the current rectangle and redraw any
 * rectangles that were partially cleared by the rectangle that
 * was deleted.
 */
/* ARGSUSED */
void
#ifdef _NO_PROTO
RectHide(display, window, rect)
Display *display;
Window window;
```

```
RectPtr rect;
#else
RectHide(Display *display, Window window, RectPtr rect)
#endif /* _NO_PROTO */
{

    Pixel background, oldColor;
    Arg args[1];

    /* Get the background of the drawing area. */
    XtSetArg(args[0], XmNbackground, &background);
    XtGetValues(drawingArea, args, 1);

    /* Save the old color for restoration purposes. */
    oldColor = rect->color;

    /* Clear the rectangle */
    rect->color = background;
    RectDraw(display, window, rect);
    appInfo->clearRect = rect;

    /* redraw the rest of the rectangles */
    RedrawRectangles(drawingArea);

    /* restore the rectangle color */
    rect->color = oldColor;

}

/* This procedure draws the stipple rectangle that is used in
 * marking the old rectangle position during a rectangle move
 * operation.
 */
/* ARGSUSED */
void
#ifdef _NO_PROTO
RectDrawStippled(display, window, rect)
Display *display;
Window window;
RectPtr rect;
#else
```

```
RectDrawStippled(Display *display, Window window, RectPtr rect)
#endif /* _NO_PROTO */
{

    register int x = rect->x;
    register int y = rect->y;
    register Dimension width = rect->width;
    register Dimension height = rect->height;
    XGCValues values;
    XSegment segments[4];

    /* Set the rectangle color */
    values.foreground = appInfo->currentColor = rect->color;
    XChangeGC(display, appInfo->rectGC, GCForeground , &values);

    /* Create the segments for drawing the stippled rectangle */
    segments[0].x1 = segments[2].x1 = x;
    segments[0].y1 = segments[0].y2 = y;
    segments[0].x2 = x + width - 1;
    segments[1].x1 = segments[1].x2 = x + width - 1;
    segments[1].y1 = segments[3].y1 = y;
    segments[3].y2 = y + height;
    segments[2].y1 = segments[2].y2 = y + height - 1;
    segments[3].x1 = segments[3].x2 = x;
    segments[2].x2 = x + width;
    segments[1].y2 = y + height;

    /* Set the line attributes and draw */
    XSetLineAttributes(display, appInfo->rectGC, 1, LineOnOffDash,
        CapButt, JoinMiter);
    XDrawSegments (display, window, appInfo->rectGC, segments, 4);

    /* restore the default line settings */
    values.line_width = HIGHLIGHT_THICKNESS;
    values.line_style = LineSolid;
    XChangeGC(display, appInfo->rectGC, GCLineWidth | GCLineStyle,
            &values);

}
```

```
/* This procedure sets the highlight rectangle and
 * redraws the rectangles.  The expose routine will draw
 * the highlight around the highlighted rectangle.
 */
/* ARGSUSED */
void
#ifdef _NO_PROTO
RectHighlight(w, rect)
Widget w;
RectPtr rect;
#else
RectHighlight(Widget w, RectPtr rect)
#endif /* _NO_PROTO */
{

    if (appInfo->highlightRect != rect) {
        appInfo->highlightRect = rect;
        RedrawRectangles(w);
    }

}


/* This procedure sets the highlight rectangle to NULL and
 * redraws the rectangles.  The expose routine will clear
 * the highlight around the highlighted rectangle.
 */
/* ARGSUSED */
void
#ifdef _NO_PROTO
RectUnhighlight(w)
Widget w;
#else
RectUnhighlight(Widget w)
#endif /* _NO_PROTO */
{

    if (appInfo->highlightRect) {
        appInfo->highlightRect = NULL;
        RedrawRectangles(w);
    }
```

```
}

/* This function creates and initialized a new rectangle */
RectPtr
#ifdef _NO_PROTO
RectCreate(x, y, width, height, color, pixmap)
Position x;
Position y;
Dimension width;
Dimension height;
Pixel color;
Pixmap pixmap;
#else
RectCreate(Position x, Position y, Dimension width,
Dimension height, Pixel color, Pixmap pixmap)
#endif /* _NO_PROTO */
{

    RectPtr rect;

    rect = (RectPtr)  XtMalloc(sizeof(RectStruct));

    rect->x = x;
    rect->y = y;
    rect->width = width;
    rect->height = height;
    rect->color = color;
    rect->pixmap = pixmap;

    return(rect);

}


/* This procedure will move the rectangle to the end of the
 * rectangle display table (effectively raising it to top of
 * the displayed rectangles).
 */
static void
#ifdef _NO_PROTO
RectToTop(rect)
```

```
RectPtr rect;
#else
RectToTop(RectPtr rect)
#endif /* _NO_PROTO */
{

    int    i, j;


    if (rect) {

        /* Get the index to the target rectangle */
        for (i = 0; i < appInfo->numRects; i++) {
            if (appInfo->rectDpyTable[i] == rect)
                break;
        }

        /* Shift the other rectangles downward */
        for (j = i; j < appInfo->numRects - 1; j++)
            appInfo->rectDpyTable[j] = appInfo->rectDpyTable[j + 1];

        /* Place the target rectangle at the end */
        appInfo->rectDpyTable[j] = rect;

    }

}



/* This procedure raises the rectangle to the top of the drawing
 * area */
/* ARGSUSED */
static void
#ifdef _NO_PROTO
RectRaise(w, rect)
Widget w;
RectPtr rect;
#else
RectRaise(Widget w, RectPtr rect)
#endif /* _NO_PROTO */
{
```

```
        RectToTop(rect);
        RedrawRectangles(w);

}


/* This procedure moves the rectangle the the end of the display
 * stack, decrements the number of rectangles, and then frees the
 * rectangle.
 */
void
#ifdef _NO_PROTO
RectFree(rect)
RectPtr rect;
#else
RectFree(RectPtr rect)
#endif /* _NO_PROTO */
{

    /* if the rectangle is registered */
    if (rect) {

        RectToTop(rect);
        appInfo->numRects--;
        XtFree((char *)rect);

    }

}


/* This procedure added the rectangle to the rectangle display
 * table (reallocing the table if necessary).
 */
void
#ifdef _NO_PROTO
RectRegister(rect, x, y)
RectPtr rect;
#else
RectRegister(RectPtr rect, Position x, Position y)
#endif /* _NO_PROTO */
```

```
{

    appInfo->numRects++;

    /* rectangles can have their x and y values reset at
     * registration time */
    rect->x = x;
    rect->y = y;

    /* realloc the table if it is too small */
    if (appInfo->numRects > appInfo->rectsAllocd) {

        /* grow geometrically */
        appInfo->rectsAllocd *= 2;
        appInfo->rectDpyTable = (RectPtr *)
            XtRealloc((char *) appInfo->rectDpyTable,
            (unsigned) (sizeof(RectPtr) * appInfo->rectsAllocd));

    }

    /* Add to end of display table */
    appInfo->rectDpyTable[appInfo->numRects - 1] = rect;

}


/* This function find the top most rectangle at the given x,y
 * position */
RectPtr
#ifdef _NO_PROTO
RectFind(x, y)
Position x;
Position y;
#else
RectFind(Position x, Position y)
#endif /* _NO_PROTO */
{

    RectPtr rect;
    int     i;
```

```
    /*
     * Search from the end of the rectangle display table
        * to find the top most rectangle.
     */
    for (i = appInfo->numRects - 1; i >= 0; i--) {

        rect = appInfo->rectDpyTable[i];
        if (rect->x <= x && rect->x + rect->width >= x &&
            rect->y <= y && rect->y + rect->height >= y) {
            return(rect);
        }

    }

    /* If a rectangle is not found return NULL */
    return(NULL);

}


/* This procedure sets the retangle's color */
void
#ifdef _NO_PROTO
RectSetColor(rect, display, window, color)
RectPtr rect;
Display *display;
Window window;
Pixel color;
#else
RectSetColor(RectPtr rect, Display *display, Window window,
            Pixel color)
#endif /* _NO_PROTO */
{

    rect->color = color;
    RectDraw(display, window, rect);

}


/* This function gets the retangle's color */
```

```
Pixel
#ifdef _NO_PROTO
RectGetColor(rect)
RectPtr rect;
#else
RectGetColor(RectPtr rect)
#endif /* _NO_PROTO */
{
    return(rect->color);
}


/* This procedure sets the retangle's pixmap. The pixmap portion
 * of the rectangle is not currently being used.
 */
/* ARGSUSED */
void
#ifdef _NO_PROTO
RectSetPixmap(rect, display, window, pixmap)
RectPtr rect;
Display *display;
Window window;
Pixmap pixmap;
#else
RectSetPixmap(RectPtr rect, Display *display, Window window,
            Pixmap pixmap)
#endif /* _NO_PROTO */
{

    rect->pixmap = pixmap; /* not currently being looked at */
    RectDraw(display, window, rect);

}


/* This function gets the retangle's pixmap. The pixmap portion of
 * the rectangle is not currently being used.
 */
/* ARGSUSED */
static Pixmap
#ifdef _NO_PROTO
```

```
RectGetPixmap(rect)
RectPtr rect;
#else
RectGetPixmap(RectPtr rect)
#endif /* _NO_PROTO */
{
    return (rect->pixmap);
}


/* This procedure gets the retangle's height and width.  */
/* ARGSUSED */
static void
#ifdef _NO_PROTO
RectGetDimensions(rect, width, height)
RectPtr rect;
Dimension *width;
Dimension *height;
#else
RectGetDimensions(RectPtr rect, Dimension *width,
                Dimension *height)
#endif /* _NO_PROTO */
{

    *width = rect->width;
    *height = rect->height;

}


/* This function creates the rectangle bitmaps for the icon. */
Pixmap
#ifdef _NO_PROTO
GetBitmapFromRect(w, rect, background, foreground, widthRtn,
                heightRtn)
Widget w;
RectPtr rect;
Pixel background;
Pixel foreground;
Dimension *widthRtn;
Dimension *heightRtn;
```

```
#else
GetBitmapFromRect(Widget w, RectPtr rect, Pixel background,
Pixel foreground, Dimension *widthRtn, Dimension *heightRtn)
#endif /* _NO_PROTO */
{

    Dimension width, height, maxHeight, maxWidth;
    GC fillGC;
    Pixmap icon_pixmap;
    Display *display = XtDisplay(w);
    XGCValues values;

    RectGetDimensions(rect, &width, &height);

    /* Get the maximum allowable width and height allowed by the
     * cursor */
    maxWidth = appInfo->maxCursorWidth;
    maxHeight = appInfo->maxCursorHeight;

    /* if the dimensions aren't within the allowable dimensions
     * resize then proportionally
     */
    if (maxWidth < width || maxHeight < height) {

        if (width > height) {
            height = (height * maxWidth) / width;
            width = appInfo->maxCursorWidth;
        } else {
            width = (width * maxHeight) / height;
            height = appInfo->maxCursorHeight;
        }

    }

    /* Create a depth 1 pixmap (bitmap) for use with the drag
     * icon */
    icon_pixmap = XCreatePixmap(display, XtWindow(w), width,
                               height, 1);

    /* create a GC for drawing into the bitmap */
    fillGC = XCreateGC(display, icon_pixmap, 0,
```

```
                        (XGCValues *)NULL);

    /* fill the bitmap with 0's as a starting point */
    XFillRectangle(display, icon_pixmap, fillGC, 0, 0, width,
                    height);

    /* Change GC to be able to create the rectangle with 1's on
     * the bitmap */
    values.foreground = 1;
    XChangeGC(display, fillGC, GCForeground, &values);

    /*
     * This draw a filled rectangle.  If only a outline is desired
     * use the XDrawRectangle() call.  Note: the outline does not
     * produce very effect icon melting.
     */
    XFillRectangle(display, icon_pixmap, fillGC, 0, 0, width,
                    height);

    /* Free the fill GC */
    XFreeGC(display, fillGC);

    *widthRtn = width;
    *heightRtn = height;

    return(icon_pixmap);

}



/******************************************************************
 ******************************************************************
            Functions used in Drawing Outlines:
 ******************************************************************
 ******************************************************************/

/*
 * This procedure changes the GC to do rubberband
 * drawing of a rectangle frame .
 */
static void
```

```
#ifdef _NO_PROTO
SetXorGC(w)
Widget w;
#else
SetXorGC(Widget w)
#endif /* _NO_PROTO */
{

    unsigned long valueMask = GCFunction | GCForeground |
                              GCLineWidth;
    XGCValues values;

    values.function = GXxor;
    values.foreground = GetColor(DRAW_AREA_BG_COLOR);
    values.line_width = 1;
    XChangeGC(XtDisplay(w), appInfo->rectGC, valueMask, &values);

}


/* This procedure returns the GC to it's initial state.  */
static void
#ifdef _NO_PROTO
SetNormGC(w)
Widget w;
#else
SetNormGC(Widget w)
#endif /* _NO_PROTO */
{

    unsigned long valueMask = GCFunction | GCLineWidth |
                              GCForeground;
    XGCValues values;

    values.function = GXcopy;
    values.foreground = appInfo->currentColor;
    values.line_width = HIGHLIGHT_THICKNESS;
    XChangeGC(XtDisplay(w), appInfo->rectGC, valueMask, &values);

}
```

```
/* This procedure returns the values of the current rectangle
 * outline */
static void
#ifdef _NO_PROTO
OutlineGetDimensions(x, y, width, height)
Position *x;
Position *y;
Dimension *width;
Dimension *height;
#else
OutlineGetDimensions(Position *x, Position *y, Dimension *width,
Dimension *height)
#endif /* _NO_PROTO */
{

    if (appInfo->rectX < appInfo->rectX2) {
        *x = appInfo->rectX;
        *width = appInfo->rectX2 - *x;
    } else {
        *x = appInfo->rectX2;
        *width = appInfo->rectX - *x;
    }

    if (appInfo->rectY < appInfo->rectY2) {
        *y = appInfo->rectY;
        *height = appInfo->rectY2 - *y;
    } else {
        *y = appInfo->rectY2;
        *height = appInfo->rectY - *y;
    }

    if (*width < 0)
        *width = 1;
    if (*height < 0)
        *height = 1;

}


static void
#ifdef _NO_PROTO
```

```
OutlineDraw(w)
Widget w;
#else
OutlineDraw(Widget w)
#endif /* _NO_PROTO */
{

    Position    x, y;
    Dimension    width, height;

    OutlineGetDimensions(&x, &y, &width, &height);

    XDrawRectangle(XtDisplay(w), XtWindow(w), appInfo->rectGC,
                x, y, width, height);

}


/* This procedure sets initializes the drawing positions */
static void
#ifdef _NO_PROTO
OutlineSetPosition(x, y)
Position x;
Position y;
#else
OutlineSetPosition(Position x, Position y)
#endif /* _NO_PROTO */
{

    appInfo->rectX = appInfo->rectX2 = x;
    appInfo->rectY = appInfo->rectY2 = y;

}


/* This procedure resets outline end position */
static void
#ifdef _NO_PROTO
OutlineResetPosition(x, y)
Position x;
Position y;
```

```
#else
OutlineResetPosition(Position x, Position y)
#endif /* _NO_PROTO */
{

    appInfo->rectX2 = x;
    appInfo->rectY2 = y;


}


/* This action procedure begins creating a rectangle at the x,y
 * position of the button event if a rectangle doesn't already
 * exist at that position.  Otherwise is raises the rectangle
 * to the top of the drawing area.
 */
/* ARGSUSED */
void
#ifdef _NO_PROTO
StartRect(w, event, params, num_params)
Widget w;
XEvent *event;
String *params;
Cardinal *num_params;
#else
StartRect(Widget w, XEvent *event, String *params,
          Cardinal *num_params)
#endif /* _NO_PROTO */
{

    Display *display = XtDisplay(w);
    RectPtr rect;
    Position x = event->xbutton.x;
    Position y = event->xbutton.y;

    rect = RectFind(x, y);

    /* if there isn't a rectangle at this position, begin creating
     * one */
    if (!rect) {
```

```
        appInfo->creatingRect = True;
        /* set gc for drawing rubberband outline for rectangles */
        SetXorGC(w);
        /* set the initial outline positions */
        OutlineSetPosition(x, y);
        /* Draw the rectangle */
        OutlineDraw(w);


    }
    else
        RectRaise(w, rect);

}


/* This action procedure extends the drawing of the outline
 * for the rectangle to be created.
 */
/* ARGSUSED */
void
#ifdef _NO_PROTO
ExtendRect(w, event, params, num_params)
Widget w;
XEvent *event;
String *params;
Cardinal *num_params;
#else
ExtendRect(Widget w, XEvent *event, String *params,
           Cardinal *num_params)
#endif /* _NO_PROTO */
{

    if (appInfo->creatingRect) {

        /* erase the old outline */
        OutlineDraw(w);
        /* set the new outline end positions */
        OutlineResetPosition(event->xbutton.x, event->xbutton.y);
        /* redraw the outline */
        OutlineDraw(w);
```

```
    }

}


/* This action procedure creates a rectangle depending on the
 * dimensions set in the StartRect and ExtendRect action procs.
 */
/* ARGSUSED */
void
#ifdef _NO_PROTO
EndRect(w, event, params, num_params)
Widget w;
XEvent *event;
String *params;
Cardinal *num_params;
#else
EndRect(Widget w, XEvent *event, String *params,
        Cardinal *num_params)
#endif /* _NO_PROTO */
{

    Position     x, y;
    Dimension    width, height;
    RectPtr      rect;


    if (appInfo->creatingRect) {

        /* erase the last outline */
        OutlineDraw(w);
        /* return GC to original state */
        SetNormGC(w);

        /* Get the outline dimensions for creating the rectangle */
        OutlineGetDimensions(&x, &y, &width, &height);

        /* don't want to create zero width or height rectangles */
        if (width == 0 || height == 0){
            appInfo->creatingRect = False;
            return;
```

```
        }

        rect = RectCreate(x, y, width, height,
                GetColor(RECT_START_COLOR), XmUNSPECIFIED_PIXMAP);

        RectDraw(XtDisplay(w), XtWindow(w), rect);
        RectRegister(rect, x, y);
        appInfo->creatingRect = False;

    }

}


/* The procedure assigns new translations the the given widget */
static void
#ifdef _NO_PROTO
SetupTranslations(widget, new_translations)
Widget widget;
char *new_translations;
#else
SetupTranslations(Widget widget, char *new_translations)
#endif /* _NO_PROTO */
{

    XtTranslations new_table;

    new_table = XtParseTranslationTable(new_translations);
    XtOverrideTranslations(widget, new_table);

}


/* This procedure handles exposure events and makes a call to
 * RedrawRectangles() to redraw the rectangles
 * The rectangles at the top of the table are drawn first.
 */
/* ARGSUSED */
static void
#ifdef _NO_PROTO
HandleExpose(w, closure, call_data)
```

```
Widget w;
XtPointer closure;
XtPointer call_data;
#else
HandleExpose(Widget w, XtPointer closure, XtPointer call_data)
#endif /* _NO_PROTO */
{
    RedrawRectangles(w);
}


/* This procedure sets up the drawing area */
static void
#ifdef _NO_PROTO
CreateDrawingArea(parent)
Widget parent;
#else
CreateDrawingArea(Widget parent)
#endif /* _NO_PROTO */
{

    static char da_translations[] =
        "#replace <Btn2Down>: StartMove() \n\
        <Btn1Down>: StartRect() \n\
        <Btn1Motion>: ExtendRect() \n\
        <Btn1Up>: EndRect() \n\
        c <Key>t: XtDisplayTranslations()";

    Arg             args[10];
    int             n = 0;
    XtTranslations  new_table;

    new_table = XtParseTranslationTable(da_translations);

    /* create drawing area at the top of the form */
    n = 0;
    XtSetArg(args[n], XmNtranslations, new_table); n++;
    XtSetArg(args[n], XmNtopAttachment, XmATTACH_FORM); n++;
    XtSetArg(args[n], XmNleftAttachment, XmATTACH_FORM); n++;
    XtSetArg(args[n], XmNrightAttachment, XmATTACH_FORM); n++;
    XtSetArg(args[n], XmNwidth, 295); n++;
```

```
        XtSetArg(args[n], XmNheight, 180); n++;
        XtSetArg(args[n], XmNresizePolicy, XmRESIZE_NONE); n++;
        XtSetArg(args[n], XmNbackground, GetColor(DRAW_AREA_BG_COLOR));
        n++;
        XtSetArg(args[n], XmNforeground, GetColor(DRAW_AREA_FG_COLOR));
        n++;
        drawingArea = XmCreateDrawingArea(parent, "drawingArea", args, n);
        XtManageChild(drawingArea);

        /* add expose callback to redisplay rectangles */
        XtAddCallback(drawingArea, XmNexposeCallback, HandleExpose,
                     (XtPointer) NULL);

}


/* This procedure sets up the area for obtaining rectangle colors */
static void
#ifdef _NO_PROTO
CreateColorPushButtons(parent, separator)
Widget parent;
Widget separator;
#else
CreateColorPushButtons(Widget parent, Widget separator)
#endif /* _NO_PROTO */
{

        static char label_translations[] = "<Btn2Down>: ColorRect()";
        Widget          bulletinBoard;
        Widget          children[6];
        XmString        csString;
        Arg             args[10];
        int             n = 0;

        /* Creating an empty compound string so the labels will have
         * no text. */
        csString = XmStringCreateSimple("");

        /* Creating 6 color labels */
        n = 0;
        XtSetArg(args[n], XmNtopAttachment, XmATTACH_WIDGET); n++;
```

```
XtSetArg(args[n], XmNtopWidget, separator); n++;
XtSetArg(args[n], XmNtopOffset, 2); n++;
XtSetArg(args[n], XmNleftAttachment, XmATTACH_FORM); n++;
XtSetArg(args[n], XmNrightAttachment, XmATTACH_FORM); n++;
XtSetArg(args[n], XmNwidth, 295); n++;
bulletinBoard = XmCreateBulletinBoard(parent, "buletinBoard",
                                    args, n);
XtManageChild(bulletinBoard);

n = 0;
XtSetArg(args[n], XmNx, BOX_X_MARGIN); n++;
XtSetArg(args[n], XmNy, BOX_Y_MARGIN); n++;
XtSetArg(args[n], XmNwidth, BOX_WIDTH); n++;
XtSetArg(args[n], XmNheight, BOX_HEIGHT); n++;
XtSetArg(args[n], XmNlabelString, csString); n++;
XtSetArg(args[n], XmNbackground, GetColor(LABEL1_COLOR)); n++;
XtSetArg(args[n], XmNborderWidth, 1); n++;
children[0] = XmCreatePushButton(bulletinBoard, "PushButton1",
                                args, n);

/* add translations for manipulating rectangles */
SetupTranslations(children[0], label_translations);

n = 0;
XtSetArg(args[n], XmNx, BOX_X_MARGIN + BOX_X_OFFSET); n++;
XtSetArg(args[n], XmNy, BOX_Y_MARGIN); n++;
XtSetArg(args[n], XmNwidth, BOX_WIDTH); n++;
XtSetArg(args[n], XmNheight, BOX_HEIGHT); n++;
XtSetArg(args[n], XmNlabelString, csString); n++;
XtSetArg(args[n], XmNbackground, GetColor(LABEL2_COLOR)); n++;
XtSetArg(args[n], XmNborderWidth, 1); n++;
children[1] = XmCreatePushButton(bulletinBoard, "PushButton1",
                                args, n);

/* add translations for manipulating rectangles */
SetupTranslations(children[1], label_translations);

n = 0;
XtSetArg(args[n], XmNx, BOX_X_MARGIN + (2 * BOX_X_OFFSET)); n++;
XtSetArg(args[n], XmNy, BOX_Y_MARGIN); n++;
XtSetArg(args[n], XmNwidth, BOX_WIDTH); n++;
```

```
XtSetArg(args[n], XmNheight, BOX_HEIGHT); n++;
XtSetArg(args[n], XmNlabelString, csString); n++;
XtSetArg(args[n], XmNbackground, GetColor(LABEL3_COLOR)); n++;
XtSetArg(args[n], XmNborderWidth, 1); n++;
children[2] = XmCreatePushButton(bulletinBoard, "PushButton3",
                                 args, n);

/* add translations for manipulating rectangles */
SetupTranslations(children[2], label_translations);

n = 0;
XtSetArg(args[n], XmNx, BOX_X_MARGIN); n++;
XtSetArg(args[n], XmNy, BOX_Y_MARGIN + BOX_Y_OFFSET); n++;
XtSetArg(args[n], XmNwidth, BOX_WIDTH); n++;
XtSetArg(args[n], XmNheight, BOX_HEIGHT); n++;
XtSetArg(args[n], XmNlabelString, csString); n++;
XtSetArg(args[n], XmNbackground, GetColor(LABEL4_COLOR)); n++;
XtSetArg(args[n], XmNborderWidth, 1); n++;
children[3] = XmCreatePushButton(bulletinBoard, "PushButton4",
                                 args, n);

/* add translations for manipulating rectangles */
SetupTranslations(children[3], label_translations);

n = 0;
XtSetArg(args[n], XmNx, BOX_X_MARGIN + BOX_X_OFFSET); n++;
XtSetArg(args[n], XmNy, BOX_Y_MARGIN + BOX_Y_OFFSET); n++;
XtSetArg(args[n], XmNwidth, BOX_WIDTH); n++;
XtSetArg(args[n], XmNheight, BOX_HEIGHT); n++;
XtSetArg(args[n], XmNtopWidget, children[0]); n++;
XtSetArg(args[n], XmNlabelString, csString); n++;
XtSetArg(args[n], XmNbackground, GetColor(LABEL5_COLOR)); n++;
XtSetArg(args[n], XmNborderWidth, 1); n++;
children[4] = XmCreatePushButton(bulletinBoard, "PushButton5",
                                 args, n);

/* add translations for manipulating rectangles */
SetupTranslations(children[4], label_translations);

n = 0;
XtSetArg(args[n], XmNx, BOX_X_MARGIN + (2 * BOX_X_OFFSET)); n++;
```

```
    XtSetArg(args[n], XmNy, BOX_Y_MARGIN + BOX_Y_OFFSET); n++;
    XtSetArg(args[n], XmNwidth, BOX_WIDTH); n++;
    XtSetArg(args[n], XmNheight, BOX_HEIGHT); n++;
    XtSetArg(args[n], XmNlabelString, csString); n++;
    XtSetArg(args[n], XmNbackground, GetColor(LABEL6_COLOR)); n++;
    XtSetArg(args[n], XmNborderWidth, 1); n++;
    children[5] = XmCreatePushButton(bulletinBoard, "PushButton6",
                                     args, n);

    /* add translations for manipulating rectangles */
    SetupTranslations(children[5], label_translations);

    /* Managing the children all at once helps performance */
    XtManageChildren(children, 6);

    /* Freeing compound string.  It is no longer necessary. */
    XmStringFree(csString);

}


/* This procedure initializes the rectangle display table */
void
#ifdef _NO_PROTO
InitializeRectDpyTable()
#else
InitializeRectDpyTable(void)
#endif /* _NO_PROTO */
{
    /*
     * Initialize display table.  This is used to maintain the
     * order in which the rectangles are displayed
     */
    appInfo->rectDpyTable =
            (RectPtr *) XtMalloc((unsigned)sizeof(RectPtr));

    /* Initialize rectangle counter.  This is used in reallocing
     * the tables */
    appInfo->rectsAllocd = 1;

}
```

```
/* This procedure creates the components to be displayed */
void
#ifdef _NO_PROTO
CreateLayout()
#else
CreateLayout(void)
#endif /* _NO_PROTO */
{

    Widget    mainWindow, form, separator;
    Arg       args[10];
    int       n = 0;

    /* Create main window */
    mainWindow = XmCreateMainWindow(topLevel, "mainWindow", args, n);
    XtManageChild(mainWindow);

    /* Create form for hold drawing area, separator, and color
     * labels */
    n = 0;
    XtSetArg(args[n], XmNwidth, 300); n++;
    form = XmCreateForm(mainWindow, "form", args, n);
    XtManageChild(form);

    /* Create area for drawing rectangles */
    CreateDrawingArea(form);

    /* Create separator to separate drawing area from color labels */
    n = 0;
    XtSetArg(args[n], XmNtopAttachment, XmATTACH_WIDGET); n++;
    XtSetArg(args[n], XmNtopWidget, drawingArea); n++;
    XtSetArg(args[n], XmNtopOffset, 5); n++;
    XtSetArg(args[n], XmNleftAttachment, XmATTACH_FORM); n++;
    XtSetArg(args[n], XmNrightAttachment, XmATTACH_FORM); n++;
    XtSetArg(args[n], XmNwidth, 300); n++;
    separator = XmCreateSeparatorGadget(form, "separator", args, n);
    XtManageChild(separator);

    /* Create color labels for changing colors of buttons */
    CreateColorPushButtons(form, separator);
```

```
    /* Make form the work window of the main window */
    n = 0;
    XtSetArg(args[n], XmNworkWindow, form); n++;
    XtSetValues(mainWindow, args, n);

}


/* This procedure initializes the GC for drawing rectangles */
void
#ifdef _NO_PROTO
CreateRectGC()
#else
CreateRectGC(void)
#endif /* _NO_PROTO */
{

    XGCValues     values;

    values.line_style = LineSolid;
    values.line_width = HIGHLIGHT_THICKNESS;
    values.foreground = appInfo->currentColor =
                    GetColor(RECT_START_COLOR);
    appInfo->rectGC = XCreateGC(XtDisplay(topLevel),
                    XtWindow(drawingArea),
                    GCLineStyle | GCLineWidth | GCForeground,
                    &values);

}
```

Glossary

accelerator

A key or sequence of keys (typically a modifier key and some other key) that provides a shortcut, immediately accessing a program function.

action

A procedure associated with a widget and invoked by the Xt event dispatcher when the widget receives an event of a given type. The widget's translation table associates event descriptions with actions.

activation

Invocation of a component's primary action. For example, the user activates a PushButton by pressing **BSelect** on the PushButton.

anchor

> A position in a collection of selectable objects that marks one endpoint of an extended selection range.

atom

> An identifier that is unique to the display and is associated with a given name. Common uses are to identify properties, types, and selections.

bitmap

> A pixmap with a depth of one bit.

callback

> An application-defined procedure that a widget invokes at some specified time. Often the widget invokes a callback from an action routine when the widget receives an event of a given type. Widgets that invoke callbacks have resources whose value is a list of callback procedures.

character set

> A set of characters that, either individually or in combination, represents meaningful words in a language.

class

> A group of elements all of the same type. A resource class represents a group of resources with different names. A widget class represents the procedures and data structures shared by all widgets of that class.

client

> A program written specifically for use with the X Window System. Clients create their own windows and know how to resize themselves.

clipboard selection

> A selection often used to cut or copy data from one client and paste it into another client or another window of the same client.

clipping

> The restriction of output to a particular area of the screen by a given boundary. For example, windows are clipped by their parents.

code set

> The set of binary values needed to represent all the characters in a language.

colormap

> An association between pixel values and colors. Each color is represented by a triple of red, green, and blue values that result in a particular color on a particular screen. Each window has an associated colormap that determines what color is used to display each pixel.

composite

> One of a group of widgets that can have child widgets and can manage their children's geometry.

compound string

> A byte stream consisting of tag-length-value segments and representing zero or more pieces of text. A compound string has components that contain the text to be displayed, a tag (called a font list element tag) to be matched with an element of a font list, and an indicator denoting the direction in which the text is to be displayed.

cursor

> A graphical image, usually a pipe (|) or block, that shows the location where text will appear on the screen when keys on the keyboard are pressed or where a selection can be made.

destination

> The location at which transfer actions place data.

dialog

> A widget that provides a means of communicating between the user and the application. A dialog is a popup that usually

asks a question or presents some information to the user. A dialog can be modal, suspending the application until the user provides a response, or modeless, allowing the user to interact with the application during the dialog.

display

An abstraction that represents the input and output devices controlled by a single server. Usually a display consists of a keyboard, a pointing device, and one or more screens.

drag and drop

A transfer mechanism where data is dragged from a source to a drop site using mouse motion.

drag icon

A graphic that is generated using pixmaps and is moved during a drag operation. The drag icon is composed of a source pixmap, a state cursor, and an operation cursor.

drag initiator

The client within whose window the user starts a drag transaction. See also **drag source**.

drag source

The object whose graphical representation is being dragged and whose data the user wishes to transfer.

drawable

An entity that can be the source or destination for a graphics operation. Both windows and pixmaps are drawables.

drop site

An area of the screen on which the user can drop a drag icon.

event

A means by which the server notifies clients of changes of state. An event may be a side effect of a client request, or it may have a completely asynchronous cause, such as the user's pressing a key or moving the pointer. In addition, a client may send an event, via the server, to another client.

event handler

A procedure called by the Xt event dispatcher when a widget receives an event of a given type. Event handlers provide input processing at a lower level than callbacks or action routines.

event loop

A program loop in which the application receives an event, handles the event, and then waits for the next event. An event loop usually does not end until the user terminates the application. Xt provides an event-dispatching loop suitable for most applications.

export target

A type of object that a drag source can process.

focus

See also **keyboard focus**.

font

A collection of glyphs and associated metrics usually used to display text.

font list

A list of entries, each of which consists of a font list element tag and either a font or a font set. When Motif displays text, it associates the text with a font list element tag in a font list and uses the corresponding font or font set to render the text.

font list element tag

A string associated with a text segment of a compound string or with a font or font set in a font list. When Motif displays text, it associates the text with a font list element tag in a font list and uses the corresponding font or font set to render the text.

font set

A group of fonts often representing the fonts needed to display text in the encoding of a particular locale.

gadget

An object that is like a primitive widget in most respects except that it has no associated window or translations. A gadget depends on a manager parent for its colors and for input dispatching.

GC

See **graphics context**.

geometry

The elements of a widget's layout, including its size, location, and stacking order.

geometry management

The process by which the user, parent widgets, and child widgets negotiate the actual sizes and locations of the widgets in an application. In general, a child widget can ask its parent to change its geometry but cannot make any changes on its own. A parent can grant or reject a request from its child and can force changes on the child at other times.

grab

A client's assertion of exclusive use of a keyboard key, the keyboard, a pointer button, the pointer, or the server. Applications usually do not use explicit grabs, but toolkits and window managers often use them to implement such features as menus and accelerators.

graphics context (GC)

A collection of attributes that determine how any given graphics operation affects a drawable. Each graphics operation on a drawable is executed using a given graphics context specified by the client. Some attributes of a graphics context are the foreground pixel, background pixel, line width, and clipping region.

hotspot

> The location in a cursor that corresponds to the coordinates of the pointer position.

I18N

> See **internationalization**.

import target

> A type of object that a drop site can process.

input context

> The mechanism used to provide the state information flow between an application and the input method.

input focus

> See **keyboard focus**.

input method

> A layer of mapping between the keyboard keys (or combination of keys) that the user types and the text data that is passed to the application.

insertion cursor

> The graphical symbol that provides the visual cue to the location of the insertion point in a Text component.

internationalization (I18N)

> The process of generalizing programs or systems so that they can handle a variety of languages, character sets, and national customs.

keyboard focus

> A state of the system that indicates which component receives keyboard events. A component is said to have the focus if keyboard events are sent to that component.

keyboard traversal

> The set of actions, usually invoked from the keyboard, that

cause focus to move from one component to another within an application or between applications.

localization

The process of providing language-specific or country-specific information and support for programs.

manage

To place the geometry of a child widget under the control of its parent. In general widgets are eligible to appear on the screen only after they are managed.

manager

One of a group of widgets that can have children and can manage their geometry. Managers provide colors and input dispatching for gadget children.

map

To mark a window as eligible to be visible on the screen. A window actually becomes visible when all of its ancestors are mapped and when it is not obscured by an ancestor or by another window.

menu

A popup widget usually allowing the user to make a single selection from a constrained set of choices. A menu is usually modal, suspending the application until the user makes a selection or dismisses the menu. When torn off, a menu becomes modeless, allowing the user to interact with the application while the menu remains visible.

mnemonic

A single character (frequently the initial character) of a Menu selection. When the Menu is displayed and the user presses the key that corresponds to that character, the Menu selection is chosen.

modal

A state of a dialog that requires the user to interact with the dialog before interacting with other parts of the application or with other applications. Three modal styles exist: primary application modal, full application modal, and system modal. See also **modeless**.

modeless

A state of a dialog that does not require the user to interact with the dialog before interacting with other parts of the application or with other applications. See also **modal**.

off-the-spot

A location for the pre-edit area in an input method. The input data is displayed in a window within the application window but not at the point of insertion.

over-the-spot

A location for the pre-edit area in an input method. The input data is displayed in a window immediately above the point of insertion.

pane

A widget that is a child of a PanedWindow. The user adjusts the size of a pane by means of a sash.

pending delete

A state of a Text component in which some user actions cause the current selection to be deleted.

pixel

A unit of height and width for a window or pixmap. Each pixel has a number of bits or planes equal to the depth of the window or pixmap. Thus, each pixel has an integral value whose range depends on the depth of the drawable. The pixel value is used as an index into a colormap to determine the color to display for that pixel.

pixmap

A two-dimensional array of pixels, all of the same depth. Like a window, a pixmap is a drawable, an entity that can be the source or destination for a graphics operation.

popup

A widget that is outside the normal widget hierarchy. Any widget can have popup children, and the widget does not manage these children. A popup's window is a descendant of the root window, and the popup is not clipped by the parent widget. A popup usually appears on the screen temporarily in behalf of its parent. Dialogs and menus are the most common popups.

pre-edit area

An area that displays the intermediate text characters for languages whose characters may require more than one keystroke to complete.

pre-editing

Creating characters in a particular language by using individual keystrokes or combinations of keystrokes.

primary selection

The principal selection, used to transfer data from one client to another or to another window of the same client.

primitive

One of a group of widgets that usually do not have children.

property

An entity associated with a window and consisting of a name, a type, a data format, and data. Properties are often used for communicating between clients and between a client and the window manager.

realize

To create windows for a widget and its managed children.

receiver

The client containing the destination of a drag and drop transaction.

resource

> An element of a database representing options or values for attributes of an application. A resource is a triple, consisting of a name, a class, and a value. A name and class may consist of components, each identifying the name or class of a particular level of a hierarchy. A widget can also have resources, whose values are derived from the resource database or set directly by the application.

root window

> A window that covers the entire viewable extent of the screen and is the ancestor of all other windows on the screen.

root-window

> A pre-edit area (or window) that is a child of the root window and not a part of the application window.

sash

> A control with which the user changes the sizes of panes in a PanedWindow.

screen

> An abstraction that represents a single bitmapped output device on a display.

secondary selection

> A selection, usually transitory, used to transfer data from one client to another or to another window of the same client without disturbing the primary selection.

selection

> A mechanism for transferring data from one client to another or to another window of the same client. The principal types of selection are primary, secondary, and clipboard. The display contains only one selection of each type. It is owned by a client or by no one and, if owned, is attached to a window of the owning client.

sensitive

> Eligible to receive input events. Xt does not dispatch most input events to insensitive widgets.

server

> The component of the X Window System that manages input and the visual display.

shell

> One of a group of widgets that envelop the top-level widgets, including dialogs and menus, in an application. A shell usually has only one managed child, and its window is often coincident with the managed child's window. A shell usually handles communication with the window manager.

status area

> An input method output-only window thaqt identifies the input style (phonetic, numeric, stroke and radial, etc.) and the current status of an input method interaction.

tab group

> A widget or set of widgets to which the user traverses by means of the **<Tab>** key. Within a tab group, the user traverses to non-tab-group descendants by means of the arrow keys.

translation

> A mapping from an event description to one or more actions. When a widget receives an event, Xt searches the widget's translation table for a matching event description. If it finds such a description, it invokes the associated action or actions.

traversal

> See **keyboard traversal**.

virtual binding

> An assocation between an abstract key or pointer button, known as a virtual key or virtual button, and a physical key or button on the display.

virtual button

An abstract representation of a pointer button that is independent of any physical button. A virtual button is associated with a physical button by means of a virtual binding.

virtual key

An abstract representation of a key that is independent of any physical key. A virtual key is associated with a physical key by means of a virtual binding.

widget

An object used to hold data and present an interface to the user. A widget is a combination of state and procedure. Each widget is a member of a class, which holds the procedures and data structures common to all widgets of that class. A widget instance holds the procedures and data structures particular to that single widget. Each widget class typically provides the general behavior associated with a particular kind of interaction with the user.

window

A data structure that represents all or part of the display screen. Visually, a window is represented as a subarea of the display screen.

window manager

A program that controls the size, placement, and operation of windows on the workspace. The window manager includes the functional window frames that surround each window object and may include a separate Menu for the workspace.

Index

Symbols

A

B

D

K

L

M

Q

R

S

V

W

X

Notes

Notes

OPEN SOFTWARE FOUNDATION™

INFORMATION REQUEST FORM

Please send me the following:

( ) OSF Membership Information

( ) OSF/Motif™ License Materials

( ) OSF/Motif™ Training Information

Contact Name _____

Company Name _____

Street Address _____

Mail Stop _____

City _____ State _____ Zip _____

Phone _____ FAX _____

Electronic Mail _____

MAIL TO:

Open Software Foundation
11 Cambridge Center
Cambridge, MA 02142

Attn: OSF/Motif™

For more information about OSF/Motif™, call **617 621 7300.**